stubborn twig

We are come to rest and push our roots more deeply by the year, but we cannot push away the heritage of having been once all strangers in the land.

—*Oscar Handlin*

stubborn twig

THREE GENERATIONS IN THE LIFE
OF A JAPANESE AMERICAN FAMILY

by Lauren Kessler

OREGON HISTORICAL SOCIETY PRESS
PORTLAND

Oregon Historical Society Press
1200 SW Park Avenue, Portland, OR 97205, USA
www.ohs.org

The paper used in this publication is acid-free. It meets the minimum requirements of American National Standard for Information Sciences—Permanence of Paper for Printed Library Materials, ANSI Z39.48—1984. ∞

Distributed by the University of Washington Press

COVER DESIGN: Chris Michel
PRINTER: Friesens

COVER AND INTERIOR PHOTOS:
All photographs are from the private collections of Homer Yasui and Kuka Yasui Fujikura and are reproduced here by permission.

Library of Congress Cataloging-in-Publication Data

Kessler, Lauren.
Stubborn twig : three generations in the life of a Japanese American family / by Lauren Kessler.
p. cm.
Includes bibliographical references and index.
1. Yasui family. 2. Yasui, Masuo--Family. 3. Japanese Americans--Oregon--Biography. 4. Japanese Americans--Oregon--Ethnic identity. 5. Japanese Americans--Oregon--Social conditions. I. Title.
CT274.Y39K47 2005
929'.2089956073--dc22
                                                2005024552

To the memory of Kay
and
to Tom, shinyu

contents

preface to the new edition

We want to be proud to be Americans—not with aggressive jingoism but with sincerity, with respect for land, people and principle. But it is sometimes difficult, for our past is clotted with ugly episodes: invasions, land-grabbing, forced marches, slavery, lynchings, mass internment. We have blood on our hands, and it is little solace to most of us that other countries have done worse. We would like to believe that America is a beacon for freedom and equality, but it sometimes seems as if the evidence is less than overwhelming.

Still, some people want and need to believe that our past is unblemished, that our national story is a simple one, a tale of great men and great deeds, of both moral and economic successes, of obstacles surmounted, dreams fulfilled. Bigger, better, more. Is it wrong—is it unpatriotic—to believe otherwise? Is it possible to be clear-eyed and critical, to acknowledge, admit and *own* a checkered past without defaulting on one's love of country? I think it is not only possible, but it is essential to our collective mental health, to our standing in the world and to our humanity.

I grew up learning a certain story of America, a narrative in which pioneers and presidents loomed large, Indians appeared long enough to sell Manhattan and attack wagon trains, African Americans toiled silently until Abe Lincoln solved their problems, and women sewed flags, rolled bandages and kept the home fires burning. In the version of my country's past that I read in high school textbooks, America opened its arms wide and welcomed immigrants. The metaphor then was America-as-melting-pot. The Irish, the Italians, the Greeks, the Russians, the Jews—they arrived speaking their own languages, eating their own foods, tethered to their homelands. Into the melting pot they jumped and, within a generation (or less), the fires of the national caldron simmered away their differences, merging these once-distinct ingredients into an American stew. I loved this story. It was the story of my southern and western European grandparents, a story of hope and idealism, of fitting in and making good.

But later, in college, I was exposed to another story. A new generation of historians had painted a vastly different national portrait, one of greed, exploitation and intolerance, of marginalization, disempowerment and shame. In this version of the American story, we Americans do nothing right. In this version, we are a people so diverse in culture, politics and religion, in homelands, customs and allegiances, that we cannot hope to understand, tolerate, or live in peace with each other. In fact, we live in fear of each other, suspicious and wary of our differences. Diversity, it seems, is just another word for tribalization, and the United States is nothing more than a nation of warring tribes. The events following 9-11, from the demonization of Arab Americans to the Patriot Act to the color-coding of the country into Red and Blue, are part of this dark and disturbing story.

There is, I think, some truth to both these versions of our national story. In order to understand our country, we must first understand that. And we must see that it is possible—necessary, even—to accept America as both hero and villain. The story of the Yasui family, a window on the immigrant experience in the United States, illustrates that point because it speaks to both the promise and the peril of America. The Yasuis' story, the Japanese story, is both typical—the wide-eyed young immigrant stepping off the boat with big plans and empty pockets—and unique. A string of nativist legislation, from an eighteenth-century edict that denied Asians naturalized citizenship to the Immigration Act of 1924, which banned further Japanese immigration, plus the mass internment of more than 110,000 people of Japanese ancestry during World War II, shows in no uncertain terms that the Japanese were treated differently from other willing immigrants to America.

It is an unsettling story, this century-long narrative of the Japanese experience in America. At first considered "alien" and "unassimilatable," Japanese immigrants like Masuo Yasui, the family's patriarch, were actually feared for being the opposite. They were, just decades after arriving in this country, beating Americans at their own game. They practiced the Protestant ethic with greater energy and resolve than many of their white neighbors. They devoted themselves to work, taught their children the meaning of hard labor and delayed their own gratification. They were the new Puritans, and the old Puritans didn't like it.

Yet, despite racism and wartime hysteria—the dark side of this American tale—the Yasuis and tens of thousands of other Japanese families like them succeeded. This country, grudgingly, unhappily, too slowly, gave them that chance. While never forgetting how unnecessarily tortuous the path was for families like the Yasuis, we should also not forget that the path existed. And so we can believe in both versions of America: the light and the shadow, the country that provides opportunity and then works overtime to prevent some people from gaining access to it.

The Yasuis' story is marbled with tragedy that reflects poorly on all of us. Yet it is also studded with success, which reflects well on us. This story has a happy ending, an America-as-hero ending, with the Yasuis becoming doctors, lawyers and teachers, entrepreneurs, artists and activists. A century ago Masuo Yasui dreamed the American Dream of equality, freedom and physical comfort. Today his children, grandchildren and great grandchildren are living it.

acknowledgments

In Japan you are born owing ancestral debts that can never be repaid, and as you make your way in the world you accumulate new obligations, kindnesses and favors owed to family, friends, colleagues, neighbors, even strangers. This web of obligation connects people in ways that both include and transcend kinship and friendship.

When I started working on this book, I entered such a web. My debts are many, but none is as deep or abiding as the one I owe Homer and Miyuki Yasui. Their early and enthusiastic support for the project opened many doors, both literally and figuratively. They granted me unlimited access to family papers in their possession, helped me establish ties with other family members, lent me armloads of books, spent long hours talking candidly about the past and even longer hours responding to my many questions. They helped me understand Japanese traditions and Japanese American concerns. They even corrected my spelling. But beyond this, they taught me, by example, the meaning of family. For that lesson as much as for their invaluable help in making this book possible, I am forever obligated.

Other family members actively supported my efforts and trusted me with their stories, taking time from hectic lives to talk and correspond at length: Chop Yasui, keeper of the family flame, and his wife, Mikie, who spent many hours with me at her kitchen table; Yuka Yasui Fujikura, one of the family's most caring historians; Min Yasui, a public animal to the last, granting me interviews even as he was dying; Michi Yasui Ando, whose participation in her college graduation ceremony forty-four years after the fact first piqued my interest in the family; Robert (Shu) Yasui, who sent me extensive clippings from his files; Maija Yasui, who opened her home to me and helped me understand Hood River; Tom and Flip, the third generation on the land; Holly, Lise and Barbara Yasui, so generous with both their time and encouragement.

I am indebted also to a number of people who grew up with members of the Yasui family and either corresponded with me or sat for the extensive oral history interviews that provided much of the material in the book: Kenneth Abraham, Margaret Cooper Annala, Min Asai, Frieda Paasche Barnes, Suma Tsuboi Bullock, Ruth Finney Crawford, Bonnie Parker Edstrom, Ruth Guppy, Robert Hackett, Jane Smithson Irwin, George Jacobson, Paul Keir, Catherine Kelly, Suma Kobayashi, Malcolm Kresse, Frances Maeda, Eleanor Middleton, Kats and Kiyo Nakayama, Don Nance, Torno Saito, Margaret Smithson Schulz, Eiko Tadakuma, Elburna Volstorff, Hisako Yoshinari, Kumeo Yoshinari. Barbara Bellus Upp, fellow historian and Yasuiphile, told me wonderful stories about the family and by the force of her own commitment deepened mine.

I owe thanks to librarians and archivists who went out of their way to help me: Tom Stave and Keith Richard at the University of Oregon; Carla Rickerson, Nan Cohen and Janet Ness at the University of Washington; Louis Flannery at the Oregon Historical Society; Sandy Macomber at the Portland *Oregonian;* and Bernard Bergland, my FoIA angel at the Department of Justice. Support from Ed Bassett, John McMillan and Jim Carey helped secure a Freedom Forum grant, which aided in the early stages of the book. I am grateful to Valerie Brown for transcribing the oral history interviews with precision, care and enduring interest.

Peggy Nagae Lum, Shirley Kishiyama and Duncan McDonald, by their encouragement and the warmth of their friendship, helped keep me going. Nat Sobel, my agent, knew how much this book meant to me and made it happen. Andrea Harding worked hard for me. I owe much to Bob Loomis at Random House, who published the first hardcover edition; Julia Serebrinsky at Plume, who published the softcover edition; and Marianne Keddington-Lang at Oregon Historical Society Press, who brought this book back to life. I am deeply and lovingly indebted to Tom Hager not only for his abiding interest in this project and his careful and expert editing, but also for very much more: his unconditional support, his unselfish enthusiasm and, perhaps most of all, his steadfast good cheer.

part one

Issei
The First Generation

Japanese Immigrants to America

1

Spacious Dreams

They called it "a little kingdom of comfort" and "the perfect pocket of paradise." And they weren't exaggerating much, these early enthusiasts of Hood River Valley. Tucked into a six-mile-wide pleat in the skirts of the densely timbered Cascade Mountains of western Oregon, the valley sprawled twenty-five miles, its floor a patchwork of infrangible forest and manicured orchards, the thick canopy of yellow pine, spruce and fir yielding to neat rows of apple and pear trees that bloomed paper white in the spring. At the foot of the valley, the Columbia River cut a mile-wide swath through thousand-foot basalt cliffs. At the head stood Mount Hood, a solitary, snowcapped alp towering eleven thousand feet above the valley floor. An icy stream, narrow, quick and clear, sliced across the valley, connecting mountain to river as it carried the melting snows of Hood's glaciers thirty winding miles to the roaring Columbia.

The town of Hood River stood hard by the banks of the Columbia, in 1900 a "sprightly little city of 700 who dwelt under a natural thatch of stately oaks in cozy cottages and unique villas," according to a boastful local newspaper editor. The fine new homes, built on the rise above town, were impressive. But the town itself was just another frontier enclave: young, raw and big on promises. Downtown was only six blocks long and two blocks wide, with rutted dirt streets that turned to choking dust in the summer and ankle-deep mud in the winter. Descendants of a tribe Lewis and Clark encountered on their journey west still lived on a nearby bluff and came to town on Saturdays to barter and shop. But the jumble of frame-and-clapboard stores was slowly yielding to more permanent structures like the new bank, the town's first two-story brick building. By 1904 a second bank had opened, and four years later three

banks with almost a million dollars in deposits served the valley. The local fruit industry was booming. Affluence was in the air.

Stern-wheelers navigated the still-undammed Columbia, bringing
people and goods sixty-five miles upstream from Portland. But the valley's main connection to the outside world was the train. Four of them
rumbled through town each day, stopping briefly at Hood River's pretty
Victorian station on their way west to Portland or east to as far as Chicago. The train brought laborers, farmers, shopkeepers, entrepreneurs,
investors and dreamers. And one spring day in 1908 it brought Masuo
Yasui.

He was a small, slight man in a trim, dark suit and a Chaplinesque
derby. The derby added a bit of height to his five-foot-two-inch frame,
and from a distance the suit made him look a little older than his twenty-
one years. But he had the serene, unlined face of a youngster, with clear,
coppery skin, full lips and a high, broad forehead. Behind wire-rimmed
glasses, his eyes were dark, intense, serious, like those of a student intent
on passing an exam.

Although born and reared in Japan, Masuo was no stranger to America. He had already been in the country four busy years, working three
jobs, attending school, learning English and converting to Christianity.
Now, like so many immigrants before him, he had a small bankroll and
big plans. Stepping from the train into the mild, apple-blossom-scented
afternoon that spring, he was ready to lay claim to the American dream.
But he was no dreamer.

Masuo had chosen Hood River not for its considerable beauty but
for its business opportunities. He had seen the town a number of times,
possibly as early as 1905, and had once spent a few days there soliciting
donations from local *issei* (first-generation Japanese immigrants) for a
float for Portland's Rose Festival Parade.

What he found was a sizable, although scattered, community of Japanese men. Some were working on a new railroad line that would soon
connect the town of Hood River to tiny settlements in the upper valley.
Others were employed by the local sawmill, and as many as three hundred worked for valley farmers, picking and packing fruit and helping
to clear the land. Many of the men had emigrated from Okayama, the
same prefecture (state) Masuo had come from. Life for them was hard
and lonely. Their one link to one another and to the culture they left
behind was a little store run by a man named Motoji Niguma. Operating out of a small clapboard building on one of the town's two main
business streets, the store had been selling a small selection of Japanese
goods and foodstuffs to the valley *issei* since 1905. Niguma was an en-

terprising sort. In addition to selling groceries and general merchandise to his countrymen, he endeavored to increase his potential clientele by operating a one-man employment agency for Japanese laborers. Above the store was a boardinghouse for new arrivals or men who needed to spend a night in town. And as the almost exclusively bachelor workforce increased, Niguma added another upstairs sideline—a brothel.

Masuo Yasui considered the situation. Here was an area with yet-to-be-developed agricultural riches that had already attracted a substantial population of his countrymen. The men working in the valley would continue to need goods and services, and their needs would expand as their numbers grew. There was room, he was sure, for another store and perhaps for other ventures. Masuo was ready for the challenge. He came from a long line of practical, enterprising men and women to whom hard work and frugality had an almost religious imperative.

Kinbei Yasui, Masuo's great-grandfather, was born in the last quarter of the eighteenth century in the small agricultural village of Nanukaichi in the southwestern region of Honshu, Japan's largest island. But Nanukaichi was more than a colony of a few hundred families tending rice paddies. In the days of the shogunate, it was a relay station on an important road to the shogun's headquarters in the ancient city of Edo. Feudal lords and samurai traveling to and from Edo stopped at Nanukaichi to refresh themselves, change horses and replenish provisions. The outdoor market bustled seven days a week in the small village, and entrepreneurism thrived.

Western Japan in general was known—and sometimes derided for—its freewheeling capitalism. To the more dignified, traditional Japanese of the eastern region around Tokyo, westerners seemed crude, crass and blunt. To westerners like the villagers of Nanukaichi, eastern Japanese seemed rigid, stodgy and straitlaced. A century later and an ocean away, the same scenario would be played out in the United States, where sophisticated northeasterners tsk-tsked the coarse frontiersmen and brash pioneers who settled the American West. But in Japan, a country so small that east and west were separated by as little as one hundred miles, this cultural fault line contributed to intrigues, rebellions and even civil wars over the course of generations.

Kinbei may not have been brash, but he certainly knew how to take advantage of the opportunities that presented themselves. In the propitiously situated village of Nanukaichi, he operated an inn that functioned as a way-station for traveling dignitaries. Family legend has it that he was also a labor contractor and a wholesale rice buyer. Whatever his various financial endeavors, he was apparently both successful and pop-

ular, for he received important symbolic recognition of his place in local society. Until the mid-nineteenth century, few Japanese were allowed
to use surnames, and only nobility and samurai were permitted to wear
swords. But as a mark of recognition, Kinbei was granted the authority
to wear a short ceremonial sword (but not the longer sword of the samurai) and to take a surname. Like the savvy businessman he was, Kinbei
chose the name Yasui, meaning "cheap" or "economical," thus becoming a walking advertisement for his own enterprises.

Kinbei's second daughter, Ume, married a local youth named Kamegoro, who, following an oft-employed Japanese custom, was adopted
into his wife's family and took the name Yasui. But he did not inherit his
father-in-law's businesses; they went to Kinbei's firstborn son, or *chonan,*
an honored position within the family. Kamegoro, like most of Nanukaichi's villagers, was himself a rice farmer. The first of his and Ume's six
children was a boy, Ikunojyo, whose position as *chonan* under Japan's ancient primogeniture laws made him sole heir to his father's holdings. He
was a scholarly boy who showed great promise and was thought to have
a bright future, but he died young, leaving the second son, Shinataro, as
the leader of the next generation of this branch of the Yasuis.

Born in the mid-1850s, Shinataro came of age during Japan's headlong rush into modernity known as the Meiji Restoration. This sweep-
ing set of changes and reforms catapulted the country from its medieval
past into the contemporary world in less than a generation, Shinataro's
generation. Before the 1868 revolution, Japan had been at the mercy
of warring shoguns who established elaborate and incessantly schem-
ing courts, a rigid social hierarchy and, above all, a strict military dicta-
torship. For three and a half centuries, the country remained locked in
isolated feudalism as Japan's rulers prohibited virtually all contact with
foreigners.

When Commodore Matthew Perry anchored his squadron of four
ships in lower Tokyo Bay in 1853, he set in motion the most dramatic
changes in Japan's long history. Within a year, shogunate officials signed
a treaty permitting trade with America; within ten years, powerful barons, disgruntled by the recent foreign intrusions, demanded the creation of a new modern and militarized government that would protect
Japan against European and American imperialism. Ironically, protection from Western encroachment meant adopting Western ways, particularly industrialization. Fourteen years after Perry's incursion, the shogun surrendered to the emperor, and Japan began to pursue a program
of modernization with the same fervor and intensity it had previously
guarded its isolation. No country has ever moved more swiftly or more

single-mindedly into the modern world than Japan of the late nineteenth century.

The two decades following the Meiji Restoration, the decades of Shinataro's young manhood, were exciting and unsettling times. Like virtually all Japanese, Shinataro had seen nothing, heard nothing, of the world outside his village. Now he was inundated with tales of America. Yukichi Fukuzawa, Japan's foremost advocate of Western learning, wrote two celebrated and widely read guides to the West and launched a Tokyo newspaper that he used as a forum to encourage young men to venture abroad. Other books and pamphlets urging emigration and touting life in the United States made the rounds. Shinataro's spirit of adventure was awakened. In Nanukaichi, his future was set—he knew just how his life would unfold. Abroad, the future was unknown, unlimited. He must have been sorely tempted.

But he had family obligations, which in Japan came before all else, including self. He was, after all, *chonan,* the oldest surviving son, and that meant more than his right of succession to his father's property. It meant duty to the family, the responsibility of caring for his parents, an obligation to carry on the Yasui name. So Shinataro set his sights closer to home, settling into village life, helping to farm and manage the family lands and marrying Tsuya Katayama. In the late 1870s, their son Taiitsuro was born, followed four years later by another son, Renichi, and on November 1, 1886, their third and last child, Masuo.

But as Shinataro's responsibilities at home grew, so too did the impetus for journeying abroad. "Come, merchants! America is a veritable human paradise, the number one mine in the world," read a popular guide to the United States published in Japan the year after Masuo's birth. "Gold, silver and gems are scattered on her streets. If you can figure out a way of picking them up, you'll become rich instantly to the tune of ten million and be able to enjoy ultimate human pleasures." Hyperbole aside, America did, in fact, offer comparatively large rewards to adventuresome Japanese men. An unskilled laborer in Japan could expect to make less than twenty cents a day; a skilled carpenter might earn thirty or thirty-five cents. A teacher with college training brought home perhaps five dollars a month. Even highly placed government officials such as the governor of a major prefecture earned only forty dollars a month. To Shinataro and thousands of men of his generation, the dollar a day promised Japanese laborers by U.S. railroad companies seemed unbelievably munificent.

It was a time when Western railroad companies urgently needed men. The newly tamed Northwest was just beginning to be tethered to the rest of the United States, and transportation barons were busy planning thousands of miles of new track. American bosses liked Asian labor. The Chinese were industrious, willing to work for low wages and generally uncomplaining about working conditions—traits that made them simultaneously appreciated by employers and despised by unions. But thanks to the Chinese Exclusion Act of 1882, that source of cheap labor was evaporating. The situation was so desperate that labor contractors for American railroads began to dispatch agents to Japanese port cities to recruit laborers, offering them three to five times the wages they were making at home and in some cases advancing them money to purchase steerage tickets to Seattle or Tacoma, Washington.

As these princely sums beckoned the unsophisticated villagers, their own government's policies seemed to conspire to push them from their homeland. To finance the industrialization and militarization of Japan, the Meiji government began requiring farmers to pay a fixed annual tax on their land, while at the same time enacting policies that depressed the price of the farmers' rice. Caught in the middle, more than three hundred thousand families lost their land. Farmers in the southwest, where the Yasuis lived, were particularly hard hit. Although the family kept its property, it was neither a profitable nor a happy time to be a rice farmer in Nanukaichi.

Then there were the stricter conscription laws of the 1880s, followed by the draft for the Sino-Japanese War of 1894. All males up to age forty were subject to military service. In earlier years, heads of households and only sons were exempt, and those who could afford to buy their way out of service were permitted to do so. But by the late 1880s the government had clamped down, and only young men studying abroad were granted exemptions. Shinataro Yasui, nearly forty years old with three sons, was still eligible for the draft.

Enticed by tales of a promised land, facing both an unpromising future as a farmer and possible conscription into the army, Shinataro made his move. Leaving his wife and three sons behind, he traveled with a friend from their home prefecture of Okayama—where a strict governor and a long waiting list made it difficult to secure a passport—four hundred miles north to Niigata. With passports in hand, they traveled back south, boarding a steamship in either Kobe or Yokohama for the long, grueling journey to America. Like most of the twenty-seven thousand other Japanese who emigrated in the decade before the twentieth century, they saw themselves as *dekaseginin*, or temporary sojourners. Their plan was simple: work hard for three to five years, saving every penny they could; then return triumphantly to Japan to either re-buy the land they lost to taxes or expand their holdings and fund new ventures. The sacrifices would be great, but the rewards greater.

Shinataro arrived in America sometime in the mid-1890s, and like more than a third of the Japanese men who landed on the shores of the Pacific Northwest, he immediately went to work for the railroad, laboring on crews along remote stretches of the intermountain West. On his half-day off a week, Shinataro wrote enthusiastic letters back to Tsuya, and, a few years later, hoping either to increase his nest egg or shorten his stay in America or both, he sent for his two older sons. When the steamship *Olympia* arrived in Tacoma in May 1897, nineteen-year-old Taiitsuro and his fifteen-year-old brother, Renichi, were on board. Masuo, only eleven at the time, stayed at home.

With her husband and older sons off on an indefinite adventure, Tsuya Katayama Yasui concentrated on surviving in the shrinking village. So many husbands and older sons had left Nanukaichi for America that her situation was far from unique. But that didn't make it any less unsettling. In a traditional Japanese family, the woman was always and in all ways subservient to the man, first her father, then her husband, later even her eldest son. But Tsuya, like many village women, had to find other ways to function. She relied first of all on her own resourcefulness, but she also sought the counsel of one of the village's few remaining older men, Ichiro Miyake. Considered a local father figure, Ichiro helped Tsuya with various business concerns and family matters. Ten years later, the two would be connected in a deeper way when Ichiro's only daughter accepted the marriage proposal of Tsuya's youngest son.

While Masuo went to high school, Tsuya operated a little store—actually more like a booth or a kiosk—selling candy, notions and other small items. She could read and write, a rarity among village women her age, and helped other wives by reading the letters their husbands sent them and by writing letters for them to be sent abroad. She doted on Masuo, not just because he was her one remaining son or because he was the youngest. A number of years before, when Masuo and his older brother Renichi were wrestling and scuffling, Masuo had fallen into the hibachi, severely burning himself. Tsuya spent many weeks nursing him back to health, and the experience deepened the relationship between mother and son. Tsuya cannot have been pleased to realize that Masuo, too, had dreams of leaving for America.

But she should not have been surprised Masuo was a bright and ambitious boy whose future was severely circumscribed by his environment—and he knew it. Japanese society of the early twentieth century, although in the throes of significant change, remained extremely structured. The feudalistic class system endured, and one's place in society, regardless of personal strengths and weaknesses, regardless of ambitions and desires, was predetermined. Duty and responsibility to family dominated one's life. A series of obligations, both passively and actively incurred, directed all relationships. Even in comparatively "freewheeling" western Japan, the individualist had little place. To Masuo and to other young men of the new century, personal freedom was an abstraction, a wish that could never come true if they remained in their native land. "I heard that the United States was a huge country—and that it was a country where one could act as he wished," one of Masuo's compatriots later recalled with awe.

Beyond this, Masuo's position in the family as third son did not suggest a particularly promising future. Taiitsro, the *chonan*, stood to inherit the Yasui land, home and business. The two younger brothers would have to start with nothing at a time when rice farming, the business they knew, had become at least temporarily unprofitable. America sent a powerful beacon.

And, as Masuo entered high school, "America fever" hit Japan full force. The newly formed Japan Enterprising Society published a series of guidebooks to the United States. *Guidance for Going to America*, issued in 1901, sold two hundred copies a week. In Okayama City, the nearest urban center to Nanukaichi, the Western Accessories Shop sold Western suits, and the Golden Horse Theater showed nascent Hollywood's version of the West: rugged, solitary cowboys living their lives against a landscape so vast it was almost beyond the imagination of a Japanese villager. And the horses! No one had ever seen so many horses. In schools, teachers actively encouraged second and subsequent sons to emigrate. For most of his boyhood, Masuo had been reading his father's letters about life in America. In 1903, when Shinataro sent for his third son, Masuo was more than ready to come.

But it wasn't that easy. A prospective émigré had to apply formally for permission to leave, a complicated bureaucratic procedure involving considerable paperwork and two separate screenings. Masuo enlisted the help of village elder Ichiro Miyake to plow through the paperwork. For the screenings he traveled to the inland seaport of Kobe some eighty miles from the village. Certain ports were quite difficult to leave from; others had reputations for being easier, with more lenient inspectors, more efficient bureaucrats and more scheduled boats. Kobe was one of the "easier" departure points, but Masuo still had to submit to what amounted to a morals examination by a special review board designed to determine the desirability of each applicant. The examiners made sure that Masuo was literate (he was, in fact, in his third year of high school), of good character and capable of maintaining Japan's national honor abroad. These boards were the government's attempt to ensure that Japanese immigrants would conduct themselves ethically, virtuously and conservatively. Thus, Japanese officials reasoned—incorrectly, as history would show—their countrymen would be treated better than the Chinese immigrants who had preceded them. Masuo also had to undergo a physical exam for trachoma and hookworm, widespread diseases among those who lived in villages with unsophisticated sanitary systems, and for syphilis.

It was common for prospective travelers to wait months for clearance to leave, and popular port cities like Kobe did a thriving business in "emigrant houses" that sheltered (and sometimes took financial advantage of) the young men eager to make their-way to America. And there were thousands of them. Masuo left Japan riding the crest of the country's greatest wave of emigration. From 1901 to 1907, almost 110,000 Japanese—most of them young, male, literate, rural and from the respectable farming class—ventured to America.

Masuo left from Kobe in the spring of 1903, a sixteen-year-old boy with a few possessions carefully packed in a wicker trunk and little idea of what lay ahead. The voyage itself was a test of both his will and his stamina. The ship, the *Ryojun Maru*, was a decrepit steamer, and Masuo, like virtually all his countrymen, traveled steerage, or third class, in common areas belowdecks. In the open spaces, netting hung overhead, so that when the boat pitched and rolled—which it did almost continuously during Masuo's rough thirty-day crossing—the men could cling to the nets to keep from being thrown against the walls. The hatch was closed in bad weather, which meant that no air circulated belowdecks, sometimes for days. The men slept in three-tiered wooden berths "like a rackful of silkworms," voyagers later recalled, with the person on the top tier sandwiched so close to the ceiling that his nose almost touched it. They ate meager meals of stale, spoiled, or unfamiliar food: rice so hard they couldn't chew it; side dishes greasy with lard; lumps of strange, unpalatable butter on odd, spongy bread. They bathed by occasionally going on deck and pouring buckets of cold water over their heads. Lice were everywhere.

Masuo battled seasickness so severe that it was the one memory of the voyage he carried with him for decades. Yet, like the other young men in steerage, his spirits were high. There was a great deal of talk belowdecks, speculation as to what their new life would be, jokes, fledgling attempts to learn English from little phrase books. "Day of spacious

dreams!/I sailed for America/Overblown with hope," wrote one po-
etically minded traveler of his transpacific voyage. Despite the terrible
crossing, Masuo, too, was overblown with hope.

When the *Ryojun Maru* landed in Seattle on June 12, Masuo walked
down the gangplank with his trunk on his back, fourteen dollars in his
pocket and no English at his command. He was greeted not by his father
or brothers, then almost a thousand miles away working on the railroad,
but by Methodist missionaries who, in those few brief years of peak immigration, met each ship and offered shelter to the new arrivals. Masuo's
first night in America was spent in the dormitory of a Methodist mission. There he remained, getting his bearings, until he joined his family
on a railroad crew.

He met up with them somewhere in Oregon, Idaho, or Montana,
for they worked on different lines in all three states during the early
years of the century. The Northern Pacific and Great Northern railroads actively competed for Japanese labor, recruiting out of Seattle
and Tacoma as well as in Japan itself. The Yasui men also at one time or
another worked for the regionally based Oregon–Washington Naviga-
tion and Railroad Company as well as the Oregon Short Line. Laborers commonly moved from one line to another, following promises of
a few more pennies a day or improved working conditions. And when
construction schedules demanded it, companies would "steal" laborers
from their competitors by sending recruiters to their camps. So serious was this problem of ever-shifting and changing work crews that
the railroad magnates, despite being notorious skinflints, resorted to
offering small bonuses to men who worked through an entire season.
By the early 1900s, when Masuo joined his father and brothers, more
than thirteen thousand Japanese men were working on the railroad in
the western states.

It was backbreaking work hoisting and positioning eight-foot-long
ties from seven in the morning until six at night. The square logs bit
cruelly into the shoulder. The mountain winters were like nothing the
Japanese had ever experienced. They wrapped towels and gunnysacks
around their feet to ward off frostbite. In all weather the men camped in
remote construction sites along the track, living in tents or boxcars converted to bunkhouses and working ten- or eleven-hour days for $1.10.
From this wage, the labor contractor, generally a fellow Japanese, took
ten cents a day as a commission and a dollar a month for an "office fee."
Contractors also levied a fifty-cent-a-month medical fee and made a tidy
sum charging the men inflated prices for food supplies (delivered at a
discount by the railroad) and money orders for remittances sent back to

Japan. The men worked six and sometimes six and a half days a week, living with an almost unimaginable frugality. In most camps, laborers spent less than four dollars a month on food for themselves, subsisting on a diet of thin soup with flour dumplings.

The sacrifices were extreme, but the men were willing to endure almost anything to save as much money in as short a time as possible. Perhaps as many as two thirds of all Japanese immigrants in these early years were *dekaseginin*, sojourners who had no intention of making America their permanent home. The dreamers imagined returning to Japan in triumph, their pockets bulging with new wealth. The pragmatists hoped to return with the funds necessary to rescue their families from debt, buy additional land, or set themselves up as small businessmen—which, in fact, was what Shinataro soon did, followed several years later by his eldest son, Talitsuro. Masuo, with no land or business to return to and fewer family obligations to meet, had different plans. But plans of all kinds required money, and railroad work was relatively lucrative.

Masuo may have at various points worked as a section hand like his father and brothers, but the stories he later told of his railroading days were of his work as a cook's helper. As a sixteen-year-old, Masuo was not yet five foot two and barely 120 pounds, too slight for holding up his end of a 200-pound railroad tie or effectively wielding a sledgehammer. So he worked at chopping wood, making fires, scrubbing pots and helping prepare and deliver meals to the crews. The food was meager, generally ill-prepared and lacking in basic nutritional value. Many men suffered night blindness from vitamin A deficiency; Renichi, for the rest of his life, attributed his poor eyesight to railroad-camp food. There were no real cooks employed on the line, just young bachelors like all the section hands. The products of nineteenth-century Japanese upbringing, these men had never learned to cook, nor would they have known anything about nutrition and diet. That was women's concern. Their culinary ineptitude was worsened by the problems of getting fresh vegetables and meat to the remote camps and the constant urgings of the men to scrimp on costs.

Awakening before the rest of the crew, the cooks and their helpers would start the fire, prepare breakfast, then clean up and immediately start on the next meal. It was Masuo's job to deliver the noon meal to section crews working two or three miles down the track by pumping himself along in a handcar. The teenager became a minor hero for his skill at throwing a monkey wrench from the moving handcar, striking unwitting jackrabbits that—much to the joy of the meat-starved crew—made it into the next day's soup. He claimed to be a dead shot up to sixty feet.

But killing rabbits and scrubbing pots were not what Masuo had in mind when he dreamed of a future in America. As a third-born son whose tomorrows weren't handed to him as a birthright, he had to take control of his own future. Unlike the *chonan* who knew their place—and for most it was back in Japan—subsequent sons like Masuo and Renichi were at loose ends. Of necessity, they had to be more self-reliant and more forward-thinking. While fathers and older brothers worked toward a swift return across the Pacific, the younger boys saw their future in America. And surely, thought Masuo, this country has more to offer a bright, ambitious young man than the isolated pauperism of a railroad camp.

In 1905, after two years on the railroad, he set off to discover what it was. Striking out on his own, he first worked in a salmon cannery in Astoria, Oregon, and then settled in Portland, where he hoped not only to make money but also to learn something about America and its ways.

In the early years of the new century, Portland was a bustling metropolis of one hundred thousand. The largest city in the state and one of five major urban centers on the Pacific Coast, Portland was a hub of both commerce and culture. Thousands of immigrants speaking dozens of languages walked its streets in search of a new life. More than half of the twenty-six hundred or so Japanese immigrants in Oregon lived in Portland, segregated in a northwest district that was quickly dubbed Japantown. In a twenty-square-block area near the river, the immigrants lived, worked and played in a self-contained world of their own design, a city within a city that eventually grew to include more than a score of small hotels and dozens of businesses—from groceries, dry goods, restaurants and tofu manufacturers to bathhouses, barbers, tailors and pool halls.

When Masuo arrived in 1905, the Japanese community was in its infancy. Technically, Japanese had been in Oregon since 1834, when three shipwrecked seamen washed ashore near Cape Flattery. But the first permanent Japanese resident of the state—a girl brought back to Portland by a sea captain—did not arrive until 1880, and there was no significant immigration until the turn of the century. Even then, the numbers hardly compared with the Japanese influx into California or even Washington. In 1902, for example, only 130 of the more than 5,000 Japanese who immigrated to the three western coastal states came to Oregon. In Portland, the pioneer *issei* were just getting their bearings, and one of the institutions helping them do so was the Methodist Church, whose missionaries had enjoyed some success in Japan. In Portland, a Japanese

Methodist church was established in 1893—ten years before the first Buddhist church opened its doors. The Methodists also operated a mission a few blocks west of Japantown and sponsored a dormitory for young men. This was where eighteen-year-old Masuo Yasui settled in soon after his arrival in Portland.

The mission and dormitory were safe havens for the lonely, disoriented young men, most of whom knew neither the language nor the customs of their new country. Here might be the only place they could find a friendly white face, a person who could help them understand and cope with the challenges they faced. Here they could find clean and inexpensive housing and help securing employment. And here they were exposed to the Methodists' moral guidance and religious teachings. Masuo was befriended by the Portland minister, who was apparently impressed with the young man's character and seriousness of purpose. For his part, Masuo was impressed with the depth of the minister's faith. After a year of discussion and study, Masuo took his first major step toward adopting the ways of the country he wanted to call home: he converted to Christianity and was baptized in the Methodist Church. Undoubtedly it was a decision that came from his heart—and undeniably his religion became an important part of his life—but converting was also a shrewd move. While the vast majority of *issei* laborers kept the faith of their homeland, a number of the most successful Japanese immigrants were leaving Buddhism behind. Their acceptance of a Western faith seemed to make them more "palatable," or at least somewhat more comprehensible, to white society. It took the edge off their foreignness and gave them something in common with the dominant society in which they had to function. At nineteen, Masuo probably never thought of it this way, but becoming a Christian would help him gain acceptance by the white community.

While he tutored the young man in religious studies, the minister also found Masuo a job as a houseboy for the family of a prominent Portland attorney. Japanese boys—and, later, girls—often took domestic jobs with white families not so much for the money, which was not as good as agricultural or railroad work (their only other choices), but because it exposed them to American customs and language and helped them more quickly acclimate to their new world. For Masuo, this lowly job as dish- and diaper-washer was his introduction to life in the American upper middle class; and for a village farm boy who had just spent two years in remote railroad camps, it must have been an eye-opening experience.

Most houseboys lived with the families they worked for, receiving room and board plus a small monthly stipend, but Masuo probably continued to live at the Methodist mission. During the day, he performed routine domestic chores. At night, he began the second major step toward his Americanization by entering the night-school program at John Couch School in northwest Portland, which offered evening classes for foreign-speaking immigrants of all nationalities. Masuo already had two years of Japanese high school behind him and he was bright, but learning a new language at nineteen was no easy task. He approached it with the same intensity and drive that would characterize his entire adult life. How long he actually attended classes is not known, but within two years he was fluent.

Masuo's life was busy and ordered: he worked hard all day as a houseboy, went to school at night and came home to study until early morning. It was a full schedule, but he found time to be lonely. Some evenings he would walk to the Burnside Bridge and look down at the Willamette River, thinking that this same water found its way to the Pacific Ocean and eventually to Japan. Later he would tell his children that it comforted him to think of the tears he spilled in that wide river drying on the shores of his homeland. The youngest son missed his mother.

But he concentrated on the task at hand: Americanization. Following an immigrant custom that cut across all races and ethnicities, he Americanized his name, signing the letters he wrote to his father and brothers "Frank M. Yasui" and addressing Taiitsuro as "Frank T." and Renichi as "Fred R." This change was short-lived, but the process it represented was ongoing. In between housecleaning and child care, Masuo had the opportunity to spend time in the family's library, which included an extensive collection of legal volumes. As he struggled to read the books, he not only sharpened his language skills but also quickly developed an affinity for the law. He even entertained dreams of becoming a lawyer in America but soon discovered that the legal profession, like many others, was barred to noncitizens. In fact, more than five hundred varieties of urban jobs requiring licenses were closed to noncitizens. And Masuo, like his fellow Asian immigrants, could not become an American citizen. The Naturalization Act of 1790—which would not be nullified until 1952—barred them from the rights enjoyed by their European and African counterparts.

Masuo could learn English and he could become a Christian, but he could not remake himself into an American, as did millions of early-twentieth-century European immigrants. Welcomed by the Statue of Liberty, the Europeans could shed the ways of the Old World. They could change their speech, their customs, their citizenship, even their names. In time, they could be, if they wanted to be—and as so many first-generation immigrants did—indistinguishable from others who had been in the country for generations. But the Statue of Liberty showed her back to the Orient, and this was more than a symbolic gesture of exclusion. Although arrivals from Asia were sometimes welcomed as cheap labor, regardless of how long they lived in America and how Westernized they became, their faces would forever mark them as foreigners. But Masuo was blinded to the barrier created by his racial differences. He believed intensely, almost single-mindedly, in an idealized version of America, the classic immigrants' version, where race, class and ethnicity mattered little in a land of unparalleled opportunity, a nation founded on the principles of equality. And while this willful ignorance of the reality of twentieth-century America enabled him to go forth in the world with energy and optimism, it also imbued in him the false hope that he could Westernize himself into full acceptance by the white community. Almost four decades later, he would find out how wrong he was.

After more than two years in Portland, Masuo once again sensed that it was time to move on. The years had been well spent, but his future was not in domestic service. If he could not be a lawyer, then he would be a businessman. He looked for opportunities and a new home. He found Hood River.

Masuo liked to tell his children that as a young man he heard about a place called "Shin-shin-no-chi," the Japanese pronunciation of Cincinnati, which translated as "new, new land." Fascinated by the name and what promise the city might hold, he boarded a train in Portland heading east for Ohio. But—and here he would pause for dramatic impact—when the train snaked through the Columbia River gorge approaching Hood River, he stared out the window and was transfixed by the beauty of the passing scenery. The dense green valley sloping back to touch the base of a snow-capped peak that looked like beloved Mount Fuji reminded him so much of Japan that he got off the train then and there, declaring Hood River his new home.

It was a fanciful—and completely fabricated—story, a little fairy tale invented for his children. Undoubtedly he thought the valley was lovely, and many immigrants remarked on the similarities between Mount Hood and Mount Fuji, but Masuo was a pragmatist, not a poet. Hood River offered opportunities for an ambitious young man.

He traveled up the railroad line, probably to Montana, to talk with Taiitsuro and Renichi about opening a store to serve the *issei* of Hood River valley. (By this time, their father, Shinataro, had already returned to

Japan with savings that would allow him to live as a prosperous farmer and landowner.) Their railroad wages may have been meager, but the older brothers had spent the past nine years working steadily and living frugally, and they probably had a fair sum put away. They listened closely to Masuo's plans and decided to part with at least some of their savings to form a partnership. Together they would open the Yasui Brothers Store in Hood River.

Masuo returned to Portland to gather his belongings and, in the spring of 1908, once again boarded the train east to Hood River, eager now, at twenty-one, to make his mark in America.

2

Paradise

The Hood River that greeted Masuo in 1908 and would be his home for the next thirty years was a prosperous small town with a weekly newspaper, three banks, two lawyers, three doctors, two undertakers and a twelve-hundred-volume library. Alongside the candy emporiums (two), millineries (four), livery stables (two) and farm implement stores (five) were two major hotels built for the summer trade—Portlanders or more distant urbanites who, if ill, came to "take the air" and, if hardy, came to venture up the slopes of Mount Hood. Two restaurants, a lunch counter and two saloons served the thousand or so townspeople whose lives were made more pleasant by divertissements both sophisticated and humble. A pair of downtown movie theaters offered the latest two-reel adventures, while dozens of talent shows, choral-group performances and lodge dances filled out the social calendar. Local dramatic productions, deemed "outrageously bad" by one native son, flourished nonetheless. Wholesome types flocked to Grange picnics and church socials, while their less virtuous neighbors frequented one of the town's several pool halls. There, as one local put it, "gambling is under the ban, but tobacco smoke and its accompaniment of undesirable language and anecdotes are not."

Although in those days still geographically remote, Hood River was not, like many northwestern towns its size, a backwoods outpost. In addition to the four trains and two to four steamers that daily linked the town to the outside world, the city boasted five hundred telephones (with "continuous service provided by three on-duty operators") and an extensive rural free-delivery system. By the year Masuo arrived, all in-town businesses and homes had electricity, and a new waterworks provided city dwellers with clear mountain water for domestic use.

The city and valley were booming with industry. Columbia River salmon runs were legendary, and commercial fishing was a major enterprise in town. At the same time, a $350,000-a-year lumber industry provided jobs for more than a thousand men——many of them Japanese——in logging camps scattered throughout the valley and at three large sawmills. Fish were so plentiful and the forests so vast that no one could imagine their demise. A 1905 pamphlet produced by the town's Commercial Club, a forerunner to the Chamber of Commerce, bragged of the "millions of feet of standing lumber . . . an amount sufficient to keep the big mills cutting 200,000 feet a day for fifty years to come." But the forests toppled faster than that and were not replanted. And logging practices, dams and overfishing depleted within a single generation the salmon runs that had nourished countless generations of Indians. The one industry that endured in the valley was specialized agriculture—what locals dubbed "fruit ranching." Masuo may have initially come to Hood River to open a store, but he was soon to realize that his future, like that of the valley's, was in the fruit business.

When he arrived in 1908, only 10 percent of the valley's available farmland was under cultivation as orchards. Agriculture was still very much in its infancy, but the budding apple business was enjoying enormous success, an early boom that would be unequaled in the history of Hood River. In the first few years of the twentieth century, the valley's fruit industry changed quickly and dramatically, from a few orchardists supplying local markets to a core of serious, innovative growers marketing to national and international buyers.

Hood River apples—huge, crisp and able to maintain their perfection through the winter—practically sold themselves. Eastern buyers discovered the valley's Spitzenbergs and Newtons in the 1890s at countless agricultural exhibits throughout the country, from the Pan American Exposition in Buffalo to the World's Fair in Chicago to the St. Louis Fair, where Hood River apples took the grand prize, the gold medal and twenty-seven other medals. At the Columbian Exposition in 1892, Hood River Valley received sixteen awards, more than any other region, including a prize for the largest apple, a six-and-a-quarter-inch-high, thirty-three-ounce Spitzenberg as big around as a cantaloupe.

While amassing these agricultural accolades, local orchardists were busy pioneering a new system of apple packing, where the produce was placed carefully in boxes, not, as had been the usual method, crammed into barrels. Each box contained the same number of identically sized, hand-selected apples arranged in uniform layers and was packed by independent packers, not by the growers themselves. This revolutionary system went a long way toward establishing the Hood River apple's reputation for quality and excellence.

In 1900, responding to interest generated by the awards and contacts made through the expositions, growers freighted their first shipment of apples to New York. Five years later, 90 percent of the valley's apple output was being shipped east for the "fancy trade," with thousands of boxes heading across the Atlantic to markets in England, Germany and France. The valley's produce continued to gain in international prominence and became, as a *Pacific Monthly* article noted, the only fruit sold at English auctions "where buyer and bidder had such confidence in the quality and grade that they made their purchases without opening a box to examine the contents." From 1900 to 1910, the entire crop of valley apples sold while still on the trees, two months before they were ready to be picked and packed. In 1906, while other apples brought less than a dollar a box, Hood River produce was selling—and selling out—at three times the price. In 1907, civic boosters claimed that Hood River apples sold for "the highest price the world has ever known." With only twenty-eight hundred acres in mature, producing orchards and tens of thousands of good, tillable acres yet to be developed, there were fortunes to be made in the valley.

Prosperity—or the promise of such—brought an influx of easterners to the area, men with money and the desire to make more. Between 1907 and 1916, sixty-eight "tenderfeet" from New York settled in the upper valley, investing in prime orchard land. A scion of a Philadelphia cabinet-manufacturing magnate came to diversify the family fortune. One of the Vanderbilts ventured west to carve an extensive orchard from the valley floor. Billy Sunday, the fiery evangelist, summered on an impressive estate nearby. A prominent San Francisco architect, a well-known landscape artist, and the Northwest's pioneer botanist all bought land and settled in. Throughout the valley were scores of "remittance men," a common term in those days for ne'er-do-well sons whose wealthy families had banished them westward but kept them solvent through regular monetary remittances. These gentlemen orchardists would parade through town in their jodhpurs and puttees, leaving the work of running their enterprises to others—principally hundreds of Japanese fieldhands. Meanwhile, the gentlemen and ladies associated with their own kind at the city's thriving University Club, which in 1910 boasted 135 members with baccalaureates from Harvard, Yale, Princeton, Cornell, Vassar and Wellesley.

The arrival of the upper crust to the upper valley, as well as an influx of men of more modest means, was due in large part to the efforts of

Hood River's unrelentingly boastful Commercial Club. Masuo had undoubtedly read club-inspired stories of the glories of Hood River in the
Portland newspapers. By the time he arrived, the club was in its eighth
consecutive year of a civic promotion campaign so intense that the efforts of Phineas T. Barnum paled by comparison. "Without exaggera-
tion," proclaimed the club in one of the many booklets it published, "it
can be truthfully said that no spot in the world has perhaps been more
benignly smiled upon by Dame Fortune than the city and valley of Hood
River." The club's 1908 pamphlet featured full-page, hand-tinted photographs of stately homes, impressive school buildings and trees laden
with apples so large and perfectly formed that they looked more like co-
lossal Christmas-tree ornaments than fruit. Yet another booklet enticed
potential settlers with a litany of Hood River's many conveniences—
from good schools to sanitary sewer systems—beckoning them to "enjoy life in a region of wonderful scenic beauty and pleasing climate."

Climate was a major selling point, for Hood River, nestled at the
juncture of western and eastern Oregon, suffered neither the extreme
aridity of the east side nor the incessant sogginess of the west. As another booster pamphlet put it in 1900, hawking the climate like a bottle
of patent medicine:

> The summers are ideal. Even in the hottest part of summer, the nights
> are deliciously cool, insuring sleep and rest. The winters are neither long
> nor severe. The climate will perhaps be best suited to invalids, who, from
> long residence in high or windy regions, have suffered from that ner-
> vousness so common to such sections, and to busy men and women in
> general. . . . Such people are usually sufferers from insomnia, loss of ap-
> petite and digestive power. The effect of this climate on such is to induce
> sleep and improve the assimilating functions. Sufferers from general ma-
> larial affections will almost invariably be cured, as will also most cases of
> dry catarrh.

The entry went on to claim that Hood River's climate could cure rheu-
matism, "heart affections," and consumption as well as provide a "practical immunity" to childhood diseases and "acute inflammations."

But city boosters were more interested in attracting healthy entrepreneurs than invalids. "For the person willing to work, there is always
an opening in the Hood River valley," proclaimed one booklet. "A warm
welcome awaits the homebuilder who wishes to engage in horticulture,"
stated another. "To the man of small means who is industrious, Hood
River offers peculiar inducements," began a club pamphlet from 1900.
Land——mineral-rich volcanic soil well irrigated by the river and a system of ditches—was the major inducement. And while the few thou-

sand acres of land developed into successful apple orchards might sell
for as much as $4,000 an acre, unimproved land could be bought for as
little as $50 an acre. It might cost $100 an acre to clear and plow the land,
$20 to plant it and $15 a year to care for it; but by the fifth year a person
could grow enough apples to meet expenses, and after ten years a single
acre of good trees could bring a $400 profit.

"The Hood River fruit industry has within the past ten years made
fortunes for scores of men. It has placed hundreds of others in positions of independence," claimed a 1908 promotion pamphlet. On pages
filled with itemized calculations, investors with big dreams and common folk with more humble aspirations could figure how a small investment might yield an eye-opening profit. Other booklets detailed individual success stories, from the transplanted New Yorker who cleared
ten thousand dollars in a single year to the penniless German immigrant
who arrived in the valley as a field hand and fifteen years later owned
orchards worth sixty thousand dollars. "There is such a heavy margin of
profit," claimed the civic boosters the year Masuo arrived in Hood River,
"that present prices could . . . stand a material reduction and still leave
the growers with a nice, healthy independent business."

Many of the growers, particularly the gentlemen from the East, managed to clear these heavy margins of profit by taking advantage of cheap
Japanese labor. An almost entirely male *issei* workforce had originally been
imported to Hood River in 1902 to work on a local railroad line. But the
work was intermittent during the ten years it took to build twenty-five
miles of track up the valley; and when the railroad gangs were laid off,
the men labored in the orchards. They put in ten- to twelve-hour days
for a dollar and change, carefully tending young orchards and performing stoop labor in the fields. The whites claimed the Japanese were well
suited to this backbreaking work because their short stature meant they
were closer to the ground. Other men found employment in the local
lumber mills, although at first mill owners and their foremen thought the
Japanese men were too short and slight for the heavy work. To persuade
them otherwise, Japanese folklore in the valley has it that one *issei* volunteered to prove he could not only handle the work but do it for three
days and nights without stopping. He did—and the mill then consented
to hire him and his countrymen. The story is probably more myth than
fact, but it has the ring of a larger truth: the Japanese were frequently
called on to prove themselves and did so by outperforming their Caucasian counterparts.

The most grueling work—but ultimately the work that helped the
Japanese establish a permanent place in the valley—was clearing stumps.

Thousands of acres of virgin forest on the valley floor had been logged off by local lumber companies, who left the land choked with brush, brambles, rocks and stumps. Converting this so-called stumpage to profitable orchard land required enormous effort. From November through March, when the rains kept the ground soft enough to work with, as many as six hundred Japanese laborers axed down heavy stands of willow and alder, grub-hoed roots and dynamited and burned stumps for white landowners. It might take two or three days to remove just one stump—blasting it, splitting it, pulling well-anchored pieces from deep in the ground with a steel cable hitched to a workhorse. And there might be as many as one hundred stumps on an acre.

Some men of small means bought this cheap land and spent the next five years clearing it themselves while simultaneously working in the mills to put food on the table. But many of the valley's future orchardists hired Japanese to do the work, often paying them not in dollars but in small tracts of the least desirable, uncleared land. Although they certainly weren't getting a bargain—some of the stumpiest land farthest from the river sold for as little as five dollars an acre—Japanese were able to become landowners with no capital investment. By 1911, eight farms in the valley were operated by Japanese.

But the roots they were putting down were agricultural, not emotional. Most of the men were bachelors who planned to return to Japan after saving a nest egg. In the meantime, they lived crudely in tents and shanties, venturing into town only when they needed supplies or when they had enough money to hire one of the girls employed at Niguma's for an hour on a Saturday night. The men knew almost no English and had few interactions with the whites of Hood River.

For Masuo Yasui, the experience was immediately different. He came to town not as a day laborer but as an incipient businessman. He came already Westernized, a Christian who spoke and wrote fluent English. And he came to stay. Wasting no time getting started, Masuo and his two brothers opened their store for business on June 16, 1908, in a small wooden building on Third Street, just off the main business thoroughfare in downtown Hood River. Although by that time Japanese owned more than 3,000 business establishments on the West Coast, almost all of them were in urban centers. The Yasui Brothers Store was one of only 120 or so Japanese-owned provision stores in the United States and one of perhaps two or three Japanese businesses in Hood River. In addition to the Niguma Store, with which the Yasuis ran direct competition, there were at various times in the early 1900s a laundry, a noodle shop and a combination lunch counter-tofu "factory."

The sign below the front display window read YASUI BROTHERS CO. ALL
KINDS OF JAPANESE GOODS, but from the beginning the tiny store carried
an eclectic inventory, including just about anything, foreign or domestic,
a Japanese worker might need. There was *shoyu* (soy sauce), black and fra-
grant, ladled from a heavy reed tub, imported rice in metal-lined boxes
and long knobby roots of *gobo* (burdock) stuck in tall, sawdust-filled
boxes. There were bins of special rice flours and shelves stacked with
jars of sauces and condiments and cans of pickled vegetables. In the
glass display cases that lined the walls there were delicate vases, kimonos,
fans, tea sets, little wooden toys and rice-paper stationery. But there were
also work boots, pots and pans, watches, knives, handkerchiefs, gloves,
suspenders and overalls for sale. Penny candy, both American suckers
and sourballs and soft Japanese caramels wrapped in edible rice paper,
filled large apothecary jars. The air was thick with the smells of the old
country: green-leaf tea, dried fish and incense.

The store was Renichi's domain. For sixty hours a week, from eight-
thirty in the morning until six at night on weekdays and until nine on
Saturdays, he worked the counter and the cash register, exchanged pleas-
antries with the customers, dispensed candy to the children and generally
took care of daily operations. Although the eldest brother, Taiitsuro, had
contributed some of his savings to start the store, his heart apparently
wasn't in the venture. Early on, he decided that being a shopkeeper was
not for him, and he either persuaded his younger siblings to give him
most of his money back or he simply demanded it, as would be his right
as *chonan*. At any rate, he was never an active participant in the store.
In fact, soon after it opened, he returned to Japan with savings sizable
enough to bankroll a new venture. Fulfilling the dream of hundreds of
thousands of his fellow sojourners, he went back to his home village,
started a new business (a denim factory), built a walled estate, raised a
large family and became increasingly wealthy.

In Hood River, the two remaining brothers formed a legal partnership that equally divided all profits from the store. But while Renichi was
the man behind the counter, Masuo was the man behind the scenes, ordering the merchandise, paying the bills, keeping the books—and keeping his eye out for other opportunities. It was an odd relationship, with
Masuo, the younger brother, in essence the boss and Renichi, the older
brother, the employee. In Japan, family hierarchy was inflexible, and a
younger brother would never be in a superior position to his older sibling. But their relationship as brothers was not that clear cut. In fact,
Renichi had spent much of his youth as a member of another family—as a *yoshi,* or adopted son. In a country where name and property

were handed down only through the male line, it was common practice for a childless couple to adopt the son of a family blessed with several sons, giving him their name and thus ensuring the future of that family for another generation. In his boyhood, Renichi had been adopted by the Fujimotos, who lived in a tiny village about eight miles from the Yasuis. He was Masuo's blood brother, but his passport read "Renichi Fujimoto." Perhaps his status as *yoshi* made a difference in the relationship between the two brothers, softening the rigidity of the customary hierarchy. Or perhaps they were able to play by new rules because they were in a new land. Whatever the internal dynamics, the brothers apparently came to an early understanding of their particular strengths and positioned themselves accordingly. Renichi was a hard and tireless worker, dependable, kind and self-effacing. Masuo was the ambitious one. No one could remember their exchanging harsh words.

From the moment the store opened, Masuo dressed like a successful businessman in a proper dark suit and tie. But Yasui Brothers was not an instant success. The going was so tough in the early days that Masuo was forced to take a second job just to keep the store afloat. He worked as a janitor for the nearby Butler Bank, under the condition that he could do all his cleaning at night. That way the good folks of Hood River wouldn't see an up-and-coming young businessman pushing a broom. The brothers kept their living expenses to a minimum, rooming together in the back of the store and preparing meals from their own merchandise in a makeshift kitchen. Within two years, a combination of their frugality, Masuo's business sense and an increase in the valley's Japanese population put the business on firm footing. Soon Masuo was deluged with entreaties from Sears, Montgomery Ward, Congoleum and others to feature their products in the store, and the range of the Yasui Brothers' inventory increased accordingly.

As the store began to establish itself in the *nikkei* (Japanese) community, Masuo, ever enterprising, turned his attention to new opportunities. As one of the very few *issei* who could both speak and write fluent English, he began to see his value as a go-between and quickly discovered that he could make money from several side businesses. He worked for the Oregon Apple Company of Hood River as a labor contractor, recruiting Japanese workers to clear land, negotiating their wages and mediating disputes. He also became an agent for the Occidental Life Insurance Company of California, signing up his fellow countrymen for modest insurance policies that they could later borrow against during hard times.

Even in these early days, with Masuo barely out of his teens, he began to assume a leadership role in the Japanese community, helping *issei* with both business and personal matters and becoming intricately involved in their lives. A man might fall ill or have an accident and need a doctor, but he didn't know whom to go to and he couldn't make himself understood. So the man went to Masuo, and Masuo found the doctor—usually Dr. Abraham, whose office was a few doors down from the store—and acted as interpreter. He helped his friends keep their finances straight, writing and answering letters for them to the bank. He guided them through what to them was the incomprehensible paperwork that made up much of American life. And as he talked to the men, he tried to persuade them to think of Hood River as their home. "Your future is not in seasonal or contract labor," he would tell them when they visited the store to buy supplies. "Settle here. Buy land. Make this your home." In this, Masuo was echoing the advice of the single most respected *issei* leader in the United States, Kyutaro Abiko, publisher of the leading Japanese-language daily newspaper in the West. Abiko used his California paper to disseminate the idea of permanent settlement, consistently advising Japanese laborers to take up farming and even publishing yearbooks listing *issei* farmers and their holdings. In 1906, he pioneered a Japanese farming colony in California by purchasing 3,200 acres of undeveloped land and selling it in small tracts to his countrymen.

Masuo tried the same thing in Hood River on a smaller scale. In 1911, he and two silent partners put a down payment of eight thousand dollars on 320 acres of undeveloped Hood River Valley land with the idea of selling off small, affordable plots to laborers wanting to put down roots. Within five months of buying the property, Masuo had already sold a third of it in eight- to ten-acre tracts, generating more than six thousand dollars cash and holding notes worth more than another six thousand dollars. In mid-1911, he bought several downtown city lots. But his ambition overreached his still-modest means, and by the fall of 1911 he was asking the bank for extensions on three notes.

He managed to squeak through, supported by profits from the Yasui Brothers Store and fueled by new enterprises. Late in 1911, John Leland Henderson, the attorney who had sold him the 320 acres, wrote to ask for Masuo's assistance. Henderson would give Masuo a thousand-dollar commission for finding Japanese buyers for a large plot of land he owned north of Portland.

Certainly he could make money acting as a real-estate go-between, but he could also achieve a higher purpose: helping his countrymen find a permanent home in America. Time and again he urged the *issei* bachelors to settle down, build houses and marry. And in 1911, three years after his arrival in Hood River, with his ventures going well and his influence expanding, he was ready to take his own advice.

Shidzuyo Miyake was born the same year as Masuo in the same small village of Nanukaichi. Her father, Ichiro, was the elder who had helped Masuo fill out his emigration papers and counseled Masuo's mother during the years her husband and older sons were in America. Shidzuyo was his *chojo,* or eldest daughter, and he doted on her from the moment of her birth, when he chose her comely name—Shidzuyo means "peaceful, loving and calm"—and throughout her early life. Unlike the Yasuis, who were a moderately prosperous, landowning family, the Miyakes were poor. Ichiro was a netmaker by trade but a poet and philosopher at heart, a man who would rather gaze out over the rice paddies and compose *tanka* poetry than tend to his business. Though respected as a wise and kind man in the village, he had difficulty supporting his family.

Shidzuyo, like virtually all children of Meiji-era Japan, attended six years of grammar school. But few went beyond this free and compulsory early education. Shidzuyo, however, had both the ambition and the talent to continue—and she may have felt the necessity to take her future in her own hands. Her family's economic status would not help her get along in society and might even preclude a good marriage. After a few more years in a village school, Shidzuyo had gone as far as she could go and needed to move to nearby Okayama City to continue her high school education. Ichiro had no money to support this endeavor, but he did write letters to several people trying to line up a "housegirl" job for his daughter. Finally, an eye doctor in the city agreed to give Shidzuyo room and board in exchange for her services as a domestic. But there was some confusion about what was expected. Apparently the doctor assumed Shidzuyo would both clean the house and care for the small children in the hours she wasn't at school. This left her no time to study. When she did take the time she needed, the doctor promptly wrote to Ichiro, telling him that his daughter wasn't performing well and asking him to come get her.

Ichiro traveled to the city to reclaim his daughter, disappointed not that she had shirked some of her domestic duties but that he was not able to offer financial support for her schooling. As they waited together at the station for the train home, Shidzuyo and her father ran into a young girl from the home village. She was Shidzuyo's age and had been in her class in grammar school. On that day she was wearing a lovely dress and carrying an armload of books, full of enthusiasm about the new high school she was going to in the city and her plans for the future. Writing in his diary at home that night, Ichiro mourned his inability to give his daughter the same opportunities as that girl. But not all of Shidzuyo's family was as interested in her education as her father. Her paternal grandmother, for example, expressed the more common view of the day: "Why does she need an education? She's just a girl."

When Shidzuyo came home to the village, this grandmother insisted that she take most of the responsibility for caring for her much-younger brother, even though Shidzuyo's mother and maternal grandmother were both available. "This is the kind of education she needs," the grandmother insisted. Shidzuyo, the dutiful daughter, obeyed. But she was terribly unhappy. When the chance came to return to school in Okayama, she took it gleefully. And in March of 1905, while an ocean away Masuo was struggling to learn English in night school, Shidzuyo graduated from an Okayama City high school.

Immediately looking to the future, she traveled to Hiroshima to take an examination that would certify her to teach. But her first attempt was unsuccessful. She was mortified. She sent a telegram to her father, telling him of her failure and saying that she could not come home and face her friends and neighbors. Instead, she would be taking the train from Hiroshima to her uncle's home in another village. In his diary, Ichiro recounted that he had been in the fields when a boy came to deliver the wire and that he immediately put down his hoe and started walking to a little town where the Hiroshima train would make a stop. He wanted Shidzuyo to know that he was still proud of her, that she had nothing to be ashamed o, and that she could come home. He arrived in time to intercept the train and persuade his daughter to return home.

But the tiny village of Nanukaichi had little to offer a girl intent on becoming a teacher. She soon left again to continue her education, this time enrolling at the Tokyo Women's Christian College and becoming the first girl in her village ever to go past secondary school. At the college, a two-year teacher-training school sponsored by the Congregational Church, she took sewing, painting, flower arranging and a variety of arts-and-crafts courses considered central to the life of a cultured Japanese woman. As she pursued her degree in home economics, she lived with a professor's family, doing chores on the side to earn her room and board. At the same time, undoubtedly due to the Congregationalist influences at the college, she converted to Christianity. At school she worked hard and showed real talent, especially in poetry, her father's first love. In fact, she self-published a thin volume of *tanka* poetry. When the course of study was completed, she sat for another teacher-certification examination, this time passing it and becoming one of only four students from her entire prefecture to do so.

In April of 1910, Shidzuyo secured her first position, as an eleventh-grade teacher in a girl's high school in her home prefecture, teaching tea ceremony, flower arranging, *sumie* (a black-and-white painting technique) and sewing. A photograph from this time shows her—upswept hair framing a proud, serene face—standing above a group of dark-kimonoed students. She had grown into a pretty woman, a few inches shy of five feet tall, with a strong, purposeful face that belied her tiny stature. She had high, very prominent cheekbones, lively dark eyes and a resolute jaw that might have been overpowering had it not been balanced by the mass of jet-black hair she wore piled on her head in a traditional high roll. Her students called her *Sensei,* a term of respect, meaning teacher or master. At barely twenty-four, she lived up to the name.

In the fall of 1910, Shidzuyo moved a hundred miles from her home to the tiny island of Awaji in the Inland Sea to teach at a girls school in Sumoto, a small village at the southern tip of the island. As she continued instructing pupils in the cultured domestic arts, she began what would be a two-year correspondence with a home-village boy, a young man she had grown up with, gone to grammar school with, and whose family had interacted with hers for years: Masuo Yasui.

It is doubtful that the two had been teenage sweethearts before Masuo left for America. The culture of their time would not have permitted such independence of action. After puberty, girls and boys were essentially segregated and interaction between them was minimal. In any case, romance was not, at least initially, a part of any pairing. Marital matches were arranged by outside intermediaries who might take many factors into consideration, but generally not the personal feelings of those they would be uniting. Virtually all marriages were arranged. Masuo, therefore, took a bold, independent step in beginning to correspond with Shidzuyo sometime late in 1910. He was probably encouraged by Renichi, who felt it was time for his younger brother to settle down. In Oregon, women made up less than 4 percent of the Japanese population, and *issei who* wanted brides had to import them. Shidzuyo, in answering and encouraging Masuo, also took a bold, independent step. Women of her day were supposed to sit back and wait for their families to arrange their futures.

Ichiro, proud of his only daughter for her accomplishments, was not pleased to learn that she was corresponding with a young man struggling to make a living some five thousand miles away. In his diary, he wrote of his great anger as he set off to see her, intent on quashing the relationship and any plans the two might have made. It was not an easy journey for him. First, he had to travel from Nanukaichi some eighty miles to the port city of Kobe. There he caught a ferry to Awaji and probably had to walk the length of the small island to the town of Sumoto. By the time he got to Shidzuyo's school he had worked himself into a lather, planning to lay down the law immediately and demand that his daughter end the correspondence and the relationship. But Shidzuyo was teaching when he arrived, and he spent the afternoon pacing the floor of a nearby inn instead. When she finally arrived, as he later confided to his diary, she was beaming, overjoyed to see her father on this surprise visit. Looking at her smiling face, he realized how much he loved her and wished her to be happy. And at that instant, *"Toketa* (I just melted)," he wrote in his diary. "What are you doing here?" Shidzuyo asked delightedly. "Isn't it wonderful that you've come." The two settled into a warm visit during which Ichiro said not a word about Masuo and the letters he knew were being exchanged. Only much later did Shidzuyo realize the intended purpose of her father's visit.

Meanwhile she and Masuo continued their correspondence, which was getting even more serious than Ichiro had suspected, and in mid-April 1911, a very special letter arrived. It was a handmade card on thick paper tied with yellow and green ribbons.. Inside, in careful script in the language of his new country, Masuo had written:

> To Miss S. Miyake.
> Heartily accept
> your purest love,
> and engage to
> unite in future.
> > Your beloved
> > M. Yasui
> > at Hood River, Ore.
> > U.S.A.

Shidzuyo knew no English, but the simple beauty of the card needed no translation.

She must have spent quite some time considering this proposal of marriage. On the one hand, she was supporting herself with a job she enjoyed and was respected for. She had made a place for herself through the force of her own intelligence, ambition and perseverance. On the other hand, she was twenty-five, quite a few years past what was then considered the marriageable prime.

But her dilemma was more complicated than that. In the Japan of her day, women often lived in fear of marriage because it meant becoming a daughter-in-law in the husband's family—and there was no lower status. The trials of the daughter-in-law were legendary. She was assigned the most menial and onerous tasks, rising in the morning before the rest of the family and doing her mother-in-law's bidding all day. Isolated from her own friends and family, she lived to serve and procreate. If she was fortunate enough to bear a male heir, her status improved somewhat, but she would have little control over the household in which she lived—or, for that matter, over her own life—until she became a mother-in-law herself and benefited from the system. Shidzuyo, unlike many of her female contemporaries, had already experienced years of independence. Marrying a Meiji man, if one could be found who would consent to unite with a twenty-five-year-old spinster, was not an attractive proposition. If Shidzuyo was to be a wife, she would have to look across the ocean to a new society.

She had other grounds for giving serious consideration to Masuo's proposal, even though accepting it would mean leaving her job, her homeland, and, most important of all, her father. One émigré bride, a contemporary of Shidzuyo's, wrote about the reasons she and thousands of others came to America in an article later published by a Colorado magazine. In addition to "fear of mother-in-law in Japan" and "anxiety of those who have passed marriage age," she contended that women journeyed to the West for many of the same reasons men did: curiosity, hopes of becoming rich, dreams of an idyllic new land and lack of ability to support oneself at home. The last would not have pertained to Shidzuyo, but there is every reason to assume that she, like Masuo and countless others, was affected by "America fever."

In fact, Japanese women were actively being recruited for emigration by their government during the second two decades of the twentieth century. Until this time, emigrants were almost solely Japanese men, either young bachelors like the Yasui boys or older men like Shinataro who left their wives behind. But the home government soon realized it would have to take steps to avoid the problems of a bachelor society abroad, the same problems that had helped sour Westerners on the Chinese (whose population in America at one point numbered twenty-seven men to each woman): prostitution, gambling and drunkenness. Thus, when the Japanese and American governments consented to the restrictive Gentlemen's Agreement of 1908—a pact that halted the "invasion" of Japanese laborers—they left a large loophole, allowing unrestricted immigration for the wives (as well as children and parents) of male workers already in America. Some, of course, had left wives behind and could call for them, but most were young bachelors without the resources to return to Japan to look for wives. By the second decade of the twentieth century, these erstwhile sojourners were beginning to realize that they weren't going to make their fortunes and return home as quickly as they had originally planned. Apart from any sentimental desire for family life, the men needed women to help them make money.

And so was born the "picture bride" arrangement, a modification of Japan's traditional matchmaker system. Village go-betweens still matched the marriageable children of compatible families—in this case Japanese women with *issei* men—but the pair met only through letters and photographs. If the families agreed to the marriage, a mock wedding took place in the home village with a stand-in for the groom, and the woman's name was transferred to the man's family register. Then, making use of the loophole in the gentlemen's agreement, the new wife or picture bride could secure a passport and journey to America to see her husband for the first time. Between 1909 and 1920, when the so-called Ladies' Agreement halted the immigration of picture brides, almost forty-five thousand Japanese women came to America. Most, like the men who preceded them, were young southern Japanese from respectable farming families.

Of course, Shidzuyo and Masuo knew each other, and their relationship was of their own making, not the result of a go-between, but the picture-bride system worked for them as well. When she finally accepted Masuo's long-distance marriage proposal, Shidzuyo, like thousands of women of her generation, married an absent groom in a Japanese ceremony in order to qualify for a passport. At twenty-six, she became Mrs. Masuo Yasui, married to a man she hadn't seen for at least ten years. In the fall of 1912, almost a year and a half after Masuo's ribbon-tied proposal, Shidzuyo packed her silk kimonos, her delicate tea-ceremony equipment and her prized *koto* (a traditional stringed musical instrument) and boarded a steamer in Yokohama bound for Tacoma. Her father was heartbroken, composing these verses on his daughter's departure:

> *Sad is the life that is left behind*
> *Unable to take one's leave ahead*
> *Little did I ever dream*
> *This parting of our lives.*

> *Who would have thought at all*
> *At this age of sixty years or so*
> *That I would feel so utterly lost*
> *At the parting of our lives.*

For the next three weeks, Shidzuyo's world was the swaying steerage hold of a picture-bride ship, where the young women—like the men who preceded them a decade before—slept in stacked bunkbeds and breathed squalid belowdecks air. Almost eighty years later, another Hood River-bound bride could vividly recall the low ceilings, dim light and toilets that were no more than holes with sea water rushing in to take away the excrement. For Shidzuyo, an educated and accomplished woman who had spent her days instructing attentive girls in the fine domestic arts, this would be the first of many culture shocks.

The boat arrived in Tacoma in mid-September, and Masuo was there to meet it, carrying in his pocket a twenty-five-dollar diamond engagement ring he had bought from a Montgomery Ward catalog. Within days Shidzuyo was "Westernized," her comfortable kimono and slippers traded for a high-necked dress and pointy-toed boots. And as soon as paperwork would allow, on November 4, 1912, she and Masuo married again, this time face-to-face, tying the knot in a legal and official U.S. ceremony. Then it was off to Hood River, where Masuo had purchased a small house on Columbia Street for his bride and himself. There would be no more makeshift living in the store with his brother.

Masuo was now a true settler, ready to embark on a future more auspicious than he could have hoped for. The Yasui Brothers Store was already a fixture in the valley's sizable *issei* community, and Masuo's recent ventures into real estate and other businesses held the promise of both increased income and status. With a wife, he could sink his roots more deeply in the valley he was coming to regard as home. But for Shidzuyo, Hood River meant something quite different: a strange, new place where people chattered in a language she would never truly understand; a place where her future, which had fleetingly been her own, was now in the hands of the man by her side.

3

Roots Sunk Deep

Laced in her first corset, with a mail-order diamond ring on her finger and her past packed away in a wicker trunk, Shidzuyo arrived in Hood River early in the winter of 1912. Stepping from the train into a new world, she was in the vanguard of the most important change in the short history of Japanese immigration to America. Her arrival, like that of the tens of thousands of other brides who reached Western shores in the second decade of the twentieth century, marked the beginning of a new era. The day of the pioneer sojourner, the single male, was over. The day of the settler—and the family—had begun.

In the Hood River valley, this meant a significant decrease in the *issei* population, as the influx of brides was more than countered by the departure of *dekaseginin*, the temporary immigrants who had been working on the railroad or in the orchards. By 1920 one in four of the Japanese who had lived in the valley ten years earlier were gone. (But those who remained were there to stay: during the same decade the number of farms operated by *issei* increased ninefold.) When Shidzuyo arrived in 1912, she joined a settlement of perhaps 450 of her compatriots. Yet it was dissociation, not a sense of community, that awaited her, for the Yasuis—then, and for the next thirty years—would be one of the very few in-town Japanese families. To Masuo this mattered little. He had daily encounters with store customers and regularly traveled throughout the valley on business. But to Shidzuyo it meant immediate and severe isolation. The informal female network that ordinarily would have welcomed a downtown merchant's new wife with teas and invitations to join auxiliaries and church groups existed for white women only. Its Japanese equivalent, to the extent that there was one in those early years, operated

35

out in the valley, fifteen or twenty winding miles down bad dirt roads. And Shidzuyo didn't drive.

The initial cultural shock was overwhelming. Everything was different in America, from the peculiar language and strange food to the simplest everyday activities: sleeping on an elevated bed, keeping your shoes on in the house. Could it be that America had no dirt? wondered the *issei* women. Why else would people wear shoes into their homes? Shidzuyo's first days were undoubtedly both disorienting and lonely, but at least she was spared two of the most unhappy surprises that often greeted her sisters: their new husbands and their new homes.

Unlike most of her contemporaries, Shidzuyo was not a true picture bride, a woman who first glimpsed her husband when she walked down the gangplank onto a new land. A surprising number of these brides were so distraught at seeing their new spouses—many of whom were twenty or more years older than the photographs they had sent to Japan—that they pleaded (unsuccessfully) to be let back on the ship and returned home. The relationships that grew from these blind unions between young girls, who felt they had been tricked, and desperate middle-aged men, who lied about themselves and their prospects to attract a mate, were often uneasy, unhappy ones. Shidzuyo, on the other hand, began her married life comfortably with a man her own age, a man she had known as a child and, through two years of correspondence, had come to know as an adult. And, while many Hood River brides were shocked to find that their new homes in America were nothing more than tents or shanties set out in the raw land, Shidzuyo at least had a real house, however small, to settle into.

Even within the walls of that house, however, she found life far different from what she had known. In Japan, she had been the daughter of a doting father whose love allowed her much latitude and many freedoms. But in America she was the wife of what *issei* women called, sometimes with exasperation but mostly with resignation, "a real Meiji man." This was a man who, the true product of his times, saw himself as the undisputed head of the household and expected his wife to subordinate her wishes to his own, to cater to all his needs while rarely helping her with any of her duties. In Japan she had been a *sensei*, a respected teacher whose students revered her. In America she was a housewife, her only status derived from her husband's position. And perhaps most significantly, in her native land she had developed into a cultured woman, a writer of poetry, an amateur musician, a woman who took pleasure in arranging flowers and performing the elaborately ritualized tea ceremony. These were not the skills she would need in Hood River. And they set her apart from the *issei* women in the valley who didn't have her education or level of sophistication and whose dawn-to-dusk toiling precluded much of a cultural life.

But, like her husband, Shidzuyo had been well schooled in the value of hard work, self-sacrifice and perseverance. These tenets of the Meiji ethic were etched into the psyches of nineteenth-century Japanese just as the Protestant work ethic, with its same nose-to-the-grindstone philosophy, was a part of the American consciousness. Shidzuyo called upon these values during those first hard months, and in the moments when they may have been insufficient in the difficult task of adjustment, she could fall back on a distinctly Japanese sense of resignation. *Shikata ga nai* (It cannot be helped), the *issei* used to say, shaking their heads about any situation over which they had no control. *Shikata ga nai* allowed them to quietly persevere, to stolidly endure.

Soon Shidzuyo had little time to sit and ponder the contradictions of her new life. A good Japanese wife was expected to produce a male heir as quickly as possible, and Masuo Yasui's wife exceeded all expectations: thirteen months after arriving in Hood River, she gave birth to the Yasuis' first son, the *chonan*, Kay, in the bedroom of their Columbia Street house. Within sixteen months a second son, Tsuyoshi, was born; Minoru, a third son, followed a year and a half later. Then, after what would be the longest hiatus in her reproductive life—just over two years— Shidzuyo gave birth to five more children in six years. In all there would be nine Yasui *nisei* (second generation), six boys and three girls, born over thirteen years. A photograph taken in the early 1920s shows the growing family: Masuo, with his hairline in retreat, stares straight ahead, calm and satisfied; Shidzuyo, broader now both in the face and hips, sits with her fifth child on her lap; the other children are spread out in front of them, perched on homemade toys. Four-year-old Minoru's arm is flung around the tiny shoulders of his two-year-old sister, Yuki.

In America, *issei* re-created the only family structure they knew, the traditional Japanese *ie*, or household of which they themselves had been products. With its rigid hierarchy ordained by gender and age, the traditional family operated by strict rules: The eldest male was accorded ultimate authority. Outside the family, he was its sole representative and spokesman. Inside, his rule was absolute. The price he paid for this power was the formality of his relationships with the rest of the family. His children were obedient and deferential, but their relationship to their father was dictated more by fear than love. Masuo was this kind of father: a distant authority figure and a stern disciplinarian. And Shidzuyo became in most ways a traditional Japanese wife and mother. She put her husband's needs before her own, serving him first at the table, not eating until he ate, waiting up for him before she went to sleep and often calling him Danna-san, which translates both as "head of household" and "my lord." Although she too was strict with the children, her relationship, especially with her older sons, was very close. In the traditional Japanese family the mother often shielded her male children from the harsh discipline of the father.

Shidzuyo's life, although perhaps not as physically grueling as that of an *issei* farmer's wife, was nonetheless demanding. She was up at six to light the stove and start breakfast, waking the rest of the family at seven. During the day she cared for her many children, hand-washing unending baskets of laundry, sewing and repairing piles of clothes, canning countless jars of fruits and vegetables and even making her own soap. In the evening she fed all the children, put them to bed and then waited— sometimes past midnight—to eat with Masuo when he returned from his long business day. When the children were a little older, she worked in the store. And after the Yasuis bought farmland of their own, the entire family worked in the fields during the summer harvest, with Shidzuyo doing stoop labor for twelve to fifteen hours a day in addition to her domestic chores.

In those days before sophisticated health care, vaccinations or even central heating, mothering a large family also meant dealing with disease. During the course of a single winter, Shidzuyo nursed one son whose cold became life-threatening pneumonia, watched helplessly as her baby contracted bronchitis and battled a 106-degree fever and then cared for one of her daughters who for three weeks suffered from mysterious "intestinal complications." As soon as they recovered, the entire brood contracted measles.

Although their family structure was imported from the old country, the Yasuis tried in other ways to take on the trappings of their adopted land. The family celebrated *o-shogatsu*, the Japanese New Year, and Shidzuyo set out rows of dolls for Girls' Day and flew carp kites for Boys' Day. But the family also learned to enjoy Thanksgiving and, as Christians, regularly celebrated Christmas and Easter. Their house was decorated with Japanese paintings and pictures, but all the other furnishings were American. Masuo stocked the family bookshelves with a ten-volume *World Book Encyclopedia*, a fifteen-volume *Book of History* and a twenty-volume set of *The Messages and Papers of the Presidents*. Unlike many *issei* who were threatened by their children's growing Americanization, the Yasuis encouraged it.

Insulated from the world outside her home by traditional family structure, her prodigious domestic responsibilities and her inability to speak or understand more than rudimentary English, Shidzuyo nonetheless tried to find a place for herself in the larger community. In doing so, she trod the line between the old world and the new. On the one hand, she somehow found the time to establish, with another *issei* woman, an informal orientation center for newcomers, instructing them in everything from American table manners to Western child-care methods. On the other hand, she kept alive her cultural heritage by teaching flower arranging and the Japanese tea ceremony to *issei* ladies in the valley. At home, in the evenings after the children were in bed, while she waited for Masuo to return from the store, she wrote poetry.

During the years his wife was struggling to adapt herself to a new way of life and his family was increasing at the rate of a child every eighteen months, Masuo Yasui was hard at work creating the beginnings of an empire. A year after returning to the community with his bride, he bought out the local competition, the Niguma Store, and moved his main operations to a new location on Oak Street, Hood River's main business thoroughfare. The new store was more visible and better integrated into the business district than the old building, which he continued to maintain as a "branch store" for a number of years.

The new Yasui Brothers sat on a busy corner at the east end of downtown, across the street from a barber shop and one of the town's thriving supply stores, Moore's Electric. Mt. Hood Hotel was across the other street, and around the corner, conveniently located for the *issei* farmers who came in from the valley to do their shopping at the store, was a combination tofu "factory" and *meshi-ya* (lunch counter). But just as important as location was the size of the new store. It took up the entire ground floor of a large three-story wooden building, which gave the brothers two to three times more floor space than their original outlet. There were large display windows that let in the ample southern light and room for four rows of glass cases and a greatly expanded inventory. In addition to everything the old store carried—from imported food to Japanese knickknacks to everyday domestic supplies—Masuo and his brother, who did much of the day-to-day work at the store, now added an eclectic array of new items: sewing machines, diamond rings, typewriters, woolen underwear, heaters, musical instruments, gold watches, raincoats, soda pop, chewing gum. Behind a partition in the back was room for a small office, where Renichi kept track of inventory and Masuo took care of business correspondence, paid bills and planned new enterprises. In the corner was a potbellied stove surrounded by wooden benches. Here the customers would sit, sipping tea provided by Renichi and alternately discussing this year's fruit crop and news of the old country.

All of the Yasuis' customers were Japanese, except for a few white children, who braved what they thought of as the overwhelming foreignness of the place, to buy candies, trinkets and toys. Although in fact the store was well stocked with the kind of routine, recognizable merchandise one would find in any general store, the children experienced the place as an exotic adventure, remembering only the Buddha incense burners with smoke wafting up from a bowl in Buddha's lap and the little packets of tightly pressed paper that blossomed into flowers in the water. When Kenneth Abraham, son of the doctor who ministered to the Japanese population, returned home from a visit to the store, his older sister would sniff his clothing disgustedly. "You've been around that Japanese place again, haven't you?" she would ask him accusingly. To the *hakujin* (Caucasians) of Hood River, the Japanese were indescribably foreign. Everything about them, from their faces to their food, was startlingly—and disturbingly—different. Their names were unpronounceable and unspellable. When Masuo received business letters, they were addressed to Mr. Yafui, Mr. Yatsui, Mr. Asu, Mr. Yashi, Mr. Yazuir and dozens of other variations.

To the whites, Yasui Brothers may have been an odd, unpleasantly odorous establishment catering to inscrutable foreigners, but to the *issei* it was home base; it was action central. Here they not only bought food, supplies and gifts but also exchanged news of the day, often picked up their mail (addressed "c/o the Japanese Store in Hood River") and conducted much of their business using Masuo as an intermediary. The store was at the core of the local *issei* economy, providing a basis for ethnic cohesiveness and self-reliance.

Business was good at Yasui Brothers. The increasingly stable Japanese population, settling in, fixing their homes, raising their families, needed the merchandise Masuo and his brother were selling: the imported food they could get nowhere else in town. And although they could have purchased many of the routine items at other stores, the language barrier—and their growing sense of loyalty to Masuo—meant that they did virtually all of their shopping at the Oak Street store. Even during World War I, when rice, sugar and other staples were in short supply, Masuo and his brother turned a respectable profit. In 1918 the brothers sold more than $20,000 worth of merchandise. The next year, sales increased to almost $34,000, netting them an income in excess of

$4,000—more than four times what an *issei* farmer could expect to clear in a good year. In 1920 their income was up 10 percent, and they reported owning an inventory worth more than $21,000.

Success was a result of both brothers' contributions: Renichi's good nature and stability; Masuo's shrewdness as a businessman. Masuo pored over scores of catalogs and read stacks of promotional literature, always looking for new merchandise to carry or new opportunities to pursue. He wrote to national companies like Victrola, asking to be the local or regional representative for their products. He kept a keen eye on prices, making sure the Yasui Brothers secured the most favorable deals from wholesalers. In a 1915 letter to his supplier of Carnation milk, he complained that he was being charged more than Portland grocers and threatened to send back the order unless he received the same deal as his urban counterparts. "We are not so blind . . . ," he scolded another Portland supplier, pointing out that the price Yasui Brothers paid for sugar was higher than what he believed other merchants paid.

Masuo generally paid his bills on the last possible date, sometimes because he just didn't have the money, other times because he was diverting store profits to fund other ventures. One time he sent an entire order of goods back to San Francisco because it was accompanied by an invoice with payment due in sixty days. "Your agent said we had ninety days to pay," Masuo said by way of explanation. Another time he chided a Portland wholesaler for insisting that a bill for sugar and beans was due fifteen days before Masuo thought it was. "This is only a small amount, and if we so desire to pay it, we can easily do, but you are not right about this at all," wrote the ever-vigilant Masuo. The overheated reply he received may have had more to do with race than business. "You very bad man to do business with," answered the angry wholesaler, in purposely pidgin English. "If you ship these goods back they will stay at the Depot we will never accept them and you will pay for them or we will close your Store. You cannot make a fool of us, as we know you very hard man to do business with, not square like other man. . . ."

Masuo may have been at times a tough man to do business with. But this came from his dogged attention to detail, not from unscrupulous behavior. One time he received a shipment of goods marked "Cash on delivery" for which he had already prepaid. The supplier, realizing his error, immediately sent back Masuo's money order. A few days later Masuo wrote a polite but insistent letter asking to be reimbursed for the forty cents he had spent on the money order.

He was a prolific and fastidious business correspondent. Sitting at his desk at the back of the store, sometimes late into the night, he neatly typed and made carbon copies of all his letters, carefully filing them by date in cabinets that stretched along the far wall of his cramped office. He wrote with an odd mixture of nineteenth-century formality ("Yours of the 14th inst. at hand") and fractured English ("Thanking you for your order and trusting this delay does not make you any way inconvenience"). In small cloth-covered books, he kept careful account of his own daily expenditures, penciling in the five cents he spent for hot milk or the fifty cents he paid for a haircut. Each day he began with cash on hand and proceeded to track every penny—a habit he later tried to instill in his children with some success. In financial matters he may have been plodding and detail-oriented, but he also had a sense of business flair. Yasui Brothers advertised in the local newspaper with seasonal sales and special bargains announced in bold type. There were also, from time to time, raffles, contests and other giveaways. Although as time passed he had many other irons in the fire, Masuo continued to devote a great deal of attention to the store. It provided a natural springboard for other ventures while furnishing the capital to make them possible.

When the brothers first bought out Niguma, they closed the upstairs brothel—much to the disappointment of many *issei* bachelors—and converted the ten small rooms into short-term rentals for visiting valley farmers or monthly accommodations for newcomers. This logical business outgrowth of the store and its position in the Japanese community was just the beginning of a slew of sidelines Masuo diligently pursued. Because he was one of the few Japanese fluent in English, he could connect with the white community in ways others among his countrymen could not. English was a difficult language for Japanese to learn, with its unusual sounds, inconsistent pronunciation and alphabet-based rather than ideogrammatic system. Most *issei* were already young adults by the time they came to America, making acquisition of a new language even more difficult. But their isolation from white society—a result of both the clannishness of all first-generation immigrants, regardless of ethnic background, and the outright ostracism the Japanese in particular suffered—was undoubtedly the reason few *issei* became fluent in the language of their new land. Masuo, as an in-town businessman, had many opportunities and much incentive to sharpen his own language skills. He became relatively comfortable dealing with the *hakujin* (white people), and they increasingly depended on him to act as a middleman with the *issei* community. When white businessmen needed Japanese labor, they came to Masuo. From the early days, he had operated as a one-man employment agency, but now because of his growing visibility as a businessman, his services were even more in demand. He was contracted to provide pickers for orchardists both in the valley and elsewhere and asked by one of the local lumber companies to organize a "crew of Japs" to cut wood in the upper valley. A lumber company more than a hundred miles away wrote asking him to find a "Jap boy" to work as a camp cook, and various Portlanders requested his help in hiring young men or women for domestic duty.

Because the store was not just a business but a meeting place for most of the valley's *issei*, Masuo was in a unique position to know—and capitalize on—the needs of his community. Once they became established, *issei* commonly paid regular visits to Japan to discharge filial obligations and to show off their growing families. Masuo quickly seized this opportunity to become a travel agent for as many as four different steamship companies, selling steerage tickets to his countrymen for a 5 percent commission. Because many *issei* sent money back to their relatives in the homeland, Masuo applied for and received an American Express money-order franchise, which he operated from the back of the store. And as the farmers and their picture brides began to raise typically large rural families, life insurance increasingly became a concern. Masuo had started selling policies to *issei* early on, but now his business grew, and he signed on as a commissioned agent for a national company. Carefully tracking the *issei*'s increasing needs (and income), Masuo arranged with a local car dealership to steer prospective *issei* buyers to them, for a fee. He even collected commissions for sending business to a local stonecutter who chiseled grave markers.

His daily interaction with dozens of valley farmers—both as friend and merchant—alerted him to their ongoing financial concerns. He knew who was making money and who needed it. He knew that *issei* in the valley were collectively depositing as much as five thousand dollars a month in Japanese savings banks, either ignorant of local banks or too intimidated by language and culture barriers to use them. In 1913 he founded and became the first (and only) president and manager of the Japanese Savings Association. Legally incorporated as a savings and loan institution with capital stock of fifty thousand dollars and reams of elegant letterhead stationery, the association operated out of the back of the Yasui Brothers Store for six years.

With his hodgepodge of moneymaking enterprises, Masuo certainly profited from the needs of the Japanese community, but he was hardly a cold-blooded businessman. In fact, he spent an enormous amount of time voluntarily and without recompense helping his own people. He was the Red Cross, the welfare agency and the legal aid society rolled into one. He was in many ways the head of not only his own household but also the extended *ie*, the kinship community that spanned the valley. He was father to his own children and, in a tradition both Japanese and Italian, "godfather" to the community.

His proficiency in English and growing knowledge of the way American business and government worked also meant that he was in great demand whenever *issei* had to interact with the larger society. A decade earlier he had dreamed of becoming a lawyer; now he found himself taking care of an array of legal paperwork for his friends. When they wanted to return to Japan for a visit, he helped them obtain passports and secure the reentry permits necessary for their return. He helped the *issei* with the paperwork that accompanied everyday life in America: applying for a driver's license, securing a gun permit, filling out tax forms, filing accident reports. Government officials throughout the state sent letters and documents in care of the Yasui Brothers Store, corresponding directly with Masuo about matters involving scores of his countrymen.

Masuo was enmeshed in their business lives as well, interceding with the local banks to help them get credit, writing letters of introduction and recommendation and acting as an all-purpose financial intermediary. After the Japanese Savings Association folded, Masuo steered the *issei* to Hood River's Butler Bank, where he had an amicable business relationship with Truman Butler, the bank president. Whenever the bank had a problem with an *issei* client—an overdrawn check, a missed or tardy loan payment—Butler or one of his cashiers wrote directly to Masuo. He was called on countless times to explain the situation to whoever had made the mistake, find out what the problem was and somehow resolve the issue. When one of the bank's customers had problems with an *issei*, Masuo's counsel was immediately sought. "One of your boys named Yamada owes our customer Mr. Boorman some money on a mortgage," a Butler Bank cashier wrote to Masuo in 1915. "Will you kindly give us such information as you can concerning Yamada and if possible bring him into the office with you in order that we may determine for Mr. Boorman what can be done for him?" When three *issei* signed up with the local telephone company, Masuo received a lengthy letter explaining the installation of the phones, the service and the charges. "We shall expect you to make these conditions known to your friends," wrote the company president, who also suggested that Masuo be responsible for collecting the monthly service charges.

Beyond helping with business affairs, Masuo took personal responsibility for the members of his community, helping to establish a local Japanese Welfare Society that aided those in times of need. He set up doctor's appointments for *issei*, in both Hood River and Portland, and frequently found himself in the middle of other people's medical concerns. In 1920 a local doctor wrote directly to Masuo, detailing the serious medical problems of an *issei* patient and prescribing treatment. Masuo was to explain all this to the man. Throughout the late 1910s and early 1920s when Japanese families in the valley were rapidly growing, Masuo often accompanied the local doctor to home births. There he acted as translator and sometimes assistant midwife—a skill he used again and again in his own home. He also frequently suggested the name for the new baby. After children were born, he wrote the letters and prepared the forms necessary to register these births with the state—a vital service, for an official birth certificate. was proof of the American citizenship of this new generation. In the days before hospital births, with their attendant paperwork, were the norm, it was common for births to go officially unrecorded. But to the *issei*, prevented by law from becoming American citizens, the legal standing of their children was their anchor in the new world. Without official documentation, their children, according to Japanese law, would be citizens of Japan.

The role of intermediary and "godfather" came naturally to Masuo, for he came from a culture that stressed group identity over individualism, that emphasized, above all else, a sense of duty and responsibility to others. The Japan of Masuo's youth was a culture based on personal ties, a great network of mutual indebtedness in which everyone incurred obligations that must be repaid. Japanese men and women were born "wearing an *on*" (carrying an obligation) to the emperor, to the local lord and to parents and soon incurred additional obligations to teachers and other contacts in daily life. Fulfilling one's obligations—from the lifelong responsibilities of family to timebound repayments of even casual favors—was defined as the supreme task of life. The society was threaded together by *osewa* (aid, help or indebtedness), a meshwork that connected people to one another across families and across generations. That is how Japan functioned.

The world of Hood River, Oregon, was not the world of Japan, yet in many ways Masuo was the *oyabun* (foster father) of the *issei* community. His language skills and business acumen propelled him to a position of leadership, and to a Japanese man of his generation, that meant duty to others. Motivated by this sense of obligation, especially to those he had persuaded to settle down and whose business kept him in business, Masuo repaid his debts in countless ways, both personal and professional. He mediated in personal and business disputes, lent money, extended credit, made introductions, gave advice, sent presents and generally kept tabs on both the fiscal and physical health of his community.

His voluntary labors as leader of the *issei* community, although enormously time-consuming, didn't prevent him from expending prodigious energy as a businessman. With Shidzuyo shouldering all of the domestic responsibilities and Renichi taking care of the store, Masuo turned his attention to real estate, making his mark both as an agent for others and as a landowner himself. Locally and throughout the West, Masuo was becoming known as the person to contact if you wanted to sell or lease your land to a Japanese. As early as 1913 he was receiving letters from out-of-towners who had years before invested in undeveloped valley property and now, with the apple business booming, wanted to cash in. "It is my understanding that you are in touch with most of the Japanese farmers of Hood River and from time to time are in a position to arrange for the leasing of farms by your friends," an absentee landowner from San Francisco wrote to Masuo, asking for his help in renting his valley property. "I am informed that you are an agent for the Japanese colony," wrote a Washington man looking to sell his Hood River orchard. "I have been told that you are interested in getting cheap land for the Japanese," wrote a Portland attorney with a 140-acre plot to sell. From California, Washington, Wyoming, Colorado and Illinois they wrote him: did Masuo know of any "Japanese boys," any "progressive, energetic Japanese" or simply "any of your people" who would like to buy or lease the land? The First National Bank of Hood River funneled real estate queries from some of its customers to Masuo. Throughout the pre-and post-World War I years, he was involved in arranging scores of real estate deals, from land sales to long-and short-term leases to speculation opportunities.

For his efforts he generally received a 5 percent commission, but he made money in other ways as well. He might loan an *issei* farmer all or part of the down payment for a piece of land in exchange for part ownership of the property or a percentage of the crop. Sometimes he financed a standard real estate loan, charging interest and collecting payments every month. However he turned a profit, Masuo worked hard for his money, hammering out countless contractual details for his *issei* clients. He not only negotiated what he considered to be a fair purchase price, but also worked out all the specifics, from standard concerns like down payments and interest rates to tax questions and water rights. Given his assiduous attention to detail and his personal as well as professional commitment to his countrymen, these transactions sometimes took months. Even after the deal was closed, Masuo continued to be involved, more often than not receiving no recompense for these extra services. If an *issei* orchardist had a particularly bad year and could not come up with a full interest payment, it was Masuo who wrote to the white mortgage holder, Masuo who offered multi-page explanations of early frosts and sizzling summers and insect infestations, Masuo who related the sad litany of accidents, illnesses and deaths. Those for whom Masuo had arranged leases had other problems. Perhaps they were late paying the rent; perhaps they needed permission to cut down sickly trees; maybe they needed new equipment. Masuo wrote the letters.

But it wasn't just his *issei* friends who depended on him. The white landowners and businessmen involved in the deals also used Masuo as a go-between. He often received letters from absentee landlords asking him to check on the condition of their orchards and houses, expedite a payment or arrange to extend or terminate the lease. When one white absentee landlord wrote that he had not received payments from his Japanese renters, Masuo traveled up the valley and personally collected the rents. The burden of the responsibility he had taken on—or was thrust upon him—as leader of the community was staggering. When a single Japanese orchardist did not make good on a $150 debt at the local fruit cooperative, the president of the co-op wrote to Masuo:

> For a number of years we have taken quite an interest in financing various Japanese who have gone into the strawberry and fruit business in Hood River Valley and have done so largely because they have been connected with your firm more or less by acquaintanceship or in a business way. . . .
>
> We understand that this man has been well able to pay this account, but has left the valley and if this is the manner in which the Japanese boys intend to transact their business they will certainly get in very bad standing. I call your attention to this matter for the reason that I feel you are interested in the success and the business enterprise of the Japanese boys. . . . I am going to leave it up to you to get a settlement on this plan. . . .

While he was involved in arranging deals and taking direct responsibility for their outcome, Masuo was also buying land himself. He had purchased his first property in 1911, a 320-acre section that he immediately subdivided into eight- and ten-acre parcels and sold to a dozen or so *issei*. Now, in the late 1910s, using profits from the store and his other ventures, Masuo began to acquire land for his own use. He bought both small plots of already producing orchard land as well as larger acreages that needed to be developed. Then he either hired men to work the land or leased it to farm families, sometimes white, sometimes Japanese.

Regardless of high-yield production techniques brought over from Japan (where a half-acre might have to provide food and income for an entire household) and plain hard work, farming was not always profitable, and Masuo was smart enough to keep his other ventures going even as he expanded his agricultural holdings. The nationally touted Hood River apple boom began to level off after 1914, and prices declined. "We are suffering financial difficulties as same as rest of people," Masuo wrote to a creditor in 1915. And despite claims of perfect weather, the climate sometimes did not cooperate with farmers. In 1919 a frigid winter killed almost half the apple crop in the lower valley. In 1922 four feet of snow blanketed the area, cutting off telephone, telegraph and railroad services, and destroying countless acres of young fruit trees. The Japanese who depended entirely on farm income sometimes lived lives of poverty and disease. During a particularly bad year one *issei* family cleared thirty-seven dollars, couldn't afford shoes for their children and lost a daughter to pneumonia. So, although Masuo, Shidzuyo and as many of the children as were able trekked out to their orchards in the valley to help during harvest time, the Yasuis did not become a farm family. Nevertheless, by 1920 Masuo owned or was a partner in five "fruit ranches" in the mid- and upper valley—and had stationery printed proudly proclaiming the fact. "Well," wrote one of his white acquaintances, a Portland insurance agent he sometimes worked with, "I hope you will not buy all the land in Hood River county before I get back there."

It looked for a while as if he might. In 1922 he arranged to buy 160 acres of orchard land bordering the Columbia River east of town, a huge tract compared with the average twenty-acre plots in the valley. The owner, W. H. Weber from Chicago, was a wealthy man who summered in Switzerland (where he took hydrotherapy treatment for his arthritis), wintered in Daytona Beach and thought nothing of loaning Masuo twenty-five thousand dollars to buy his ranch. After the deal was done, Masuo contracted with a number of *issei* to tenant-farm the land, which was mostly in apples but also produced pears, cherries, asparagus and melons. Two of his other ranches specialized in strawberries, a crop the Japanese were particularly fond of because, unlike fruit trees, it returned an immediate investment. In fact, by the early 1920s, strawberries accounted for more than 60 percent of the Yasuis' farm income. Masuo had become one of the largest strawberry growers in the .valley.

Naturally, he also became involved in the business and marketing end of the local fruit industry. In 1913 valley farmers formed a shipping, marketing and distributing cooperative called the Apple Growers Association, although it dealt with many different fruit crops. The cooperative secured the best prices for fruit each season by making large-scale deals with wholesalers. Then it bought the fruit to fill these or-

ders from its members and packaged and distributed it under the Hood
River Apple Growers Association label. The cooperative used its collective buying power to purchase machinery, fertilizer, chemicals and other
goods its members needed and sometimes advanced payments on next
year's crops to farmers who were having a hard time making it through
the winter. From its earliest days the organization was open to Japanese
farmers—it had to be, given the relative size of the *issei* farming community and the impact it had through high-yield crop production. Although
the cooperative's motives for including the Japanese may not have been
egalitarian, the result often was. Being part of the association meant the
issei were not in direct competition with their white counterparts. In the
neighboring state of California, where successful Japanese farmers went
head to head with the *hakujin*, the result was escalating violence and legislation that restricted Japanese landownership. In Hood River, at least
on the surface, Japanese and white farmers cooperated—mostly through
the voluntary efforts of a single person, Masuo Yasui, who acted as an
intermediary by negotiating prices, straightening out accounts, explaining procedures and trouble-shooting potential conflicts.

Regardless of their inclusion in the Apple Growers Association, the
Japanese farmers must have had some concerns of their own, for in
1916 Masuo helped organize fifty *issei* into the Japanese Farmers Association of Hood River, probably for the purpose of marketing the one
crop Japanese farmers had majority control of in the valley, strawberries. The organization, all of whose members belonged to the Apple
Growers, made every effort to appear unthreatening. "Our board of
directors respectfully ask you for your advices on our members for their
cultivation and care of their fruit orchards," Masuo wrote to the general
manager of the Apple Growers Association in the winter of 1916. "We
want your advice: We want your suggestion. We want to stay with you."
A few years later, Masuo organized his countrymen into the Mid-Columbia Vegetable Growers Association, a cooperative that specialized
in marketing asparagus—another of the Yasuis' successful crops—to
Eastern cities.

But not all of his activities depended on his countrymen. Beginning
in the 1910s, he became an entrepreneur in his own right, crossing over
into the white, mainstream economy. He became an important regional
exporter of strawberry plants, the very successful, hardy and nationally
known Clarks' Seedling variety that he grew on his ranches. When out-
of-state farmers wrote to Hood River's fruit cooperative asking about
strawberries, they were invariably steered to Masuo Yasui. "Any plants
that are guaranteed by them [the Yasui Brothers] to be correct, you can

rely upon. . . ." a representative of the fruit cooperative wrote to a Washington farmer. Like many small businessmen in the heady decades before the Depression, Masuo looked to stocks and bonds as a way to increase his wealth. He regularly received fliers from a bond and trust company in Portland that offered investment opportunities and stock market news. At various times he may have invested in everything from irrigation-district, school-district, road-improvement and general-obligation bonds to stock in an Indiana manufacturing firm and the Willys Jeep company. In 1919 he bought twenty-five shares of stock in a film production company.

As he moved from struggling entrepreneur to middle-class businessman, Masuo's ties to the white community strengthened. He became a member of both the local and state chambers of commerce, and during the World War I years he made himself a visible patriot. For the city's traditional Independence Day parade, he organized a Japanese contingent. On July 4, 1917, to the enthusiastic applause of their *hakujin* neighbors, dozens of *issei* men and women, dressed in their finest, promenaded down Oak Street singing "Auld Lang Syne" in Japanese. In 1918 he was appointed a member of the Third Liberty Loan Committee, a local group in charge of selling war bonds. The next year he donated five hundred dollars to another war-bond drive. When the war was over, a mix of American patriotism and a Japanese sense of obligation compelled him to send a box of hand-selected Hood River apples ("the last word in apple perfection") to Woodrow Wilson. "As a Japanese resident of the United States, I greatly desire to show appreciation and gratitude in my small way to President Wilson for his efforts in affecting world peace," Masuo wrote in an accompanying letter.

On a personal level, he was developing a handful of strong friendships with whites. With King Tyler, a Portland man who worked for the same insurance company as Masuo, he traded lighthearted letters. The two were long-distance business acquaintances whose relationship warmed over time. When Tyler scolded him good-naturedly for not writing often, Masuo, in a rare expression of jocularity, replied: "You no doubt will be surprised when you get letter from me. I hope everything is alright with you except you don't make very much money. If you are making any, you must send me some." A few weeks later, Tyler answered, calling Masuo "Old Top" and "a good scout" and concluding warmly: "I hope always for you to be my friend." In another letter, Masuo told Tyler, "I have no better friends (than you) among our own Japanese."

Out in the valley, in the tiny settlement of Parkdale, Masuo had a particularly fervent supporter, a Mrs. Bailey, who wrote to him often, inviting him to her house and the community's church, and ordering special items from the store. Barbara Bailey was apparently a devout Methodist who, through the church, was connected to the Japanese Christian community. "My only desire is to show my love and friendship for Japanese here and everywhere," she wrote to Masuo in one of her many hastily scribbled letters.

In town, at least two of Masuo's business relationships deepened into something more. Down the street from Yasui Brothers was the office of Dr. V. R. Abraham, who agreed to examine most of the Japanese applicants for the life insurance policies Masuo sold. A pillar of the community, the first commander of the local American Legion Post, the second president of the Rotary Club, Abraham was also a true liberal married to a lifelong leftist. While other local doctors avoided contact with the Japanese, Dr. Abraham became an ally, and from 1910 through the early 1920s, when he and his family moved to California, he ministered to the *issei* community and had frequent and friendly contact with Masuo. Abraham's son, Kenneth, was a good friend of Masuo's oldest sons.

But Masuo's closest and most enduring friendship was with Ernest C. Smith, a Hood River lawyer. "E.C." took care of all of Masuo's legal concerns from the early days through World War II, also advising him on real estate transactions and even entering into a few with him. Through Masuo, Smith developed a sizable and loyal Japanese clientele, including a number of *issei* for whom he helped buy land. The two exchanged hundreds of letters, from pro forma legal memoranda to warm thankyous for Christmas presents, continuing to address each other formally as "Mr. Smith" and "Mr. Yasui" long after the relationship had deepened into true friendship. They had respect for each other both as businessmen and as men, trading information about their families and their health and often visiting each other's home. Smith sacrificed much to be loyal to Masuo and his Japanese clients.

Although Masuo didn't know it at the time, people were whispering behind Smith's back, calling him a "Jap lover" and taking their business elsewhere. The town dentist's wife confided in the town doctor's wife that Mr. Yasui had gone to Mr. Smith's home one night. "And do you know that Mrs. Smith served him coffee? Can you imagine that? Served him?"

His friendships with *hakujin* along with his new status as a middle-class burgher gave Masuo a false sense of security about his and his countrymen's position in the local community. His success temporarily insulated—or perhaps blinded—him from the growing anti-Japanese sentiment in Hood River. Racism had long been etched into the American psyche, and various anti-Asiatic movements had been popular up and down the West Coast since the mid-nineteenth century. As Japanese became permanent, landholding neighbors, as they became successful agricultural competitors, whites became increasingly less tolerant of their presence. In Hood River, in the years following the Great War, "natives" eyed "aliens" with growing suspicion. An undercurrent of racism was about to flood the valley.

4

The Yellow Scourge

"New plague threatens us," warned a headline from the San Francisco *Gazette*. The story below, which cautioned against what West Coast alarmists would soon be referring to as the Japanese Question, the Japanese Problem, the Japanese Menace, the Yellow Peril and the Yellow Scourge, was more than a bit premature. The year was 1869, a full three decades before Japanese would emigrate to America in any visible numbers. "These people came to literally take root in the ground," said the newspaper story, referring to the handful of immigrants who had just arrived in Southern California to start the Wakamatsu Tea and Silk Colony. "Shall Los Angeles be made a tea garden and Santa Barbara a mulberry field?"

The already well-formed prejudice that greeted the Japanese when they began to arrive on America's western shores in the late nineteenth century was the legacy of years of bigotry and discrimination against the Chinese, who had come in great numbers during the five previous decades. Beginning in 1849, tens of thousands of impoverished Chinese peasants emigrated to a place they called *Gam Saan* (Golden Mountain, their name for California) in hopes of literally striking it rich. "Money is in great plenty and to spare in America," claimed one of the many circulars distributed in Chinese port cities during the heady California gold-rush years. "[Americans] want the Chinaman to come and make him very welcome." The United States did, in fact, initially encourage this immigration as a necessary source of cheap labor, especially during the early railroad-building days. But the honeymoon very quickly ended.

White workers soon perceived the Chinese as a serious economic threat, and organized labor enthusiastically led an anti-Chinese crusade.

American Federation of Labor president Samuel Gompers went so far as to write a pamphlet calling for the exclusion of "congenitally inferior" Asians. Others, threatened by the thought that the West Coast would be less racially homogeneous than they wanted, found support from powerful newspapers, local politicians—and soon the federal government, which responded to the groundswell of racism by passing the Chinese Exclusion Act of 1882. Chinese laborers may have been prohibited from entering the country by this piece of legislation, but the need for cheap labor, especially on the railroads, persisted. A mere six years after the exclusion act, Japanese labor was first introduced in California.

But the new Asian immigrants soon met the same fate as their predecessors. Initially welcomed to America and even praised by the Immigration Commission for their "great eagerness to learn," the Japanese quickly fell victim to established race hatred. At the peak of Japanese immigration—when Masuo and thousands of other young men ventured across the ocean during the first seven years of the twentieth century—Japanese represented less than 2 percent of all immigrants to America. Yet politicians called it an "invasion." The San Francisco *Chronicle* called it "the problem of the hour." The Sacramento *Bee* was less temperate in its reaction: "Now the Jap is a wily an' crafty individual—more so than the Chink . . . they try to buy in the neighborhoods where there are nothing but white folks," said a local resident interviewed by the capital city's influential daily. "The Jap will always be undesirable," he concluded. The sentiment was widely shared.

In 1900 protesters gathering at the first large-scale demonstration against Japanese immigration heard the mayor of San Francisco proclaim that "the Japanese are not the stuff of which American citizens can be made." American citizens, meanwhile, roamed the streets of that city, roughing up Japanese and vandalizing their stores and homes. In 1905 delegates from sixty-seven organizations met in San Francisco to create the Asiatic Exclusion League, headed, ironically, by a first-generation immigrant from Scandinavia. Three years later, 231 different California organizations—from Granges to chambers of commerce to scores of trade unions—were affiliated with the League, which was pressing hard for federal legislation to halt all Japanese immigration.

In Washington, D.C., Teddy Roosevelt balked, wanting to preserve amicable relations with Japan. But racial tensions, sharpened by the San Francisco school board's resolution to segregate Japanese pupils in the public schools, precipitated a crisis Roosevelt could not ignore. Through an exchange of notes collectively known as the Gentlemen's Agreement of 1907-1908, the Japanese government agreed to cease issuing passports to laborers bound for the continental United States, while the U.S. government promised to discourage any law limiting Japanese immigration.

If Roosevelt thought the gentlemen's agreement would put a lid on anti-Japanese feelings in California, he was wrong. Almost immediately, the Asiatic Exclusion League, an omnibus organization that made bedfellows of traditional enemies like the American Legion and organized labor, renewed its efforts for restrictive federal legislation and mounted a campaign for an amendment to the U.S. Constitution that would deny citizenship to even American-born Asians. The Sacramento *Bee*, under the editorship of V.S. McClatchy, intensified its invective. "The Japs . . . will increase like rats" if they are allowed to settle down and own land, he warned his readers. Testifying later before the U.S. Senate, McClatchy claimed that Japanese were "less assimilable" and "more dangerous" than other immigrant groups. "They come here specifically and professedly for the purpose of colonizing and establishing the proud Yamato race. . . . In pursuit of their intent to colonize this country with that race, they seek to secure land and found large families."

While they had no intention of "colonizing," it was true that Japanese immigrants were interested in securing land. Unlike the Chinese who came before them, many of whom came from the destitute peasantry, Japanese immigrants tended to be from the comparatively prosperous farming class. They were accustomed to owning land and making their living from it. In America, landownership was a goal for many.

Thus land—and who had a right to own it—became a focus for California nativists, who saw their national efforts at exclusion at least temporarily stymied by what they considered the far too moderate gentlemen's agreement. In their home state, however, they met with quick and dramatic success: both houses of the legislature voted overwhelmingly in 1913 to adopt the Alien Land Law, prohibiting landownership by "aliens ineligible for citizenship" (a category that, because of an eighteenth-century naturalization law, included only Asians) and limiting their lease of agricultural land to three years. "A careful study of the subject will convince anyone who will approach it with an open mind that the attitude of California . . . is not only justifiable but essential to the national welfare," declared members of a coalition of Western congressmen in a report to the U.S. House of Representatives. Oregon agreed. And in the years that followed, California became its model.

"Every honest means should be used to stop Oriental immigration to our country. It is a menace to all our institutions," stated Oregon's labor commissioner in a 1909 report. While politicians were talking, citizens took matters into their own hands. When the supervisor of an eastern Oregon woolen mill imported a few Japanese laborers, locals were so incensed that they literally ran the Japanese out of town. A few years later a mob of sixty-five Willamette Valley men descended on a railroad camp, telling the Japanese work crew there to get out by morning or their section house would be blown up with them in it. Farmers in central Oregon were calmer but no less insistent in their anti-Japanese sentiments. In one county, potato farmers unanimously proclaimed their opposition to Japanese field laborers. In another, 150 ranchers and businessmen passed a resolution stating that they were "unalterably opposed to any Japanese coming in here, either as laborers or so-called experts, or any other occupation or vocation whatsoever." Traveling through Oregon in the wake of California's Alien Land Law, a visiting journalist interviewed "many ranchers, businessmen and others" and "was surprised at the unanimity of local opinion that the Japanese should be restricted."

Adopting the tactics of the state's neighbor to the south, Oregon politicians and newspapers issued dire warnings about the "Japanese invasion" that would soon engulf the state. But in fact there was no invasion. Oregon attracted only a small fraction of the Japanese immigrants who settled on the West Coast. In 1900 there were only twenty-five hundred Japanese in the state; ten years later the number had increased by only six hundred. In the decade following the passage of California's landownership law, while anti-Asian rhetoric in Oregon escalated, the percentage of the state's Japanese population actually declined. Ignoring the official census data, the state's labor commissioner cautioned that "the Oriental, unless stopped, will by reason of his large numbers undertake to control the political as well as the economic affairs of the country."

The "problem" was not that Japanese immigrants were flooding the state but that many of those who began to call Oregon home—like Masuo and Renichi Yasui—were beginning to achieve a modicum of success. When "the little brown men," as a Portland *Oregonian* story called them, rented farms from the whites, their owners "realize more money each year than they did when running the farms themselves." But when Japanese started buying scrub and stump land, when they started farming it intensively and out-producing their white neighbors, they stopped being good workers and started being competitors. Their successful high-yield farming techniques were criticized as purposeful attempts to "rob the [ground] of its fertility." Their frugal ways were proof of their inferiority. "They live on a fraction of what it costs a white person, and dwell in places that are not only unsanitary but criminally so," wrote the labor commissioner in an attempt to explain the Japanese farmers' success.

Politicians might argue about statistics and life-style, but what it came down to was race. What was "wrong" with the Japanese was they weren't white, and regardless of how they dressed, talked or behaved, regardless of how many years they spent in America, they would never be white. "The Japs' good points have been dwelt upon recently," wrote the editor of a central Oregon newspaper, "and the fact that he pays his bills, is reasonably law abiding and works hard is the sum total of his assets . . . but a Jap's a Jap . . . and the melting pot never even warms him."

In a speech before the state legislature in which he sang the praises of Oregon's pioneer heritage, the governor concluded that "[the Japanese] are not our people. We cannot assimilate them and they cannot assimilate us." Oregon exclusionists repeatedly returned to this theme of the overwhelming and abiding separateness of the Japanese. They cast the *issei*'s love of their native land and attachment to its culture—a common trait of first-generation immigrants from virtually all lands—in a sinister light: Not only would the Japanese never be "true" Americans but they didn't want to be. Theirs was a "naturally dominating instinct," according to an article reprinted in the Hood River *News*. "A patriotism possesses them that is second to that of no other country or race, and inspires them with a passionate determination to extend the governmental, commercial and cultural influence of Nippon into all parts of the world." Across the Pacific, Japanese leaders were, in fact, following expansionist policies in Korea, China and Manchuria. American racists extrapolated from this that all people of Japanese descent were inherently, indeed genetically, driven to dominate.

But while the Japanese were being criticized for wanting to control rather than join American society, for not taking on the trappings of their new home and for being visibly and unalterably different, they were in actuality feared for the opposite reason: they were beating Americans at their own game. In California, in Oregon and in Hood River, *issei* were practicing the Protestant work ethic with an intensity that overwhelmed their white neighbors. The Japanese were devoting themselves to work, teaching their children the meaning of hard labor, delaying their own gratification. They were the new Puritans. And the old Puritans didn't like it.

Members of the Oregon legislature, both reflecting and leading the anti-Japanese push, tried hard to convert fear and prejudice into law by mimicking California's efforts. In 1917 the first measure aimed at prohibiting landownership by Japanese was introduced by George Wilbur, a lawyer, a prominent member of the American Legion, vice president and legal adviser of the newly established Anti-Alien League—and Hood River's representative in the state Senate. Initially received with enthusiasm, the measure was scuttled in committee through the efforts of the Portland Chamber of Commerce, which had an interest in preserving a decent business relationship with Japan. But early in the next biennial session the bill reappeared. Again, the business community exerted its influence, arguing not that Oregonians should rethink their attitudes toward the *issei* in their midst but rather that anti-Japanese legislation would jeopardize one of Oregon's major overseas markets.

The exclusionists persisted. At a special session called the next year, they proposed a joint resolution that "no Japanese who is not a citizen" could own property or lease it for more than ten years. While this resolution once again, due to economic pressure, died in committee, the Oregon legislature did manage to find an outlet for its anti-Japanese attitudes that year: both the House and the Senate voted unanimously to issue a statement supporting a change to the Fourteenth Amendment to the U.S. Constitution that would deny citizenship to American-born children of parents who themselves were barred from citizenship (a group that included only Asians). During the 1921 legislature yet another alien land bill was introduced, this time by a Portland attorney and longtime American Legion activist who got so carried away in his defense of the measure that he suggested America should declare war on Japan. The bill passed the House 34 to 25 and moved to the Senate, where its passage seemed imminent. But at the last minute, one of Oregon's U.S. senators sent a telegram pleading with the state legislature to postpone passage of the bill lest it interfere with federal action on the matter.

In the midst of this flurry of legislative activity, anti-Japanese sentiment in the hinterlands was reaching fever pitch. In 1919 the "Japanese situation" was considered so troublesome that the governor felt it necessary to dispatch a prominent state senator to make a thorough study of the problem. Frank Davey visited all parts of the state, gathering statistics and interviewing businessmen and local politicians. His report, while attempting to present a realistic, objective view of the Japanese in the state, turned out to be patronizing, racially tinged and condescending to its subject. The report took for granted fears of a Japanese takeover of the state and claimed, widespread evidence to the contrary, that "antis" were neither abusive nor bitter toward the Japanese. On the one hand, it presented the Japanese as a threat; on the other, it occasionally praised *issei* for being "quiet" and "well-behaved." Few Davey talked with expressed temperate views; most "didn't want the Japs as neighbors." And nowhere in Oregon did he find more virulent anti-Japanese sentiment than in the Hood River valley.

"Dear Sir," began a letter to the editor of the Hood River *News* in the winter of 1919, "Have been up here but a short while from California, where there is a lot of opposition to the Japs, but I have never seen it quite so strong any place as it is here." Walking down the main street of Hood River, *issei* and their young children were told to "go home, Jap," while more aggressive townsfolk threatened to "beat up all Japs" and "spit on them." One valley resident's hatred ran so deep that he contrived to cause an automobile accident with a Japanese truck driver. An anonymous witness to this "dirty frame up," as he called it, wrote to Masuo that the man "hates all Japanese people, calls them slant eyed S.B. and Yellow Bellies and all kinds of bad names." Other forms of prejudice were more subtle. Tadao Sato, a Japanese elementary school teacher who emigrated the year after Masuo, encountered "frozen cold" attitudes when he did his shopping at downtown stores. Barbara Bailey, the upper-valley matron who was a friend to Masuo and others of his countrymen, complained of the "taunts and jeers" she encountered because of her quiet support for the *issei* through her church work.

The people of Hood River were reacting to what they considered a foreign invasion. As one newspaper article in 1919 put it: "Japanese farmers have swarmed into the Hood River valley like an army of conquest." The valley was small and self-contained, and the few hundred Japanese who lived there were a visible presence. In earlier years hundreds more worked on railroad crews or as seasonal laborers, but now, in the years immediately after World War I, their population declined. By 1920 only slightly more than 4 percent of the valley's population was Japanese. But those fearful of an *issei* takeover had little use for these official statistics. Instead, they gathered their own figures, which showed an alarmingly high Japanese birthrate. While married *issei* made up only 1.5 percent of the population, they accounted for 10 to 20 percent of all the births in the county, according to local alarmists. JAPANESE STATISTICS FOOD FOR THOUGHT, announced a front-page story in the Hood River paper. What the "antis" forgot to figure into the equation was that, unlike the white female population, virtually all *issei* women were of childbearing age and, as relatively recent brides, were at the height of their procreating years. And virtually all were raising farm families, which, regardless of race, were larger than city families.

But what worried the whites of Hood River most was that the *issei* were buying land. What worried them was Masuo Yasui, who was both a landowner and the unofficial real estate agent to the *issei* population. By 1920 he owned or had interest in five orchards in and near the valley and had assisted dozens of his countrymen in purchasing or leasing land. "Extensive purchases of farming lands in the Hood River valley . . . by Japanese cannot be ignored," warned a newspaper article in late 1919. "The Hood River valley is one of the paradises on earth. Just as surely as two times two is four, that whole valley will pass ultimately into the hands of Japanese owners." Meanwhile an anonymous bit of doggerel was circulating around town:

> *Hood River, Golden Valley in the hills,*
> *Who is to possess its acres and rills?*
> *A horde of aliens from across the sea?*
> *Or shall it be a paradise for you and me?*

The 1920 Davey report also focused on this imaginary turf battle between whites and Japanese. "Sooner or later," stated Davey in the document that was later forwarded to Washington, D.C., "that wealth-producing spot must become either a white or a yellow settlement."

But official statistics told a different story: in 1920 Japanese farmers owned less than 2 percent of the tillable land in the valley. "Antis" not only ignored the facts but also conveniently forgot that much of the land owned by the Japanese was given to them by white orchardists in payment for earlier stump-clearing labor. Other white landowners unloaded undesirable land on Japanese because no one else would buy it. In an apologetic letter to the Hood River *News*, one man explained that he leased 320 acres to a Japanese family because the water was bad, there was no public road near the property and "no white person would consider it."

But a number of valley farmers were convinced that their paradise would soon be lost, and in the fall of 1919 they took the first step to convert local anti-Japanese sentiment into anti-Japanese action. On September 5 at 8:00 PM, fifty orchardists met at Library Hall downtown. Despite the drenching rains that persisted all evening, growers drove in from remote rural districts to listen and take part in a discussion entitled "Shall Hood River Valley be peopled by Americans or Asiatics?" Not surprisingly, the question was quickly answered, and the group moved on to its real agenda: establishing Hood River's own Anti-Asiatic Association. In a small upper-valley settlement, as the Hood River *News* later reported, "practically every white resident" came to a similar meeting. "From the outset it was apparent that the feeling of the meeting was practically unanimous in opposition to further Japanese ownership," according to the news report. After testimonies from a number of orchardists who maintained that "the Japanese leave something to be desired as congenial neighbors," the group unanimously pledged its cooperation with the newly formed Hood River Anti-Asiatic Association.

A few months later, anticipating a lecture on the problem of Japanese immigration and ownership, a large number of growers and businesspeople gathered for a talk at the downtown Congregational church. But, as the *News* reported the next day, they were "disappointed" to find that the evening's speaker, an export merchant named W. D. Wheelwright, spoke instead of Japan's advanced laws, low illiteracy rate and developed sense of business morality. At a local Grange meeting soon thereafter, growers found the speakers more to their liking. Addressing "The Japanese Problem," a Professor Gibson was greeted with applause when he said that "the Japanese people take no interest in nor are they sympathetic towards any phase of our American institutions or ideals." A second speaker, up from California for the occasion, maintained that the Japanese had "pushed out the native inhabitants" of his state. In the city of The Dalles, Hood River's neighbor to the east, "the hall rang with cheers," according to a news report, when a representative of the Anti-Asiatic Association of Hood River told Oregon and southern Idaho farmers: "Let the Mongolian have the eastern hemisphere, but save our United States for Americans." Back in town, Hood River pioneer Wilson Ross Winans copyrighted and distributed a six-stanza poem entitled "America for Americans . . . Americans for America" that began:

> There's a rift in the lute of the U.S.A.
> A Japanese horde in the vale,
> Americans swear they must go their way,
> No more land to the Japs is for sale.

And ended with this bit of aggressive patriotism:

> Americans stand! for home, native land,
> Let each to his country prove true;
> "Divided, we fall, united, we stand,"
> Ever true to the Red, White and Blue.
> Here's to foreigners all, with unlimited gall,
> And intriguers bland, the curse of our land,
> Take a hunch or you'll hear something fall,
> Get a move to your own native land.

But the Japanese had some supporters in the white community. Ulysses Grant Murphy, a Methodist Church administrator who traveled throughout the Northwest (with numerous stops in Hood River) tending to a scattered Japanese flock, called his parishioners "a bright and thrifty race" in a self-published pamphlet that argued against restrictions on immigration or landownership. J.B. Lister, a Hood River resident for seven years, wrote a long, temperate letter to the *News*, praising the Japanese for their hard work and calling for peaceful coexistence between the races. Masuo's friends Ernest C. Smith and Barbara Bailey were consistent supporters. Even the local newspaper sometimes struck a moderate tone, as in one editorial that called the Japanese "law abiding, thrifty, hard-working, up-to-date in their methods, and if one remembers the language obstacle, not entirely impossible as neighbors." But in the end, the *News* shifted with the prevailing winds. "[W]e cannot countenance a further increase from the outside of a race, however admirable may be their qualities, which cannot be assimilated into the American body politic," the editor wrote in the winter of 1919.

The Anti-Asiatic Association, meanwhile, busied itself with meetings, speeches, statements and pledges. In September 1919, thirty-eight orchardists and businessmen signed an oath to "protect and preserve America for Americans" by prohibiting Asian immigration and restricting landownership to native-born or fully naturalized citizens. They agreed in writing not to sell or lease any of their land to Japanese and further pledged to "use every means in their power" to halt others from selling to *issei*. The association sought and quickly received the hearty and enthusiastic support of the local American Legion post. And, in a special statement to the Hood River *News*, the group appealed to the general citizenry: "To us of Hood River, great is our inheritance. . . . The poet's beautiful dream has already come true. Let us, citizens, join hands and see to it that this dream of the yellow peril does not also come true."

But "the poet's beautiful dream" had come true not just for a few dozen white orchardists. It had—or was coming—true for a handful of Japanese immigrants as well, especially Masuo Yasui. His stature in the *issei* community, not to mention his position as a major landowner, put him squarely in the spotlight of the local controversy. He was, claimed the exclusionists, the "emperor" of the valley, the leader of "the Yellow Invasion."

Masuo accepted the role of leader while quickly moving to refute the idea of an invasion. Given the context of the time, arguing on the basis of racial equality or the ability of Japanese to assimilate was out of the question. If Masuo was to defend himself and his compatriots, he would have to accept the white's definition of "the problem" and argue the particulars. So, to the Anti-Asiatic Association's claim that more than

800 Japanese lived in the valley, he responded with a survey of his own that found only 362 local *nikkei* (all people of Japanese ancestry). (A year later, the official U.S. census confirmed Masuo's findings, putting the number at 351.) When the association warned that Japanese were running whites out of the valley, Masuo countered with the fact that only seventy Japanese owned farmland, which accounted for only 2 percent of the land available for cultivation. When locals claimed that "all profits made by Japanese farmers go straight to Japan," Masuo responded with his own estimate that perhaps 15 percent of the *issei*'s income was spent on foreign products. (A government report a few years later estimated a much lower 3 percent.)

The Hood River *News*, which allowed ample space to the activities of the Anti-Asiatic Association, did not seek out Masuo for a public response. But the Idaho *Farmer*, a Boise weekly, did. In a lengthy, generally sympathetic interview headlined M. YASUI, CO-CALLED "EMPEROR" TALKS FREELY, Masuo was allowed to painstakingly explain everything from the demographics of the Hood River Japanese population (it was declining) to the particulars of the valley land owned by him and his countrymen (small plots, much still in timber). "If there's anything that M. Yasui, the so-called 'emperor' of the Japanese colony at Hood River, doesn't know about his countrymen there, he'll look in a book and tell you, for he has it all down in oriental black and white, and can figure it out with an exactness which would do credit to the political boss of a city ward," wrote the anonymous "staff correspondent." The writer was clearly impressed with the "so-called emperor," remarking that he displayed "many [characteristics] which would stamp an American as a careful businessman, an enthusiastic fruit grower and a lover of home and family." The problem, suggested the author of the November 1919 newspaper story, was that Hood River whites considered Masuo "too blamed enterprising." He was "the forerunner of nobody knew how many other Japanese like himself, cultivating the soil with equal or greater success than many white men. . . ."

In a second interview in the same paper a month later, Masuo was given the opportunity to refute a long litany of accusations: the Japanese government was urging its citizens to buy American land; Hood River *issei* were being bankrolled by Japanese money; all *issei* were sending their children back to Japan to be educated; Hood River Japanese were not improving their properties. But the stories—if indeed anyone in Hood River read the Idaho newspaper—did little to defuse the explosive local situation. The Anti-Asiatic Association vigorously continued its campaign.

During the fall and winter of 1919 Masuo attended several of the meetings, offering what should have been comforting statistics about the decline in Japanese population in the valley. But the growers were in no mood to listen. Instead, they responded by temporarily shifting their argument. For a month or two they stopped talking about the Japanese "invasion" and developed a new damning thesis: the valley *issei* were undesirable neighbors because they lived in "unsightly homes" and were failing to improve them. Eager to establish some common ground, Masuo "admitted the justice of the charge" at one of the association's meetings that fall. "The failure on the part of Japanese to improve their home surroundings . . . is true," he told the growers. But it was the lack of money, not the absence of middle-class values, that was preventing the *issei* from making the necessary improvements. Focusing on this seemingly resolvable conflict, Masuo pledged to lead a "better homes and gardens" movement among his countrymen.

When this suggestion was quickly tossed aside, Masuo responded by developing a three-part proposal that essentially capitulated to all the association's demands. First, current *issei* residents would promise to prevent any more Japanese from coming into the valley. Second, Japanese landowners would promise not to buy any more land. And, third, they would "improve their homes up to the standard set by their neighbors." Masuo hoped his proposal would quell the association's biggest fears, put a lid on local anti-Japanese activities and avert disaster in his own community. He called a meeting in January of 1920, at which Japanese landowners, after expressing their desire to "live in peace with their white neighbors if humanly possible," decided to forward the proposal to the Anti-Asiatic Association. At first the group rejected the proposal because it was "indefinite" and asked Masuo to submit a detailed plan in writing. When he did, the group rejected the proposal outright. "A strong majority is opposed to any form of compromise," reported the Hood River *News*.

The situation in Hood River was widely known at the time, attracting considerable attention from both Oregon and out-of-state newspapers. Several out-of-towners even wrote to Masuo offering their support. "I am informed that there is a movement on foot in the Hood River valley to prevent any Japanese resident from purchasing land," a southern Oregon man wrote in the fall of 1919. "So far as I have observed, the Japanese mind their own business and are industrious and peaceable citizens and I would certainly prefer them for neighbors to Italians, Greeks, Germans and many other foreigners." From Illinois came another letter: "I note the recent agitation in Hood River valley over the race question, and will say that I had Japanese neighbors for some years and found them very good citizens. Therefore, I do not sympathize with the recent movement which I think is activated by jealousy of the success of the local Japanese farmers."

But many—both in Hood River and in the nation—did sympathize. And by the early 1920s their persistent anti-Asian and anti-Japanese activities finally began to pay off. In 1922 Congress passed the Cable Act, which essentially punished American women for marrying Asian men by taking away the woman's citizenship. "Any woman citizen who marries an alien ineligible to citizenship [an Asian] shall cease to be a citizen of the United States," stated the legislation, which was amended slightly in 1931 (and repealed five years later).

Also in 1922 the Supreme Court decided the Ozawa case, which up to that point had kept alive the remote possibility that Japanese, like other immigrants, could become naturalized citizens. In 1914 Takao Ozawa, a Japanese immigrant who had made the United States and then Hawaii his home for twenty years, applied for citizenship. When his application was denied, he appealed to the U.S. District Court for the Territory of Hawaii, which found him "in every way eminently qualified under the statutes to become an American citizen," except one: he was not white. Six years later, when his case made it to the Supreme Court, Ozawa informed the justices that he was educated in American schools, spoke only English, attended an American church, raised his children as Americans and was, "at heart . . . a true American." The Court denied his petition, based on a 125-year-old naturalization law that declared nonwhites ineligible for citizenship. "The slim hope that we had entertained . . . has been shattered completely," editorialized a Japanese American newspaper of the day.

The following year began with a major defeat for Oregon's Japanese residents, and Masuo in particular. During the first day of the 1923 state legislative session, the thrice-defeated Alien Land Law was once again introduced, this time to a legislature dominated by Ku Klux Klan and Federation of Patriotic Society members. "We cannot and we must not submit to the peaceful penetration of the Japanese. . . ." Oregon's governor, who had run on an anti-Japanese platform, told the legislature in a formal address. "Who owns America anyway? Who does this country belong to?" asked the American Legion, which once again ardently supported the bill. This time, although business interests continued to speak against it, the bill was met with overwhelming enthusiasm on the floor. The Senate passed it unanimously; in the House there was only one dissenter. After six years, Oregon exclusionists, who owed a great debt to the Anti-Asian League of Hood River and the town's local American Legion post, scored their first official triumph.

But the federal government did them one better the very next year. In 1924 Congress passed an immigration quota bill, the National Origins Act, the purpose of which was to restrict immigrants from "undesirable" areas while encouraging "good" immigrants. The bill set annual quotas from various countries. From Ireland (in "good" northwestern Europe), 17,853 immigrants would be allowed; but from Poland (in less desirable eastern Europe), the limit was 6,524. The annual allowable quota from Japan: 0. Wives of Japanese citizens already in America were no longer permitted to enter (as they had been through a "loophole" in the 1907 Gentlemen's Agreement). Even U.S. citizens could not bring into the country their Asian spouses, who were classified as "aliens ineligible for citizenship."

Up and down the West Coast the Japanese community reeled from the combined blows of 1922, 1923 and 1924. In Hood River, as the Anti-Asian Association celebrated, one of Masuo's countrymen captured the quiet bitterness of the *issei*, as he came in from the orchards to write:

> *A wasted grassland*
> *Turned to fertile fields by sweat*
> *Of cultivation:*
> *But I, made dry and fallow*
> *By tolerating insults.*

5

Mat Yasui, Cottage Industry

In Japan, protesters marked the passage of the 1924 immigration act with a National Humiliation Day. In America, the Japanese-language press advised its readers to "remain calm" and "avoid unnecessary indignation." The *issei* turned to each other with purposefully impassive faces. *"Shikata ga nai"* (It can't be helped), they said, nodding slowly. "You have to bite your tongue," they told each other. "The nail that sticks up gets hammered," they said. *"Gaman-suru"* (Persevere/be patient). So they settled back into their lives after the triple blows of the early 1920s. But for most *issei,* life in America was never the same: they saw the new immigration law as the culminating act of rejection by the United States, the definitive sign of their failure to win acceptance.

For Masuo the defeat was a personal one. He had led the Hood River *nikkei* in a concerted effort to counter the strongest local anti-Japanese agitation in the state. He had arranged for speakers, scheduled meetings, negotiated compromises and finally, when all else failed, submitted a plan to local exclusionists that capitulated to all their demands. But even that was not enough. Neither his very visible example as a "model citizen" nor his actions as a community leader were able to dam the current of racism in his own community. Yet Masuo's reaction to the triple blows of the early 1920s was not that of a defeated man.

Immigration exclusion did not directly affect him and his family, and he might have at least temporarily accepted the white argument that halting the flow of Japanese immigrants would ease tension between the races. But the Alien Land Law was another matter entirely. At first, it seemed as if a law making it illegal for *issei* to own land would have an immediate impact, both on the future of Masuo's own land acquisitions and on his position as unofficial real estate agent for his countrymen. But he quickly managed to accommodate to the new situation, finding that there were ways around the restrictions. There was, in fact, a major loophole: Masuo—or any *issei*—could continue to buy land if he recorded it in his children's names, for as native-born American citizens the *nisei* could be legal landowners. His friend, the Hood River lawyer E.C. Smith, helped him and other *issei* do just that. Smith also put his own name on at least one piece of property that he helped Masuo buy after the passage of the land law.

The new law didn't put a dent in the number of letters Masuo received from out-of-towners looking for Japanese buyers. It just changed the wording of the requests. Landowners, with full understanding of how to manipulate the law, now specified that Masuo find "American-born Japanese" to buy their properties. Others suggested under-the-table arrangements. "I think we can make some kind of an agreement to make it seem as tho' your man were not exactly renting the place, just let that be between us," Mrs. E.S. Klossner wrote to Masuo in the summer of 1924. Because the new law was so easy to circumvent, Masuo dismissed it as unimportant. This attitude allowed him to continue his entrepreneurial life with unabated enthusiasm, yet it also blinded him to the long-term significance of the legislation: following the lead of its West Coast neighbors, Oregon had legalized and legitimized racism, laying the foundation for what would be much harsher treatment of Japanese residents some twenty years later. Because the new laws halted most of the virulent anti-Japanese activity of the 1910s, Masuo and his countrymen failed to see that race hatred continued to smolder just beneath the surface.

But in the early 1920s Masuo felt insulated from the new laws and the thinking they reflected; he felt protected by his own business savvy, by his place in the community, by his ongoing friendships with prominent whites—and by his distinctly American "can do" attitude. While other *issei* may have resigned themselves to second-class status and pinned their modest hopes for acceptance on their children, Masuo chose to look at the victory of the anti-Japanese movement not as a defeat but as a "challenge." He listened to the *New World Daily,* a large-circulation Japanese-language newspaper, when it lectured its readers to "rise to the challenge and demonstrate the true character of the Japanese people." Despite formidable evidence to the contrary, he maintained his unshakable belief in the egalitarian ideals of America. "We cannot be Americans legally, but we are 100 percent American at heart in every way," he told a group of fellow Methodists in 1925 in a speech at an upper-valley

church. "To our mighty God there is no difference in races or nationalities on this globe but merely all brothers and sisters. . . . We hope to
forget racial differences and live on this earth as good friends and neighbors."

Masuo brought this hopeful message home with him, and against
the backdrop of prejudice that continued to be the subtext of daily life
in Hood River, he worked hard to convince his children that they could
be successful. He had great hopes for his children—and even greater
expectations.

Kay, the *chonan,* born in 1913, was already proving to be an immensely curious, bright young boy, a nature lover, a collector of insects,
birds' nests and rocks, an insatiable reader and a gifted student. Tsuyoshi,
the second son, born sixteen months later, was in many ways Kay's opposite: as short and stocky as Kay was tall and slender; as gregarious as
Kay was reserved. Energetic, mischievous and, above all, good-natured,
Tsuyoshi showed himself early on to be adaptable in a way his older
brother would never be. In grammar school the white kids nicknamed
him "Chop" because they thought "Chop Yasui" sounded like "chop
suey." The nickname both called attention to his racial heritage and mis-
identified it—chop suey is a Chinese, not a Japanese, dish—but Tsuyoshi
not only ignored the implied insult but embraced the name, reclaiming it
from his would-be detractors. Although Masuo and Shidzuyo continued
to call him by his Japanese name, his siblings and his friends, for the rest
of his life, would call him Chop.

If Masuo was disappointed that Chop was more interested in fishing
and playing pranks than in doing well in school, he was pleased that his
third son, Minoru, more closely fitted his ideal of a Yasui *nisei.* A year
and a half younger than Chop, Min, as the family called him, was an intellectually curious, extraordinarily determined boy who studied hard.
Fiercely competitive, stubborn and confident, Min would be a leader.

"Children are gifts from God," Shidzuyo used to say. "And my children make me truly a rich woman." But in 1922 one of these gifts was
taken away. The Yasuis' fourth child and first daughter contracted influenza that fall when an epidemic swept through the valley. At dawn on
October 27 four-year-old Yuki, whom Masuo called "our graceful and
loving daughter" and "our most beloved and beautiful girl," died. They
buried her in the segregated Japanese section of Idlewild Cemetery, a
grassy expanse up the hill from town, where on clear days visitors could
take solace from breathtaking views of Mount Hood to the south and
Mount Adams to the north. The family mourned its loss and visited the
grave regularly. But by the time Yuki died Shidzuyo had already given

birth to two more children. Michi, born in the summer of 1920, when her sister was not yet two, and Roku, born eighteen months later. Less than a year after Yuki's death, Shu was born, and fourteen months later, Homer. In January of 1927, in her forty-first year, Shidzuyo gave birth to her ninth and last child, a girl they named Yuka.

By the late 1920s the internal family dynamic was set: Kay, Chop and Min, the three older boys, formed a tight-knit trio at the top of the sibling hierarchy. Below them, in another exclusive trio, were the three youngest boys, Roku, Shu and Homer. In between was Michi who grew up part tomboy, running after her older brothers, and part "little mother," nurturing her younger brothers. Yuka, separated from her only sister by almost eight years and from her oldest brother by more than thirteen, was doted on by all, the pampered baby of the family.

The Japanese culture that formed Masuo and Shidzuyo's parental attitudes sent ambivalent messages about child rearing. On the one hand, parents expected much of the *chonan* and the boys in general. They should be examples of rectitude, reflections of and testaments to their parents' proper values. But on the other hand, Japanese children were given extreme latitude in their early years. Little children, especially boys, could do no wrong. They could be boisterous, naughty, disobedient, even rude to parents and elders, and all would be tolerated. Sometime between the extreme permissiveness of early childhood and the high expectations of adolescence and beyond, all the rules changed, and both parents and children were expected to change with them.

Children were a vital part of the family, both economically and emotionally, and women of Shidzuyo's generation were trained to sacrifice everything for their sons and daughters. *Kodomo no tame ni* (for the sake of the children) was an unquestioned imperative for *issei* women. Yet Japanese culture did not allow for the physical expression of strong emotion. Even if she had not been too busy with her own domestic chores and the added responsibilities of the store and the farms, Shidzuyo would not have spent time hugging, kissing and proclaiming motherly love. Such open demonstrations were simply not a part of Japanese culture. Instead, she showed her love by working for the children, sewing their clothes, darning their socks, making their meals.

Masuo was even less a presence, both physically and emotionally, in their lives. Generally out of the house before they awoke and still at work when they went to sleep, he spent most of the little time he did interact with the children either instructing them to do chores or lecturing them on the need to excel. For warmth, for acceptance—and most of all, for fun—the children went not to their parents but to their uncle. While Masuo was busy being a father to his community, his brother Renichi was father to the Yasui *nisei*.

Uncle Ren, whom the children called Chan (the suffix *chan* is a diminutive and a term of endearment), was everything their father was not: mild, considerate, even-tempered and easygoing. While Masuo was busy and ambitious, his brother lived a slower, less harried—and far less public—life, working at the store, closing up at six and spending many long evenings at the Yasuis' home. He was generous and thoughtful, surprising the children with dollar bills tucked into decorative packets for their birthdays or holidays, buying Yuka a red dress with brass buttons that she admired in the window of J.C. Penney, taking the older boys on camping trips, spending hours with Shu and Homer telling them ghost stories of old Japan. They would all fall asleep in Chan's big bed, and in the morning he'd fix them his specialty, *eggi-meshi* (eggs, rice and soy sauce) and fried baloney. He spent so much time with them and lavished so much affection on them that each child grew up thinking he or she was Uncle's favorite.

They also grew up thinking Chan was a bachelor. He lived alone in a small house next door to the Yasuis and took many of his meals with the family. Shidzuyo did his laundry and mending. Never in all the stories he told the children of the old country did he mention a woman named Matsuyo Senno, a woman he had married by proxy in 1904. The two had not seen each other in decades, nor had they ever lived together as man and wife; they had "married"—that is, Matsuyo's name was added to the registry of Renichi's adoptive family, the Fujimotos—when he was working on railroad crews in the Northwest and she was back in her tiny home village in Okayama prefecture. But their union was legally sanctioned, and Matsuyo had spent all the years since her marriage quietly fulfilling her traditional wifely duties, living with and caring for her mother-in-law and father-in-law. She had married at age eighteen, but it wasn't until she was forty-four, when the Fujimotos died and Renichi returned to Japan to collect her, that she joined her husband and became part of the extended Yasui clan. From 1931 on, Obasan (aunt) and Renichi lived together in a basement apartment below the Oak Street store, he continuing to operate Yasui Brothers, she working silently in the fields during harvest time. They never had children of their own.

In the 1920s the steadily expanding Yasui family lived in close quarters in a modest house on Third Street next door to their own branch outlet, with their closest neighbors a feed store, a furniture emporium, a bakery and a meat market. Although located within the downtown core, the property included a sizable backyard with room for a chicken coop.

The house itself was a cheaply constructed wood building with two sleeping areas: a downstairs bedroom, where Masuo, Shidzuyo and all the younger children slept, and an unfinished attic, shared by the three older boys. The older boys got to their room by climbing up a crude staircase that led to a hole cut in the ceiling. But they loved the privacy of their quarters, and they especially loved the little window that opened onto a shed roof, allowing them to come and go as they pleased. In the downstairs room one or more babies were in cribs, while the older children slept in single beds pushed against the wall. Heat came from a potbellied stove in the front room and a wood cookstove in the kitchen. When the children awoke on winter mornings, they could see their own breath and peel frost from the inside of the windows. One morning they awoke to find that the water in the fishbowl had frozen.

Although Masuo was becoming increasingly successful, the family lived frugally, spending very little money. Their rice and canned food came from the store, their produce from one of their farms or the farms of other Japanese who frequently brought them fruit or vegetables as gifts or as payment for goods from Yasui Brothers. Fish came from the Columbia; mushrooms came from the nearby forests. Shidzuyo canned and pickled all summer. She sewed all of the family's clothes on a Singer treadle machine, from the boys' underwear to the girls' school dresses. When she wasn't making new clothes, she was patching and darning.

As with most immigrant families whose offspring are born in America, the Yasuis lived a bicultural but increasingly Americanized life. Masuo and Shidzuyo spoke Japanese to each other, and Shidzuyo spoke Japanese to her children. But, as the children grew and attended public school, they quickly replaced the old language with English. Soon they were speaking only English to one another, and the younger kids grew up learning very little Japanese. For years the family ate a traditional Japanese diet of rice, vegetables and very little meat. *Okazu* (a generic mixed vegetable and meat dish) was standard dinner fare. Rice and pickled vegetables was lunch. But the children started bringing home new ideas—macaroni and cheese, corned beef and cabbage, Jell-O—which became mealtime staples as soon as Michi began taking over the cooking chores in junior high school.

American culture seeped into the house on Third Street in other ways as well. Masuo subscribed to *Life, The Saturday Evening Post, Newsweek* and *Collier's*. Kay received dozens of sporting-goods and natural history collector's catalogs. The boys fished, hunted, camped, joined the Boy Scouts and played baseball. Michi, who was learning to play piano, bought the latest sheet music, from fox-trots to show tunes. And in the front room sat a Montgomery Ward Airline console radio that was tuned in nightly for the news. When he was home, Masuo would sit and listen raptly to the *Richfield News Report,* mimicking the baritone-voiced newscaster when he announced that the program was "brought to you by Richfield High Octane."

In one extremely important aspect of their lives, Western ideas dominated: religion. The family went to church every Sunday and prayer meetings every Wednesday evening, sometimes driving miles to attend gatherings in the homes of valley *issei.* They said grace before meals, and Michi, at her father's prompting, learned to play every selection in the Methodist hymnal. Shidzuyo found time to do church work, distributing Japanese-language Bibles to non-Christian *issei* women in the valley, collecting funds for mission work and acting as the treasurer of the Japanese Methodist church for many years. Masuo, who made it clear that he thought smoking, drinking, gambling, card-playing and dancing were sins, cared not just about the religious health of his immediate family but also of the larger community as well.

During the early and mid-1920s, he was instrumental in arranging numerous visits by traveling clergy to preach to the Hood River Japanese. In 1927 he noted with pleasure in a letter to a Methodist administrator that "four more" of his friends wanted to convert to Christianity. "It is my pleasure to inform you that the Christian influence among our community is surely growing stronger ," he wrote. That same year Masuo and a handful of other *issei* Christians helped bring the Japanese American community a full-time pastor. The Reverend Isaac Inouye, himself an *issei,* had been in America for eight years, four of them as a theological student in Boston. A bachelor with seemingly endless energy, Inouye preached a regular Sunday service, led a weekly children's Bible study, taught Japanese-language classes all Saturday morning and traveled throughout the valley during the work week, teaching and preaching in a different farming community each day. But if their Christianity connected the Yasuis to American life in important ways, it also highlighted their separateness. The Japanese Christians of Hood River were not granted special acceptance because of their beliefs. They did not flow into the mainstream of the white Methodist community. Instead, they supported their own pastor and generally worshiped separately from their white counterparts.

More than the rest of the family, Shidzuyo, because of her lack of direct contact with white culture, remained essentially a stranger in a foreign land. When an eight-year-old friend of one of her sons visited the house, she startled him by bowing a greeting. And despite the rest of the family's growing Americanization—from Masuo being called Mat by white business acquaintances to Michi sending notes to friends SWAK (Sealed With A Kiss)—the Yasuis continued to hold on to some traditional Japanese customs. They made *mochi* (sweet rice cakes) for New Year's and celebrated all day, alternately feasting and visiting up and down the valley. They participated in the yearly *undo-kai,* a summer picnic and games day that attracted the entire *nikkei* community. And they maintained contact with the old country.

In June 1926 Masuo received word from his father that Tsuya, his mother, was seriously ill. Within days the dutiful son had arranged passage for himself and his entire family, and very soon thereafter Masuo, Shidzuyo (who was three months pregnant with Yuka) and their seven children traveled steerage class on the S.S. *President Grant* from Seattle to Kobe. They spent the entire summer in Japan, walking the countryside, visiting relatives and paying their respects. Roku, Shu and Homer, at age four, three and two, respectively, were too young to be affected by the trip. But for Michi and the older boys it was both a window to their cultural heritage and a clear vision of how different they as *nisei* were from the children of Japan. Masuo returned with a renewed appreciation of the economic opportunities of his adopted country.

In the decade before the Depression, Masuo continued his full-steam-ahead pursuit of the American dream. A veritable cottage industry unto himself, he continued orchestrating real estate deals for others, arranging labor contracts and employment, booking transpacific travel and selling insurance policies. In the mid-1920s he added a new sideline: for fifty cents a report, he supplied "unbiased information" about *nikkei* applicants for a New York life insurance company. Money was also coming in from rentals, both the farms he leased to others and the rooms above the store he rented by the month. The store itself continued to do well. And it was a good thing, too, because increasingly Masuo needed the money to fund his agricultural activities, which were not turning out to be as prosperous as he had hoped.

In fact, he was bleeding the store to support the farms. Although his books showed the store was operating at a profit of about three thousand dollars a year throughout the 1920s, he began to pay store accounts so late that creditors hounded him, albeit in the polite language of the day. "Perhaps the pressure of business has made it inconvenient for you to meet the balance of your account," one letter suggested diplomatically. "We presume this matter has escaped your attention," wrote another courteous but insistent creditor. "We cannot believe you are deliberately withholding payment from us," wrote a distributor who asked for payment on a four-month-overdue account. Several creditors, receiving no satisfaction from Masuo, found it necessary to draw drafts against his account at the Butler Bank in town.

Masuo may have been deliberately withholding payment as a normal business strategy—in the past he had routinely paid late, using the money for other purposes—or he may have, from time to time, simply run out of money. Throughout the 1920s, he was seriously overextending himself, buying more real estate and incurring tens of thousands of dollars of additional debt. In Hood River in those days, few mortgages went through banks. Instead, owners and buyers commonly signed private land-sales contracts, with the buyer promising to pay monthly interest and principal payments directly to the owner. Masuo entered into a number of such contracts, both as a principal and as a partner. He owned two orchards with a Mr. Tamura and was, at various times, partners with Messrs. Kuga, Hishikawa and Kiyokawa. Other partnerships went unrecorded, as when he lent money to *issei* orchardists who couldn't make payments on their own notes in exchange for a percentage of their crop. In the mid-1920s, he held two sizable notes for others, one for $4,500 and a second for $7,500, in addition to payments he was committed to make on 170 acres of his own land.

He was trying hard to mount a successful second career as an orchardist, growing apples, cherries and pears on five "ranches" throughout the valley. But a farmer's existence was always fragile. One year an early frost would decimate a crop; another year it was insects. Some years everything went right, too right. Fruit flooded the market and depressed the prices. In the 1920s Hood River orchardists were having a particularly difficult time. The trouble had actually begun years ago when the apple boom of the early 1900s led to hundreds of acres being planted with apples chosen for their appeal to Eastern markets rather than their suitability to the region. Beginning in 1919, several harsh winters showed that these varieties were not hardy enough for the valley. Soil depletion and water erosion, the results of over planting in the good years, were also becoming problems. And, as always, orchardists faced an unpredictable, often wildly fluctuating market.

In 1923 Hood River apples brought seventy cents a box—but cost growers $1.10 a box to raise and harvest. The next year a good crop brought $1.35 a box, with comfortable profits of twenty-five to twenty cents a box. But in 1925 Masuo's apple orchards lost money because everyone's trees produced so well that a glutted market paid the cheapest price ever for Hood River apples. The next year an uncharacteristically rainless spring and scorching summer dried up the lake Masuo used to irrigate his largest orchard, and the sun blistered his apples. As the 1920s continued, the bad years outnumbered the good, and Masuo, among others, lost faith in the once mighty Hood River apple. "I give up hope to raise any apples to make any profit," Masuo wrote to W.H. Weber in 1927. Weber held a $25,000 mortgage for Masuo on a huge tract of orchard land east of Hood River. "I tried last four years and every year I have suffered a big loss. The only hope I have ever to make a success on the farm is to raise early vegetable such as tomatoes, beans, asparagus and cantaloupe." He asked Weber's permission to cut down acres of apple trees and replant the land with these more profitable crops, especially asparagus. Others throughout the valley were making the same decision. From 1925 to 1930 the number of bearing apple trees in Oregon (most of which were located in the Hood River valley) decreased more than 40 percent as farmers replanted with pears, cherries and row crops.

In the early 1920s, seeing the handwriting on the wall, Masuo had begun researching the possibility of growing asparagus, a crop that was just beginning to be commercially raised in the area. With his usual thoroughness, he wrote to chambers of commerce in Washington and Idaho to get names of locally successful asparagus growers, then corresponded with them, asking pointed questions about cultivation, fertilization, weather and diseases, and requesting roots of their stock, which he planted experimentally. By 1924 he had eleven acres planted in asparagus east of Hood River and was ordering ten thousand more plants for spring delivery. By 1927 he had forty acres in asparagus and was the area's leading grower. By the end of the decade the crop he had pioneered was so successful that Masuo established the Mid-Columbia Vegetable Growers Association to market the fifty thousand crates of asparagus he and other *issei* farmers were producing.

He was also devoting increasing time and acreage to strawberries, always a popular crop with the Japanese. At first, economic necessity dictated the choice: *issei* orchardists just starting out had planted strawberries between the rows of young apple trees as a cash crop while waiting out the five to seven years it took for new trees to produce enough to support their families. But even after the trees began producing, Japanese farmers found strawberries to be a dependable crop. By the mid-1920s, about seventy *issei* growers—led by top producer Masuo Yasui—were producing two thirds of the valley's berries. "It requires very patient and skillful work, particularly back-breaking hoeing," he explained to a Portland man in 1927. "White farmers do not like to perform such stooping, back-ache hoeing." But neither did Masuo. He hired pickers, and during peak times Shidzuyo, the boys and later Obasan provided much of the labor. Masuo himself was more manager than farmer. In fact, the only real farming he did was at his twenty-acre Pine Grove orchard, his pride and joy, in the lower valley. There he changed his dark business suit for overalls and got his hands dirty pruning pear trees and spading the earth.

In the other orchards he and Shidzuyo oversaw seasonal workers, many of whom were young white men. The Yasuis treated their help well, and many wrote to them during the winter asking for fruit-picking or asparagus-cutting jobs for the upcoming season. "We sooner work for you people than any of our own countrymen," Julius Hausinger, an overseer who had worked for the Yasuis for several seasons, wrote to Masuo in 1926. "I know you are honest people." (Years later Masuo repaid the loyalty by making a small personal loan to Mrs. Hausinger after her husband died. "Please feel easy about that loan and do not worry about it, as I will never press for payment," he wrote her during the dark days of the Depression.)

Although Masuo tried to counter his losses in apples by devoting an increasing percentage of acreage to asparagus, strawberries and pears, it wasn't that easy. He had scores of acres in apples and could not afford to replace them all. Nowhere did he experience worse luck with what had been the premier crop of the valley than at his 160-acre Mosier farm, the orchard land east of town bordering the Columbia River that he was purchasing from the wealthy Chicagoan W. H. Weber. In 1922 Masuo put a $10,000 down payment on the land and signed a contract with Weber for an additional $25,000. Two years later, he wrote to Weber claiming he had already lost almost $20,000 on the ranch. In 1924 with his labor costs almost four times his income, Masuo asked for an extension on his mortgage payment for the first of what would be many times. Weber responded with understanding and generosity. "We can arrange to give you all the leniency unreasonable conditions in the industry may require," he wrote to Masuo in the fall of 1924. "We have every confidence that when [conditions] become anywhere near normal you will be able to make a very satisfactory success of your undertaking. So do not lose any sleep on our account."

In 1926 much of the apple crop failed. In 1927 a hard frost damaged the pear and cherry crops. Masuo wrote despairing letters to Weber and borrowed money from Renichi to help pay the interest on his loan. The hard luck seemed endless. Each season there was a new crisis: equipment failures, labor problems, bad weather, family illnesses. Each season there were more plaintive letters asking for extensions on the loan payments.

Weber continued to be sympathetic. "There is no need of worrying," he counseled Masuo in the spring of 1926. "You need have no fears of our taking any advantage on account of your being in arrears with your payments. We will be patient. . . ." Yet it was difficult for Weber to be unceasingly patient in the face of Masuo's unbroken litany of problems. "I cannot understand what has gotten into the Mosier apple business," Weber wrote with only veiled exasperation in the winter of 1926. "Up to the last three years we always had good fruit. . . . During my seventeen years connection with the Mosier district I never saw anything approaching the failures that you have met with." Yet in the end, Weber did understand and always granted the extensions. Throughout the 1920s he allowed Masuo to pay—almost always late and often only partial—interest-only payments on the loan. He never paid on the principal at all.

In the spring of 1927 Masuo was beset by the most serious problem to date. He was only forty, but after years of pushing himself both mentally and physically, after the cumulative strain of the losses at Mosier and the continual difficulty in keeping up with his many loans and bills, his health failed. In March he spent three weeks in Good Samaritan Hospital in Portland with pneumonia so severe the doctors doubted his recovery. But he pulled through and was home recuperating in Hood River by mid-April. "I am very weak and unable to walk as yet," he wrote to Weber. In the very next sentence, however, he promised that "in the next few days" he would go down to his office to attend to business. He pushed himself too early, and the recuperation was long and slow. In May he was back in his sickbed, writing to Weber of his "dispared" mind and "constant worry." In June Shidzuyo insisted that he stay at the house on the Mosier property to get away from the press of business in town. But he brought his work with him: From his bed he dictated business correspondence to his oldest son, thirteen-year-old Kay, and arranged mortgages on his other properties to keep the Mosier operation afloat. "I will stick to my job until the very last minute so long as your helping hand extends to me," he wrote to Weber. It wasn't until the next spring that Masuo fully recovered.

Although his own business was suffering, he continued to help others with theirs. His ties to the Butler Bank were particularly important for the *nikkei* community. "The bearer of this letter wishes to ask you for a loan," he wrote on the behalf of a fellow *issei*. "He is an honest and industrious man and you can depend on his business dealings." The bank made a variety of loans to Japanese farmers based on Masuo's recommendation and depended on him to intercede if there were any problems. "Very frequently we find it necessary to refer our troubles to you," bank president Truman Butler wrote, asking Masuo to help straighten out an account with a local *issei*. The phone company also depended on Masuo to ensure prompt payment by its Japanese customers. And increasingly his position as chief counselor to his community was becoming known outside Hood River. A civil engineer from Portland wrote to him, requesting his presence at a meeting with two Japanese farmers. "I shall be glad if you would be present at the interview that we might have a complete understanding of any transaction that might be concluded." A Portland lawyer wrote, asking for Masuo's help in resolving a dispute with a valley *issei*. "I am informed that you sometimes act as interpreter and advisor for your fellow countrymen," he noted.

Out in the community, Masuo continued his "godfather" role, helping with everything from finding in-town domestic jobs for young *nisei* girls to arranging credit for farm-equipment sales to securing a patent for two farmers who had designed new fruit shears. When a local woman was threatened with deportation and a warrant issued for her arrest, Masuo and Renichi posted bond. When another woman tried to blackmail a respected member of the *issei* community, Masuo interceded on his behalf. When two families eyed each other's children as marriage prospects, Masuo was enlisted as a go-between. He and Shidzuyo led the community in collecting funds and clothing for victims of a particularly devastating Japanese earthquake. Shidzuyo was active in the Fujinkai (Japanese Women's Club), and Masuo helped organize and sponsor a summer "open-air camp" for Japanese young people throughout Oregon.

But perhaps their greatest contribution to the *nikkei* of the valley during the 1920s was their leadership in creating the Japanese Community Hall in Hood River. Constructed on a piece of in-town property the Yasuis owned, financed by seven thousand dollars of contributions by the Yasuis and other Japanese families, the building was completed in August of 1926 and quickly became a cultural and educational hub. Previously, ceremonies, festivities and gatherings had taken place in church basements or halls rented from sometimes reluctant whites. Now, a generation after their arrival in Hood River, the Japanese finally had a visible "home" in their adopted land, tangible proof of the prosperity and endurance of their community. Here in the modest wooden building out on West Sherman Street, they gathered for traditional celebrations like *Tenchosetsu* (the emperor's birthday) as well as Christmas pageants. Here the women's organization and the welfare society met. Here Shidzuyo taught flower arranging. And here the young *nisei*, driven into town from their valley ranches, gathered on Saturday morning to learn their parents' language, a language most of them had quickly forgotten as they entered

public school. Reverend Inouye rode herd over some thirty children
each Saturday, walking up and down the aisles of desks, stopping to listen to pronunciation, to correct writing or, most often, to quiet a restless
or overexuberant student who would rather have been out playing that
morning. Other language classes were taught in upper-valley community
halls. In Portland, Seattle, San Francisco and other urban centers with
sizable Japanese populations, language classes often met every day after
public school, with instructors teaching not only language but Japanese
ethics and morals. They served to socialize the next generation into traditional ways. But in the Hood River valley, the Japanese population was
too scattered for this approach. And although Masuo honored many traditional values himself, he was more interested in the Americanization
of the next generation than in their link to the past.

Throughout the 1920s Masuo worked hard in the service of his community, concerned with both the general welfare of his countrymen and
the asparagus and strawberry industries they now dominated. Long considered a leader by the local community, he was recognized as such in the
mid-1930s when the exclusive Japanese-based Nippon Industrial Society
gave him an award for his "outstanding effort towards improving relations between the U.S. and Nippon, for his progressive work in farming
and for service in behalf of his own nationals." Bestowed by a hierarchi-
cal society long on ceremony and tradition, the commendation—hith-
erto given to only two other Japanese in North America—was a serious
honor. Masuo was feted at a formal dinner in Portland, where the consul
general personally congratulated him, and speeches were made on his
behalf. The Hood River *News*, calling the award a "well-earned recognition," praised Masuo as "an outstanding man." Soon afterward, a hundred or more *nikkei* jammed the Japanese Community Hall to present
Masuo with an engraved loving cup commemorating his "dedicated service." Masuo was extraordinarily proud of the awards. And in the mid-
1930s, in the grip of the Great Depression, he needed such a boost.

On the eve of the Depression, Masuo was, by the standards of his day,
a wealthy man, with assets of more than $140,000, almost three quarters
of which was real estate. He owned $1,200 of stocks and bonds and was
holding notes or credit vouchers for almost $20,000. His farms were op-
erating at a net loss, but steady income from the Yasui Brothers Store,
other enterprises and rentals more than made up the difference. He was
$42,000 in debt, almost all of it connected with real estate purchases.
When the Depression arrived, he barely noticed it. Like all farmers, he
was used to bad years, fluctuating prices and unstable markets. In any

case, those first years were more than kind to him. He did so well during the 1929-30 season that he was able to payoff a $2,000 note at the Butler Bank. And early in 1930 the Texaco Company contacted him with a lucrative offer for leasing the corner lot on Oak Street. The Yasui Brothers Store sat on the lot, but the offer was so good that the brothers signed the lease, demolished the old wooden building and constructed a new three-story edifice next door. The new store opened in August.

As the Depression deepened around him, Masuo worked even harder to maintain his various business ventures, especially his "cash cow," the store. He was at the store very late most evenings, taking care of orders, tallying accounts and handling correspondence, sometimes until midnight. He and his brother began to make a special effort to court customers, both white and Japanese. At Christmastime, Yasui Brothers ran a large display advertisement in the local newspaper, calling the *hakujin*'s attention to "beautiful gifts direct from the Orient" and "toys that children will appreciate." Inviting customers to "spend an hour with us," the ad promised "stock . . . so different that you will want to see it." The Yasuis' trade had been almost always exclusively with the Japanese. Here was an obvious attempt to broaden the appeal.

To hold on to and increase business among *nikkei*, Masuo's brother, Renichi, and his second son, Chop, solicited special orders in the valley. In preparation for New Year's, a visiting and feasting day for the Japanese, the two drove up and down the valley after school and on Saturdays, taking orders for the imported delicacies that would grace *nikkei* tables during the holiday. They made the extra effort to ensure that customers wouldn't do mail-order business instead with one of the large import houses in Portland or Seattle. The strategy worked. While Furuya Company, the biggest, most successful Japanese store in Seattle, went bust in 1931, and other smaller shops closed down one after another in the cities, business at Yasui Brothers held steady during the worst years of the Depression. From 1931 to 1935 the store maintained a $6,000-$7,000 inventory and brought in $2,000 or slightly more in net annual income. Although this was less than their pre-Depression business, it was better than many small businesses were able to do. When a Los Angeles firm specializing in "business opportunities"—in actuality, carpetbaggers who made low-ball offers for Depression-damaged businesses—contacted the Yasuis in the spring of 1932, Masuo was able to turn them down without a second thought.

That same year Masuo himself was quick to take advantage of a Depression-created opportunity to expand his holdings. When the county foreclosed on Willow Flat, a 120-acre fruit ranch in the mid-valley, because its owner was unable to pay several years' worth of delinquent taxes, Masuo and his lawyer friend E.C. Smith rushed to the sheriff's sale on the steps of the county courthouse. With E.C. contributing the bulk of the money, and the friends agreeing to a long-term business partnership, the two bought the land, under Smith's name, in April. Masuo hired an *issei* to live on Willow Flat and act as foreman, with Chop commuting sixteen miles round-trip every day to learn the farming operation—which in those days was done with mule power—from the ground up.

At first Willow Flat was unprofitable. During the 1932 season, Masuo listed just over $19,000 in income from Bartlett, Cornice and D'Anjou pears and six varieties of apples, but his expenses totaled almost $21,000. He was, however, determined to make a success of this operation. The key was direct involvement. During harvest season he and Shidzuyo would go out every day to both work and supervise. Chop began to stay at the ranch all summer, taking increasing responsibility as he moved into his late teens. By the mid-1930s, he was in charge, and Willow Flat was paying its own way. During the 1936 season the ranch produced 40 percent more fruit than anticipated and employed twenty-eight full-time pickers to bring it in. In 1938 it took six weeks to pick and pack the more than thirty-five thousand boxes of apples and pears produced at Willow Flat with some workers making as much as two hundred dollars—a veritable fortune at the time—for the harvest.

But the Depression only intensified problems at Masuo's other large operation, the 160-acre Mosier property. In 1930 the price for asparagus and green beans, two mainstays of the farm, was so low that Masuo considered the crop "not worth picking," and there was almost no market for tomatoes. "I am trying very hard to meet my obligations," Masuo wrote to W. H. Weber that spring, "but in these times of hardest financial depressions I am just struggling for bare existence both physically and financially." Weber consented to yet another delay in interest payment. "I surely will remember you and your kindness as long as I live," Masuo gratefully replied. He was able to send a small check to Weber at the end of 1931, but throughout the next year his letters were filled with dire details of a failing farm and pleas for continued extensions. Weber remained sympathetic, although he himself was feeling the pinch of the Depression. "If you could from time to time send me a little, say $100, it would help a great deal," he wrote Masuo in 1932. But soon Masuo was forced to figure out other arrangements. In February of 1933 W. H. Weber died, leaving his less solicitous son-in-law in charge of his estate, which Masuo owed twenty-five thousand dollars "and a great deal of interest unpaid," as the son-in-law was quick to point out. From now on he would somehow have to find the resources to keep at least his interest payments current.

By the mid-1930s the combination of depressed prices and shrinking markets was affecting all of the Yasuis' operations, the ranches as well as the store. "The time is awful hard down here and business is just dead," Masuo wrote to an acquaintance in the winter of 1931. The reduced income from the store, which was being used to make up operating deficits on the farms and had to support the Yasuis and their eight children as well as Renichi and Obasan, was stretched beyond its limits, and Masuo seemed to be operating hand to mouth. When a payment became due, whether it was for merchandise, mortgage or taxes, he wrote for an extension or tried to renegotiate the terms. He paid late, paid partial or paid not at all. In 1931 he was forced to lay off employees at various ranches. That year and the following one he failed to pay any property taxes. In 1932 his cash flow was so poor that he stopped paying his life insurance premiums, as he wrote to Weber, "in spite of the fact that I have eight dependents, but what else can I do when you can get no money from anywhere."

The only thing holding together the business and farming communities of the valley was the fact that everyone was in trouble: farmers were pleading with merchants to extend them credit; merchants were pleading with suppliers to extend them credit; and everyone was pleading with the bank. Masuo was both debtor and creditor, owing the bank, Weber's estate, his suppliers and others tens of thousands of dollars, but also being owed thousands by customers who bought on credit and farmers for whom he held notes. As he pleaded poverty to others, so others told their sad tales to him. He responded with leniency. An *issei* to whom Masuo lent money to buy an orchard consistently asked for—and got—extensions on his payments. Tenants leasing some of his orchard land had to be forgiven a year's worth of interest. Two other men defaulted on loans for $1,500 and $700. Masuo held notes and mortgages totaling more than $20,000 in 1934 but was consistently unable to collect not only the principal but also interest payments throughout the Depression. At the store a Washington man who ran up a sizable bill could not afford to make good on his account because he had "a low wage job, no assets and can barely afford to pay for groceries." Dozens of *issei* customers who had no cash for purchases deluged the Yasuis with crates of produce from their land.

Perhaps because he was accustomed to frugality, perhaps because Japanese culture, with its entreaties to *gaman-suru* (be patient, persevere), its recognition of *ganbatte* (constant struggle) and its attitude of *Shikata ga nai* (It can't be helped) preconditioned him, Masuo was not one of those devastated businessmen who contemplated jumping out a window when the Depression lingered and deepened. "Do you know, Mr. Yasui, I have realized for a long time that you owe your present good state of health both mental and physical to your unusual capacity in patience and endurance in spite of depressing conditions," wrote an out-of-towner who was working with Masuo to sell his valley orchard land. Wrote Butler Bank president Truman Butler in 1931: "It has been my privilege to get a little better acquainted with you and your family each year, and I have watched with great pleasure the development of those fine traits of character which have enabled you to withstand some very severe strains."

Less than a year later the Butler Bank went under, taking with it more than eleven thousand dollars of Masuo Yasui's money. He had been on the depositors' committee that had tried in vain to keep the bank open, even extracting promises from those with accounts to take a 35 percent reduction in their deposits. But the bank was too far gone for any remedy. "It is beyond anyone's imagination about this Depression," he wrote to an acquaintance two months after the bank went bust.

Conditions continued to worsen for Masuo and all the valley's agriculturalists when the fruit industry took a precipitous dive in 1932 and didn't recover for most of the rest of the decade. That year it cost four dollars more a ton to grow and harvest Bartlett pears than they brought at the marketplace; cash income from apples was down 50 percent from pre-Depression days, and income from strawberries—Masuo's most dependable crop—was off almost 60 percent. Local growers lost money on their crops continuously through 1935, as both domestic and foreign markets shrank. "If we do make enough money to pay this year's growing and harvesting expenses, we will be mighty lucky," Masuo wrote to one of his sons in the spring of 1935. Prices were up slightly the next year, and Masuo made enough money to pay delinquent taxes and interest on a few loans. But 1937 was bad again, "the most disastrous year as far as our financial condition is concerned," Masuo wrote. "We lost heavily on all our operations." In fact, with apples selling for sixty-three cents a box less than they cost to produce, the Yasuis lost seven thousand dollars on one orchard alone, and once again Masuo was forced to ask for extensions on his loans. But the following year, 1938, showed promise. Ideal weather resulted in one of the largest strawberry crops Masuo had produced in more than two decades, so although prices were still bad, he was able to turn a profit. The next year the outbreak of World War II all but wiped out the lucrative European markets for Hood

River fancy fruit. Listening to the news every night, Masuo, like the rest of America, followed the conflict that was raging many thousands of miles away.

While Masuo appeared in public to take the hard times equably, at home the strain showed. Always stern, he became more so, the pressure of business and the burdens of leadership welling up in him until he lost his temper, raged at the children, meted out harsh punishments, even threw china. Shidzuyo—always self-sacrificing—became more so, leading the boys out into the strawberry fields, where, bent over a hoe, she labored with them all day, returning at dusk to her considerable domestic duties. The children never saw her idle. She saved everything: rubber bands, string, used tape, food that was going rotten. Farmers with accounts at Yasui Brothers were paying in sacks of cabbage, bushel baskets of *daikon* (white radish) and crates of smelt that the Yasuis could barely keep up with. The *daikon* Shidzuyo put in a fifty-gallon wooden tub in the basement with water, salt and pickling spices. After months the homemade solution began to grow mold, the odor of which was so intense that it wafted up through the floorboards and permeated the house. The Yasui children were embarrassed to bring white friends home. Apple boxes full of smelt were down in the basement too, kept fresh, in those days before refrigeration, by huge blocks of ice. But the fish spoiled faster than the Yasuis could eat it, even though they ate it almost daily. Eventually, the children told Shidzuyo they couldn't face another smelt. She buried the fish as fertilizer under the backyard roses.

The family economized in other ways. When Michi needed clothes for school, Shidzuyo, who sewed everything for her large family, bought enough yardage to make four new dresses. But the dresses were identical, for Shidzuyo bought many yards of the same fabric, which was apparently cheaper than buying smaller quantities of different material. The younger children wore hand-me-downs. The family never owned a new car, never took a trip together, not even to Portland, never ate at a restaurant and rarely spent money for entertainment (although occasionally one or two of the children would be given ten cents for a matinee at the Rialto, Hood River's downtown movie palace). If a child asked for money to buy a soda, he or she was told that it was *"fukeiki* time" (hard times, depression) and there was no money to spare.

Yet despite—or more likely because of—this life-style, the Yasuis actually held their own during the Depression while many of their neighbors went under. In fact, Masuo's protestations of poverty to the contrary, he found the wherewithal to pay for piano lessons for Michi, dancing lessons for Yuka and private-language instruction for the younger children.

Even during the depths of the Depression, he dipped into the store's inventory to send valuable gifts to friends and business acquaintances. And at the same time he was decrying his lack of funds to his creditors, he moved the family to a much larger, much nicer home in a prime residential neighborhood. The new house, which, unlike their old place, sat on a quiet, tree-lined avenue rather than across a busy downtown street from a feed store, had three luxurious bedrooms upstairs and room for a huge garden in the back. For the Yasuis it was an important move "uptown" and into the middle class; for their white neighbors it was an unwelcome intrusion. It was one thing to have Japanese living in shacks out in the valley (or next to their stores downtown); it was quite another to have them living next door.

During the toughest years of the Depression, Masuo and Shidzuyo also found the money to pay for college for several of their children. "Your most important job is to get the best education you possibly can," Masuo had been telling his children for years. The importance of schooling had been drummed into him in the old country, where education was heavily promoted as the way for Japan to move from a medieval to a modern society. And as a culture, Japan had long revered learning and literacy. Masuo knew also, from his experience in America, that his children needed an edge. "You must outperform your detractors," he instructed them. (Most of the children responded by placing at the top of their class in the Hood River public schools.) "A man may leave you, a man may lose his job—but if you are well educated you will always be able to take care of your children," Masuo lectured his oldest daughter, Michi. "Study hard, be conscientious," Shidzuyo told her children, passing along her own passion for education. "Nobody can take your brains and education away." While he struggled to meet other bills and put off paying loan payments for years, Masuo supported Min as an undergraduate at the University of Oregon from 1933 through 1936 and in law school for three years after that. He paid for a year at Oregon State University (then known as Oregon State College) for Chop, four years at the University of Oregon for Michi and four years at Northwestern University for Roku.

"Of course you realize how hard it is to send a son to college in time of Depression like it is now," Masuo wrote to Min in 1937. "But we keep fighting awfully hard to meet ends. Do not worry of your financial affairs. Your dad certainly will take care of you." He did, too, coming up with one hundred dollars a year for tuition, twenty-five dollars a month for room and board and an additional twenty-five dollars to forty dollars a month for expenses. He insisted that the children keep the same kind

of detailed daily expense accounts he kept and urged them, in letter after letter written late at night at his desk at the back of the store, to be
frugal. "As you know, it is still hard time prevailing as ever and it is very
difficult to make money," he wrote to Chop in 1935. "Be careful of your
spending and try to cut down expenses. And every month you send me
your expense account so that I can go over it." To Michi, whose neatly
printed expense sheets showed her to be as conservative as he hoped,
Masuo wrote in 1938: "I appreciate your full understanding of our present financial difficulties. . . . In spite of all our unbalanced financial affairs, we are trying to struggle through somehow, at least for the time
being, in order to carry out our business as well as give good education
to our children."

And struggle through they did, thanks to Shidzuyo's management
of the household, the diversity of Masuo's enterprises, the cooperation
of his creditors and thirty years' worth of business savvy. Throughout
the 1930s, while others succumbed to worldwide economic forces that
raged out of control, Masuo not only survived but enhanced his status.
In 1931, reflecting both his standing as one of the area's largest growers and the *issei's* formidable presence in the local fruit industry, he was
elected to the Board of Directors of the Hood River Apple Growers
Association, the first Japanese ever to fill this position. Four years later
he was reelected to the board with the highest vote total of all thirteen
candidates and continued to serve as the board's only Japanese member
throughout the Depression.

He also broke the race barrier at the local Rotary Club, attending
the group's regional convention in Seattle in 1932 and coming home to
become an active Hood River member. He arranged programs for the
Rotarians, from films of pearl culturing, *origami* and fan-making that he
specially requested from the Japanese embassy in Seattle to more home-
grown entertainment: his own two daughters singing and playing the piano. In the late 1930s he served as a member of the club's International
Service Committee. He took other civic responsibilities seriously, donat-
ing time and five hundred dollars to a Chamber of Commerce campaign
to build a bridge across the Columbia at Hood River and, during a particularly bad Depression year, buying one thousand dollars' worth of
bonds to help construct a new local hospital. By the end of the decade
he alone of all the four hundred *nikkei* in the valley had become an active participant in mainstream Hood River society.

To do this, he had to bury the memory of the virulently anti-Japanese 1910s and his own and his community's defeat. He had to show
himself to be more than a law-abiding thirty-year resident, more than a

successful businessman, more than a civic booster; he had to make himself personally acceptable to the whites. With the same energy and intensity he brought to his ventures, he worked to create a new public persona for himself. At home he was still the same stern, unemotional Meiji man he always had been. But out in Hood River society, he presented another face. Out in Hood River society, he was voluble, gregarious, in the words of his youngest son a "good old boy," who could more easily slap some acquaintance on the back than show emotion to his own children. Out in Hood River society, he was Mat, the Anglicized name his business acquaintances gave him, which he started calling himself in the late 1930s.

He was rewarded by a number of seemingly sincere friendships. "I love these children of yours," wrote one of his white friends in a 1932 Christmas letter, "but best of all I like you." Another praised him for his "wholesome influence which has been of inestimable value to this community."

By 1941 Masuo owned, co-owned or had interest in close to one thousand acres of orchard land, had a financial stake in one out of every ten boxes of apples and pears shipped out of Hood River and was the area's biggest grower of several row crops. He had operated a successful store in the heart of downtown for a generation. He had a nice house on a quiet street in a middle-class neighborhood. One son was married and taking over some of the farm operations; another had a law degree. Three children were in college. With only Homer, a senior at Hood River High School, and Yuka, a sophomore, at home, Masuo and Shidzuyo were looking forward to a quieter life and, soon, a comfortable retirement. But history refused to cooperate.

6

Paradise Lost

As the winter of 1941 blanketed Hood River valley with its first snow, Masuo found himself even busier than usual. His business ventures, now recovering from the worst of the Depression, kept him working late most nights. His community service, expanding as his own stature continued to grow among the *hakujin* (whites), demanded more time than ever. He was still the only Japanese member of the Apple Growers Association Board of Directors, representing scores of his countrymen who would otherwise have been voiceless in the organization that determined their livelihood. He was a model Rotarian. Now, with the war escalating in Europe and draft boards all across America readying themselves for the inevitable, Masuo was asked to perform yet another vital service as a link between Hood River's selective service board and *nisei* boys who might be called for military duty. The board wrote to him dozens of times throughout the fall of 1941, asking for Masuo's recommendations on various draft-eligible *nisei*. What was their family situation? Were they necessary to the operation of their farms? Should they be exempt from service? The board depended on Masuo's intimate knowledge of the community as well as his personal integrity. He responded promptly and succinctly, most often recommending against exemption.

During the first week of December he was busy checking special orders for the hectic Christmas season. On Saturday evening, December 6, he, along with many members of the *nikkei* community, stayed late at the Japanese Hall rehearsing their annual Christmas show. The next day, early in the afternoon, he got a call from Hugh Ball, editor of Hood River's weekly newspaper, telling him that the Japanese had attacked the U.S. Pacific Fleet at Pearl Harbor. Masuo was dumbstruck. After a long moment, he managed to ask: "Is that an authentic report? Has that been verified?" Ball said yes.

Masuo's first thought was to tell his countrymen. He grabbed a heavy winter coat from the closet and ran more than a mile to the Japanese Community Hall, where many of the valley's *nikkei* were gathered for a church service. "Remain calm," he told them, trying to keep his own voice steady. "Return to your homes." He ran home himself, panting and almost wild-eyed, stopping by a vacant lot where his sixteen-year-old son Homer was playing football with several neighborhood boys. Homer had never seen his father so agitated. "I didn't know what was going to happen," Homer remembered, "but I knew it wasn't going to be good."

Masuo's next thought was for his son, Minoru, working in Chicago at the time. Min had gone through ROTC at the University of Oregon—the first two years were required of all men; he chose to continue for the final year—and held the rank of lieutenant in the reserve army. After shepherding Homer back home, Masuo ran downtown to the Western Union office to fire off a telegram to Min:

AS WAR HAS STARTED YOUR COUNTRY NEEDS YOUR SERVICE AS A UNITED STATES
RESERVE OFFICER I AS YOUR FATHER STRONGLY URGE YOU TO RESPOND TO THE
CALL IMMEDIATELY

That night Masuo and the rest of America learned the details of what President Roosevelt was calling "a day that shall live in infamy": more than two thousand Americans were dead; 150 aircraft and nineteen ships were destroyed. And that same night, the rumors began: the Hood River Japanese had known about the bombing beforehand; they were gathered at the Community Hall late the night before planning a victory celebration; they were flashing radio messages to Japanese submarines lurking off the coast of Oregon; they were plotting to blow up Bonneville Dam; they were conspiring to poison the town's water supply. The Hood River Japanese—the men and women who had lived, worked and raised their families in the valley for the past three and a half decades—were the enemy.

On Monday, December 8, as Homer and Yuka sat in their Hood River High School classrooms feeling anxious, confused and somehow ashamed, Taiwan-based Japanese bombers struck two American airfields in the Philippines, destroying more than half of the U.S. Army's Far East aircraft. Fueled by rumors, propelled by panic, the gears oiled by a century of racism, the federal machinery jump-started. The day after Pearl Harbor the Treasury Department ordered all Japanese-owned businesses closed and all *issei* bank accounts frozen. In Hood River, armed treasury agents boarded up the Yasui Brothers Store and posted sentries at the front door. Masuo and Renichi had to get formal written permission to remove anything from the store, including perishable food items for family use.

On Tuesday, December 9, FBI agents began arriving in town, and for the next two days, as Hood Riverites sat glued to their radios listening to reports of the Japanese invasion of the Philippines, government agents fanned out throughout the valley, searching selected *issei* homes and confiscating firearms, radios, cameras and anything that looked suspicious to them. At the Yasuis' home, one of the first to be searched that week, agents confiscated an elegant Japanese scroll certifying Masuo's completion of judo training (at age fourteen), along with drawings and maps the children had completed as homework assignments. Later in the week, agents returned to arrest two valley *issei,* Mr. Akiyama and Mr. Watanabe, both of whom were active in the local Japanese Welfare Society, an all-male self-help and cultural association that sponsored picnics and parades. If there were any charges against the two men, no one was told what they were. The *nikkei* watched in stunned silence. The whites watched also. To them the arrests seemed to legitimize the worst rumors: there *were* "Jap spies" in the valley.

The searches and arrests may have come as a complete surprise to West Coast communities, but such actions had long been planned by top federal officials. Five months before Pearl Harbor a special Department of Justice committee, with assistance from the FBI and the Office of Naval Intelligence, was busy preparing lists of Japanese and Germans "with something in their record showing an allegiance to the enemy." The so-called ABC List, which numbered two thousand by mid-1941, included "known dangerous aliens" whom the FBI had individually investigated (the "A" list), others about whom the government had suspicions (the "B" list) and hundreds of men with clean records who had never been investigated but whose position or occupation made them "suspicious" (the "C" list). By midsummer 1941, federal officials had created a comprehensive interdepartmental plan that, in the event of war, called for the FBI to arrest "potentially dangerous" aliens, the Department of Justice to run hearings to determine their loyalty and the Immigration and Naturalization Service to take custody of those deemed disloyal. During the week after Pearl Harbor, more than a thousand *issei* men were arrested up and down the West Coast. The FBI singled out community leaders, religious leaders, educators. They arrested businessmen, officers in Japanese associations, editors of Japanese-language newspapers,

Shinto and Buddhist priests, teachers in Japanese-language schools. And, on December 12, they came for Masuo Yasui.

He knew they were coming. There was little doubt in the Yasui household that Masuo, the most powerful and visible leader of the state's second largest *nikkei* community, would be picked up. Fourteen-year-old Yuka was in a state of "sheer panic" all that week. She'd walk home from school for lunch, tense, breathless, wondering: "Is he gone? Did they take him today? What will become of us? What will I tell people? What will they think if my father is arrested?"

At 6:30 PM on the Friday after Pearl Harbor, the waiting ended. Two armed agents took Masuo from his home. There were no charges. The family was not told where he was being taken. As the FBI saw it, Masuo was "a wealthy, prominent Japanese merchant and farmer" who "it is reported . . . is strongly Japanese and wants to do something for that government."

Immediately after his arrest, the rumors personalized and intensified. His white neighbors reasoned that if Masuo was picked up, he must be guilty of something. The award he had received in 1935 from the Japanese Industrial Society honoring his business and agricultural achievements, the award the Hood River *News* called "a well-earned recognition," became, in the minds of some, a military award. (The head of the society was the prince of Japan who also held a military title, which may have been the source of this rumor.) Then the rumor mill transformed this imaginary "military award" into a commission in the Japanese navy. The Montgomery Ward console in his living room became a shortwave radio used to transmit coded messages either, as one rumor had it, directly to Japan or, as some were saying, to Japanese submarines in the Pacific. His business success was now thought to have been "funded" by the Japanese government, a carefully orchestrated plot to elevate him to a position of trust and authority in the community. Within days, "Mat" Yasui, the veteran businessman who had lived peacefully in Hood River for thirty-three years, became Masuo Yasui, the Jap spy. As Joseph Meyer, the mayor of Hood River, said after all the Japanese were removed from the West Coast: "Ninety percent of us are against the Japs! Why? Well, because we trusted them so completely while they were among us, while all the time they were plotting our defeat and downfall. They were just waiting to stab us in the back. One of our leading merchants was Yasui. He was a member of our Rotary Club. But I'm sure he was working for Tokyo—probably he even knew that Japan was planning to attack us! Anyway, he's now in the hands of the FBI."

He was in the hands of the FBI, but that was all the family knew. Rumors raced through the *nikkei* community, the most persistent of which were that those rounded up would be shot or immediately deported to Japan. Chop Yasui, living on the Willow Flat orchard with his wife, Mikie, tried to find out where the agents had taken his father. He went to the local sheriff, who didn't know. He questioned the treasury agents in town, who wouldn't say. Then he called the U.S. district attorney in Portland. Meanwhile, Min, using his contacts from law school, was also making inquiries. Between the two of them, they managed to discover that Masuo was being held at the Multnomah County Jail in Portland. For an as-yet-to-be-determined time, he would be alien number 5 439 151.

Multnomah County Jail was just a few blocks from Japantown and a two-minute walk from the Foster Hotel, where Min, back from Chicago, would soon set up his law practice. Masuo was held there without charges, without bail and with no outside communication from December 12 through December 27. On his second day in jail, he was questioned by an INS inspector who grilled him about ties to his native land.

"How many trips have you made back to Japan?" asked Inspector C.J. Wise.

"Just once since the first time I came," replied Masuo.

"What relatives do you have in Japan?"

"I have one brother," answered Masuo.

"How long has it been since you've written a letter to this brother?"

Masuo's last communication with his older brother Taiitsuro had been after the Yasuis returned home from their one and only trip to Japan in the late summer of 1926. "I wrote one letter informing him of my safe arrival," answered Masuo. "That is all."

The inspector persisted. "How long has it been since you've written to any person in Japan?"

"The last letter I wrote to Japan was last year, 1940, in August."

"Who did you write to?" asked the inspector.

Masuo named a few names.

"What was the purpose of writing these letters?"

"My girl made a trip to Japan last summer," answered Masuo, referring to Michi, "and I wrote to express my appreciation."

"Have you written to any person in Japan concerning the military condition in the United States?"

"Absolutely not," answered Masuo.

On the basis of this sworn statement and unsubstantiated "reports" of his allegiance to Japan, Masuo became, in the parlance of the day, a "detainee." On December 27, 1941, he and a group of fellow detainees being held at the jail were taken under guard to Union Station and put on a train bound for Fort Missoula, Montana, where the Department of Justice was conducting hearings to determine the loyalty of Japanese aliens. It was an eight-hundred-mile overnight trip that began with heartbreaking familiarity as the train snaked its way up the beautiful Columbia River gorge through the town of Hood River and then through mile after mile of the bleak and windblown dry lands of eastern Oregon and Washington.

Fort Missoula was a small, old army post with the standard forty-bed wooden barracks, mess hall, canteen, assembly hall, hospital and laundry. But the compound was customized for its new purpose, encircled by a heavy galvanized iron fence dotted with floodlights and punctuated by tall guard towers, where armed sentries stood watch around the clock. When Masuo arrived on December 28 with, as the Department of Justice carefully cataloged, "one box, one suitcase, one bundle," the air was frigid, the ground was covered by a thick blanket of snow. The converted facility had been operating for only ten days. Eventually Fort Missoula would be a temporary home to more than twelve hundred Pacific Coast *issei* as well as an almost equal number of Italian aliens.

Through the winter and early spring, while the Japanese were held with no charges and no hint of what the future would bring, life at Fort Missoula settled into a pattern. Department of Justice officials organized the Japanese contingent into a self-governing unit with representatives elected from each barracks, and a mayor, assistant mayor, treasurer and secretary as spokesmen for the whole group. Committeemen were assigned to oversee the operation of supplies, mail, the mess hall and other services. During the day some detainees worked in the mess hall or the laundry, where they washed and ironed not only their own clothes and bedding but those belonging to the Italians. But most men had little to do. During the bitter cold winter days, they stayed in the barracks playing *go*, chess and *hana*. In nicer weather they played baseball against the Italians or strolled the compound collecting unusual stones that they later polished. Masuo, neither a card player nor a hobbyist, spent his days thinking, praying and writing letters. On Sunday morning he attended nondenominational Christian services; on Monday evening there was hymnal practice and on Wednesday evening a prayer meeting. Time passed slowly.

As the winter dragged on with no change in his status, Masuo began to worry seriously about family finances. With no income from the store and his assets frozen, meeting bills and his children's tuition expenses required careful planning and mountainous paperwork. Each month he had to itemize and justify every family and business expense for government officials and apply for these funds to be unfrozen and disbursed. He worried about the burden that fell on Shidzuyo, the decisions she would have to make in his absence. He worried about his own fate, about his future. But mostly he kept his worries to himself, writing reassuring letters to his family. "We are all spending our days comfortably, without inconvenience, day after day. Please never worry about me," he wrote to Shidzuyo. "I am getting along very nicely under the circumstances, and keeping my usual good health," he wrote to his son Roku. But it was impossible for him to hide all traces of anxiety and confusion. "Who would have predicted such an unexpected misfortune would strike us?" he wrote to his wife after he had spent two months behind the high fence at Fort Missoula.

Meanwhile, Masuo's relatives in Japan were desperately trying to discover what was happening to the American branch of their family. Taiitsuro, Masuo's older brother, sent at least three telegrams during the early part of the war, hoping for news and reassurance. "How are you getting along? We are all worrying day and nite," read one. ". . . Have inquired about your safety but no reply as yet," he wrote a month later. "We are worried." Masuo received the telegrams, which were sent through the auspices of the Red Cross of Japan, carefully translated and then vetted by government censors, but he did not reply. The INS inspector in Portland had made it clear from his questions about letters Masuo wrote to Japan that any correspondence to anyone in that country for any purpose would be suspect. "Have sent you two message but no answer. We are all worried," Taiitsuro wrote again. More than two years after the first telegram, Masuo finally replied: "Thanks for your message. Though we are not living together we are well and safe."

On February 3, eight and a half weeks after being taken from his Hood River home, Masuo got his first inkling of what the future might hold when he was called before the Enemy Alien Hearing Board convened at the fort. Attorney General Francis Biddle had established a national network of these hearing boards early in the year for the purpose of questioning some twelve thousand aliens whose loyalty was suspect. Some two thousand were *issei* leaders; the rest were either Germans who belonged to pro-Nazi groups or Italians who were members of fascist organizations. Each three-member board, staffed by a U.S. attorney or assistant attorney and representatives from both the FBI and INS, was empowered to conduct what the government was calling "informal hearings." There was no judge, no specific statutes to guide the proceedings and no legal counsel permitted for the alien "suspect." Everything about the hearings was casual except the outcome: after questioning the detainee and discussing the case, the board had the power to decide the man's future—unconditional freedom, parole or internment. Fewer than half of the Italians and Germans were ordered interned; more than two thirds of the Japanese spent some or all of the war years in detention camps.

Min, back in Portland, wrote to the superintendent of alien detention requesting permission to attend his father's hearing. Cautioning him that he could not act as legal counsel and could not meet with any other *issei* at Fort Missoula, officials allowed Min to sit in. He found the hearing a "complete farce" and "a kangaroo court." The proceedings began with a recitation of seemingly innocuous facts: Masuo Yasui was "an influential leader in the Japanese community" who had "extensive property interests." He had visited Japan once in 1926 for three months. But it quickly became clear that the government official running the hearing saw nefarious connections between Masuo and his homeland. The official made much of a wooden cup Masuo had received from the Japanese government, as if it were proof of his disloyalty rather than a symbol of his efforts to foster good relations between the two nations. And the official made a case that Masuo had strong, recent ties to Japan through the Japanese consulate in Chicago. It was true that his son Min had secured a job there after law school, thinking that a diplomatic career might be in his future. And it was true that Masuo had written a letter of introduction for his son. But it was not true, as the official implied, that Min was hired because his father had great influence or connections in high places. Masuo did not.

Min tried to argue the point. "I had an excellent record in college," he told the members of the hearing board. "I was Phi Beta Kappa. I had won speaking contests. That's why I was hired." In fact, several people had written letters of recommendation to the consulate for Min, including Wayne Morse, dean of the University of Oregon Law School during Min's tenure there.

But the most damning "evidence" against Masuo came when one of the hearing officers produced drawings the FBI had confiscated during the search of the Yasuis' home.

"Mr. Yasui, what are these?" he demanded, showing Masuo a stack of childishly drawn maps and diagrams with the name of one of his children scrawled on the bottom of each page.

Masuo looked at the drawings. "Those look like drawings of the Panama Canal," he said.

"They are," said the official. "These were found in your home. Can you explain why they were in your home?"

"If they were in my home, it seems to me that they were drawings done by one of my children for his schoolwork," Masuo replied.

"Didn't you have these maps and diagrams so you could direct the blowing up of the canal locks?"

Masuo was visibly taken aback. "Oh, no," he almost shouted. "This is just schoolwork of my young son."

"We believe you had intent to damage the Panama Canal."

"No, no, no."

"Prove that you did not intend to blow up the Panama Canal," demanded the official.

Min was incensed at the treatment his father received. But Masuo accepted it stoically, not so much with a sense of *shikata ga nai* (it can't be helped) but with stubborn faith that the American system would work for him, that eventually the truth would be known, his innocence confirmed and his name cleared. Min reported to his younger sister that Masuo was "very philosophical" about his situation and "willing to accept whatever the U.S. government told him to do." As a Japanese national in federal custody, he had little choice.

Finally, a month after the hearing and almost three months after his arrest, Masuo was informed of the government's decision. Based on the recommendation of the hearings board, he was pronounced "potentially dangerous to the public peace and safety of the United States." Above the signature of the attorney general on the official order of March 6, 1942, were the words that would determine his life for the next four years: "It is ordered that said alien enemy be interned."

One month later, without warning or explanation, Masuo was transferred to Fort Sill, Oklahoma, where he and four hundred other Japanese men were housed in tents and issued sets of olive drabs with their internee number stenciled on each article. "My dear Shidzuyo," he wrote soon after he arrived in mid-April 1942, "I am here in Oklahoma. I spend my time being as useful as possible, although there isn't much to do but eat and sleep." When Shidzuyo failed to answer after several weeks, Masuo wrote to his son Chop: "Since my arrival in Oklahoma . . . I have heard not a word from home, . . . Naturally I am worrying about my folks." He had good reason to worry. Shidzuyo hadn't written because she was busy preparing for the family's forced evacuation from Hood River.

During the three and a half months since Pearl Harbor, as first Hong Kong and then Manila fell to the Japanese and as the Japanese navy triumphed over Allied forces in the Java Sea, the federal government had decided that all persons of Japanese ancestry living on the West Coast, aliens and American-born citizens alike, should be removed from their homes and interned for the duration of the war in special inland "camps." These were not people who had been or would ever be formally accused of acts of disloyalty, espionage or sabotage. These were people, as one *nisei* later wrote, whose "only crime was their face." (In fact, no person of Japanese ancestry living in the United States, Alaska or Hawaii was ever charged with or convicted of any act of espionage or sabotage during the entire World War II period.)

In the spring of 1942 Masuo was transferred again, this time to Camp Livingston, Louisiana. As Min wryly remarked to his sister, "When it's cold, they ship 'em to Montana where it's thirty below; when it gets hot, they ship 'em to Louisiana for the summer."

Masuo did, in fact, arrive at Camp Livingston just as the muggy summer began. Cicadas screeched all day in the 100-degree heat; humidity thickened the air until it turned almost solid. Then, with both regularity and high drama, a late-afternoon thunderstorm brought temporary relief. Built at the edge of the Kisatchie National Forest in central Louisiana, a hundred miles southeast of Shreveport and a hundred miles northwest of Baton Rouge, the camp was, quite literally, in the middle of nowhere. The Japanese lived in fifteen-man barracks with latrines and showers under a separate roof. As in Fort Sill, there wasn't much to do. Masuo worked in the kitchen and mess hall every so often, and during the dog days of summer sometimes went outside the compound with work crews to load heavy logs. At age fifty-six, he found that "it was certainly a hard work for me, and we are wet with drenching sweat," as he wrote Chop in mid-June.

Masuo spent much of his time writing letters, both to members of his own family and to the wives and children of a number of his fellow inmates who could not write in English. As in Hood River, his language proficiency set him apart from the others and conferred elevated status. If he could, he would have written his family every day, but Department of Justice regulations stated that internees could write only two letters and two postcards each week. The letters had to be written on a standard government form, one side only, no more than twenty lines. Men were told they could write to their families about "matters of mutual interest" but not about camp conditions. Both incoming and outgoing mail was extremely slow, as letters made their way through thick layers of government bureaucracy, sometimes crisscrossing the country on their journey past translators, multiple censors and various camp officials. It was common for a letter from Shidzuyo or Yuka to take a month and a half to reach Masuo.

But they did not let the delay stop them. All the children kept in close contact, especially keeping their father apprised of their academic achievements. Yuka wrote her father every two or three days, often sending him candy and other little gifts. The girlish letters, with their optimistic recitation of daily life and their obvious affection, served double duty, as a voice for her mother and as her own effort to keep the family connected. They cemented Masuo's already close relationship with his youngest child. "I am happier to have you as my own girl than to own the whole world," Masuo wrote to her from Camp Livingston.

One person Masuo did not write to throughout his internment was his good friend E.C. Smith, although Smith wrote him "many kind and comforting" letters. After the war, after his long internment was over, Masuo confided to his friend that he broke off contact because he thought Smith could be compromised by receiving mail from, as Masuo sardonically called himself, "a potentially dangerous enemy alien."

Beginning in the fall of 1942, soon after the government announced a plan to allow rehearings for aliens who felt they were unfairly interned, Masuo began pressing for a new hearing. He petitioned the Department of Justice to allow him to join his family, who had by this time been transferred from a temporary assembly center to a permanent internment camp on the California-Oregon border. Throughout the fall and into the winter and following spring, the wheels of bureaucracy turned with agonizing slowness. In December of 1942 the Department of Justice sent Masuo application materials for a rehearing, which he dutifully completed and returned. Three months later he received word that the department would "hold the matter in abeyance" until it received "further directions concerning policy." That spring Min began a separate campaign to get his father paroled from Camp Livingston. He wrote to a number of Masuo's Caucasian friends and close business acquaintances in Hood River, asking them to send letters of recommendation for Masuo to be used at his rehearing. Of the twenty men he asked to help, most ignored the request, including Hood River *News* editor Hugh G. Ball. At least three wrote back "some pretty unpleasant things." Only two responded positively—the ever-faithful E.C. Smith and Truman Butler, erstwhile president of the defunct Butler Bank and now a successful insurance agent.

Still, Min thought his father's application would be "fairly well received." As he wrote to his brother Chop, "I personally feel that Dad has better than a fair chance of being released. Mom, of course, is sure that Dad is coming back." But, unbeknownst to Min, his request for letters of support may have done more harm than good. The news that Masuo was applying for a rehearing became an occasion for others, particularly members of Hood River's virulently anti-Japanese American Legion, to write their own negative letters to the government about him. They may have sincerely believed Masuo to be a dangerous "Jap spy" or they may have seen the war and Masuo's plight as an opportunity to rid their valley, once and for all, of its "yellow invaders." In any case, in April, the government added to Masuo's file "letters received from representative citizens of the Hood River valley opposing modification of the order of internment." Even the local chamber of commerce chimed in, with chamber secretary R.E. Steele writing to "vigorously protest" the possibility of Masuo's release.

The new hearings were to be scheduled for late May or early June, but on May 26, 1943, more than half a year after Masuo had first submitted his petition, his application for rehearing was denied. "I know that your conscience is clear, and that you have nothing to be ashamed of," Min wrote his father in consolation. Like Masuo, his faith in the American system was unshakable. "There is reason to believe that justice is not dead, and that though the wheels may grind slowly, they grind exceedingly fine," he wrote. Eight days later, without warning, Masuo was transferred for the fourth and last time to Santa Fe Detention Station in New Mexico.

Located on a hillside overlooking the town of Santa Fe, the facility was the largest exclusively Japanese detention camp in operation during the war. Masuo was part of a contingent of five hundred *issei* transferred west from Camp Livingston who joined more than fifteen hundred men already there. Constructed on a former Civilian Conservation Corps encampment site, the twenty-acre compound was a hodgepodge of buildings procured from agencies throughout the federal bureaucracy as well as four-man prefab dormitories dubbed "victory huts." Inmates, issued World War I-vintage army clothes, slept in long bunkhouses on narrow army cots, the millionaire farmer from California next to the Shinto priest from Seattle. Each man had a single wooden shelf for his belongings; each barrack had a single potbellied stove for warmth. Surrounded by a twelve-foot-high, double-strand barbed-wire fence and guarded by armed INS border patrolmen, Santa Fe was nonetheless the most pleasant facility Masuo had been assigned to. "The scenery here is the most magnificent and beautiful," he wrote Yuka a few days after arriving. "The water is pure and good. The climate is very healthful and comfortable."

At Santa Fe, Masuo could finally receive visitors. But arrangements were not a simple matter. There were no official visiting days; each time a family member wanted to see Masuo he or she had to write a formal letter stating who wanted to visit, exactly when and why. The request took several weeks to be processed and was followed by a formal, written notification of approval. Visitors had to arrive on the specified day and, once there, had to limit their visits to one hour in the morning and one hour in the afternoon.

Nonetheless, once they figured out how to operate within the bureaucracy, family members made frequent pilgrimages to see Masuo. On one particularly eventful fall morning in 1943 Masuo hurriedly changed from bib overalls to "Sunday pants and a neck-tie" and rushed to the reception center to see his daughter Michi for the first time in two years. With her was her new husband, Toshio Ando, whom Masuo had never met. A few months later, Chop and Mikie visited bringing with them eighteen-month-old Joanie. Masuo held his first grandchild in his arms and was clearly delighted. "She is not so much bashful," he reported to his wife.

Shidzuyo herself visited a number of times, as did Min, who not only conferred with his father on legal matters but also acted as a communications link between a number of Santa Fe inmates and their families. Yuka and Homer saw their father several times. Roku, now an army sergeant bound for the Philippines, received special permission to visit Masuo—both trying to ignore the obvious irony of the situation.

In between the excitement of family visits, Masuo had to contend, long distance, with his crumbling business empire in Hood River. In his absence the farms were in the hands of white caretakers and renters, some who pruned, sprayed, irrigated and harvested with care, others who neglected the land almost entirely. "I am glad you people cannot see the farm now," a valley orchardist wrote in the spring of 1944 after visiting the 160-acre Mosier ranch. "You would be terribly disheartened. Everything is a helter skelter disarrangement. The orchards have had no care and insufficient water." Another orchard was being cared for and profitably harvested, but the renter had paid the Yasuis no rent at all for two years. A business that had rented downtown property from Masuo for years stopped paying entirely right after Pearl Harbor and had to be persuaded more than once by government officials to make good on its standing contract.

Although the flow of income slowed to a trickle, Masuo still needed considerable funds to keep current with taxes on his many properties and keep the children in college and support Shidzuyo. With enormous reluctance, the Yasuis began to consider selling off their holdings.

It was not a seller's market. Whites in Hood River and up and down the West Coast understood well the desperation of their Japanese neighbors following Pearl Harbor. In the months after the attack, as it became increasingly clear that ethnic Japanese on the West Coast would be forcibly evacuated inland, *nikkei* farmers and businesses rushed to liquidate their property. Some whites, perhaps seeing an opportunity to even the score with these foreigners who had previously been so disturbingly successful, rushed to buy Japanese land at bargain-basement prices. Masuo sold his valuable downtown property—the three-story building that housed the store and a floor of apartments as well as the prime corner lot rented out to Texaco—for only $25,000. He sold the Mosier ranch, the 160-acre property he had contracted to buy for $35,000 in the early 1930s and had just finished paying off before the war, for $10,000. When the offer came in the spring of 1944, he wrote to Shidzuyo: "It seems to me . . . that this is nothing but a giveaway deal. However, in view of the current chaotic and uncertain conditions under which we are now placed, I decided to consider the proposition." The Pine Grove orchards, where Masuo had gotten his hands dirty tending young pear trees, sold for half its original purchase price. He signed an agreement to rent the Japanese Community Hall for one hundred dollars a year. When the feeding frenzy was over, the Yasuis were left with only one farm, the Willow Flat orchard that Chop had lived on before the war.

Meanwhile, in Santa Fe Detention Center, the grinding routine of life continued. Masuo wrote letters. He hand-copied newspaper articles into a looseleaf notebook. He read the Bible. He sat on his bunk in silent prayer. He went to religious services and prayer meetings, becoming the unofficial chaplain of his group. Occasionally, like all the other men, he awoke before dawn for a morning of K.P. duty. Mostly he counted the days and once again worked toward getting a new hearing.

In September of 1943 Min wrote a formal letter for Shidzuyo requesting the details of the charges against Masuo in order to apply for a new hearing. "Records show that the subject was apprised of charges against him at the time of the original hearing and given the opportunity to explain them," replied the government somewhat testily a few weeks later. Nevertheless, officials explained that Masuo needed to "supply new evidence" and "clarify his connections" to certain groups and individuals in order to get a new hearing. They seemed particularly troubled by Masuo's membership in the Nippon Society of Portland, although why they would have been is a mystery. The society was a group of *issei* leaders and white businessmen formed in the 1930s to "preserve the fine friendship and understanding between Japan and the United States." Operating from the offices of the Portland Chamber of Commerce, the group sponsored exhibitions of Japanese artists and entertainers and held public receptions for visiting Japanese university students. Government officials also demanded an explanation of Masuo's connection to a group they identified as the Sokoku Kai, an organization of young men interested in fostering loyalty to the homeland and eventually repatriating to Japan. But he didn't belong to the group, and given that its popularity was confined to a few hundred *nisei* held at a California internment camp, he may not have even heard of it.

And despite Masuo and Min's explanations at the original hearing, the government continued to suspect an insidious relationship between Masuo and the Japanese consul general in Chicago. The wooden cup Masuo received as an honor from the Japanese government also continued to deeply trouble them. If Masuo was to get a new hearing, the government wanted "definite proof of the subject's loyalty . . . rather than character references."

By the spring of 1944 the paperwork for the new hearing was complete. And despite an angry letter from Penn Crumm, a Hood River optometrist and American Legionnaire who took it upon himself to write the government protesting any change in Masuo's status, the Department of Justice authorized a rehearing in late April. In addition to whatever material Masuo supplied, the government could depend on a variety of reports concerning his behavior during internment. One such document, dated May of that year, gave him high marks in virtually every category. His attitude toward officials was "respectful." His deportment was "very good." He was "active" and "cheerful" and a "leader in activities." Most important, Santa Fe officials found that he "evidences loyalty to the U.S." and "does not wish to be repatriated."

The rehearing took place July 3, 1944, three and a half years after his arrest. Masuo thought it went well. "I was very fortunate in having been able to present my case to the Board in such a way to satisfy them. The entire Board members were very kind and patient in permitting me to take plenty of time to explain my side of the case," Masuo wrote to his son Shu a week and a half later. His instincts about the proceedings were correct. When the special hearings board wrote its report, it stated that "the internee explained to the Board's satisfaction his activities in his community" and also apparently managed to satisfy the officials on the matter of the wooden cup, which, the board stated, "seems to be the chief factor in his internment." After praising his "good record" at Santa Fe and making note of his many, well-educated and productive offspring, the board recommended parole. "[I]f this man were paroled," the report concluded, "he would not constitute any danger to the internal security. . . ."

But back in Oregon, the local hearings board—undoubtedly influenced by rumors of Masuo's disloyalty still being spread by Hood River American Legionnaires—steadfastly disagreed. "We doubt the advisability of paroling a man of this type," Portland officials wrote to their colleagues in Santa Fe. "He should have strict supervision, and we doubt this can be properly done outside of an internment camp." A later internal memo recommended parole "but not to return at present time to his home in Hood River, Oregon, solely for public relations reasons." For months Masuo languished while Department of Justice officials decided how to reconcile the conflicting recommendations. In early September, more than two months after the hearing, when Shidzuyo wrote to Santa Fe officials asking for news of the outcome, they replied that recommendations were "now being considered." Hearing nothing, she wrote again in November and once more in December. On January 29, 1945, the government finally responded: "No change will be made in internment status." Masuo would continue to live behind barbed wire at Santa Fe.

The family's hopes for his release had been high, and their disappointment was palpable. But whatever anger and bitterness they felt was immediately channeled into renewed efforts. Shidzuyo, Michi, Roku and Homer bombarded the Department of Justice and Santa Fe officials with letters requesting Masuo's release. Meanwhile, Min, as a lawyer with connections in both the *nikkei* and white communities, orchestrated a separate letter-writing campaign. In March, Joe Grant Masaoka, a regional leader in the Japanese American Citizens League (JACL), wrote to the government requesting Masuo's release. In April, Saburo Kido, national president of JACL, wrote both a formal letter to the department, stressing that Masuo was "not dangerous," and a personal appeal to Edward Ennis, chief of the department's Enemy Alien Control Unit. In July, Wayne Morse, Min's old law school dean, who was now a U.S. senator from Oregon, joined the fight, requesting that Masuo's case be reviewed. "Every effort will be made to proceed with care and to make certain that no injustice will be done," replied the government to Morse's inquiry. An internal memo a few weeks later recommended parole.

On August 14, a week after the cities of Hiroshima and Nagasaki had been leveled by atomic bombs, the war in the Far East was over. On September 2, millions of Americans celebrated V-J Day as the Japanese formally surrendered aboard the U.S.S. *Missouri* in Tokyo Bay. But in Santa Fe, despite the best efforts of the family and supporters, Masuo remained interned. In September, asked again whether he wanted to be repatriated, he answered a resounding "no" and took the opportunity to make yet another case for his own release. The inspecting officer noted that his application had "outstanding merit" and praised his "loyalty" and "attitude toward the United States." Late that fall the government told Michi, Roku and Homer that their father's case "will be reconsidered . . . in the near future." The winter came. Masuo spent his fifth Christmas behind barbed wire.

Then, on January 2, 1946, four and a half months after the war ended and four years and three weeks after he was first taken from his Hood River home, Masuo was told by the camp commander that he would "soon be released." The U.S. attorney general had signed the order the week before. "This is rather a surprising but a very pleasant news," he wrote to Min, as if he could not yet believe it himself. But six days later, holding his official letter of release from the Department of Justice's Immigration and Naturalization Service, he was put on the morning train bound for Denver.

He was now sixty-one. During his years of being shuttled from army forts to prisoner-of-war camps to detention centers, he had lost his house, his business and all but one of his farms. He had missed the birth of his first two grandchildren and the wedding ceremonies of a daughter and a son. He had missed four college graduations and his own thirtieth wedding anniversary. The family was scattered. Shidzuyo, Michi and her husband Toshio were in Denver to greet him and take him "home" to the cramped rooms they rented on the top floor of a house. But Min was in Chicago; Roku was serving as a language specialist in Japan with the occupation army; Homer and Shu were in medical school in Philadelphia; Yuka was at the University of Oregon in Eugene. Only Chop had returned to Hood River.

"I have no definite plans for the future," Masuo wrote his friend E.C. Smith soon after he arrived in Denver. "As you know we all love Hood River so well not only because it is a very beautiful place to live but because we spent most of our life there." But he questioned the advisability of returning, wondering "how many of former friends . . . still can be counted on as loyal and true." E.C. responded warmly, telling him that those who disbelieved in his innocence "will know the facts and regret lack of faith" and offering a pep talk: "Knowing you as I do," he wrote Masuo, "I am sure that you will waste no time in thinking too much [about internment], will mark it down as one of those inevitable mistakes that go along with the hazards of war, and that you will take up your useful life with loved ones. . . ."

But it wasn't as easy as that. Masuo's life had changed forever. His reputation was permanently tarnished. Most of the whites he had considered friends had deserted him, concluding that his internment—and especially the length of his internment—proved his guilt. He would live for another nine years, but he would never again call Hood River home. He would never again be the "emperor" of the valley.

part two

Nisei
The Second Generation

American-Born Children
of the Issei

7

A Shadow Across the Canvas

On weekday mornings the older boys would dress in corduroys and V-necked sweaters, the younger boys in knickers, the girls in freshly ironed dresses, and they would walk in twos and threes to Coe Primary, Park Street School, Hood River Junior High and Hood River High School, returning home at noon for a home-cooked lunch. After school the eight Yasuis kept to their sibling cliques, Kay, Chop and Min at the top of the hierarchy, as inseparable as Roku, Shu and Homer at the bottom. Michi and Yuka, the two girls, although six and a half years apart, found themselves bound both by mutual interests and the common cultural expectations of gender.

After school the older boys played tag, catch and kick-the-can in the vacant lots near their downtown home. The younger boys constructed cardboard villages out of the empty boxes behind Cobb's ten-cent store. The girls practiced their music lessons. Some afternoons Roku, Shu and Homer would wander down to the railroad tracks and play by the switching yards, explore the roundhouse, pick up old iron spikes, place pennies on the track. Or they might spend hours skipping flat rocks across the sloughs and ponds below Hood River where the hoboes camped. Sometimes the hoboes invited them for a cup of stew. Kay, Chop and Min would fish near the mouth of Hood River, where in those days the trout and salmon ran so thick that a casual afternoon outing would net sixty or seventy fish. After the novelty of quantity wore off, the boys learned to be fussy, bringing home only the largest specimens, which Shidzuyo would dutifully clean and cook. When the weather turned warm, the older boys would roll their blankets, loop rope around the ends, sling their homemade sleeping bags over their shoulders and venture into the woods for a night of camping.

Once a week there were Boy Scout or Campfire Girl activities. On Saturdays, ten cents would buy a seat at the Rialto Theater for the latest Keystone Kops adventure. On Sundays there was church followed by Sunday school. In the dead of winter there was sledding on the State Street hill just above the Yasuis' house. On hot summer afternoons there was swimming at Koberg's Beach, the Coney Island of the Columbia, where the children splashed in a protected cove, played on a white-sand beach and ate a picnic lunch under the shade of cottonwood trees.

It was in many ways a childhood straight out of an Andy Hardy movie or a Norman Rockwell painting, a quintessential early-twentieth-century rural American childhood. And yet, there was always a subtext, an undercurrent, a shadow across the canvas. Behind closed doors, Hood River parents would lecture their children: "Now, don't you go playing with those Japanese kids." The scoutmaster who led the troop the three older boys belonged to told potential recruits, "I've got to warn you, we have Japanese boys here." At the Rialto Theater, the Yasui children sat in the unofficially segregated balcony.

Although they had a few white playmates, the Yasui children were rarely invited into *hakujin* homes. One particularly good friend of Kay's never asked him into his house because his mother was afraid of Kay. He looked so strange, so foreign, she told her son. She wasn't sure what Kay would do or how he would act. "What in the world would I serve him?" she asked her son, as if Kay were a tourist from an exotic land. After primary school the Yasui children were never invited to the parties of their *hakujin* classmates and never attended school dances or socials. Interracial dating was unheard of. Even interracial friendships between girls and boys were vehemently discouraged.

Their seemingly all-American pre-Depression childhood was in fact a time of deep conflicts and unresolved contradictions. Despite the Scouts and Sunday school and the old fishing hole, it was not a Rockwellian childhood. It was a childhood unique to their heritage. It was a *nisei* childhood.

To be a *nisei* was to be two people: a dutiful child of Japan who honored parents and respected authority as well as an adventuresome, independent-minded American youngster who tested limits. Sometimes the *nisei's* own parents didn't recognize them. "I feel like a chicken that hatched duck's eggs," an *issei* mother once told an anthropologist. Sometimes the *nisei* didn't recognize themselves. They talked, dressed and acted like their white counterparts, but when they looked in the mirror a "foreign" face stared back at them.

To be a *nisei* was to participate fully in American life—school, church, sports—and, as Homer remembered, "to eat Wheaties and drink Ovaltine." Yet it was also to be told and treated as if you were irredeemably different. In Hood River the *nisei* were every bit as American as their second-generation Finnish and German counterparts who sat next to them in school. Yet the white kids and their parents thought of the *nisei* as foreigners. When parents told their children not to play with "any of those Japanese," the Japanese they were referring to were in fact native-born American citizens like their own children.

Some *nisei* openly admitted it, others effectively buried the experience, but they all grew up feeling their "two-ness." There was, of course, a positive side to this biculturalism: an appreciation of two life-styles, an opportunity to know two languages, an escape from the small-town provincialism of their peers. But the Hood River *nisei* had little chance to appreciate these gifts: born into the virulently anti-Asian atmosphere of the late 1910s, they came of age during wartime evacuation and internment.

They might try to ignore it, but two-ness was at the core of their lives. It was not just that they were roasting turkey at Thanksgiving and toasting *mochi* at New Year's, not just that they were banzai-ing to the emperor on his birthday and pledging allegiance to the flag every morning. The duality ran deeper than that. It was a question of basic values and norms. Although the Meiji ethic of their parents and pervasive Puritan ethic of their birthplace both stressed frugality, sobriety, hard work and delayed gratification, there were significant differences in values that created for some a lifelong identity crisis and for all a degree of internal conflict. Their parents' culture emphasized the importance of consensus and conformity, the good of the community over the rights of the individual. But American culture, particularly its Western incarnation, made a cult of individuality. One was responsible first and foremost for oneself in American society; one could mold one's own life. But the *nisei*'s parents had grown up in a society where each person was born indebted to others, where future actions and relationships were determined by past obligations. American culture valued spontaneity, self-expression and robust self-confidence. Japanese culture taught reserve and self-effacement. Americans took thumbing their nose at authority as a God-given right—it was certainly a constitutional one. To the Japanese, respect and obedience were the keys to success. The American-born *nisei* had to come to terms with these contradictions in ways their parents, many of whom spent their whole lives in protected *issei* enclaves, did not. They had to invent themselves, create a hybrid personality and in the process define a generation of hyphenated Americans.

Growing up *nisei* anywhere was difficult. Growing up *nisei* in Hood River, epicenter of anti-Japanese agitation, was even more trying. But growing up a Yasui *nisei* in Hood River, the offspring of the city's only Japanese businessman and the valley's undisputed *nikkei* leader, was the toughest of all.

Masuo was not an easy father to have. In his house he was absolute ruler. He didn't spend much time with his children, and the time he did spend was most often devoted to delivering stern lectures and meting out even sterner discipline. He didn't ask his children to do chores; he told them. He didn't discuss; he ordered. They obeyed without question, or they suffered the consequences.

One evening he came home late from the store, as he usually did, to find Roku, Shu and Homer playing in the kitchen. It was nine or ten o'clock, and the boys had school the next day. "Go to bed!" Masuo shouted when he walked into the room. The boys, deep in their game, kept playing. Masuo became enraged, screaming at Roku and Shu to go upstairs and grabbing his youngest son, Homer, and pushing him out the front door. It was a cold winter night. Out in front of the house, Masuo stripped Homer to the waist and threw handful after handful of snow at his bare back and chest.

His quick temper, which he effectively repressed in public life, went virtually unchecked within the walls of his own home. Mostly his rage found expression in heated lectures to his children in which he alternately admonished them to uphold the moral precepts of Confucianism and shamed them for their offending behavior. The *issei*'s most common method of disciplining their children was to tell them they would bring shame to the family. When his anger could not be contained by words, he threw china, he smashed a lamp. The few domestic arguments that Masuo and Shidzuyo had throughout their long marriage were arguments over his severe treatment of the children.

His Japanese upbringing stressed the father's role as strict disciplinarian, and the reigning philosophy of child rearing in Japan showed little mercy toward children. Parents were instructed to *kuro o katte mo, sase!* (make the children suffer even if you have to buy suffering for them!), for it was thought that through suffering a child matured and came to understand life. The severity of the Japanese father was a national cliche. According to one proverb, the things one had most to fear were *"jishin, kaminari, kaji, oyaji"* (earthquake, thunder, fire, father).

Masuo's anger flared when his children failed in any way to meet his lofty expectations. Perhaps a child had committed the serious crime of receiving a low grade in school or misbehaving in class; perhaps a child composed a poorly written letter. Some offenses were so egregious, such as Min coming home tipsy one night, that Masuo's rage lasted for days. "I grew up thinking: I can't do a bad job. It's got to be good. It's got to be better than good," remembers Michi. The boys had to meet even higher standards, and the older boys, as the leaders not only of their siblings but of the valley's *nisei* generation, were held to higher standards still. It made their already difficult lives even more so.

Kay, Chop and Min were the *nisei* pioneers: the first Japanese American children to attend Hood River elementary schools, the first to attend Methodist Sunday school, the first to enroll in Boy Scouts. And because the Yasuis were for many years the only Japanese family in town, the children remained oddities through most of their childhood. It was not until high school, when the rural *nisei* throughout the valley were bused in to attend the area's only secondary school, that the Yasuis had any Japanese American classmates. The older boys were oddities in another way that distanced them from potential white playmates: when they were growing up, the family lived in the middle of the downtown business district, blocks away from residential streets. The few white children they came into contact with were the sons of nearby merchants who sometimes hung around their fathers' stores after school.

Mostly, the Yasui boys played with one another, and the bonds of their shared isolation drew them closer. They shared a big attic room, which they reached by means of a jerry-built staircase and sometimes exited on the sly by means of a window that opened onto the shed roof of an attached building. The room was lined with wooden shelves, the shelves crammed with the artifacts of boyhood: snakeskins, owls' nests, beehives, seashells and thunder eggs. The boys had rock collections, butterfly collections, knot-tying displays, mounted birds, hunting knives, fishing lures and, buried under a stack of Indian curio catalogs, a single French postcard. They divided their time between school, chores, scouts, sports and outdoor adventures. During the summer they worked long hours in the family's orchards. During the winter they spent time with their uncle Chan, who listened to their troubles, surprised them with candy from the store, bought them fishing poles and, at night, kept them on the edge of their seats with Japanese ghost stories.

One spring when the boys were in their mid-teens, Chan suggested that they all take a camping trip to Yellowstone Park. The thousand-mile trek seemed like a journey to the ends of the earth to the youngsters, and in those days, it almost was. There were no through highways. Beyond the narrow band of civilization that surrounded a town, all the roads were dirt and gravel. Rest stops were clearings under the trees that bordered the rutted, dusty roads. In preparation for the trip, Chan bought Chop a Model T Ford coupe. At fifteen, he was too young to legally drive, but Kay, who had a license, was a poor driver, and Min was barely thirteen. Chan himself had neither the language skills nor the eyesight to pass a driving test.

All that spring, Chop practiced his driving skills, terrorizing the countryside with his love for speed and adolescent penchant for taking chances. The local speed cop, a short, dapper fellow who rode his big Harley Davidson dressed in breeches and military boots, chose to ignore him. Perhaps it helped that the cop was also the older boys' scoutmaster.

The Model T was fun, but when it came time to ready themselves for the trip, Chop persuaded his uncle to trade it in for a larger Chevrolet, a used but still classy four-cylinder hardtop convertible. After the school year ended, the boys and their uncle headed off, Chop at the wheel, Chan beside him, Kay and Min in the rumble seat and all their camping and fishing equipment tied to the fenders. All day they bumped along the terrible roads, Chan entertaining them with stories about his days working on the railroad; at night they pulled out their bedrolls and built fires of sagebrush and mesquite. As they drove through eastern Oregon, Idaho and Montana, Chan would occasionally direct his nephew to drive up winding, unmarked dirt roads where, relying on thirty-year-old memory, he would find the graves of *issei* railroad workers. Despite heat, dust and three flat tires, they made it to Yellowstone, where they spent two glorious weeks loafing, fishing and exploring.

But for all their shared experiences and fraternal intimacy, the three older boys were distinct individuals. Min, the youngest, was small and wiry, an intense, headstrong youngster who, while he played the role of a dutiful son, loved dares and challenges and had little patience for life's refinements. His speech was blunt, his manner with fellow *nisei* sometimes pugnacious. Instead of wooing a *nisei* girl for whom he was carrying a torch, Min instead taunted her with a series of dares: who could go without sleep the longest, who would jump off a nearby bridge, who could memorize the most number of words in the dictionary.

But he realized, early on, what his father expected, and he gave it to him. "Will obey your instructions to the dot, so no need of useless anxiety," Min, at fifteen, assured his father in a letter written during a trip to Seattle. At home, he drove himself to perform academically. Independent, self-contained and confident, he had a talent for extemporaneous speaking and was blessed with a photographic memory that he used both to help him stay at the top of his class and later as a way to entertain his friends. At Hood River High, he was serious, studious and thought of as a "brain," signing on for the tough courses, taking an overloaded schedule and setting high academic goals for himself. And, although he had a brilliant high school career, finishing the four-year program in three and graduating as salutatorian, that was not good enough for him. A half century later, he was still mulling over his "failure" to graduate as valedictorian. "I was so close," he told a friend at their fiftieth high school reunion. He put his forefinger and thumb together, almost touching. "I was really that close."

Min's older brother Chop, on the other hand, was easygoing, affable and happy-go-lucky, with a broad smile and ready laugh. He was generous and had a gentle sense of humor that he often turned against himself for good effect. Kind, understanding and solicitous of his younger siblings, he seemed to model himself after his uncle rather than his father. Even their body types were similar. Chan and Chop both grew broad and stocky as they aged, while Min and Masuo were slim and spare. A poor or, at the very least, unmotivated student, Chop spent more time playing than studying. He took great pleasure in athletics, although his short, thick body didn't make him a prime candidate. For several years he was the second-string halfback for Hood River High's football team in the fall and the manager of the school's basketball squad in the spring. When the valley *nikkei* organized a sports league, Chop quickly signed on as catcher. The all-*nisei* team, self-proclaimed "baseball nuts," would spend their weekends traveling to Portland, Salem, Seattle and eastern Oregon in the back of pickup trucks to play triple-headers, mostly against other *nisei* teams. One year Chop and his teammates, dressed in their usual attire of well-worn street clothes, faced a neighboring city's all-white team bedecked in sparkling new uniforms. Much to everyone's surprise, the *nisei* team won. Another year Chop's team swept the Mid-Columbia Tournament.

But his greatest love was hunting. The Hood River *Guide,* the high school's weekly newspaper, took great pleasure in reporting the antics of Chop and his hunting buddies, poking fun at them for bagging "four teals, one mallard, two pheasant, one goose and three good colds." Concerning another duck-hunting excursion where the only targets to sustain direct hits were empty pop bottles at the city dump, the paper reported that "Malcolm Kresse blames the clear weather for lack of ducks. Vic Howell attributes his failure to an old superstition of no ducks on Friday, and [Chop] Yasui says his failure was due to the bad company in which he went hunting."

Chop was enormously popular with both *nikkei* and *hakujin,* thought of as "a jolly good fellow" and "a good-time kid" with a "teddy bear personality." At a *nikkei* young people's regional Christian conference held in Hood River one year, the organizers composed a ditty that went: "C is for Choppy, Hood River's personality boy." This exuberant personality found an outlet in pranks and tricks that often got Chop in trouble both at school and at home. At Coe Primary, Chop and his friend Hershey Gross conspired to be the class clowns. Miss Cornelius, the venerable first-grade teacher whom the kids secretly called Miss Corncob, would have none of it, administering quick justice with a rubber hose. Every week she would find it necessary to lean one or the other of the boys across her desk to give him five or six swats. Hershey always got off easier than his friend because with the first swat he would let out a bloodcurdling scream that stopped Miss Cornelius in her tracks. Chop, who took some pride in accepting his punishment silently, got the full six whacks. But that was mild compared with the dressing down he would get at home that night from his father. One day he and Hershey, in a creative attempt to get out of school, ate raw onions, cloves of garlic and Limburger cheese. They smelled so bad that the principal sent them home immediately. In high school, when he was tooling around Hood River in his old jalopy, Chop would look over at whoever his hapless passenger was that day, say "Let's take a shortcut," and swerve off the road for a wild ride over open country that miraculously never ended in disaster.

Yet for all his surface joviality, Chop was not an entirely happy boy. In fact, his laughter masked the deep insecurities of a *nisei* childhood. In his mid-teens, when he took a standard personality test, he checked such items as "troubled by shyness," "think people make fun of me," "lack self-confidence," "depressed over low marks at school" and "feel unusually unlucky." Accepted and befriended by whites, he still checked "often feel self-conscious because of physical appearance." As a *nisei* in Hood River, regardless of one's lovable personality, it was hard to escape the reality of being different.

One afternoon Chop and a number of his classmates stayed late at Hood River High for some event. When they left the school, it was already dark outside. Chop turned to a casual acquaintance, a fifteen-year-old white girl, and told her he didn't think she should be walking home alone after dark and that he would be happy to accompany her. The two walked together for several blocks until they were stopped by the city's night patrolman. "Young lady, get in this car," the patrolman ordered Chop's friend, Margaret Cooper. "You have no business being out with a Japanese boy. Just wait until your father finds out." Margaret got in the car, giggling. She knew she wouldn't get into any trouble. Her father knew of her friendship with Chop and had no objections. To her, the incident was humorous. But Chop was humiliated.

His poor scholastic performance, although he joked about it for his whole life, must have also been a source of embarrassment for an older son in a family that prized academic achievement above all else. "[Chop] has the ability but not the effort to meet the assignments," his English teacher noted on a slip that warned of his imminent failure in the class. Later, his civics teacher noted that Chop had not been doing passing work in the class "due to lack of proper preparation." While his brother Min finished the four years of high school in three, it took Chop five years to get through the program. He said he chose to stay beyond his senior year to continue to play football—apparently a somewhat common thing to do in those days. But the truth was, as a substitute player, he wasn't that much in demand, spending the year, as he said himself, "gathering splinters on the bench." In fact, he probably needed to stay an extra year to earn enough credits for graduation. And in any case, he was in no rush to graduate, for he had no plans to continue his education.

Masuo, of course, had other ideas. "Oh no," he told his son sternly when Chop said he didn't want to go to college. "Things are just not going to be that way." As a first step, he got Chop to agree to attend a local business college, but the three-night-a-week schedule still left too much time for loafing, his father thought. Masuo had a solution. He owned about five acres of land west of the high school. It had several hundred pear trees, a small barn, a rental house—and thousands of rocks. "I have news for you, son," Masuo informed him. "If you're not going to go to school, you're going to clear that land." With a crowbar, a team of horses and the help of a hired man, Chop spent an entire summer digging and hauling rocks and using them to build a wall around the property. When the job ended, he decided going full-time to college wouldn't be that bad after all.

If Chop was content to be a social animal rather than an intellectual force, it may have had more to do with the considerable abilities of his older and younger brothers than any lack of intelligence on his part. Watching Min come up quickly behind him and Kay set impossible standards ahead of him, Chop decided early to opt out of the competition and instead create a unique niche for himself. Competing with Kay, in particular, would have been disastrous. Kay was not just smart, he was brilliant.

Kay was *chonan* (eldest son), which meant he had a position of power, respect and considerable responsibility in the family. He was conscious of his place—both his parents and the weight of centuries of Japanese culture made him so—and he was proud of it. But his responsibility went beyond the family. In an important sense, he was *chonan* to the entire *nikkei* community of Hood River. His father was the community's leader and one of its earliest true settlers, and Kay was one of the first male children born into that community. With him the *nisei* generation began. As if to exemplify the strength and promise of that generation, the mix of Japanese blood and American soil, Kay grew to be a tall, athletically built young man, towering not only over his siblings but, by his mid-teens, over his father as well. Standing six inches taller than Masuo and outweighing him by forty pounds, Kay looked like what others said he would someday become: the outstanding leader of the second generation of Japanese in Oregon.

If Masuo had high expectations for all his children, he had monumental ones for his firstborn son. Kay must be a role model for his siblings. He must do more than succeed; he must never fail. When, at age ten, Kay visited Portland for a few weeks and wrote his father a letter detailing his activities, Masuo responded by chiding him: "It was not well written as I expected. You must be more careful when you write a letter." Kay internalized his father's lectures on *bushido,* the feudal code of conduct that taught self-control, self-discipline and dispassion. When he was sixteen and away from home at a combination athletic/military boys' camp for a few weeks, he was stung by mosquitoes on both cheeks. The bites got infected, his face swelled, his pulse raced, his fever reached 103 and he was hospitalized for several days. But he waited until he had weathered the crisis, in stoic samurai tradition, before he wrote to his father. "I didn't want to give you any cause for worry," he wrote from his hospital bed. "Now since I am almost fully recovered, I'll make full explanations."

Masuo had every reason to be proud of his firstborn son, for Kay quickly showed himself to be an extraordinarily bright and curious boy with wide-ranging interests and enthusiasms. A born naturalist, he was acutely observant of the world around him, collecting rocks, fossils, birds' nests, butterflies and other insects, and teaching himself nature photography. He was an American Indian enthusiast with a collection of arrowheads, baskets and curios as well as a tall stack of collector's catalogs. He was a voracious reader, from boys' magazines to Edgar Rice Burroughs to fly-fishing manuals. He loved to fish the local rivers and go duck hunting with his brother Chop, but he was also intensely interested in other lands. As "the most popular and lively member" of an international pen-pal club sponsored by a Japanese American newspaper, he corresponded with a number of boys. "My dear friend in Panama," he wrote to one of them, "I've never been to Panama or even Central America, so I'm naturally curious—more than curious—to learn about your country. Panama—it's a magic word. I have in mind a view of jungles; the tropics, wild animals. Oh if I could but get a chance to see Panama."

Kay's teachers thought of him as the brightest of all the Yasui children, not insignificant praise given Min's and a number of his other siblings' accomplishments. Described variously by his contemporaries as "brilliant," "a brain" and "a genius," Kay consistently made the honor roll in high school, generally earning either the highest or second highest average in his class. The good grades came easily for him, leaving him time to play first-string football and run for the high school track team. Kay wanted to be first in everything, and it really bothered him when he wasn't. He took his few failures hard—not making Eagle Scout because he wasn't a strong enough swimmer, never learning to be a crack shot with a .22.

His biology teacher saw him as the leader of the class, but Kay's interest, early on, was writing. At the junior high school he was editor in chief of *The Tickler,* a mimeographed student newspaper. Early in his high school career he entered and won a national essay-writing contest. As a sophomore he was granted special permission to enroll in the school's junior/senior journalism class, an introduction to reporting that the kids called "the newsies." In January of his sophomore year he was elected vice president of the Oregon High School Press Conference, an annual statewide gathering of student journalists in Eugene. In February one of the newspaper editorials he wrote for "the newsies" won fourth place in the nation in the prestigious Quill and Scroll (the national journalism honorary society) competition. Throughout his sophomore year he wrote regularly for the weekly student paper, the *Guide,* racking up more column inches of copy than any other reporter that year. The next year, for the first time in the history of Hood River High, a junior was named editor in chief of the student paper: Kay Yasui.

Kay took his job at the *Guide* seriously, each week neatly typing out lists of stories and the writers he had assigned to cover them. And he took his own development as a reporter seriously as well, scouring books about good writing and constantly referring to his own dog-eared style manual to make sure his grammar was flawless. His journalism was good: compact, clear, informative. When he covered an event, such as the visit of a Civil War veteran or the concert of a Japanese diva, he recognized its newsworthiness and wrote about it simply and professionally, with a degree of clarity and restraint unusual for a high school journalist. When he editorialized, he selected weighty questions, such as "Why study history?" ("You and I are making history," he concluded).

At home, as the oldest in the family, Kay was expected to do the toughest chores, from chopping and hauling wood for the family's use to laboring in orchards and fields during harvest time. He also had a major domestic responsibility all year round—taking care of his seven younger siblings when Shidzuyo worked in the store or helped in the fields. In this role he modeled himself after his father: he was strict, stern and had no patience with misbehavior. He never hit his younger brothers and sisters, but he often yelled at them. Most of the kids were in awe of him. It seemed to Michi that Kay, like her father, knew everything, that if Kay said it, it must be right. It seemed to Homer, the youngest boy, that nothing he did pleased his big brother. One time, when Homer was four or five years old, Kay tried to teach him to tell time. Pointing to the Seth Thomas clock on the living room wall, Kay quickly ran through the lesson: "All right," he told Homer, "if the big hand is here and the little hand is here, that means fifteen minutes after twelve. Or sometimes it's called a quarter after twelve, or a quarter past noon." He went on for a while, explaining half-past and a quarter-to as Homer looked on with increasing confusion. "Okay, now," Kay said after the brief lesson was over, "if the big hand was here"—he pointed—"and the little hand was there, what time would it be?" Homer shook his head. He had no idea. "Well, you just stand there and think about it," Kay yelled, stomping out of the room. Homer stood there for what seemed to him like hours.

Kay was somewhat kinder with his *nisei* contemporaries, who saw him as outgoing and confident, and recognized him as a leader. But some thought his self-confidence bordered on arrogance and his self-assurance approached cockiness. When the *nisei* got together at the *undokai,* the annual summer athletic meet, Kay would climb up a tree and challenge the other kids to try to get him down. But when anyone got near, he would kick at them, yelling taunts. Sometimes a friendly wrestling match in the grass turned dead serious when Kay confronted an arch rival from a neighboring town, another *chonan* who was never quite able to best him in the day's races.

With *nisei* girls, his self-confidence took a softer tone: he was charming and witty. He wrote love poems to one girl who lived out in the valley, sending her gifts of handkerchiefs and little pins from the store.

With another, who actually had eyes for his younger brother Chop, he teased and flirted, at least in print: "The great love I formerly expressed for you is false," he wrote in a spoof billet-doux when he was fifteen. "Of course I have a heart to bestow, but I do not want you to imagine it at your services and whims." He teased the same girl by composing a six-stanza song to the World War I tune of "Mademoiselle from Armentieres" to welcome her back from a trip to Japan.

> *Oh Eiko Yamaki crossed the sea*
> *Parlez-vous*
> *She ate lots of rice and drank green tea*
> *Parlez-vous*
> *She got seasick and nearly died*
> *Bill said so, but I guess he lied!*
> *Hinky Dinky Parlez-vous!*

One Christmas he typed a three-page letter to Eiko's family, close friends of the Yasuis, detailing the mock gifts he was presenting them, including "gold nuggets . . . found in early '89 in the Yukon Gold Fields" and a wooden box "made by Jimmy Tenno in 1035 B.C. (maybe) . . . and found at the South Pole by Byrd."

Kay—bold, self-confident, even imperious with *nisei*—showed another side of himself when he interacted with *hakujin*. In school he was quiet, reserved, almost diffident, a well-mannered gentlemanly youngster who tried, his classmates thought, never to seem out of place. But his Japanese-ness did set him apart. In junior high he was asked to demonstrate the Japanese tea ceremony at a school carnival. Undoubtedly coached by his mother, he went through the ritual in full kimono regalia as his classmates stared open mouthed. In high school, as part of an assignment for "the newsies," Kay brought in an advertisement from his father's store featuring sukiyaki. None of the kids knew what it was.

The *hakujin* girls thought of him as extremely shy, and with them he undoubtedly was, given the prevailing attitude toward interracial dating or even girl-boy friendships. But Kay did take a special liking to Frieda Paasche, a girl from a rural family who, along with her sisters, picked strawberries for the Yasuis during the summer. Acting as straw boss in the fields, Kay would sometimes talk to Frieda—he taught her the Japanese word for strawberry—and sometimes walk ahead of her in the row, stooping to pick and leaving her little piles of berries for her bucket. After strawberry season, when Kay went away for a few weeks to Camp Hurlburt, a military/sports camp for boys, he wrote to Frieda. She was thrilled; it was the first letter she'd ever received from a boy. Her mother forbade her to reply.

Kay had felt the sting of rejection before. When he arrived at Camp Hurlburt in the summer of 1930, the only Japanese American among hundreds of teenaged boys, he found he wasn't assigned a bed in one of the tents. The captain took aside George Jacobsen, Kay's friend from Hood River. "You know, we're having trouble finding a place for Kay to go," he told him. "Nobody wants to be with him. You're his friend. Will you take him in?" George did. Earlier that year, Kay had been chosen to represent Hood River High at a statewide convention out of town. When he arrived, again the only Japanese American, he was informed that he would not be able to room with the rest of the high school students. Kay didn't talk about his feelings or the rebuffs to his friends, but he did express his anger, at least once, in a poem he wrote early in his seventeenth year.

> You call me "Jap,"
> And boast, saying you yourself are American.
> My hair is black,
> My nose, you say, is flat.
> You insult and torment;
> You say you are my superior
> Because you are
> American.
>
> American,
> If such a thing be true,
> By what rights do you designate yourself
> American?
>
> In your blue eyes, I see the Swede,
> You have the red hair of the Irish,
> Your mother's mother was of Spain,
> Your father is from Britain's soil.
> Trace your ancestry;
> Were they Indians of America?
>
> By what rights then,
> American,
> Are you American?
> Because you were born in this land
> Are you American?
> I, too, claim this land as my birthplace.
> As much American as you,
> I, too,
> Am American.

The week of February 23, 1931, began as an ordinary week for seventeen-year-old Kay, with him and his small staff busy writing and laying out the next edition of the *Guide*. The current week's issue, which came out on Wednesday, included the usual mix of stories: a report on a school assembly, a story about a winning basketball game, a review of a student theatrical presentation. As usual, Kay had written several editorials. One suggested that the faculty recognize and show their support of scholastic excellence by entertaining honor students at waffle breakfasts. Another was an ode to spring:

> Spring is at hand! Rosebuds are out, boidies tweeting, and—well, spring is here, that's all.
>
> What is so wonderful? Why, spring is the bloom of the world's youth. It is a festival, an awakening, a celebration. Words won't say it all adequately.
>
> We hope spring's within us all. We think maybe we can get through the school year safely with spring in sight. . . .

On Thursday Kay had to deliver the layouts for the following week's edition of the paper to the offices of the Hood River *News,* where the *Guide* was printed. He and his friend George Jacobsen, who was the paper's typist, were in good spirits that day. They walked together from school to the *News* office, talking animatedly about their summer plans, and then back to the Yasuis' house, where Kay took George up to the attic room to show him some new additions to his animal-trophy collection. A few hours later, when Shidzuyo returned home from working at the store to prepare dinner, she asked Kay to run upstairs and wake up Min, who loved to take naps. But instead of awakening him, Kay played a prank on his brother, swabbing his face with black shoe polish as he slept. Shidzuyo, unamused, scolded her son, warning him that his father would hear about this.

When Masuo came home late that night and learned of Kay's mischief, he exploded, "ripping him up one side and down the other," as Homer remembers it. Only Kay and Masuo know exactly what was said that night, but one can make a reasonably accurate guess. Masuo was more than disappointed in Kay; he was ashamed of him. Kay's prank was probably seen as an act of aggression against his younger brother, and children in a Japanese family were taught to withhold aggression. Hitting, starting fights or taunting were considered shameful acts for anyone, but more so for someone like Kay who was the *chonan,* the leader, the family's bright and shining star. Masuo expected his eldest son to conduct himself with dignity, to be beyond reproach, to set an example for his siblings. Kay had failed.

Min probably joined in the scolding that night. Not only was he the aggrieved "victim" of his brother's thoughtless prank, but Japanese family dynamics would have called for him to side with his father against his brother. A child who misbehaves in a Japanese family cannot expect to find support in any quarter. "His family is a solid phalanx of accusation" who will "turn against him if he defaults his responsibilities," an interpreter of Japanese culture once wrote. With Masuo's high expectations and no tolerance for his children's misbehavior, with his sharp temper and history of militant discipline, he must have given Kay the lecture of his life. When the yelling ended, he grounded his son, forbidding him to go to school the next day.

The following morning, February 27, a Friday, Masuo left early as usual, Chop and Min headed out to the high school, Michi to junior high, the little kids to Park Street and Coe Primary. Shidzuyo went to the store. Sometime that morning, Kay came down from the attic room he shared with his brothers and rummaged through the kitchen cupboards until he found a box of white powder. Like most rural housewives of the day, Shidzuyo kept strychnine around the house for killing rats and mice. Kay spooned the powder into a glass of water and drank it.

Strychnine poisoning is not a pleasant way to die. Within fifteen minutes, twitching, intense nausea and waves of panic attacks begin. Within a half hour the body is seized by two-minute-long convulsions that occur at five- to ten-minute intervals. The pain from the muscle spasms is excruciating, and the person usually remains conscious throughout. Death comes by suffocation perhaps an hour later when the diaphragm, in protracted spasm, blocks the lungs from expanding. In death the face freezes in a distinctive grimace that doctors call the "death grin."

When Shidzuyo came home a few minutes before noon to fix lunch for her children, she found Kay on the kitchen floor, his arms and legs locked stiff, his lips pulled tight over his teeth. The doctor came; Masuo came; several of Shidzuyo's friends from out in the valley drove in. When six-year-old Homer arrived home after school, he saw Kay's body stretched out on his parents' bed in the downstairs bedroom, surrounded by Japanese women massaging his limbs in an effort to straighten them. Seven-year-old Shu was quickly hustled out of the house and told to go down to the store. Ten-year-old Michi was taken aside by friends of the family and told Kay was dead.

The coroner listed the cause of death as "strychnine poisoning self administered," adding, with sensitivity to the family rather than medical or common sense, "whether with suicidal intent or not unknown." But Masuo and Shidzuyo told the *nikkei* community that Kay had died of natural causes. And their friends—out of a combination of respect and cultural reticence—never questioned them, although many thought it odd that such a young and seemingly healthy boy would die so suddenly. The local paper reported that he died of "failure of the heart."

Masuo and Shidzuyo never sat down with their children to explain Kay's death. Their cultural upbringing precluded shows of emotion and heart-to-heart talks. And they were deeply ashamed. Better not to speak of it at all. "His heart stopped," the children were told. They were told nothing else, and their brother's death remained a dark mystery about which they never inquired. Even among themselves, they never spoke of it.

Masuo and Shidzuyo may have thought they were keeping Kay's suicide a secret—their *nikkei* friends allowed them to think so—but Hood River was a small town, and within a few days everyone knew. On the Monday after Kay's death when Homer was walking home from school, a little girl came up to him on the street. "I heard your brother died," she said. "Yes," answered Homer. Then she said, "I heard he committed suicide. Aren't you ashamed?" This was how Homer found out the truth of his brother's death. At Hood River High, there was no official announcement of the death, no explanation, no opportunity for kids to talk about it. But they did talk about it. The rumors flew.

Some said Kay committed suicide over a bad grade. Others said his father had told him he had to resign as *Guide* editor. One boy said he heard Kay had taken his life because his father wanted him to return to Japan. (More than a decade later the rumor mill churned out another version: Kay had killed himself because he discovered his father was spying for Japan.) But these initial explanations lacked teenage drama. It was almost impossible for the white kids to imagine that a seventeen-year-old boy would kill himself because his father was angry with him. And it was equally impossible for them to imagine what a deeply conflicted life Kay was leading. The kids had to come up with a more plausible explanation.

The more cautious of them said that Kay had been spurned by a girl. Those with more imagination maintained that Kay was in love with a white girl and that both families forbade the two from seeing each other. A few of the most daring kids suggested the unthinkable: Kay had gotten a white girl pregnant. The rumor quietly wormed its way into Hood River lore. Four years later Masuo received an anonymous note warning him that a member of the fruit cooperative was not playing fair with the Japanese growers. This same man, stated the note, "says your son committed suicide cause he had a white girl in trouble and you have the kid now." Sixty years later classmates were still trying to figure out who this nonexistent girl was.

A few *nisei* came closer to the truth, whispering among themselves about Masuo's harshness with his children and a family fight the night before Kay's death. They understood more than the *hakujin* ever could the potent mixture of anger and shame in a Japanese family. In a culture where keeping one's name and reputation spotless was of the highest priority, being shamed carried an enormous burden—a burden that was so intolerable that the remedies were both drastic and dramatic. One was taking vengeance upon the person who impugned one's good name, which would have been impossible for Kay because that person was his father. The other was clearing one's name and redeeming one's reputation by committing suicide.

No one but Kay knows what went through his mind that night and the following morning. There was the immediate incident with his brother to think about; there was his father's disappointment, anger and powerful disapproval. There was the shame of his fall from grace. But there was also, layered beneath that single incident, years of conflict, confusion and two-ness. Kay may have wondered, not for the first time that night, where exactly he fit in. As firstborn, his psychological ties to the land of his parents would have been stronger than those of his younger siblings, and his sense of conflict deeper. Was he Japanese or American? To what extent was it possible to be both? At seventeen, Kay had already had several pointed experiences that forced him to confront his duality and showed him in no uncertain terms how the world saw him. He knew he was bright, and he was bright enough to know that his future would be circumscribed by his race.

Masuo and Min guarded the knowledge of that night, and shouldered the blame for Kay's suicide. On the third anniversary of his death the father and third son exchanged sad letters. "As you say," Masuo wrote to Min, who was in college at the time, "yourself and father are directly responsible for the loss of our dearest one. Your feeling and thought of the 27th day of February meet exactly with mine." Masuo was unsparing. "You will surely feel very keenly toward your responsibility [for Kay's death], and I feel just as much as you do. There lies our common sorrow and great pain which we must suffer for the rest of our lives."

Kay's funeral was March 8. It would have been sooner, but the family was waiting for Chan to return from a trip to Japan. He had gone several months before to escort Obasan, the wife he had married by proxy more than twenty years before, back with him to America for the first time. But when the two arrived in Tacoma, there were some problems with

Obasan's papers, and Masuo had to take the train up to Washington to help his brother straighten things out. He took four-year-old Yuka with him, and on the short trip she suddenly became dangerously ill. The two stopped off to see a Japanese doctor in Portland, where Masuo, beside himself with worry and guilt, wrote home: "How can I tell your mother that she not only has a dead son but also a dead daughter?" But Yuka pulled through; Masuo managed to unsnarl the immigration paperwork, and the four returned to Hood River toward the end of the first week in March.

Kay's funeral reflected his father's power and position within both the *nikkei* and *hakujin* communities. There were more than eighty wreaths, flower arrangements and *koden* (traditional gifts of money to the bereaved) from family friends and Masuo's business associates, from the Hood River High junior class, from Kay's Boy Scout troop. The family received two dozen telegrams and almost one hundred letters of condolence from up and down the West Coast and as far away as Denver and Chicago. "Our great sympathy to you," wrote Masuo's friend E.C. Smith. "Command anything we can do." But there was nothing that would console Masuo. "My wife and I are in poor physical condition due to sorrow and grief over which we have no control," he wrote to a business associate a month and a half after Kay's death.

Sometime after the funeral there was a special memorial service at the Japanese Community Hall. A few months later, in the spring of 1931, when the high school yearbook came out, Kay's picture was on the front page. The book was dedicated to him "in memoriam." That summer, Masuo, Chop and Min attended a memorial service for Kay at Camp Hurlburt in Vancouver, Washington, the camp where none of the boys had wanted Kay as a tentmate.

The pain of Kay's death remained fresh for Masuo. He kept it fresh. Every February 27 the family made a sad pilgrimage to Kay's grave, next to little Yuki's, at Idlewild cemetery. And on February 27, for many years, Masuo wrote sorrowful, self-accusatory notes to Min. Three years after Kay's death, Masuo wrote to Min that he "could not stop hot tears rolling down from my eyes." On the next anniversary of his son's suicide, Masuo wrote to Min of his "deep sorrow that will never vanish from [my] heart." Six years after his son's death, Masuo's memory of that day was "still fresh, and our heart is greatly suffered." Thirteen years after Kay's death, when Masuo was interned in Santa Fe, he gave each person who attended the Sunday church service a small gift "as a token for [Kay's] memory." At a prayer meeting a few days later, he spoke of his eldest son's life in detail. "Everyone who heard me wept," he wrote to Yuka.

LEFT: Twenty-year-old Masuo Yasui (left) and a friend dressed in their finery for Portland's annual Rose Parade in 1907. It was while collecting donations for an *issei* float for the parade that Masuo first came to know Hood River.

LEFT, BOTTOM: Hood River valley, Oregon, was the "perfect pocket of paradise" with its glacier water, temperate climate, fertile soil and inspiring mountain vistas. During the early 1900s, hundreds of Japanese men helped transform the valley floor from the brush and stumps left behind by loggers to carefully tended fruit orchards.

RIGHT: Shidzuyo Miyake was a cultured woman who played the *koto* and composed *tanka* poetry. She was a teacher at a girls school on Owaji Island when she and Masuo Yasui began corresponding..

BELOW: Masuo and his brother, Renichi Fujimoto, opened their first store on Hood River's Third Street in 1908.

ABOVE: Shidzuyo and Masuo, married by proxy in Japan, were married again in Tacoma, Washington, in November 1912. The already Westernized Masuo posed beside his Japanese bride.

RIGHT, TOP: Shidzuyo and Masuo (in backseat) posed with another *issei* couple on their wedding day. Between 1909 and 1920 forty-five thousand Japanese women came to America as brides.

Masuo's and Renichi's store flourished as the Japanese settled in and made the valley their home. Just a few years after opening the Yasui Brothers Store, they moved the business to larger quarters on First and Oak streets.

RIGHT TOP: Yuki (left), born December 1918, was the Yasuis' first girl. "Our graceful and loving daughter," as Masuo called her, died during the influenza epidemic of 1922. Here she poses with older brothers (from left) Min, Chop and Kay.

RIGHT BOTTOM: The growing Yasui family pose in their living room in 1923: (back, from left) Min, Kay, Chop; (seated, from left) Michi, Roku, Shu (on Shidzuyo's lap).

BELOW: Shinataro (center, with derby), Masuo's father, visited the increasingly prosperous American Yasuis in 1918. He is holding grandson Chop on his lap. Shidzuyo is to his right; Masuo, to her right, holds Min. Kay, the oldest, is perched on the dog. Standing (left) is Masuo's brother, Renichi.

LEFT: When Masuo's mother's health failed in 1926, the dutiful son took the entire family to Japan for their first and only group visit. On the deck of the USS *Grant*, Masuo holds baby Homer while Min carries Shu on his back. Shidzuyo was three months pregnant with her ninth child at the time.

BELOW: While in Japan in 1926, the American Yasuis visited the ancestral family graveyard in Nanukaichi, where they posed with the extended clan. In the center, in the broad-brimmed hat, is Shinataro, Masuo's father. To his left is his wife, Tsune, Masuo's mother. Immediately behind Shinataro in the straw boater is Masuo, holding Shu. Far left, standing, is Shidzuyo, with Homer on her back. Far right, standing, is Taiitsuro, Masuo's oldest brother.

ABOVE: The older boys, among the first of the *nisei* in the valley, broke the color barrier in school, sports and Scouts. Kay (seated, left) and Chop (standing, right) were the only two nonwhites in Hood River's Boy Scout troop.

BELOW: Masuo always wore a business suit, even when he visited his orchards. Here he poses with some of his pickers at apple harvest time.

Kay, the *chonan*, or eldest son, felt the weight of
responsibility his position in the family entailed.
This picture was taken a year before his suicide,
when he was seventeen.

8

The Overachievers

The Yasui children didn't spend much time recovering from Kay's death, for in truth they had failed to experience it in the first place. The conspiracy of silence both within the family and in the larger community created a kind of amnesia about the event—and, soon, about Kay himself. To Masuo, who maintained his annual ritual of self-recrimination, and to Shidzuyo, who stolidly nursed a deep pain, their eldest son's suicide would forever remain an unhealed wound. But it was a wound they bandaged well and hid from sight. To all the children except Min, the death remained a profound mystery that, because it was never spoken of, lost its meaning in their lives. They began to forget Kay.

It was not such a difficult task. To four-year-old Yuka and her nine-, eight- and seven-year-old brothers, Kay had been, in life, a distant authority figure, an almost grown man who had little connection to their childhood. It was Chop, not Kay, who had played with them, taken them fishing, told them stories, bought them treats. And Masuo actively helped his remaining children to forget Kay by quickly moving the clan from the old house, now suffused with memories of the suicide, to a new uptown home on Twelfth and Montello. This effort to start anew, to wipe the slate clean, was largely successful. The younger children grew up in surroundings that gave no hint of their brother's existence. As the years passed, they began to mentally rewrite family history, until as adults they would tell others that their parents had raised seven children, not eight, and that Chop was the *chonan*.

Although what memories they had of Kay dimmed over the years, his legacy remained strong. He had set a standard for academic and athletic excellence that most of the others struggled to live up to. Along with Chop and Min, he had pioneered the way for the rest of the children, breaking the color barrier in school, sports and Scouts. He and his two brothers had started to clear a path, but the younger children, growing up a decade later, still found the going rough.

A few months after the move to Twelfth Street, a move that did not sit well with the Yasuis' solidly middle-class, all-white uptown neighbors, seven-year-old Homer and his eight-year-old brother Shu were walking together to the first day of classes at their new elementary school. Along the way, they passed a group of first-graders laughing and playing in a playground. When the children saw the Yasui boys, they stopped their games and grew silent. One little boy skipped over to the fence and started jumping up and down. "Look at the little Jap boys," he began chanting, as he pointed to Homer and Shu. Soon the other kids joined in, their high-pitched voices singing, "Look at the little Jap boys. Look at the little Jap boys." Homer and Shu swallowed hard and kept walking.

Still, life in their new two-story home on a quiet maple- and oak-lined street was good. Shu thought the house, with its front and back porches, its two front parlors and its formal and family dining rooms was "the most beautiful house in town." It was far from that, but it was a substantial improvement over their former cramped quarters on a downtown side street. With three upstairs bedrooms, the family could spread out as never before. And as first Min and then Chop left home, the younger boys found they had even more room. Roku, Shu and Homer, not content to share the front bedroom, fanned out through the house. Shu moved his belongings to the second-floor sleeping porch, which had an inspiring view of the Columbia River and Mount Adams beyond but lacked heat. On winter mornings he grabbed his clothes and bolted downstairs to the kitchen to dress in front of the potbellied stove. Homer established a separate space for himself in the alcove off his parents' bedroom. Roku, enjoying unheard-of luxury, had the bedroom to himself.

Compared with the unfinished attic space their older brothers had shared, the younger boys grew up in splendor. Yet their lives were in many ways more difficult. Masuo was more successful now. Between the new house, the store, the strawberry fields and the orchards, there was always hard work to do. And the Depression made it even more imperative that the boys contribute. Any form of protest against the seemingly unending chores was squelched with words like "duty" and "obligation." At home, they spent countless hours hauling and splitting wood for the stoves for cooking and heating. The family used more than six cords a year, and the boys had to cart the wood from the basement, where their older brothers had stacked it, to the main floor by pushing wheelbarrows up steep wooden planks laid across the stairs. It was exhausting, repetitive work that numbered among their least popular chores. That was why the boys were so disgruntled when Masuo volunteered them, without their knowledge, to do the same work for his friend E.C. Smith.

In the spring and summer there was much work to be done in the fields, and the younger boys started to pitch in when they were only seven or eight. On weekends in May and all through June after school let out, the family would awaken early, eat a quick breakfast and pile into the model A Ford for a drive out to one of the farms. There the younger boys would sit on their haunches to pick strawberries all day alongside the hired help. From July through September, there were scores of acres to be carefully tended by hand-hoeing. It was because white farmers refused to do this labor, considered the most backbreaking of all farm chores, that the Japanese dominated the strawberry industry in the valley. Roku, Shu and Homer, working along with their mother and aunt, did all the hoeing on the Yasuis' extensive property. The summer days were long and hot; the fields stretched out endlessly. When they rode back into town, the boys stared enviously out the car windows at kids playing stickball in the streets.

At sixteen, with his new driver's license folded neatly in the pocket of his overalls, Shu escaped the strawberry fields. His job now was to single-handedly load hundreds of crates of fruit on the back of a flatbed truck, drive twelve miles down a winding two-lane road from the family orchard to the warehouse, unload all the crates and drive back out to the farm. He would make six or seven trips a day, ending in exhaustion but also a kind of exultation that came from his new power behind the wheel.

During the late fall and winter the younger boys had more time for themselves. They belonged to the same Scout troop, went on camping trips in the mountains, accompanied Chop on duck-hunting adventures, played among themselves in the backyard, the playgrounds and parks, and along the river. With less than three years separating them, the brothers were almost constant companions. But as they moved into adolescence, their differences became marked. Roku, initially the trio's leader by virtue of birth order, became in many ways odd man out. Temperamentally different from not only his younger brothers but also the others, he was volatile, impulsive and argumentative with a hair-trigger temper that often caught his siblings by surprise. Unlike the rest of the boys in the family, he was uninterested in both sports and the outdoors. Instead, he loved to work with his hands, building model airplanes out of balsa wood, tinkering with tools, repairing appliances. An average student in a family of overachievers, he was also an intellectual misfit. He was a dutiful student, several times winning awards for perfect attendance, but few classes captured his imagination. In elementary school he excelled only in drawing. In high school he expressed a fleeting interest in journalism, even serving as editor of the Hood River *Guide*, but his true calling was elsewhere. He found out where when Masuo gave him the family's disabled Model A Ford to tinker with. Roku disappeared into the garage, spending long afternoons wedged under the chassis, taking apart the car piece by piece and painstakingly rebuilding it. He restored the engine, teaching himself mechanics along the way and losing himself in the details and precision of the work.

With Roku pursuing his own interests, Shu and Homer, only fourteen months apart, formed their own tight clique. They had been particularly close since early childhood when, at age six and seven, they would sit side by side on the curb in front of their downtown house watching the neighborhood doctor drive up in his new car. Dr. McClain cut an elegant figure as he dashed from his shiny automobile to his office, well groomed, impeccably dressed, clutching his large black leather bag. Shu and Homer instantly stopped what they were doing and looked on in awe. Later, when Shu was so sick he had to be taken to the doctor's office, his fascination with the gleaming white examination room left him more dazed than his malady. Shu never wanted to be anything but a doctor when he grew up. And Homer wanted to be whatever Shu wanted to be.

Although a leader as far as his younger brother was concerned, Shu grew up as reserved and shy as Roku was impulsive and hotheaded. Soft-spoken, diffident to the point of timidity, he agonized incessantly over his own lack of self-confidence. It didn't help that strangers sometimes laughed when they first heard his name, euphonious in Japanese but pronounced just like "shoe" in English, or that kids at school teased him about it. He was embarrassed by wearing hand-me-downs and outdated high-buttoned shoes that didn't sell well at the Yasui store. He was mortified by the haircuts his father gave him by placing the proverbial bowl over his head, and once got into a fight with a boy who ridiculed his hairstyle. He felt outside the mainstream, separated by his race, embarrassed by his difference.

One time Shu stood at the edge of a crowd while a high school bully taunted another white student. "Are ya gonna quit going with those Jap kids?" the bully shouted. The other boy, son of valley farmers, had several *nisei* friends. "No," the boy answered with some bravado. "I can choose anyone I want to be friends with." The bully hit him hard in the stomach. "What about now? Are ya gonna keep your Jap friends now?" The boy stood his ground. "They're just as good as you are," he told the bully. The bully hit him again, harder, and again. Finally, the boy collapsed in a heap, sobbing. Shu walked away, his head hung low.

His extreme shyness made him into a self-professed "goody-goody," an obedient, courteous, polite boy who never even considered misbehaving or playing a schoolboy prank. He acted not so much from moral conviction in those days—that would come later—as from a timid boy's fear of being reprimanded. He envied his high-spirited, mischievous classmates and longed to be like them. To compensate for his lack of self-confidence, he pushed himself in school, forcing himself to seek and accept leadership positions. He was seventh- and eighth-grade class president, and in ninth grade served as student-body president of the junior high. One of his responsibilities was to lead the all-school assembly, but on one occasion he was so terrified that he lost his voice a minute into the speech, and the principal had to rescue him.

In high school Shu worked unceasingly to counterbalance his shyness by excelling in both academics and athletics. He was president of the Boys' League and sports editor of the school newspaper. He ran track, lettered in baseball and, at 142 pounds, played first-string quarterback. In the opening game of his senior year he scored four touchdowns. After school, after sports practice, after chores, Shu studied diligently every night. He would much rather have had a social life than the highest grade-point average at Hood River High. But he had to settle for the latter.

At the end of his senior year he was voted "Best Boy" based on scholarship, leadership and athletics and capped his high school career by being chosen class valedictorian. Masuo, whose many responsibilities had forced him to miss most of Shu's football games during the year, was there to hear his son deliver the valedictory address. He and Shidzuyo sat in the second row. Shu's topic was the greatness of America and how the country was built by the contributions of immigrants from all over the world. He praised the nation as a beacon of freedom, justice and liberty in a world torn by age-old hatreds and prejudices. It was May of 1941. German armies had conquered most of Europe, the *Luftwaffe* was bombing London, but it would be more than six months until Japan and the United States became official enemies.

Just as Chop faced the impossible task of following Kay through school, Homer grew up in the shadow of Shu's achievements. As the last boy in the family, he could have easily been bowed by the weight of cumulative expectations, with the brilliant high school careers of not only Shu but Kay, Min and Michi preceding him. Certainly he felt great pressure, or, as he put it in his characteristically blunt way: "I knew I had to do something or I would look like a dunce." But miraculously the pressure did not translate into sibling rivalry. To Homer, Shu was an esteemed and admirable older brother, not an object of envy. Shu was everything he wanted to be, and Homer was content to try to follow in his brother's footsteps. During their childhood years the two were perhaps closer than any others in the family. Neither can remember ever having a fight.

Homer did well in school, making honor roll most quarters, and, like his brother, was involved in a number of extracurricular activities, from singing in the Glee Club to writing editorials for the school newspaper. He lettered in tennis at Hood River High, played catcher on the baseball squad and competed in football until the doctor permanently sidelined him after detecting a slight heart murmur. But his greatest love, like Chop's, was the outdoors. He was an enthusiastic Boy Scout who reveled in long hikes and overnight camping trips. He loved hunting and fishing. In the fall he would awaken before dawn, bundle up in heavy clothing, hurry down to the river and jump in a borrowed canoe he kept hidden in the rushes. The object was to hunt ducks and geese, but Homer was equally happy just floating, a slight boy in a small canoe on a big river.

Homer had more self-confidence than Shu, a bolder way of acting in the world, but he too had his diffident side. It came not so much from inborn personality but rather from an acute awareness of his different appearance and of the singularity of the Yasuis. Wherever he went— shopping, the park, the movie theater—he was conscious of being a person with a Japanese face. That realization plus years of his father's stern lectures on deportment made him quiet and reserved around *hakujin*. He was careful about what he did, what he said, how he acted.

Michi's and Yuka's lives were quite different from those of their brothers, and the shared experiences as the only girls in a large family of boys united them across their six-and-a-half-year age difference. Sports, such a big part of most of their brothers' childhoods, were completely absent from their lives, although Michi was somewhat of a tomboy. In the place of baseball, football and track, the girls were exposed to the cultural niceties of the middle class. Michi took piano lessons from age six; Yuka took both tap dancing and ballet lessons. The sisters performed together many times, Michi not only teaching her younger sister the songs but also designing and sewing costumes for her. Whenever the Rotary Club or some other group needed entertainment, the Yasui girls were called in. One of their performances was at the elegant Columbia

River Gorge Hotel, where the girls were treated to dainty sandwiches and felt sure they had made it into High Society. Another time they performed on a Portland radio program called *Stars of Tomorrow*, with Yuka dressed in pink organdy and bows.

Farm labor, which took up most weekends and all summer for the boys, was not required of the two girls. Instead they had prodigious domestic duties, learning cooking and sewing from their mother and taking over much of Shidzuyo's work in their early teens. Together, they made dinner for the entire family, with Yuka learning American cuisine from her older sister.

Although their brothers were achievers and their father was the most successful *issei* in the valley, the girls looked to Shidzuyo as their role model. In her they found not merely a domestic workhorse who could teach them what they needed to know about taking care of a home and family, but a quietly cultured woman who valued music and art and strongly believed in educating her daughters. Masuo, too, was convinced his daughters should go to college. So, while traditional Japanese families revered sons and generally considered daughters second-class citizens, Michi and Yuka were encouraged—and expected—to perform academically, continue their education and develop if not a career, a "livelihood." From the day she started Coe Primary, Michi knew she would be going to college.

The two girls shared many experiences, but birth order did make a difference in how they were treated in the family. As the older girl, Michi was expected to be the dutiful daughter who would early on relieve her mother of some of her domestic burdens. She was expected to be serious, hardworking, composed—a "little mother." Yuka, the baby, was indulged. A somewhat headstrong little girl, she was given much latitude in the large family, doted on by Chop, spoiled by her uncle and pampered by her older sister. Michi consciously tried to make Yuka's childhood better than her own. She wanted her younger sister to reap some benefit from the pioneering efforts of the siblings who preceded her. She wanted Yuka to be more accepted in mainstream society.

Like Homer, Michi was sensitive about her own place in Hood River society and the difference her race made to those around her. And she was especially aware of her position as both buffer and link between the foreign world of her mother and the white society she as a *nisei* had been born into. When Shidzuyo brought her to Coe Primary to register for first grade, Michi found herself, at age six, doing all the talking. Her mother simply could not communicate with the teacher. Michi felt awkward and afraid as she looked across the big desk at Miss Cornelius, translating for her mother, answering the best she could, not knowing if she was doing the right thing. Worse, she felt ashamed of her mother. Throughout grade school, while other little girls' mothers joined the PTA, helped organize fund-raisers and baked cookies, Shidzuyo remained aloof, the language and culture barriers too formidable for her to overcome.

But Michi herself joined in. She became part of a group of a half dozen or so girls, all of them white except for her, who walked home from school together, played in the afternoons and went to one another's birthday parties. With Ruth Finney she played "teacher," both girls taking turns at the head of the class and later talking earnestly about their desire to be real teachers someday. With Marcia Stone she played music. Most of the girls in her group took music lessons. For Michi it was part fun—she made her way through stacks of sheet music from classical etudes to "When the Swallows Come Back to Capistrano"—and part tedium. Shidzuyo would make her sit and practice piano every day, winding an alarm clock, setting it on top of the piano and instructing her daughter to practice for thirty minutes. Frequently unenthusiastic, Michi sat on the stool staring blankly at the clock and listening to it tick.

To her clique of girlfriends, who stayed together from first grade through high school, Michi was "one of the gang" and "just another girl." But Michi remembers it differently. As soon as the girls reached dating age, her social life changed dramatically. She was no longer invited to parties, which were now boy-girl affairs, and never went to dances or other mixed-gender social events at school. There were certain clubs she did not even try to join. That's just the way it is, she told herself, employing a *nisei* version of the old *shikata ga nai* (it can't be helped) philosophy. Accepting the exclusion she thought of as "just a fact of life" helped insulate her against overt rejection.

But exclusion from some parts of teenage life certainly didn't mean exclusion from all activities. Michi was, in fact, a born joiner. In high school she participated in the drama club, the pep club, the French club and the orchestra. She was assistant editor of the newspaper, served on the yearbook staff for two years and was elected secretary of the Oregon High School Press Association. When she wasn't staying after school for extracurricular activities or going off to Campfire Girl meetings, she was at home doing chores. By fifteen she was doing all of the cooking and most of the housekeeping. But despite this crowded schedule, she excelled academically, making almost straight A's through high school and earning the honor of class salutatorian. Her achievements made her and her parents proud, but ironically did little to further her acceptance at Hood River High. Behind her back the kids whispered that she wasn't really that smart, that she had to stay up past midnight every night to study, that she had to work much harder than the white kids to get the grades she did.

Michi hoped life for Yuka would be different—and it was, but not in the way Michi intended. By the time Yuka was growing up, family dynamics had changed: Shidzuyo—after giving birth to nine children and seeing two of them die, and after spending the better part of two decades raising her remaining brood—was cycling out of domestic life. During Yuka's childhood, her mother spent most of her day either working on one of the Yasuis' farms or helping out at the store. This left Yuka to come home to an empty house after school and Michi to act as surrogate mother.

In some ways given less attention than her older siblings, Yuka also reaped the benefits of being the last child. Chop in particular devoted himself to his little sister, who, in temperament at least, most resembled him. She was a high-spirited, bubbly, gregarious little girl whose singing and dancing talents earned her the sobriquet "The Japanese Shirley Temple of Hood River." She made friends easily and, although she achieved the requisite Yasui accomplishments, seemed to take herself less seriously than all her siblings save Chop.

As a nine- and ten-year-old, she would come home from Park Street School, and while Michi busied herself with extracurricular activities and the boys stayed for sports practice, she cleaned up the kitchen from the noontime meal. Then she walked downtown to the store, where Chan would invariably give her change from the till so she could run up the hill to the Safeway to buy one of her two favorite treats, peanut butter or cocktail wieners. Chan let her help around the store, but mostly she spent her afternoons playing with a little girl whose parents owned a coffee shop a few doors down from the Yasui store. An hour before dinner, she hurried home to set the table and help Michi prepare the meal. When her older sister left home for college, Yuka, not quite twelve, took over dinner preparation, trying to put into practice the skills Michi had taught her. But her brothers were less than enthusiastic about their baby sister's culinary talents. "Please send Yuka some recipes," Homer promptly wrote Michi. "She only knows how to make corned beef and cabbage."

Yuka grew up in an ever-shrinking household as, one by one, the Yasui children left home to go to college and make their way in the world. The first was Min, who, although one and a half years younger than Chop, beat him to college by sailing past him in high school, finishing in three years to Chop's five. In the fall of 1933, when Yuka was only six years old, Min left Hood River for Eugene, where he enrolled at the University of Oregon as one of half a dozen *nisei* on the three-thousand-student campus. He was only sixteen—and, with his small, wiry frame, wide-open stare and shock of black hair, looked perhaps fourteen—but he was confident, fresh from his successes at Hood River High.

"Please do not fail to be a good scholar and do not disappoint your parents who expect a great deal from you," Masuo lectured his son in a letter written a few weeks into Min's first quarter at college. "You must keep up your high ideals and noble desires. . . ." Min soon reported that he was carrying eighteen hours of credit (three hours more than a full load), studying assiduously and finding college work "harder than anything I've had before." But, he quickly added, "Dad, I'm trying awfully hard to do my best."

He lived up to his word, finishing his first term with the second highest grade average among freshmen in his dorm and, fueled by a combination of his father's expectations and tins of No-Doz, continued to make the honor roll every quarter of his undergraduate career. But Min was no mere grind. Early on he showed his talent for public speaking, placing third out of 130 students in an extemporaneous speaking contest during his freshman year. Later he would win first prize in an all-campus speaking contest and travel the state delivering lectures to civic groups and giving radio talks.

Masuo was pleased and showed his support in the most significant way he knew how: money. When his son dutifully forwarded his monthly expense sheets, detailing fifteen-cent shoe-shines and five-cent orange-ades, Masuo often responded by sending Min ten or twenty dollars more than he had requested. In the depths of the Depression the additional money represented sacrifice on Masuo's part. Min understood the implied message well and worked even harder.

But life at the university was not easy. Although there were a few other *nisei* on campus, the environment was almost as chilly as it had been in Hood River. Min happily went through fraternity rush only to be told that the national bylaws of every one of the fraternities excluded all nonwhites. In fact, Asian Americans were not admitted to any national organizations on campus except scholastic honoraries. When Min ran for the position of secretary-treasurer of his dorm, Alpha Hall, two of his dormmates let it be known that "no damned Jap would ever get to be an official of the hall." But much to their dismay, Min won anyway, and relished the victory. "Ah, ha, ha, ha!" he wrote triumphantly to his brother Shu, describing his detractors as "a tall, dour worthless old guy" and "a lantern-jawed guy." He was also elected to the Spanish honorary, became the president of the campus's international organization ("I might help in furthering the cause of Japanese-American amity," he wrote his father) and distinguished himself in ROTC.

Two years of ROTC was mandatory for all college men; the remaining year, which ended in a commission in the reserve army, was optional. Min chose to stay in the program, becoming a platoon sergeant at the end of his sophomore year, a captain in the fall of his junior year and—"in spite of my race," as he wrote his father—the commanding officer of company D that spring. "It's great sport to watch the subordinates jump at your voice," he reported in a letter home. Although he qualified for an appointment as a second lieutenant that spring, he had to wait for his commission until fall of the following year, 1937, when he finally turned twenty-one.

After three highly successful years as an undergraduate, Min became the second *nisei* ever to enroll in the University of Oregon's law school. Law may not have been his first choice for a career, or even his idea. Certainly Masuo, who as a sixteen-year-old houseboy had dreamed of becoming an attorney, exerted considerable influence on his son. "Knowing as well as I do how much you are depending on me to succeed in law school . . . I have been studying desperately hard," Min wrote to his father during his first term. "If success is based on perseverance and study, I promise you, Dad, that I'm going to succeed." But Min found law school "a bitter struggle. It is not only extremely difficult," he wrote to his father, "but I find that it is becoming monotonous and uninteresting." At the end of the term, his grade average was a disappointing 2.7 (about a B minus), but, as he carefully pointed out to his father, this was only two-tenths of a percent lower than the highest grade earned by anyone in the first-year class. Min reacted to his "failure" by establishing a punishing schedule for himself: breakfast at seven, classes until noon, studying in the law library from 1:00 until 6:00 PM and again from 7:00 until 11:00, then reading briefs and typing notes in his dorm room until 3:00 AM His determination paid off. At the end of the year he was one of two law students elected to Phi Beta Kappa, the first *nikkei* to become a member of this honor society in the history of Oregon higher education.

But law school never came easy. In his second year, he was studying twelve hours a day, forgoing vacations home—and still coming up short. He was astounded to learn that he had failed examinations in Bills and Notes and in Mortgages. In another class he anticipated an A but received a B. In two other courses, he thought he earned B's but got C's. He told his father that he was "nearly sick with fatigue" when he took the exams but nevertheless wondered if he was truly being judged on his merits. "I was talking to the son of a man who is on the board involving the law school," Min wrote to his father. "I was intensely interested to learn that in his opinion, the law faculty were prejudiced against the Japanese." Later in the letter, he referred to "insidious comments" from the faculty and "earnest assurances" from several law students that the faculty was, in fact, biased against him.

"I can stand for anything no matter what it is EXCEPT some one says: 'I heard that a son of Yasui failed.' " Masuo quickly replied. "I'll get through this course of law," Min answered. "I shan't let it be said that a son of Yasui has failed!" Min enrolled in summer school, received an A and a B for his makeup course work and became the school's first *nisei* graduate. That fall he took and passed the Oregon bar.

While Min was putting his nose to the grindstone at the University of Oregon, his older brother Chop was enjoying a far less illustrious—and much briefer—career as a student at Oregon State in nearby Corvallis. It was the state's land-grant institution, its "cow college," and, because of its agricultural focus, attracted *nisei* who came from rural families. There were perhaps a dozen during Chop's time there. College life began inauspiciously for Masuo's second son when, in the fall of 1934, he was refused entrance into the freshman dorm. Watching him and his father walk up the steps of Poling Hall, the housemother quickly interceded. "Mr. Yasui," she said, "if you would be so kind as to wait, the Dean of Men will be over to converse with you." A few minutes later, Dean Dubach arrived to inform them that Orientals were not allowed in the dorms—apparently an unwritten policy stemming from the college's experiences with a disruptive foreign student from Korea. Dubach was apologetic and even offered his own home as a temporary way station. Chop lived at the Dubachs' during his first quarter and later moved to a boardinghouse with several other *nisei* boys.

Masuo had pressured the reluctant Chop to go to college in the first place, and he kept the pressure on once his son was there. "You know how hard Minoru is studying, and you are his older brother. You should try at least to keep pace with him," Masuo wrote. But Chop just wasn't cut out for academic life. He enjoyed himself at Oregon State, "baching" it with the other *nisei* boys at the rooming house, horsing around with his new friends and going to football games, but, as he wrote his father when midterm exams loomed, "It is still quite hard for me to settle down and study." Masuo was not interested in excuses. "Please always bear in your mind that I am not sending you there to spend your very valuable young life without a definite purpose," he lectured his son.

Chop did try hard to be a good student and live up to his father's expectations. He even reported staying up until past midnight to study. But his grades were never good. "I was disappointed and ashamed of the grades I received last term," he wrote apologetically to Masuo after his second quarter at college. "I am trying to do my best to raise my grades for this term. I am not expecting as good grades as Min makes but I am studying harder." Masuo, unsatisfied, goaded his son with guilt: "When you cannot study, you just draw a picture of your poor mother and aunt with their big straw hats, with hoes in their hand bending their back in strawberry field in burning hot weather or in cold windy autumn days. Why are they doing that?" The pressure only increased in Chop's second year, when he and the other *nisei* boys were finally allowed into the dorms. Now Chop not only had to do well to please his father, but was also faced with the burden of "proving" the good name of the *nisei*. "You must be very careful what you do in the dorm," he father counseled that fall. "If you fail to keep good names in the dormitory this is the last chance Japanese students ever permitted to get in. Please keep it in your mind and try your best."

Just as in high school, Chop's warmth and joviality made him immensely popular with both *nisei* and *hakujin*. He socialized with gusto and, during the time he probably should have been studying to improve his consistently mediocre grades, played for both the intramural basketball and softball teams. Also as in high school, his high spirits and natural exuberance eventually got him into trouble. He was known for playing pranks and tricks, a favorite one being sneaking down with friends to the tunnel that connected the dorm to another building, opening the electrical panel and unscrewing all the fuses. They were caught more than once. He told one hometown acquaintance that he was kicked out of college for his involvement in a panty raid on a girls' dorm. With trademark humor, he reported to others that he was "invited to leave" for being "a bad influence." Whatever the cause of his dismissal from Oregon State, Chop didn't make it through his second year. By 1936, as Min was being tapped for Phi Beta Kappa and moving into his first year of law school, Chop came home to Hood River to farm his father's land. As it turned out, he was the only Yasui *nisei* not to graduate from college.

His younger sister Michi had a stellar college career, following Min to the University of Oregon in 1938. She wanted to be a teacher like her mother, but was almost immediately discouraged from taking education classes. "You're wasting your time," she was told by her professors. "There are no Japanese American teachers in Oregon public schools, and there won't be." She didn't give up her dream, but she did change her major to English. During her freshman year, she was the only *nisei* among seventy-five girls in Susan Campbell Hall. But aside from her race, she was the quintessential co-ed with her bobbed hair, pleated skirts, cardigan sweaters and saddle shoes.

For Michi, the first three years at the university were "the happiest years of my life." She joined the International Relations Club and was soon elected to serve as its secretary. She won second prize in an all-campus speech contest. ("However," she said in a letter home, "I cannot boast because I believe Min won first place several years ago.") She was elected to the national speech honorary and became a member of a twelve-woman symposium team that traveled throughout the state debating "Does College Training Better Fit Women for Their Place in Society?" in front of 108 different service clubs, Granges and church groups. An officeholder in the campus YWCA and a member of a prestigious women's service group, Michi was also a serious and successful student. She studied hard, staying up all night during finals week like her brother Min. And she earned top grades, consistently making the honor roll and winning election to the junior women's scholastic honorary.

While studying hard and energetically participating in campus life, she continued to be the dutiful daughter, keeping the kind of detailed monthly expense accounts that earned her father's praise and writing long letters home. "Dad, I hope your faith in me will be justified," she wrote toward the end of her freshman year. "I shall do my very best to live up to yours and Mom's expectations. To me that would be my greatest accomplishment." She often thanked her parents for sending her to college during hard economic times—the point Masuo had repeatedly tried to bring home to Chop—and this was, indeed, music to Masuo's ears. "Your mother and I are very happy to receive your lovely and well written letters," he wrote. "I draw very close attention to your very sincere appreciation and gratitude for the opportunity and privilege granted you. . . ." Even during finals week, Michi's thoughts were close to home. "I hope everyone is all right," she wrote to Masuo. "Mom can save the washing and ironing for me to do when I get home. Please tell her so."

During Michi's junior year, her next brother, Roku, headed off to college, the first of the children to go out of state. With his interest in things mechanical, Roku wanted to go to a strong engineering school, and he probably wanted to get as far away as possible from the competition of his older, more academically talented siblings. Masuo sent him to Northwestern University just north of Chicago, where he did moderately well, earning mostly B's during his first year. But he soon discovered that one of the professors at the school's Technological Institute, which housed the Department of Engineering, was determined to create barriers to his success. Impatient with school after his first year, Roku wanted to find a job in Detroit. "I went to see a few of my professors . . . for letters of recommendation," he told his father, "but found that although they were more than happy to do so, they were afraid to take any definite steps since Mr. Suelberger [professor at the Technological Institute] had advised them to not write any type of letter recommending me to any employer." Roku transferred to the University of Michigan.

Shu, eighteen months Roku's junior, was ready to start college in the fall of 1941. He chose to follow Miri and Michi to the University of Oregon, which still had only a handful of *nisei* students on campus. He was assigned a roommate who had never even spoken to an Asian American before shaking hands with Shu in the small Alpha Hall dorm room they were to share. But the two became good friends, going to occasional concerts and movies together. Mostly, however, Shu concentrated on his classes. He studied hard, earning straight A's all year as he rushed from classroom to library to the dorm kitchen, where he washed pots and pans in exchange for his meals. Still painfully shy, he mostly kept to himself.

By 1941 the Yasui *nisei*, young Americans pursuing a traditional American dream, were on their way to promising futures. Chop, now back home and married to the daughter of a local orchardist, was growing strawberries, pears and apples at Willow Flat and starting to make his own mark in the fruit business. Min, with law degree in hand, had at first tried to establish a practice in Portland, but the Depression made it tough going. When he heard about an opening at the Japanese consulate in Chicago, a writing job for a bright, young bilingual man, he immediately applied. Perhaps he could use his law degree in a diplomatic career, he thought. With his outstanding academic record and a strong recommendation from the dean of the law school, he secured the position and left for the Midwest. There in Chicago, the gregarious Min quickly became, in his brother Roku's words, "one of most popular young *nisei*" in town. "I think that after this war scare is over he could have a splendid chance to make good here, either as a lawyer, professor or diplomat," Roku wrote to his father. Michi, Roku and Shu were all in college, each avidly pursuing credentials for professional careers. Homer, a senior at Hood River High, was looking forward to following in Shu's footsteps. Yuka, a fourteen-year-old sophomore, was just coming into her own.

But the Japanese attack on Pearl Harbor changed all of their lives instantly and forever. Masuo, Shidzuyo and each of their seven children would remember exactly where they were on Sunday morning, December 7, 1941. That moment would redefine their lives, as it did the lives of more than one hundred thousand other West Coast *nikkei*, separating everything into "before" and "after," forever changing dreams, goals, relationships, careers, home, family life and sense of self. Although all of the Yasui children were jolted into new lives, no one was as transformed as Min. For Masuo Yasui's third son, December 7 marked the beginning of his life's work and what would be his enduring legacy.

9

Oriental Jailbird

Min was sacked out on the couch of his Dearborn Plaza apartment in Chicago when the phone rang early Sunday afternoon, December 7, 1941. He had been out late the night before, carousing in the bars of North Rush Street with co-workers from the Japanese consulate, where he had been working for the past year. On the other end of the line was Suma Tsuboi, the feisty hometown girl who long ago had matched wits with him, once staying up all night on a dare, another time meeting his challenge to jump off a bridge into the swift Columbia. Through the years the two had continued their easygoing, playful relationship. But this afternoon Suma's voice was dead serious. "The Japanese have bombed Pearl Harbor," she told him. "We're at war."

Min was shocked and, at first, incredulous. Although he spent every day at the consulate, he hadn't noticed anything unusual—no tension, no furtive glances, no cryptic messages, no detectable change in the office atmosphere. Dressing quickly, he went out to confirm Suma's report, checking with a *nikkei* family he knew on the Near Northside, then coming home to make a few telephone calls and, like everyone else in America that day, sit glued to his radio. At some point during the afternoon there was a knock on the door, and a Western Union boy delivered a telegram from Masuo in Hood River urging his son to report for military duty. "Your country needs your service as a United States Reserve Officer," read the terse message. Five days later Masuo would be picked up by the FBI.

Min immediately resigned his post at the consulate. It hadn't been a sensitive job or a particularly prestigious one—Min spent his days reading American newspapers and writing summaries of current events—

but he had enjoyed it and was even considering a diplomatic career. Now, of course, any connection with Japan was out of the question. Federal officers surrounded the consulate; its bank accounts were immediately frozen. Min had to mail in his letter of resignation, for no one was permitted to enter the consulate building. That was Monday. On Friday of that first week after Pearl Harbor Min learned that federal agents had come to Hood River and taken away his father. A few days later, as he was trying to figure out how best to help his family, he received official orders to report for active duty with the United States Army at Fort Vancouver, Washington.

Min cleared up his business, waited around to cash his last paycheck and then went down to the Union Pacific railroad station to buy a ticket back to Portland. The ticket agent squinted at him, giving him the once-over. "Say, are you a Jap?" he asked suspiciously. Min answered that he was an American of Japanese ancestry. "Well, I can't sell any ticket to any Jap," the agent replied. Min tried to reason with the man, pulling his official army travel orders from his jacket pocket and displaying them on the counter. But the agent could not be budged. Min wasn't intimidated; he was angry. As a lawyer, he knew his rights as an American citizen, and he understood his impending obligation to the military. He knew he had to get on that train somehow. With characteristic doggedness, he made an appointment to see one of the attorneys in the general counsel's office at Union Pacific and found himself quoting the Fourteenth Amendment to his fellow attorney to prove the constitutionality of his own American citizenship. Finally, the man handed him a written authorization to purchase a ticket.

The first leg of his journey took him to North Platte, Nebraska, where he stopped to see old friends and say his good-byes. As far as he knew, he was "off to the wars," and there were no assurances that he'd ever be back. That night, back in his hotel room, he answered a loud knock on the door. A man in street clothes pushed his way in. "You're a Jap, aren't you?" he asked Min. "No," said Min, unable to resist, "I'm bog-Irish." The man's eyes widened. "Don't get smart with me," he threatened. "I'll throw your ass in jail if you fuck around with me." "Who are you?" asked Min. The man produced a badge; Min produced his military travel orders, and the incident abruptly ended.

But despite his momentary bravado, Min was visibly shaken. Was he being followed? Were all persons of Japanese ancestry being watched? After a night of troubled sleep he boarded the train and continued west. He had a week before he had to report to Fort Vancouver, and he spent it in Hood River trying to work his way through the thickening layers of government bureaucracy that now controlled his father's businesses. Masuo was now a "detainee" at Fort Missoula, Montana.

On January 19 he took Masuo's car and drove west to Portland and then across the Columbia to Fort Vancouver to report for duty. The colonel who received him looked over his orders, leafed through his file and dismissed him: "We'll let you know when to report," he said. Of course, Min had already received official orders to report, but the military simply did not know what to do with previously commissioned *nisei*. The colonel was stalling for time. During the next few days, Second Lieutenant Min Yasui returned to the base eight times to report for duty and each time was rebuffed. Later, the army would reclassify him, as well as many other *nisei*, including his older brother Chop, as 4C: "not acceptable for service by the War Department." It was a classification based on race alone.

Min returned to Hood River in time to learn of his father's enemy-alien hearing scheduled for early February at Fort Missoula. There, in a small room facing three government officials, he listened helplessly as his father's name was muddied by innuendo and unsubstantiated rumor. In the hands of the examiners a child's homework became a spy's document, a business accolade became a military award. He watched as the two things he believed in most—his father and the law—were attacked. And he knew then that he would have to fight back. His chance came a month and a half later.

Soon after he returned from his father's hearing, Min moved to Portland, where he set up a law office on the ground floor of the Foster Hotel, a Japanese-managed establishment on the raggedy northwest edge of downtown, to help *issei* deal with the flood of paperwork the government now demanded of them. The *nikkei* community was in a panic. In the two months since Pearl Harbor there had been ugly rumors: the *issei*, as noncitizens, would be jailed; the *issei* would be deported; the *nisei* would be put in work camps. No one knew exactly what the government had in mind, but every person of Japanese ancestry on the West Coast understood they were in imminent jeopardy. Just how serious their situation was became clear on February 19, 1942, when President Franklin Roosevelt signed Executive Order 9066 empowering the secretary of war to designate sensitive "military areas" in four western states and remove and exclude "any and all" persons from them. Everyone, from the president to the old *issei* farmer, knew that the real target of EO 9066 was not "any and all persons." The real target was the ethnic Japanese, the people who had the same face as America's new enemy.

Min Yasui knew it too. And, as the only practicing attorney of Japanese descent in Oregon—and one of the very few on the entire West Coast—he knew it was up to him to find a way to stand up for his people. He was an American citizen. More than two thirds of the *nikkei* on the West Coast were American citizens. How could this government that Min had been taught to revere treat some of its citizens differently from others, merely because of their parents' birthplace?

As soon as EO 9066 was signed, Min went into action, conferring with local *hakujin* (white) lawyers, other legal specialists and federal authorities about the constitutionality of possible restrictions that singled out ethnic Japanese. During that tense post-Pearl Harbor winter, amid vitriolic anti-Japanese rhetoric and rumors that all Japanese would be forcibly removed from the West Coast, Min developed and sharpened his legal arguments in consultation with others.

"It is my belief," Min told his fellow attorneys, "that no military authority has the right to subject any United States citizen to any requirement that does not equally apply to all other U.S. citizens." They countered with the argument that a government has certain rights during wartime. But Min persisted: "If the government curtails the rights of any person," he said, "the damage is done not only to that individual but to the whole social structure."

Earl Bernard was one of the legal specialists that Min sought out. Fifty-two and then in the prime of a distinguished career, Bernard was a pillar of the Portland legal community, a member of the local gentry, a vestryman in the Episcopal church and an old-style trial lawyer who thrived on tough, controversial cases. An expert in constitutional law and, like Min, an optimist about the document's power, Bernard was sympathetic to Min's arguments. But, he told Min, in order to test a law you have to violate it. And no legal challenge would be possible until the government actually issued orders backed by criminal penalties. "Look, if this ever happens," Min informed Carl Donaugh, the local United States attorney with whom he had been keeping in touch, "we're going to start a test case."

During the next month, sandwiched between sixteen-hour days in his law office, Min began to plot strategy. In meetings with his Portland colleagues and during marathon bridge games with a close-knit group of fellow *nisei*, he reiterated what he had said to the lawyers. One of the duties and obligations of a good, patriotic American, he told them, was to challenge laws he thought unjust. "If we believe in America, if we believe in equal democracy, if we believe in law and justice, then each of us, when we see or believe such errors are being made, have an obligation to make every effort to correct such mistakes." Min saw the wartime treatment of Japanese Americans as a basic legal issue that cut to the heart of the Constitution, a document he believed should be defended at all costs. Some of his friends argued that defying a military order would be seen as disloyal, even traitorous, and would seriously hurt the Japanese community. But others quietly agreed with his position.

Min's idea was to challenge the very first government restriction, not wait for the mass evacuation order that many thought would eventually come. It didn't matter what the particular military order was, the principle—singling out a group of citizens on the basis of ancestry—was what he wanted to call to question. This meant mounting a test case, finding someone who would disobey a military order and break the law. That person, Min reasoned, should be sympathetic to the public in every way possible: "some *nisei* who had served in the army during the first World War, was married and had a few cute kids." Childless, single and turned down repeatedly for active duty since Pearl Harbor, Min was certainly not his own first choice. Anyway, he saw himself as the lawyer who would argue the case, not its guinea pig. He began combing the local Japanese community for just the right man to challenge the order. This person would risk everything: his name, the welfare of his family, his standing in the community. He would risk imprisonment, a stiff fine and, after that, an uncertain future. It was hardly surprising that volunteers didn't beat down Min's door. It soon became clear that if he wanted a test case he would have to be his own guinea pig.

But Min was not an ideal candidate in other, more serious ways—ways he either did not understand or refused to acknowledge. First there was the matter of his father, once successful and powerful, now being held as a "potentially dangerous alien." The white community was less equivocal about Masuo Yasui: they called him a Jap spy. In the heat of the historical moment, the Yasui name was already suspect. Second, and perhaps more important, Min had been working for the Japanese government in the days just before Pearl Harbor. Although his job with the consulate was routine, it too cast suspicion on Min's loyalty. Later these facts would come back to haunt him and muddy the legal waters.

But in the absence of volunteers, he mentally volunteered himself, and waited for the government to issue the first restrictive proclamation. Meanwhile, as he tended to the legal concerns of the Portland *issei*, he burned with righteous anger: the country his father had loved and zealously believed in had betrayed him, and it was now about to betray a hundred thousand others.

All through his childhood he had heard his father say: "We are born into this world to make a difference." In adolescence, after Kay died and it was clear that easygoing Chop would not be the kind of leader Kay had been destined to be, Min accepted both the burden and the honor of such leadership. He became an example not only to his younger brothers and sisters but also to his generation. His father's words took on added meaning. Here, in the spring of 1942, was a chance for Min to make the difference his father talked about.

On March 24, Lieutenant General John L. DeWitt, the man chosen by the secretary of war to carry out Executive Order 9066, issued the first blanket restrictions: an 8:00 PM to 6:00 AM curfew for German, Italian and Japanese nationals as well as for all American citizens of Japanese descent. The restrictions on Germans and Italians were widely considered unenforceable—as white Europeans they could not easily be identified as foreigners—but restrictions on ethnic Japanese were another matter. Readily recognizable by their racial characteristics, ethnic Japanese, whether resident aliens or American-born citizens, were the obvious target of the new order. This was what Min had been waiting for.

The evening of March 28 was cool and unseasonably dry. At his office in the Foster Hotel, Min neatened the piles of paper on his desk, reached for his overcoat, relit his pipe and gave final instructions to his secretary, Rae Shimojima. "Notify the FBI," he told her. "Call the Portland police. Tell them a Jap is walking up and down the streets, and he wants to be arrested."

At exactly eight o'clock, Min closed the door on his law office and set out to break the law. Calmly and purposefully he walked up and down Portland's Third Avenue, expecting at any moment to be arrested for violating the curfew order. But the minutes stretched into an hour, the hour into two, and still he walked free. At ten o'clock he saw a patrolman up ahead and rushed to catch up with him.

Min pulled a copy of the curfew order from the pocket of his overcoat. "This is Military Proclamation Number Three," he told the officer. "It prohibits persons of Japanese ancestry from being away from their homes after eight o'clock." The cop said nothing. From his other pocket Min took a copy of his birth certificate. "See," he told the cop patiently, "I am a person of Japanese ancestry." The cop just stood there. "You should arrest me," insisted Min. The cop shook his head and sighed. "Run along home, sonny boy," he said. "You'll get yourself in trouble."

Min walked on. He was tired; it was getting late. An hour later he took fate into his own hands and walked five blocks south to the squat gray building that housed both the downtown police station and city jail. There he successfully argued the desk sergeant into arresting him, and at 11:20 PM, Minoru Yasui—high school salutatorian, university Phi Beta Kappa, first Japanese American attorney in the state of Oregon, second lieutenant in the U.S. Army Reserves—was hustled into the drunk tank, where he spent the weekend. It was an inauspicious beginning to a historic legal challenge that would be both a focal point of Min's life and a milestone in *nisei* history.

On Monday morning Earl Bernard, who had volunteered to represent him, arrived at the city jail with bail money, and after two sobering nights in the drunk tank, Min was free. He walked the five blocks back to his office and immediately called his mother in Hood River. Her husband was imprisoned; the world they had spent thirty years creating was crumbling. Now her most successful son had been arrested. The Portland newspapers were calling Min a "Jap spy" and "a paid agent of Japan."

"Mom, *shimpai shiteru dessho?*" (You are worried, aren't you?), Min asked Shidzuyo via telephone that morning.

Her response was to stay in Min's mind for the rest of his life: "*Shimpai dokoru kat Susumeru zo!*" (Worry, nonsense! I encourage/support you!).

Still, he knew what he had done could affect the family adversely. The next day he wrote a letter to Chop, who was farming his father's orchards at Willow Flat. "I have received rather unpleasant notoriety in the newspapers and I regret that it was necessary to drag the family into this mess." To Shu, a freshman at the University of Oregon, he wrote: "I realize that some of my friends [at the university] will undoubtedly criticize and blame me for my attitude." Min didn't know—and Shu didn't tell him—that the situation for his younger brother at the university was much worse than that. Almost immediately after the news of Min's arrest hit the newspapers, Shu's ROTC commander began publicly hectoring him. "So, your brother's a spy, huh?" he shouted at Shu during a lineup. "I hope they hang him." The commander kept at it. Every few days he would ask, "Have they strung up that brother of yours yet?"

Min was also concerned about the financial burden his case might impose on the family. "I am prepared to go as far as my personal finances will take me," he wrote Chop, adding that "if necessary I am afraid that I shall be required to call upon you and the family to give me financial backing." Less than a week later, he received a check for five hundred dollars from Chop and his wife, Mikie. His father, too, lent his strong support. From the barracks of his Department of Justice prison camp, he wrote to his youngest daughter about Min: "I am deeply impressed with his noble spirit and high ideals. We are all very proud of him." Later he wrote directly to Min, praising him for his "fine disposition and braveness."

But the West Coast Japanese community was far from unanimous in its support. One of the community leaders Min had written to during his search for a test-case volunteer was Mike Masaoka, then secretary of the San Francisco chapter of the Japanese American Citizens League, a powerful national organization established in 1930 to promote the Americanism of the *nisei*. Masaoka, soon to be the organization's national leader, never responded, claiming later than he hadn't received the letter. That may have been true; many believed that letters to and from JACL chapters were being routinely censored. But Masaoka's silence was undoubtedly related to his appearance, just two weeks earlier, before a congressional committee examining the potential problems posed by mass evacuation of Japanese from the West Coast. Masaoka had assured the committee that Japanese Americans were willing to "move out" if given a military order. The JACL-ers believed that obeying without question was the best way to prove their loyalty and worth as American citizens.

Now, hearing of Min's arrest, Masaoka lashed out in a JACL bulletin, calling Min a "self-styled martyr" and drawing attention to his employment at the Japanese consulate. Concerned that even one resister would undercut his promise to the committee, fearful that Min's solitary act might cause others to resist and, perhaps most of all afraid that Min's case would arouse further hostility toward Japanese Americans, Masaoka steered the JACL away. "National Headquarters is unalterably opposed to test cases to determine the constitutionality of military regulations at this time," he wrote in the organization's newsletter a week and a half after Min's arrest. The JACL does "not intend to create any unnecessary excuses for denouncing the Japanese as disloyal and dangerous."

But the organization's opposition did not deter Min. In the weeks after his arrest, he wrote numerous letters attempting to drum up support not just for his own case but for a *nisei* movement to revoke or at least modify any government orders that discriminated against Americans of Japanese descent. He circulated petitions among Portland and Hood River-area JACL-ers that called for the national organization to take a united stand against forced evacuation and then sent the petitions, along with a strongly worded letter, to Mike Masaoka. He wrote to the *nisei* head of a Seattle cannery workers local, hoping to enlist union support. And he fired off a letter to General DeWitt, head of the Western Defense Command. The forceful letter, although it began, "with due respect for your position," accused the military and the U.S. government of racism in no uncertain terms. He called the discriminatory treatment of Americans of Japanese descent "an effrontery to the name of democracy" and "a blot on the escutcheon of honor of the United States of America." In arguing against what very much looked like the future— the *nikkei's* forced evacuation from the West Coast—he hammered away at the inconsistency of a nation fighting for democracy abroad but failing to practice it at home. "The President of our United States has often times repeated that we are fighting a war to preserve the four freedoms throughout the world," he lectured DeWitt. "Surely then, it is of paramount importance to preserve those self same freedoms within the United States of America." There was no response.

Meanwhile, Min reopened his Portland law office. The small room in the aging hotel on the wrong side of downtown became a central clearinghouse for the routine but suddenly important business of the local Japanese community. Again, Min was overwhelmed with tedious legal chores. With their futures uncertain, with persistent rumors of impending evacuation—but no details as to when, where and how—*issei* scrambled to get their personal papers and property in order, while *nisei* rushed to locate copies of their birth certificates and other documents, thinking that proof of American citizenship might make a difference in how they would be treated. Others enlisted the young lawyer's help in securing special permits so they might voluntarily leave the West Coast. "As [our uncle] states in his letter," four young men from Onalaska, Washington, wrote Min that spring, "we all four *nisei* boys are willing to go to Idaho and join him to do farming for our country. Will you please help us get our special permit . . . ?" Min was busy filing legal papers on April 22 when he heard that a federal grand jury had indicted him for the curfew violation.

Now, with nothing to lose, Min purposefully disobeyed another government order that severely restricted travel for ethnic Japanese. When his uncle Renichi needed to travel from Hood River to Portland to see an eye specialist for his cataracts, Min obtained the appropriate military permission for him to venture more than five miles from his place of residence. But to avoid a prohibited zone around Bonneville Dam, he would have to drive his uncle on a 140-mile detour south of Mount Hood. When he took his uncle for an examination and later for surgery, Min traveled by the roundabout route. "I didn't want him to languish in an internment camp for violating military orders," he later explained.

But, on other trips between Portland and Hood River by himself, Min deliberately drove through the barred zone, expecting—and hoping—to be arrested. "I figured that as long as they had me for curfew, I might as well ask for a test of other aspects of military orders," he explained to a friend. He was not stopped.

In early May the military finally posted the evacuation orders the local Japanese community had been anticipating: all Portland area residents of Japanese ancestry, aliens and citizens alike, were to leave their homes and report to a temporary assembly center set up north of town. They had five days. Min quickly notified the authorities that he had no intention of obeying what he considered to be "unconstitutional, illegal and unenforceable" orders. Just before the Portland *nikkei*'s evacuation deadline, he packed his legal files and few belongings in his 1935 Chevy, gave the military his Hood River address, "invited them to arrest me or stop me" and headed to his family's home.

He made it, but a few days later military authorities called the Yasui home to inform Min that an escort would soon arrive to bring him back to Portland. Min indicated he would comply—under coercion only. The military obliged, and on May 12 a sedan with a second lieutenant and a driver, along with a jeep with four armed MPs drove up Hood River's quiet, residential Twelfth Street and stopped in front of the Yasuis' home. Min was led to his own car, and with the lieutenant's car in front and the MPs behind, the caravan headed for the North Portland International Livestock Exposition Center, renamed the Portland Assembly Center, which was by then teeming with some three thousand ethnic Japanese from surrounding counties. Min took one look at it and dubbed it the North Portland Pigpen.

The Livestock Center, a huge wooden structure fronting one of the sloughs of the Columbia River, was now surrounded by an eight-foot-high barbed-wire fence with corner watchtowers, searchlights and sentries cradling 30-caliber machine guns. Families slept in what had been horse stalls or in plywood partitioned barracks; they ate from tin plates in a hastily set-up mess hall draped in yards of sticky yellow flypaper that had to be replaced daily. The place was thick with horseflies and noisy with the suddenly public lives of hundreds of families. Min hardly had time to get his bearings and settle into a bachelor dormitory when in early June he was taken to Multnomah County Jail to await trial. Then, on June 12, 1942, Minoru Yasui had his day in court.

The trial lasted only a single day, yet it involved monumental issues: an untested congressional statute, unprecedented wartime orders and uncharted constitutional waters. To Earl Bernard, the defense lawyer totally committed to his client, it was an opportunity to argue an exciting case and challenge a presidential order both he and Min felt violated the Constitution. Bernard, however, was operating without the support of two groups that should have been his natural allies. The JACL, with its heated objection to any test case, not only withheld support, but acted to undermine Min's credibility. And the ACLU, the only legal group to support court cases on wartime policy, was nervous about Min's case because of the possibility that his previous connections with the Japanese consulate might leave him open to charges of being an enemy agent. The group backed away.

To the prosecution, nominally headed by local U.S. attorney Carl Donaugh, the Yasui case was a vital part of the government's strategy to validate its policies toward ethnic Japanese—from curfew to evacuation to internment. The case was an opportunity to test the strategy the government anticipated using in later court-room challenges. Of course, Donaugh wanted to convict Min of the curfew violation, but the stakes were much higher—so high, in fact, that a special legal team representing the War Relocation Authority (WRA) was sent to Portland from Washington, D.C. And it was WRA lawyers, not Donaugh, who set the strategy and wrote the script for the trial. "Such notice by national figures to me denotes a certain concern by the Federal authorities as to whether or not they can sustain their position," Min wrote optimistically to his brother Chop before the trial.

The government's strategy depended on the premise that ethnic Japanese, whether American citizens or not, were by virtue of their "racial characteristics" predisposed to commit subversive acts. Donaugh was instructed by one WRA lawyer to use the argument that Japanese Americans had organized a fifth column of spies and saboteurs who would be used by the Japanese government as instruments of espionage. "Jap citizens are inevitably bound, by intangible ties, to the Empire of Japan," wrote a high-ranking government lawyer in a brief submitted to the judge who would oversee the Yasui trial.

As much as they wanted to test this genetic theory of loyalty, government lawyers were perhaps even more interested in seeing how successful they might be using a tactic called "judicial notice." Under this legal doctrine, lawyers are exempt from proving in court certain "self-evident" facts. Government lawyers knew there was no way they could prove ethnic Japanese were a threat to American security. There was no evidence whatsoever of a secret group of *nikkei* spies ready to carry out Tojo's orders. But would a court accept the genetic-loyalty premise and consider the existence of a Japanese American fifth column self-evident? The lawyers hoped so. It would mean curfew and other restrictive policies were justified. It would mean Min Yasui would be found guilty.

At 10:05 A.M District Court Judge Alger Fee gaveled the court to order. A native Oregonian who had worked as a War Department lawyer and a state court judge before his federal appointment a decade earlier, Fee had a reputation for being a judicial maverick. He alone would hear the case, for Earl Bernard had advised Min to waive his right to a jury trial. Min freely admitted breaking the law; it was the complex legal issues that needed to be decided, and Bernard wanted them decided by a judge, not by a group of citizens in the throes of post-Pearl Harbor hysteria. As it turned out, Fee had invited eight leading Portland lawyers to sit as "friends of the court" and help him decide on constitutional issues.

The trial began with police testimony that quickly established the fact that Min had indeed broken curfew. Throughout the rest of the morning and part of the afternoon, the prosecution called a series of witnesses who recounted conversations they had had with Min or testimony they had heard him offer during the enemy-alien hearings for his father. The focus was clearly on Min's employment at the Japanese consulate in Chicago. The aim was to imply disloyalty, the intent to undermine his U.S. citizenship. Much was made of the minor role played by Min's father in securing him the position at the consulate. (Masuo had written his son a letter of introduction.) It was Masuo's alleged "connections" that got Min the job, the witnesses said. With Masuo currently in military prison branded as a dangerous alien, this was damaging testimony. Bernard had little luck in the cross-examination. In a typical and frustrating exchange that morning, he tried to separate father from son to show that Min secured the consulate job in a normal, above-board manner.

"Do you recall [Min] saying . . . that in order to get this position . . . he also got letters of recommendation from Wayne Morse, Dean of the University of Oregon Law School?" Bernard asked one of the prosecution's witnesses.

"No, I do not," the witness replied.

"You don't recall that?"

"No, sir."

"He might have said that?" Bernard pressed.

"I do not recall."

Bernard tried one last time: "You do not recall, but it might have slipped your memory?"

"I do not recall it."

It was midafternoon before Min took the stand in his own defense. Bernard led him through a series of questions designed to demonstrate his Americanism and emphasize his loyalty. Where was he born? Where did he go to school? Had he ever voted? Had he ever received communication from Japan about his willingness to engage in military activity? Bernard had Min carefully explain the nature of his one and only trip to Japan (a family vacation when he was ten) and painstakingly describe how he secured his consulate position (not only had Wayne Morse recommended him but there were a number of supporting letters from Hood River and Portland people, including his father). Min outlined his consular responsibilities, told how he resigned his post immediately after Pearl Harbor and tried repeatedly to report for active service in the army. He swore he never pledged loyalty to a foreign power and never renounced his American citizenship.

Donaugh, of course, took a different tack. His cross-examination focused on Min's cultural ties to Japan. "Do you speak Japanese?" he asked Min. "[Did] you speak Japanese in your home?" "Ever go to a Japanese language school or Japanese school of any kind?" "Ever belong to any Japanese fencing clubs?" The prosecutor tried to portray Min's consulate job as a sensitive public relations position that had him acting as an apologist for Japan's political policies.

Bernard jumped on this immediately. "[Did] you ever make a speech or [do] anything which you consider detrimental to the United States of America?" he asked Min after the prosecutor had finished.

"No, sir," Min replied. "I have never done such a thing. I couldn't have done such a thing."

Just as Min was about to be excused, Judge Fee, who was known for such tactics, began to question him from the bench. Before hearing his testimony, Fee had openly doubted Min's American citizenship, wondering whether he had, by his actions, effectively renounced his birthright. Now Fee pursued a surprising line of questioning that showed those doubts had only intensified through the day.

"What is Shinto?" he asked Min.

"Shinto?" said Min, clearly puzzled by the question. "As I understand, Shinto is the national religion of Japan."

"Do you give adherence to its precepts?" Fee asked.

Min answered that both his parents were Methodists, that he was a Methodist and that he didn't know what the precepts of Shinto were. Fee persisted.

"Was not Shinto practiced in your household?"

"No, sir."

Still, Fee persisted. "By your mother and father?"

"It was not, no, sir."

The practice of Shinto would have, of course, tied Min to the culture of Japan and thus, the reasoning went, weakened his loyalty to the United States. But Fee was also undoubtedly reacting to American propaganda of the day, which viewed Shinto not as a religion but as military-backed mass-indoctrination designed to teach Japanese that they were chosen to rule the world.

Apparently dissatisfied with Min's responses, Fee continued grilling him on the precepts of Shinto. Did he believe the emperor was divine? Did he leave food offerings on the graves of his ancestors? Min repeated that he and his family were Methodists who—he told the judge with wry humor that went unacknowledged—put "floral offerings" on family graves. Finally, Fee moved on to a new line of questioning, trying to make Min concede that his rights as a citizen were secondary to the oath of allegiance he took during reserve officer training. But Min was unbudgeable. "At the time of my active commission, I will obey any command . . . ," he told the judge. "But . . . every American citizen has the right to walk up and down the streets as a free man."

After Min's testimony the prosecution tried to introduce two witnesses meant to buttress the government's "racial characteristics" argument: a business agent from a local lumber workers' union who was going to testify to the bad blood between Caucasian and Japanese workers and a mystery expert who was supposed to offer scholarly testimony about the racial loyalty of Japanese. But Fee backed Bernard's objections and effectively scuttled this part of the government's strategy.

Promptly at five in the afternoon, *United States of America v. Minoru Yasui* ended, and the defendant was taken back to the Portland Assembly Center. He spent the rest of the hot, dry summer of 1942 there behind barbed wire, debating his case with friends, doing unpaid legal work and playing cards. He was still awaiting word of the verdict when in mid-September he and the rest of the internees were transported five hundred miles to a more permanent facility in an isolated spot in the south-central Idaho desert—an internment camp called Minidoka.

But before he could completely settle in, he received word that he would soon be taken back to Portland to hear Fee's verdict. It was already November. The bone-cold Idaho winter was fast approaching. The judge had taken an inordinately long time to decide the case, both because of its importance—more than one hundred thousand people could potentially be affected—and the number of briefs he had received from local and national constitutional experts.

Finally, on November 14, a single U.S. marshal driving an unmarked sedan arrived at Minidoka to take Min into custody. After a long drive and an overnight stay in a central Oregon lockup, Min found himself in a corner cell at the far end of the isolation block on the fourth floor of the Multnomah County Jail in Portland. Keyed up for his court appearance, he barely noticed his surroundings. Instead, he paced back and forth most of the night, thinking of all the "marvelous and eloquent things" he would say in court.

The next morning Min was handcuffed, chained around the waist, taken from his cell and led one block to the federal building and the courtroom of Judge Fee. It was a deeply embarrassing moment for him. He found it "degrading" to be led through the public streets "like a convicted criminal" when in fact he had undertaken this entire matter on his own initiative, and was "eager to stand before the Court." Now standing before that court, Min heard Judge Fee's complex decision. On the one hand, he ruled that in the absence of martial law the military had no legal right to regulate the life of citizens. Using the forceful language of an adamant civil libertarian, Fee argued that the rights of the citizen were supreme, and that citizens of Japanese ancestry shouldn't be treated differently than any other citizens. But in the next breath, he stripped Min of his American citizenship, claiming that he had "elected" to become a Japanese citizen by his acts—most particularly his work for the Japanese consulate in Chicago. The curfew, as it applied to citizens, was unconstitutional, said Fee. But Minoru Yasui was not a citizen. He was, ruled Fee, an alien—an enemy alien who disobeyed regulations that legally applied to aliens. Fee looked around the silent courtroom and paused before passing sentence: "The court finds him guilty."

Min was dumbfounded. The judge had just confirmed all his deeply held convictions about the fundamental principles of democracy. But the verdict was against him personally. He spent most of that night, his second in solitary confinement, writing a statement to the court. The next morning, just before sentencing, he read it.

"I am compelled to pay tribute and to give my unreserved respect to this Honorable Court for its clear-cut and courageous re-affirmation of the inviolability of the fundamental civil rights and liberties of an American citizen," he told Judge Fee. "My confidence has been justified and I feel the greatest satisfaction and a patriotic uplift in the decision. . . ." Then he shifted gears. "I have lived, believed, worked and aspired as an American," he told the court. "I am an American citizen who is not only proud of that fact, but who is willing to defend that right." Calling Pearl Harbor a "treacherous" and "reprehensible" act, he said that he, along with seventy thousand other *nisei*, would be "willing, or eager, to lay down our lives, down in the streets, down in the gutters, to defend our homes, our country and our liberties.

"I would a thousand times prefer to die on a battle front as an American soldier in defense of freedom and democracy, for the principles which I believe, rather than to live in relative comfort as an interned, alien 'Jap'," he told the court.

But his words had no effect. That morning the judge gave him the stiffest sentence allowable: one year in jail and a fine of five thousand dollars. Min immediately instructed Earl Bernard to appeal the decision. Then, shackled and in handcuffs again, he returned to his cell to wait out the process.

Back at Multnomah County Jail, Min was permanently assigned the corner cell on the isolation block. The solitary confinement was for his own protection, the jailers told him. "There might be incidents if he were thrown into one of the corridors with the other prisoners," reported one of Portland's newspapers. The cell was eight by six with bars on two sides, gray painted steel walls on the other sides and a concrete floor. There was an uncovered toilet bowl, a washbasin and a double-decker steel bunk with dirty gray canvas stretched across the frame for sleeping. There were no windows. A single light bulb was screwed into a ceiling fixture. This was to be Min's home for as long as it took his appeal to make its way through the legal machinery. It could be years.

The jailers left him a thin army blanket, the clothes he was wearing and a writing tablet he'd requested. They took away his pens, gave him a pencil stub and locked the cell behind them. For the next month and a half Min was kept in the cell twenty-four hours a day, with no exercise periods and no trips to the showers or the barber. He tried to wash himself in the washbasin with rags, but after six weeks of this, he was "stinking dirty." His hair grew shaggy, unkempt and tangled. His nails grew so long that they curled inward. But to his youngest sister, Yuka, he made light of his condition, writing only that he looked like "a wild man from the mountains." It wasn't until after Christmas that he was taken out of his cell to bathe and have a shave. Thereafter he was permitted monthly baths and hair trims.

Min's daily jail routine revolved around food. At 7:00 AM a trustee would deliver four slices of dry bread, a bowl of glutinous oatmeal and a cup of chicory coffee. Every once in a while, there were a few stewed prunes. At 11:30 AM the trustee would be back with four more slices of bread and a boiled potato. At 5:00 PM, there would be a potato cubed and fried in fat, four more slices of bread and a cup of chicory coffee. Min went to sleep dreaming of lobster Newburg and dry sherry. At first he couldn't bring himself to eat jail food. But hunger changed his mind within a week.

The poor nutrition and tedium were relieved once a month when his Portland friends Buddy and Cora Oliver visited him, bringing Chinese food from a local restaurant. Once an old law-school classmate appeared with armloads of books. Min was surprised and touched by several visits from a stranger, a Quaker woman, who also brought him books. Earl Bernard visited from time to time to keep him apprised of the appeal process.

But mostly Min was alone. He went through a worn dictionary, page by page, memorizing a new definition every day. He transcribed the Bible in shorthand. He counted the gray bricks on the hallway wall facing his cell. He counted the cockroaches—"my devoted cockroach friends," he called them. He wrote to his family, cementing a special relationship with Yuka. Her cheery, gossipy letters were addressed to "my favorite oriental jailbird."

He wrote to friends, particularly Frances Maeda, a Portland girl and a "shirt-tail relative"—one of her brothers married Chop's wife's sister—who had gone to Boston to do missionary work. The long letters, written in Min's neat hand, seesawed between flirtation and high-minded rhetoric. "Hello, beautiful!" he addressed her, "Call it personality, character or soul, or what you will, you've got it." In one paragraph, he bemoaned the fact that he was six years her junior and thus not a suitable marriage prospect, in another he lectured her on the Four Freedoms and the meaning of democracy. He could be self-effacing: "Aw nuts," he wrote to her in the spring of 1943, "in discussion of principles, I'm such a dummkopf." Yet in the next breath, he would expound on these principles in language befitting an elder statesman. To Frances he poured out his loneliness and his doubts while simultaneously reinforcing his convictions. To Frances he talked about love as well as law, food as well as freedom.

He also wrote poetry—not lean verse like the kind his brother Kay used to write, or classical lines like his mother, but tidy quatrains that, belying their serious purpose, read like doggerel. He wrote about evacuation, the stockyards, Minidoka, the routines of jail life, the fellow prisoner he could hear but never saw. He wrote about nights spent behind bars:

No sun to shine, no stars to glow,
No fresh breezes in freedom blow
Where I lay down my throbbing head
And cry for sleep in a steelclad bed.

The routine of the day became fixed, and Min found himself adjusting. "I suppose one can get used to anything," he wrote. But the nights were rough. The single bulb in his cell would go out at ten-thirty; the lights in the corridors would dim. "You'd hear coughing or sneezing . . . some indistinguishable mumbling, and an exasperated 'Goddammit!' 'Shut up!' Things would get quiet for a while—then a groan . . . and in this cold, steel, concrete place, a hundred troubled souls would be trying to sleep. It was a weird and disquieting feeling," Min wrote. "Nights were bad."

But even harder to bear than the nights was the uncertainty. Min was not serving out a predetermined jail sentence. He could not take solace in putting an X through successive boxes of a calendar, crossing off the days until freedom. He was just waiting for his case to make it through the legal system. Still, the uncertainty didn't shake his confidence. As he waited, he used both poetry and correspondence to bolster his spirit, reassure himself that he had made the right decision and reiterate his principles. In "Yasui in jail," written after a little more than a month behind bars, he reminded himself:

Yes, when I ask, "Why am I here?"
I can answer with no trace of fear:
I'll let my country do no wrong,
And I'll be true to freedom's song!

In "Meditations on a Pair of Torn Pants," written in January of 1943, he cautioned himself not to be like a pair of pants that "split from stem to stern" and became "useless" because they had not learned how "to yield without breaking." Min admonished himself to "never relinquish ideals" but to "learn to accept inescapable fact."

So I'll keep my principles always right
And never sacrifice them in my fight,
I'll yield and I'll bend when troubles begin,
But at the end, I'll see that they win.

To Frances he wrote, "I am confident that I am right and that, after all, is more important than whether I win or lose." In another letter he wrote with self-assurance: "By adhering to principles of democracy, and fighting for a legal recognition of those principles even in times of war, I feel that somehow I am contributing to democracy."

With these thoughts sustaining him as the weeks and months crawled by, he turned inward for strength. A social being to his core, he at first missed talking with people and sharing ideas. But after a while, he learned that other people weren't necessary for his own sense of self. He knew who he was, and he knew what he was trying to do.

It was in early April of 1943, after almost five months of solitary confinement, that Min learned the first news about his appeal: the Ninth Circuit Court of Appeals in San Francisco had refused to review or rule on *United States of America v. Minoru Yasui*. Rather than deciding the case, the judges had invoked a rarely used procedure called "certification" to send the case directly to the Supreme Court. No one knew at the time that this unusual move was the result of a special request by the U.S. attorney general and behind-the-scenes maneuvers by Justice Department lawyers. With the war on and more than one hundred thousand *nikkei* behind barbed wire, the government wanted a speedy resolution to the constitutional issues raised by the Yasui case.

Both Min and his lawyer were stunned. They had assumed the case would take the usual several years to make its way up to the High Court. By that time, they figured, the war would be over and calmer heads would prevail. Min was prepared to sit out the war in a jail cell, convinced that the issues his case raised would get a better hearing after anti-Japanese hysteria subsided. He called the speed with which his case went to the Supreme Court "the greatest shock of my life," but he tried to find a positive side. In a letter to a friend that spring, he wrote: "I never believed that the lower courts would have sufficient moral courage or judicial integrity to abide by the principles of the U.S. constitution. My faith has always been with the Supreme Court."

On May 11, eleven months after the Portland trial and barely six months after Judge Fee announced his verdict, Earl Bernard stood before the chief justices of the United States. The Yasui case would be argued along with another related case, that of Gordon Hirabayashi, a Seattle Japanese American who, six weeks after Min broke curfew, refused to register for evacuation. Bernard's task that morning—to argue for Min's American citizenship—was not a difficult one. In fact, the government's own brief conceded that Judge Fee's ruling was in error: Min's employment by the Japanese consulate did not constitute a renunciation of his citizenship. In a low-key and workmanlike argument, Bernard merely reiterated the points he had made earlier in Portland. Then he yielded the podium to Abraham Lincoln Wirin, a Southern California lawyer who worked part-time for the Los Angeles branch of the ACLU.

Although it had shied away from participating in the lower-court trial
and had voted not to enter the case as it moved to the Supreme Court,
the ACLU, had reversed itself at the last minute and decided to join in. Wirin, outraged by the evacuation order and eager to be part of a Supreme
Court challenge, had come east to Washington, D.C., to help with the
Yasui and Hirabayashi cases.

It was Wirin's job to argue that the government's restrictions on Japanese Americans were unconstitutional, and he got right to the point.
"Race prejudice, not military necessity, was the reason for these orders,"
Wirin told the justices. He accused the government of acting in bad
faith and charged that General DeWitt, the man assigned to carry out
the government's policies, heeded "the drums of hate against persons of
the Japanese race." DeWitt was a puppet of "pseudo-patriotic groups"
and those who wanted to use the war as an excuse to acquire Japanese-
owned lands "on a song."

Charles Fahy, the solicitor general of the United States, presented
the government's arguments. A quiet, almost meek man, a man, as one
observer noted, "not given to gesture," Fahy was absolutely determined
to win the case. His major argument was that during a wartime emergency the constitutional rights of an individual must give way to the
"reasonable discretion" of the military in exercising its powers. Restrictions on ethnic Japanese were a military necessity, he stressed, focusing
on the importance of the Pacific war and West Coast defense facilities.
Using the "racial characteristics" argument, he maintained that Japanese
Americans "had never become assimilated," and it was therefore "not
unreasonable" to assume that they would aid the enemy.

After two days of arguments, Wirin told one of his ACLU, colleagues
that he thought the case was going badly for his side. Another ACLU, lawyer observing the arguments remarked that "a majority of the justices
appeared to be hostile" to the lawyers representing Min and his fellow
defendant. It seemed that everyone knew what the outcome would be,
although it took the court six weeks to announce its verdict.

On June 21, 1943, the High Court reversed both of Judge Fee's decisions. First, it unanimously ruled that the government did have the
authority to restrict the lives of civilian citizens during wartime. Then it
overturned Fee's decision to strip Min of his citizenship. The Supreme
Court decision meant Min was once again an American citizen but, by
unanimous consent, guilty of disobeying orders found to be both legal
and constitutional. Back in his Portland jail cell, Min consoled himself
as best he could. "At least I tried," Min wrote to Frances. "Too many

people go through life without ever having made an intense enough effort to be called a failure."

The case was sent back to Fee and the lower court for resentencing, but for some reason encountered substantial delays. Meanwhile, Min, still in solitary, was beginning to chafe. He had been patient long enough. Now he wanted to get out of his cell and start serving his time at a work farm. Finally, at the beginning of August, Bernard once again visited Min, this time with good news: he would not have to spend any more time in jail. Fee considered time already served while awaiting the appeal sufficient punishment under the law. Following the Supreme Court's implied suggestion that his original sentence was unnecessarily harsh, Fee also suspended the five-thousand-dollar fine. The Yasuis had spent more than twice that much to carry the case through the courts.

In the early morning of August 19, 1943, a U.S. marshal came to escort Min from the Multnomah County Jail back to the internment camp at Minidoka. After nine months in solitary confinement, he was trading one prison for another.

10

A Viper Is a Viper

Min had picked his fight. He had chosen to disobey his government's orders. But for virtually all of the other more than a hundred thousand *nikkei* up and down the West Coast, the days, weeks and months immediately following Pearl Harbor involved no choices at all. Swept from their everyday lives, propelled by forces so much greater than themselves—the war, the government, the media, the dark side of human nature—they were helpless. In Hood River, with its long history of antipathy toward its Japanese American residents, Pearl Harbor was seen as both proof that the Japanese were a scurrilous race and the justification some locals had long been searching for to rid their valley of its own "yellow scourge."

"In this solemn hour we pledge our fullest cooperation to you, Mr. President, and to our country," read a telegram sent to the White House by the Japanese American Citizens League just hours after Pearl Harbor. "There cannot be any question, there must be no doubt. We, in our hearts, are Americans—loyal to America." The Hood River *nikkei* also moved quickly to declare their loyalty. "I almost lost my mind about what to do," a prominent *issei* fruit grower from the upper valley wrote to the Hood River *News* a few days after Pearl Harbor. "But now I know very distinctly . . . I will fight against any enemy, including Japan, to protect my wife and children and defend the community in which they live." Within days of Pearl Harbor, all of the county's Japanese residents had signed a pledge to "obey American laws, policies and administration always and especially during the present situation." Published in the weekly newspaper, the oath pledged "devotion to this great Democratic America" and "loyalty to the Stars and Stripes." In the days after the surprise attack, such loyalty pledges poured in from *nikkei* up and down the West Coast.

At first, it seemed the response might be reasonable. "It is my fervent hope and prayer that residents of the United States of Japanese extraction will not be made the victims of pogroms directed by self-proclaimed patriots and by hysterical self-anointed heroes," Representative John M. Coffee declared before Congress the day after the attack. "Let us not make a mockery of our Bill of Rights by mistreating these folks." But almost as he spoke, vandals were roaming the grounds near Jefferson Memorial, chopping down Japanese cherry trees. Hysteria soon gripped the nation as its citizens—egged on by wild stories in the newspapers and the reckless, unsubstantiated statements of some military and government officials—anticipated a full-scale attack on the U.S. mainland. Watching the rumors fly at military headquarters in San Francisco, Major General Joseph W. Stilwell wrote in his diary: "Common sense is thrown to the winds and any absurdity is believed."

Hours after Pearl Harbor, rumors about *nikkei* collaboration began surfacing: they had secretly and selectively cut Hawaiian sugar-cane fields in the shape of arrows pointing to the U.S. Navy base at Pearl Harbor; they had impeded rescue efforts by forming a roadblock with their produce trucks. "Dead Jap flyers" were found with Honolulu high school rings on their fingers. The Japanese in Hawaii had carried out "the most effective fifth column work that's come out of this war. . . ." declared the secretary of the navy a week after Pearl Harbor. But within days of this public accusation, everyone from Honolulu's police chief to FBI director J. Edgar Hoover called the stories unadulterated bunk. Extensive investigations showed no sabotage of any kind before, during or after the attack. Meanwhile, Western Defense Command in San Francisco was reporting that it had "reliable information" that a Japanese attack on Los Angeles was imminent. It was thought that *nikkei* fishermen were prepared to join the attack, with Japanese Imperial Navy uniforms wrapped in oilskins hidden in their bait boxes.

In Oregon, the fear of attack was intensified when newspapers throughout the state reported as fact a rumor that the bodies of Japanese navy men were found washed up near Cannon Beach, a tiny coastal town an hour and a half due west of Portland. A week later, the story was retracted, but the damage had already been done. The harbormaster at the port of Astoria, just north of Cannon Beach, clearly fearing an imminent invasion, speculated that area *nikkei* could set fires to help guide Japanese bombers on attack runs. These local fishermen and cannery workers, most of whom had lived in Astoria for more than thirty years, could aid the enemy by "spreading confusion and panic . . . such as the turning in of false fire alarms. . . ." The American Legion, never a friend to the *nikkei* in Oregon, spread fabricated tales of caches of arms, ammunition and explosives supposedly uncovered in sporadic raids of Japanese American homes throughout the state. "This is no time for namby-pamby pussyfooting, fear of hurting the feelings of our enemies . . . it is not the time for consideration of minute constitutional rights," declared a resolution passed by the men of Post no. 97 in Portland. When a Japanese submarine did, in fact, fire a few poorly aimed shots at Fort Stevens on the Oregon coast, causing no injuries and little damage, people's worst fears seemed justified.

Still, there was some attempt to keep the hysteria in check. At the University of Oregon, where Michi and Shu were encountering the hostile stares of their fellow students, a history professor lectured his audience to deal fairly and sensitively with Japanese Americans. "We must fight this war as a nation, not as a mob," he told them. In Hood River, the weekly *Sun* fleetingly preached restraint: "Idle rumors, malicious gossip and thoughtless acts must not come into Hood River county in these trying days," wrote the editor. But the local rumor mill was working overtime, and it seemed there was nothing that could stop it.

One story was that the Japanese were going to invade the United States by sending submarines up the Columbia right past Hood River. A more fanciful version had Japanese frogmen disguised as salmon swimming up the Columbia. However the invasion would take place, one thing was clear to the rumormongers of Hood River: The local *nikkei* were poised to help. The locals would destroy the bridge over the Columbia; they would set fires in the hills; they would poison their produce; they would poison the reservoirs that provided the valley's drinking water. Always at the core of these stories was Masuo Yasui, supposedly a high-ranking officer in the Imperial Navy who received instructions' directly from Japan via a shortwave radio hidden in the back of his store.

Everything the *nikkei* did—or didn't do—in Hood River made them suspect. If they continued to work hard on their orchards and farms, they were greedy, setting themselves up to take advantage of wartime needs. But if they didn't plant crops, they were undermining the American home-front effort. If they didn't show themselves on the streets, they were busy plotting fifth-column activities. But if they did walk in town, they were collecting intelligence for the emperor. If they looked their *hakujin* neighbors in the eye, they were belligerent. If they averted their gaze, they were sneaky.

But what the *nikkei* in Hood River actually were was scared. They were every bit as panicked as their white neighbors about the possibility of air attacks. Out in the valley, children scrambled inside and hid under beds whenever they heard the distant drone of an airplane. *Issei* had other reasons to be alarmed. Their position was suddenly a terrifying and confusing one. They had lived in America most of their lives and had raised their families here, but they were still Japanese nationals. True, U.S. law had prevented them, unlike European immigrants, from becoming naturalized citizens. But this fact seemed to be lost in the hysteria of the moment, and they stood exposed as citizens of one of the most hated enemies in American history. Depressed and bewildered, half believing rumors that they would be deported, they talked of mass suicide. The *nisei*, American citizens with foreign faces, were equally anxious as they vacillated between confidence in their citizenship and fear that their birthright would not protect them from some terrible future.

And in the days that followed Pearl Harbor a string of official actions fed their fears. At first, it was the *issei* who were singled out. All business transactions between Japanese nationals and American citizens were immediately forbidden; the *issei* were ordered to apply for special identification certificates, and local officials soon announced their own restrictions. WARNING! read the proclamation signed by a county judge and the local sheriff and printed in inch-high letters in the Hood River *News*. "To Japanese nationals: You are hereby requested to remain on your own premises and not leave same unless accompanied by an American citizen." Soon the sheriff's office issued a list of contraband articles—cameras, shortwave radios, guns, ammunition, explosives, swords—and posted a deadline for turning them in. The *issei* dutifully came to town to deposit their hunting rifles and the ceremonial swords they had brought with them so many years ago from Japan. A few days after the deadline the FBI arranged to have all phone service cut to the Japanese while county and city law-enforcement officers along with federal agents methodically searched hundreds of valley barns, woodsheds, packing houses and homes looking for contraband. The agents found one radio. In another sweep they uncovered a dynamite cap, commonly used by valley farmers to blast stumps, in the corner of a barn owned by a Mr. Nishimoto. The FBI immediately took Nishimoto into custody.

Thus far the restrictions pertained only to *issei*, the noncitizens. But in March of 1942 military authorities announced curfew and travel restrictions that applied to all people of Japanese ancestry, whether American citizens or not. In Hood River, the 8:00 PM curfew was keenly felt by the young *nisei* who could no longer go to basketball games or carry on any semblance of a social life. It put yet another wedge between them and their *hakujin* classmates, accentuating differences and further isolating the *nisei*. For their parents the implications were more serious. One *issei* woman in the valley was afraid to walk outside after dark to bring in wood for the stove. She thought she might be shot for violating the curfew.

Her fear was exaggerated, but it was not without foundation. Although there were no incidents of outright violence against the Japanese in Hood River, there were threatening phone calls late at night, epithets mumbled in the streets and cars that slowly cruised by *nikkei* homes night after night. Vigilante groups formed in town vowing to protect Hood River from its Japanese residents. Armed guards were posted around dozens of reservoirs, including a small six-hundred-gallon pond up at Chop's Willow Flat property, to prevent water poisoning. Fifty men, many of them legionnaires, volunteered for round-the-clock guard duty along the Columbia. Heavily armed, they set up headquarters in a sand-and-gravel office by the banks of the river, watching for both a Japanese invasion and any suspicious activity on the part of the local *nikkei*. At Hood River High School, a *nisei* student came into shop class one day to find his project vandalized. On one of the boards ripped from his unfinished rowboat, someone had scrawled: TO HELL WITH JAPS.

The air seemed charged with hatred. There was no room for equivocation. "I am for the immediate removal of every Japanese on the West Coast to a point deep in the interior," wrote a syndicated columnist in the San Francisco *Examiner* two months after Pearl Harbor. "I don't mean a nice part of the interior, either," he continued. "Herd 'em up, pack 'em off and give 'em the inside room in the badlands . . . let 'em be pinched, hurt and hungry." In the Hood River newspaper, a writer implied that *issei* were suspect just for continuing to speak their own language. "These are the same people who profess loyalty and devotion to their adopted country. . . . If this feeling is so manifest, why can't these people . . . learn to talk and use the English language?" No such scolding was given the area's German immigrants, many of whom also spoke their native tongue. Merchants who continued doing business with their longtime *nikkei* customers were ostracized by their neighbors. People who spoke up for the Japanese were shunned. When the mother of one of Yuka's *hakujin* friends defended the Japanese to the women in her literary club, she was met with silence and stony stares. Her friends rejected her so completely that she took to her sickbed and later left town for several months to stay with her sister.

As the winter of 1941–42 wore on, the complete absence of any fifth-column activities did little to relieve the tension in Hood River or up and down the West Coast. In fact, military officials were now saying that the absence of sabotage only proved that the *nikkei* were busy plotting something big. Something was brewing, something was about to happen, they warned. They were right: something was about to happen, but it wasn't acts of disloyalty on the part of Japanese Americans.

In the months after Pearl Harbor the U.S. government had been busy planning. In less than three months, federal and military authorities had conceived, staffed and begun to implement a multibillion-dollar plan to forcibly remove all people of Japanese ancestry from their West Coast homes to vast "camps" in the country's interior. President Franklin Roosevelt decided the exclusion was necessary despite the reservations of many of his advisers. The War Department told him there was no evidence of an imminent attack. The FBI told him there was no evidence of planned sabotage. Forty years later the government's own investigative commission ruled that the policies of evacuation and internment were driven not by analysis of military conditions but rather by race prejudice and war hysteria.

Roosevelt's Executive Order 9066, issued in mid-February, officially authorized the creation of West Coast military zones from which "any and all persons" could be excluded. A day after the order, General DeWitt was chosen as Western Defense commander and empowered to carry out an evacuation plan—a plan the military had been working on for months that DeWitt had in fact proposed to the secretary of war in a memorandum a week before FDR's decree.

With the stamp of presidential approval and full military involvement, it was therefore somewhat disingenuous of the U.S. Congress to set up a series of hearings in West Coast cities to gather citizen testimony about the "Japanese problem." The so-called Tolan committee (named for chairman Representative John H. Tolan of California) was an exercise in democratic window dressing, creating for itself the wholly redundant job of discovering what to do with the ethnic Japanese, when in fact the government and the military had already formulated a "solution." But the *nikkei* did not yet know of the military's plan for evacuation, and many welcomed the hearings, hoping to convince Congress that a policy of racial exclusion was wrong.

In Los Angeles, San Francisco, Portland and Seattle in late February and early March, the committee listened to a number of witnesses, most of them white, most of them virulently anti-Japanese. San Francisco's Italian mayor argued that Italian and German immigrants could be trusted, but that all people of Japanese ancestry ought to be "removed from this community" because of "the activities of the Japanese saboteurs and fifth columnists in Honolulu." Earl Warren, who was then California's attorney general and would later become Chief Justice of the Supreme Court, agreed. "We believe that when we are dealing with the Caucasian race we have methods that will test the loyalty of them," he told the committee. "We can, in dealing with the Germans and Italians, arrive at some fairly sound conclusions because of our knowledge of the way they live in the community and have lived for many years. But when we deal with the Japanese, we are in an entirely different field. . . ."

In a way, Warren was right. At least it seemed that the committee itself had little idea of who the *nisei* actually were. The committee expressed surprise that Japanese American Citizens League representative Mike Masaoka, one of the very few *nikkei* to testify during the hearings, could speak English so well. Like all *nisei*, of course, Masaoka was born and raised in the United States. They were again surprised that he, like most *nisei*, could not speak, write or read Japanese and were amazed to learn that Masaoka was a Christian, not a Buddhist. The foreignness—and therefore untrustworthiness—of the *nisei* was an insistent theme, throughout the hearings and in the press. As a columnist in the Los Angeles *Times* asserted: "A viper is nonetheless a viper wherever the egg is hatched." When the committee moved its hearings to Portland to take additional testimony, the secretary of the war board of Hood River County summarized the area's feelings succinctly: "Generally the sentiment here is one of fear. . . ." he told the congressmen. Another state official stressed that Oregonians were "alarmed and terrified as to their person, their employment and their home." The publisher of the state's largest newspaper, the Portland *Oregonian*, claimed that the danger of sabotage was great and that it would take "just ten or twelve people . . . to burn the entire forest lands in Oregon."

But underlying the "military necessity" of removing all ethnic Japanese from the West Coast was another, older concern. "We're charged with wanting to get rid of the Japs for selfish reasons," an official of a California growers' and shippers' association told *The Saturday Evening Post*. "We might as well be honest. We do." His words echoed the thirty-year-old hostilities now revived in Hood River: "It's a question of whether the white man lives on the Pacific Coast or the brown man. They came [here] to work, and they stayed to take over."

By early March, a few weeks after the hearings ended, Hood River *nikkei* knew they were going to be forced from their homes. But they had no way to fight the power of the U.S. government even if they had wanted to—and few did. Not only was following government orders during wartime seen as proof of loyalty but also the *nikkei*'s own cultural norms emphasized conformity and stressed that strength of character came from obedience, not rebellion. They had no choice but to prepare to leave. They didn't yet know when they'd have to go or where they'd be sent, but they realized it was time to put their affairs in order. This was perhaps more difficult in Hood River than in many other places, because here the Japanese owned their land and the thousands of dollars' worth of equipment it took to farm it. Elsewhere, especially in parts of California, *nikkei* farmers leased the land they worked or owned only small truck-farm plots. But in the valley there were seventy-seven productive Japanese-owned orchards, lands that families had worked for more than three decades. With an uncertain future before them, the orchardists knew they had to do something, but most did not want to sell. And even if they did, finding buyers who would pay anything close to what the land was worth would be an almost impossible task given the climate of fear and hatred.

"Do not sell anything, goods, possessions, land or houses below the market prices," a visiting Japanese Methodist Church official cautioned his Hood River audience in mid-March. "Selfish people wish to profit by your misfortune. Carpetbaggers are already abroad." Indeed, it seemed a given that locals would try to take advantage of the *nikkei*'s vulnerable position. "Any individuals who are toying with the idea that they can turn a dishonest penny by exploiting the Japanese of Hood River valley, who are destined to be evacuated sooner or later, might as well abandon their plans to get rich quick," reported the local paper, announcing that a Federal Reserve Bank agent would be arriving in town to oversee all sales. The Farm Security Administration also sent an agent to watchdog agricultural transactions. In addition, a group calling itself the Traffic Association formed in town to see that *nikkei* fruit growers received a "square deal" for leasing or selling their orchards, and the local Civilian Defense Commission designated a Hood River lawyer to help the Japanese with contracts.

But the concept of a "square deal" was relative. To the federal government and the military, and to many of the people of Hood River, it was not just Japan that was the enemy, it was anyone with a Japanese face. And as the Imperial Navy scored a series of early victories, and thousands of U.S. soldiers fell in battle, fairness to Japanese Americans became a casualty of war as well. A number of vocal Hood Riverites had been pushing hard for more than two decades to "save" their valley from the "yellow invasion." Here was their chance. Despite well-meaning government assistance, most of the *nikkei*'s valuable orchards leased for less than what their owners had to pay in property taxes each year, and other land, such as two of the Yasuis' farms, eventually sold for a fraction of its worth. How could the *nikkei* possibly bargain for more? In fact, "evacuees," as they were to be called, left behind property worth more than $200 million.

As spring arrived and the valley turned white with apple blossoms, the *nikkei* had more than the disposition of their land to worry about. A million details consumed them: Where would they be sent? How long would they be gone? Would families be able to stay together? What should they do with their furniture, their cars, their farm machinery, and tools? Who would take care of their family pets? Would they be able to take valuable possessions with them or should they store them? Where? What tax records would they need?

The Yasuis, because they had more than most, had more to worry about. At the time of Pearl Harbor the entire family enterprise was worth more than half a million dollars, including the store, the house and more than eight hundred acres, much of it land owned in various partnerships. This was nearly half of all the Japanese-owned land in the valley. Chop worked hard to secure leases for the farms and, with his uncle's help, began selling off the merchandise in the store. The Treasury Department, which had closed down Yasui Brothers the day after Pearl Harbor, allowed it to reopen temporarily for a liquidation sale. A businessman to the last, Renichi put up posters and notices announcing the sale: "Come in and be amazed at the merchandise which we are able to offer you. WE HAVE WHAT OTHERS HAVEN'T." Exactly one month later, on April 18 at 6:00 PM. Yasui Brothers closed its doors after thirty-four years of doing business downtown. The store would never reopen.

By the third week in April, a special field agent with the army's Wartime Civilian Control Administration in charge of overseeing land transactions declared that his job was just about over. The majority of Japanese farms and orchards had now been "transferred to new operators."

On Thursday, May 7, at noon, local officials thumbtacked Civil Exclusion Order no. 49 to telephone poles in Hood River and throughout the valley. The military directive, which made definite what local *nikkei* had feared for the past two months, gave them six days to finish putting their affairs in order and pack up their belongings. On Wednesday, May 13, all area residents of Japanese ancestry, aliens and citizens alike, were ordered to report to the Union Pacific station downtown for immediate evacuation.

The local American Legion Hall, site of so many anti-Japanese activities in the past, was fittingly designated Evacuation Control Center. On May 8 and 9 all heads of households reported to the hall for preliminary registration. On May 10 families reported for medical checkups. Sixty soldiers helped process 544 *nikkei* during those hectic days, inundating them with instructions, proclamations and mandates, and burying them with the paperwork that helped convert them from individuals to numbers. The Yasuis became evacuee family no. 16261.

In the early morning hours of May 13 the *nikkei* began arriving at the station with their duffles and stuffed laundry bags, their boxes and bulging suitcases tied closed with twine. They were allowed to take bedding, clothes, toilet articles and "essential personal effects"—but only what they could carry. Yuka put on layer after layer of clothes and waddled to the station, where an armed guard joked that he should really assign her a second number because she looked big enough to be two people.

The youngsters like Yuka didn't realize what was happening to them. When she heard that her family was being sent to a "camp," Yuka thought it would be like the Campfire Girls camp she had gone to—an outing, an adventure. Homer, too, was caught up in the novelty of the moment. He and the other teenagers weren't thinking about their civil rights or the loss of their families' property; they were rejoicing in the happy fact that the school year was over for them a full month early. The young adults like Chop felt the moment more keenly and understood its larger meaning. But being young and at the beginning of their lives, they mustered considerable optimism about the future. "We leave with tears in our eyes, not because we dread the unknown ordeal before us, but because we regret leaving this beautiful valley. . . ." wrote the local *nisei*-dominated Japanese American Citizens League in a public statement issued just before evacuation. "As we go with heavy hearts, we leave with the hopeful expectations that some day soon we'll return once again to this land where the rain and the sunshine meet."

But the *issei* nurtured little such hope. They had already endured a lifetime of discrimination; they had labored hard to get where they were. Now everything they had worked for was reduced to the contents of the suitcases they held in their hands. Their families were being ripped from the valley by their roots. The fact that they quietly accepted their fate (*Shikata ga nai*) made them no less disconsolate about it. When *issei* women came into Keir's Drug Store the morning of evacuation day to buy last minute toiletries for the trip, they stared at the floor, mournful and silent. Behind the counter, young Paul Keir, whose father owned the store, watched with tears in his eyes. He had never seen people so thoroughly forlorn, so completely dejected. Shidzuyo was stoic and dry-eyed that morning, but Obasan was inconsolable.

The Hood River *News* chose to remember the day differently. Families came "in their best clothes, many of these being newly bought for the trip." There was an "evident atmosphere of holiday spirit" as crowds of onlookers watched "the colorful scene." The front-page headline read MANY WHITE AMERICANS BID FRIENDS GOODBYE. But Ken Abraham, the son of a local doctor who had ministered to the Japanese American community, surveyed the same scene and saw something quite different: One solitary white man walking slowly through the crowd of Japanese, stopping to shake a hand, pat a back or say a few words. It was the lawyer E.C. Smith, who had been such a good friend to the Yasuis and others. Of all of Homer's *hakujin* friends from high school, only one came to the station to say good-bye.

Promptly at 10:00 AM the guards began herding the families onto the train, an ancient coal burner specially commissioned for the trip by the army. In each car the blinds were drawn and armed soldiers were posted at both ends. The train pulled out slowly, following the Columbia as it flowed west to the Pacific, backtracking along the route Masuo had taken thirty-three years before. Some thought they were headed for Portland, where the government had set up an "assembly center" for Oregon *nik-kei*, a temporary facility to hold them until more permanent inland "relocation centers" were being completed. But the local JACL chapter, with Chop at its forefront, had learned a few days earlier that Hood River families were to be sent to an assembly center in California's San Joaquin Valley. JACL had objected strenuously. The Portland *nikkei* were assigned to the Portland center, constructed on the grounds of the city's livestock pavilion. The Hood Riverites had friends and family in Portland; they knew the city. Being shipped there would be less dislocating. But the Wartime Civilian Control Administration turned a deaf ear, and Pinedale, just north of Fresno, remained the official destination.

The train moved slowly through Portland and then, making a hard left, headed south down Oregon's long and fertile valley to California. Hours later it chugged through Eugene and past a young woman standing by the railroad tracks just north of the University of Oregon campus. It was Michi Yasui, who had learned that the Hood River people were being evacuated that day. As the train passed she squinted hard, concentrating on every window, hoping to get a glimpse of her family, not knowing when she'd see them again. But the blinds were drawn, and the train didn't stop. Michi saw nothing. She turned and headed back to campus.

There, life for her and her younger brother Shu had changed dramatically since Pearl Harbor. Wherever she went, Michi felt eyes on her. The
housemother peered in her dorm room every night and kept tabs on her
during the day. The students cast sidelong glances, some suspicious and
hostile, others just awkward and confused. She thought the FBI might be
watching her, especially since Min, her brother, whom newspapers had
called "the Jap spy," was now in jail. As she struggled to make it through
the last quarter of her senior year, she wondered whether the next knock
on the door might be an agent come to take her away. She briefly considered going home to Hood River to help her mother and await evacuation
with the rest of her family, but she was so close to graduating, so close
to fulfilling her parents' dream for her, that she had to stay.

Shu also was intent on completing the school year. But it was a struggle just to walk across campus and encounter the angry stares and mumbled remarks, let alone drag himself to ROTC class, where the commanding officer openly berated him. His roommate offered support, but Shu
heard others in the dorm sneering about "that dirty Jap." Whenever he
went downstairs past the usual group of men in the dorm's front parlor,
all conversation stopped. He walked by quickly, not knowing what to say
or how to act. He holed up in his room, studying with almost fanatic intensity as if he could blot out the world by this single act of will. It was
mid-May, only weeks away from Michi's graduation and the end of Shu's
freshman year. They trudged to and from classes in a daze, not knowing from one day to the next if they would be allowed to stay at school.
Time seemed to stand still.

The senior class would be graduating on May 31, and Michi wanted
desperately to attend the evening ceremonies that would celebrate her
four years of hard work. But the curfew law, the one her brother was in
jail for violating, mandated that all *nikkei* had to be off the streets by 8:00
PM. Graduation wouldn't be over until after 10:00. A sympathetic university dean wrote to county, state, federal and military officials asking for a
one-night, two-hour exception for Michi and promising that she would
be "in the custody of the Dean of Women" the entire time. The request
was denied. Michi tried to settle down to study for her final exams, not
knowing if she'd have the opportunity to take them.

Shu was waiting it out too, but he was also thinking hard about his
future. And the more he thought about it, the more he could not accept the idea of being taken to a camp and, as he saw it, "treated like a
convict." The thought of being interned somewhere, being imprisoned
in his own country for no crime was simply and irrevocably unacceptable. At eighteen, he was old enough to know his own mind and young

enough to dare to take bold action. A few days after the train carrying his family passed through Eugene, Shu went door-to-door asking all his professors to assign his final grades early because he might have to leave before the term was over. The first four teachers gave him A's. Then, with much trepidation, he entered the office of the ROTC instructor, who had given him such a rough time. He explained his situation and handed him the report card. The instructor looked at the four A's and then peered intently at Shu through narrowed eyes. After a long moment he scribbled something on the card, handed it to Shu and said, "Dammit, go on!" When he got out of the office, Shu looked at the card. It was another A.

He waited until after midnight to sneak down the fire escape of the dorm and walk hurriedly through the darkened streets of Eugene to the small downtown bus station. *Nikkei* were not permitted to be out after 8:00 PM., nor were they supposed to travel more than five miles from their home, but the elderly clerk at the Greyhound ticket window either didn't know that or chose to ignore it. In any case, he sold Shu a one-way ticket to Denver, Colorado, far east of the designated military zone, where the Yasuis had a few friends and where the state's governor had publicly welcomed and supported transplanted West Coast *nikkei*.

Shu boarded the bus carrying a small suitcase and took a seat all the way in the rear. In Portland, where the bus stopped briefly to take on a few passengers, no one noticed the young man hunched in the back. Two hours later, at a scheduled stop in Hood River, he felt sure he would be discovered. But it was the wee hours of the morning, and when no one got on or off the bus, Shu was almost weak with relief. Throughout the long trip, as the bus stopped in the sparsely settled towns of eastern Oregon, then Idaho and Wyoming, he dared not leave his seat. He ate nothing, fearing that an appearance at a lunch counter would end in arrest. He went to the rest room only when absolutely necessary. Most of the time, he sat in his seat in the back pretending to be asleep.

In Cheyenne, Wyoming, however, he had to get off the bus and wait in the station for a connection to Denver. Shu felt terrifyingly visible. He wasn't sitting there long before a large man with a star pinned to his chest came up to him and asked who he was and where he was going. Shu was sure his journey had come to an end and that he would be thrown in jail. But, as he was stumbling for the words to reply, a noisy fight broke out just outside the bus station. The deputy left hurriedly to break it up, and in a scene that could not have been better scripted by Hollywood the loudspeaker announced that the bus for Denver was now boarding. Shu ran for it, sat in the back and held his breath. The bus left before the deputy returned, and Shu made the ninety miles to Denver without further incident.

Once there, one of the first things he did was call Michi in Oregon to tell her that he'd made it and encourage her to do the same. At that point, knowing that Eugene would be evacuated any day, having held on just about as long as she could and having just heard she wouldn't be able to go to her own graduation, Michi didn't need much encouragement. Soon, she too boarded a late-night bus out of Eugene and, a day and a half later, arrived in Denver. They had escaped the fate that awaited 112,000 other West Coast ethnic Japanese. But their family—Shidzuyo, Homer and Yuka, Chop and Mikie, Renichi and Obasan—had not. They were on a shuttered train moving south to Fresno and to a life behind barbed wire.

11

Behind Barbed Wire

It took nearly two days for the old coal burner to travel the seven hundred miles from Hood River to Pinedale, California, with long hours spent waiting on railroad sidings for higher-priority trains to pass. Inside the shuttered cars the *nikkei* teetered between exhaustion and anxiety, as they sat up and talked into the night, trying to imagine their futures. But nothing prepared them for what they saw when they finally reached their destination that Friday evening, May 15, 1942.

Pinedale was eighty flat, dusty and treeless acres a few miles north of the city of Fresno. The San Joaquin Valley sun had baked the earth as hard as concrete. Stepping off the train, even long after the sun went down, was like walking into an oven. Formerly a lumberyard for a nearby sawmill, the site had only recently been leased by the government for the purpose of constructing a "temporary assembly center." What greeted the Yasuis and their Hood River neighbors that evening was a desolate, isolated quasi-military compound with more than 250 hastily built, identical tar-paper barracks laid out in endless rows. Ringing the perimeter was a ten-foot-high fine-mesh fence topped by three strands of electrified barbed wire. At each corner of the compound stood a tall watchtower manned twenty-four hours a day by military police. Searchlights made wide, measured sweeps over the barracks all night long.

Impressive security measures were in place, but the camp itself, barely a week old when the Yasuis arrived, was not yet finished: the sewer system was inadequate; there were too few mess halls; none of the barracks was furnished. But for the next two and a half months, Pinedale would be home to forty-eight hundred ethnic Japanese from Hood River, the Seattle area and two nearby California counties. It was one of sixteen

189

temporary facilities designed to warehouse West Coast *nikkei* until more permanent "relocation centers" or "evacuee communities"—as the government was euphemistically calling the massive internment camps it was busy building—could be finished.

Most of the temporary centers were in California (with one each in Washington, Oregon and Arizona), and many, like the north Portland center, were constructed on existing county fairgrounds or racetracks, with *nikkei* living in converted horse stalls. By these standards, the Hood River contingent and the others at Pinedale were luckier than most. Homer, in fact, considered himself mighty lucky. At seventeen, caught up in the "adventure" of evacuation, he looked around that first night in awe. "Boy," he said excitedly to his sister as they walked through camp, "just look at all these Japs!"

Minutes after their arrival, the Yasuis and their valley neighbors were herded into long lines, the first of hundreds they'd stand in that summer, to be assigned their block number and housing unit. A block consisted of twenty tar-paper barracks, with each of the long buildings divided into five to seven rooms. Every family was assigned a single room with one iron cot per person and one bare light bulb hanging from the rafters. The room had a concrete floor, bare stud walls and flimsy eight-foot-high partitions that stopped short of the rafters. Sound traveled easily from one end of the barracks to the other; privacy was impossible. As they got to the front of the line, Shidzuyo, Homer and Yuka were each handed an empty sack made of mattress ticking and shown the location of a large pile of straw. Real mattresses were promised but never materialized, and it would be three weeks before camp carpenters finished constructing crude barracks furniture: one bureau, one table and three benches for each family. "My feeling was something I know I can't express with words to anyone," wrote a little *nisei* girl from Hood River valley a few days after she arrived in Pinedale. "I never felt so downhearted in all my life."

As difficult as it was to adjust to incarceration, it was almost as hard for the Hood River contingent to adjust to the San Joaquin Valley climate. Accustomed to temperate weather, considerable rain, cool nights and the deep shade of the old oaks that dotted the valley floor, the *nikkei* found themselves in another world entirely: Fresno in the summer, where it would have been 110 degrees in the shade had there been any shade. The Hood Riverites found that during the day they could do little other than sit and fan themselves. People regularly fainted from the heat while waiting in line for lunch or dinner. And the nights were almost as hot as the days, making sleep difficult. Some people tried dozing under their cots at night to avoid being splattered by the hot tar that dripped from the roof. Others carried buckets of water from the laundry room to wet down their concrete floors, hoping to cool off the room. A few times that summer, camp authorities gave each family a block of ice, which was set in the middle of the floor. The families sat on benches around the melting block, fanning the cooled air in their faces and chipping off pieces of ice to suck.

The unrelenting heat soon taxed the camp's rudimentary plumbing and sewer system. People lining up to take cooling showers had to wait up to an hour to stand in an open stall, a demeaning experience that never ceased to jolt their sense of privacy. When they walked back to the barracks, they had to sidestep rivers of dirty water overflowing from the shower houses. Pinedale's mimeographed weekly newspaper noted "puddles the size of miniature lakes." Homer would never forget the smell of that stagnant, soapy water, sweet and rancid, as it pooled up between the barracks.

Access to toilets was a problem too: The camp simply had too few for its thousands of inhabitants. Long after the Hood River contingent was settled in, workers were drilling and digging ditches into the night to construct additional latrines. But even with adequate facilities, taking care of bodily needs was never a pleasant experience. In front of each shower sat a chlorine footbath meant to prevent a camp-wide athlete's-foot epidemic. It didn't. What it did do was sting feet so badly that children, with their little cuts and scratches, screamed every time they stepped into it. Open rows of latrines faced large educational posters that depicted the (harmless) male and (dangerous) female scorpion and cautioned latrine users to lift the seat and carefully examine the toilet before sitting down.

When they weren't waiting on lines to take showers, Pinedaleans were standing in the scorching sun, sometimes for an hour and a half, to get their food. Badly organized eating schedules added to the problem of too few mess halls. For the first few weeks after the Yasuis arrived, food supplies were scanty, and dinner for the entire camp was more likely than not sandwiches made with white bread, Spam and French's mustard. Even when supplies came in, the food was poor: no fresh fruit and few fresh vegetables other than the mashed rutabagas and turnips that the *nikkei* found unpalatable. The government was spending about thirty-five cents a day on food for each internee. Camp officials apparently enjoyed a different diet, for from time to time a sympathetic administrator gave Mikie, Chop's then-seven-month-pregnant wife, an apple or an orange.

The whole process of eating was unappetizing, from standing in long lines in the sun to filing past servers who slopped hot and cold food together on a metal plate to sitting on long, hard benches in the noisy mess hall. Because of the heat, food poisoning was an almost weekly occurrence. The crowded and unsanitary conditions led to outbreaks of both mumps and chicken pox a week after the Yasuis arrived.

Shidzuyo, Homer and Yuka shared one room, Chop and Mikie shared another in a distant barracks, and Chan and Obasan lived in separate quarters elsewhere in the sprawling compound. Living on different blocks and assigned to different mess halls, the members of the once-close family saw one another infrequently. Pinedale had no school and few recreational facilities. The common complaint of children—"There's nothing to do" —was true here, for both children and adults. Women sat on benches and fanned themselves; single men played poker all night long. Teen-age boys like Homer ran around camp at loose ends, alternately bored and full of mischief. Homer spent his days in idle play until Shidzuyo made him apply for a job. In the temporary camps some *nikkei* could find work as cooks, janitors, carpenters and clerical help, making from eight to twelve dollars a month. Homer, an unskilled seventeen-year-old, took the only job then available: latrine inspector. After a few terrible weeks, he traded inspecting toilets for emptying bedpans when he secured a job as an orderly in the camp's makeshift barracks hospital.

To Yuka it seemed that all the girls in camp were either older than her or just babies. She made few friends, instead spending most of her time with Shidzuyo. Her mother taught her how to embroider that summer. The two of them sat together on a bench outside the barracks staring through the fence at a patch of green, an old fig orchard located just beyond the camp's perimeter. In those dog days of summer, they took solace in the deep, glossy green of the leaves and the rustling sound they made in the all-too-infrequent breeze. "Our daily life is like a floating cloud, moving aimlessly. . . ." wrote a Seattle-area *issei* of his life behind barbed wire that summer.

Time passed with the slowness that time passes when there is nothing to look forward to, when one day is the same as the next. As July approached, the camp was rife with rumors about when the *nikkei* would leave the temporary quarters of Pinedale and where they would be taken next. No one seemed to know, including camp officials. As it turned out, by the end of the month, the almost five thousand Pinedaleans would be scattered across the country, some sent to Arkansas, some to Idaho and many, including the Yasuis and most of the Hood River contingent, to Tule Lake, an internment camp on the California-Oregon border.

That spring and summer, while virtually all West Coast *nikkei* were being held in temporary compounds, the army and the newly formed War Relocation Authority were spending a quarter of a billion dollars constructing ten permanent "relocation centers" in inhospitable desert areas or on marshlands in California, Arizona, Idaho, Utah, Wyoming, Colorado and Arkansas. But even as they were being built, the official reason for their construction—"military necessity"—was fading. In June 1942, U.S. naval forces defeated the Japanese near the islands of Midway, marking the end of Japanese naval superiority and signaling the turning point of the war in the Pacific. America now had increasingly less to fear from Japan, and the idea of a Japanese invasion of the U.S. mainland, if it had ever been taken seriously by the military, was not being taken seriously now.

Still, the construction continued. Each camp was built following a single master plan that, much like the design of Pinedale, called for row upon row of tar-paper barracks organized into vast, identical blocks, each with its own mess hall and sanitary facilities. Like the assembly centers, the permanent facilities would be ringed by barbed wire and watched over by armed sentries. But there would be important differences. Because the ten new facilities were designed for the long haul —the "duration," as the government put it —they had many of the trappings of real communities: schools, hospitals, sports programs, movies, dances, even beauty contests. Each center was a self-contained, wholly segregated city with its own government, police force and weekly newspaper. By the fall of 1942 all of the *nikkei* had been transported, again by shuttered railroad cars, to these newly built camps. With this move, the ethnic Japanese who once lived on the West Coast were now at least several hundred and as many as several thousand miles away from what had been designated as militarily "sensitive" areas.

Oddly, U.S. victories in the Pacific and the removal of the ethnic Japanese to desolate inland outposts seemed to do little to dampen anti-*nikkei* sentiment on the West Coast and elsewhere. In northeast Portland and in Hood River, more than a year after forced evacuation, vandals ransacked Japanese cemeteries, reducing more than two hundred tombstones to rubble. A group representing 125,000 Oregon, Washington, Idaho, California and Montana farmers proclaimed Japanese Americans "incapable of becoming assimilated" and recommended that Congress strip *nisei* of their citizenship and deport all ethnic Japanese. A legislator from the state of Washington proposed a constitutional amendment to disfranchise all American-born Japanese. Congressman Henry Jackson, also from that state, sponsored federal legislation to keep the *nikkei* under permanent scrutiny after the war was over.

A year and a half after all ethnic Japanese were removed from coastal California, the Los Angeles *Times* conducted a poll that found Southern Californians favored, by a 14-1 margin, deporting all *nikkei*, aliens and citizens alike, to Japan. "A Jap is a Jap," General DeWitt told the House Naval Affairs Committee in 1943. "They are a dangerous element, whether loyal or not." Meanwhile, various U.S. congressmen were calling for the army to take over control of the internment camps, because, they claimed, War Relocation Authority officials were "coddling" inmates. NIPS ENSLAVE YANKEES and HOSTILE GROUP IS PAMPERED IN WYOMING CAMP, read headlines in the Denver *Post*.

In early July of 1942 the Yasuis, along with most of the Hood River contingent, arrived at Tule Lake, a permanent internment camp just south of the California-Oregon border. After two and a half months in the parched San Joaquin Valley, they looked forward with eagerness to seeing the camp's namesake lake. But as they stepped from the buses that transported them from the train station to Tule Lake's main gate, they saw instead land as arid and desolate as what they had left behind in Pinedale. It was flat, hard, dusty land with only a single tree big enough to provide shade in the entire 7,400-acre compound. To the west was a bare, craggy ridge called Castle Rock; to the east, a treeless flat-topped butte called Horse Mountain. To the south lay acres of lava outcroppings, harsh, black and barren, more like a lunar landscape than an earthly one. Tule Lake itself was a long-dried-up lake bed. The men stepped down from the buses and rubbed their eyes. They said it was the dust, but it was tears.

The now familiar ten-foot-high barbed-wire fence enclosed rows of peaked-roof, tar-paper barracks that stretched to the horizon, each a hundred feet long, each facing its mirror image. There was an unsettling but at the same time numbing sameness to it all, the gray land, the black barracks, the endless sky. It was a city of eighteen thousand set down in a desert hundreds of miles from any sizable town. Hood River lay to the north, perhaps four hundred miles away. But it might as well have been four hundred light-years.

The families lined up to get their housing assignments: a single sixteen- by twenty-foot room for smaller groups and a twenty- by twenty-five-foot room for large families. There was no effort to keep together the extended families that formed the fabric of *nikkei* life. Shidzuyo, Homer and Yuka were assigned a unit on block 74. Chop and Mikie were given quarters a considerable distance away on block 69. Chan and Obasan were sent to what the Tuleans called "Alaska," the far north end of the camp. The weather that summer was not just hot but hot, dusty and windy. "The wind blows so hard and penetrates me," Shidzuyo wrote to her husband from Tule Lake. "Around the area, tens of thousands of geese fly in flocks to the east and west every day. This is such a sight, and when you are in the desert without even one flower, flying birds and clouds are a great comfort."

As the Yasuis settled in they found conditions much the same as in Pinedale. There were long lines at the mess hall, where, the daily fare (funded at forty-five cents a person) was mostly starch. Whatever they ate—potatoes, rice, Spam, hash, overcooked liver—the Tuleans called "slop suey," because the servers dumped it unceremoniously on their tin plates where it all ran together. Mealtime, the once-pleasant hour for the entire family to gather and exchange the news of the day, became a tiresome wait on a cafeteria line followed by a harried ten minutes eating at a long wooden table. EAT SLOWLY FOR THE SAKE OF YOUR HEALTH, admonished a large sign over the dining hall. The Tuleans laughed at the poster. They knew that those who lingered too long would find several kitchen workers waiting impatiently behind them, eager to clear the table and go home. There wasn't much reason to linger anyway. Families no longer ate together. Aunts, uncles and cousins lived in distant barracks and ate in their own mess halls. Teenagers, released from familial discipline as behind barbed wire the family lost both its purpose and its power, ate with their friends.

There were long lines for showers and latrines, too, even though *issei* women, out of modesty, often waited until after midnight to visit the facilities. They just couldn't bring themselves to sit in full view of others on one of the twelve toilets, aligned in two back-to-back rows down the middle of the long, open barracks. When they had to visit the latrines during the day, the women dragged large cardboard cartons with them, which they stood up around the toilet to form screens. Lack of privacy was a way of life. One internee later wrote: "Evacuees ate communally, showered communally and defecated communally."

As in Pinedale, poor nutrition and rudimentary sanitation meant Tuleans were often sick, from persistent diarrhea and seemingly permanent colds to outbreaks of food poisoning and childhood diseases. And, as in Pinedale, the weather was a fierce adversary. The summer had been hot, almost as hot as in Fresno, with the added discomfort of dust storms so intense that people sometimes wore goggles to bed. The thin walls of the barracks, with their cracks, knotholes and torn tar paper, were no match for the violent storms. The wind and dust would whip through the narrow canyons formed by long rows of barracks, blurring vision, stinging legs like sharp needles. In winter the temperature sometimes dipped to 20 below zero, with snow blanketing the compound for weeks. The snow turned black within hours from the soot of thousands of coal-burning potbellied stoves, one in the center of each barracks room, the internees' only source of heat.

But there were new amenities at Tule Lake: church groups, Girl Scout troops, social clubs and dozens of sports teams—for adults and children, girls and boys—from sumo to softball. There was even a camp movie theater constructed by stacking bleachers in an empty barracks. The back rows, where one's head grazed the ceiling, were one of the few places dating couples could go to get a bit of privacy.

Issei women offered classes in sewing, dance, tea ceremony and flower arranging. Arts and crafts flourished in camp, as the women, "freed" from much of their usual daily toil, began casting around for something to occupy their time. Digging in the old lake bed, the women uncovered thousands of shells, which they patiently soaked in laundry bleach, painted with nail polish and spent hours arranging and gluing into shell pictures, pins and corsages. Tuleans also busied themselves tending one of the most extensive "victory gardens" in the country, raising virtually all of the vegetables eaten in camp (their diets improved immeasurably) and exporting the surplus as part of the war effort. *Issei* men and women spent long hours creating intricate rock and flower gardens around the barracks, constructing small gates, arches and birdhouses from the graceful limbs of scavenged wood, arranging stones in pleasing patterns, planting morning-glory vines to help obscure the ugliness of their tar-paper homes. The *nikkei* knew this was going to be home for a while. They took a certain pride in carving a livable community out of the hostile land, in creating beauty where there had been only dust and rock. Most quietly settled down to the ongoing task of acclimation, but all were fed by a deep reservoir of anxiety and confusion as they worked hard to fill their days with meaning. As one internee wrote:

> *Nobody knows*
> *Which way to go*
> *They just pass their days*
> *Vacantly*

At Tule Lake, Chop began to assume the preeminent position in the family, taking care of the Yasuis' legal and financial business, sending money to Michi, Roku and Shu for school expenses, making decisions about selling and leasing the Hood River properties, acting as Masuo's attorney-in-fact and, just a few weeks after the family arrived in camp, on July 29, 1942, fathering the first of the new generation of Yasuis—the *sansei*—a daughter named Joan Kay. It had been tough for his wife, Mikie, in the last trimester of her pregnancy, to withstand the baking heat of first Fresno and then Tule Lake, the lack of privacy, the poor food, the crude sanitation facilities and, when the time came, the primitive hospital. When she craved fruit juice during her long recovery, a sympathetic nurse had brought her the only thing available: thick corn syrup from a can of peaches.

Chop threw himself into camp life, serving as block manager of his barracks section and playing regularly on the baseball team. During baby Joanie's first year he frequently volunteered for special work-release programs that took him out of camp and, along with scores of other ablebodied *nikkei* men, up into Montana to help harvest sugar beets. With most of the country's young men drafted, farmers across the country were hurting for help during harvest time. By special arrangement with the internment camps, these farmers hired crews of *nikkei* men, usually for substandard wages, to work the fields during peak season. Soon Chop, with his agricultural management skills, was much in demand. The Utah-Idaho Sugar Company hired him that first spring to recruit laborers from Tule Lake to work in the Great Falls, Montana, area. The money was poor; the working conditions were awful. But it was a chance to get out of their barbed-wire prison, and many men jumped at it.

As Chop was becoming a leader, his baby brother Homer was fast becoming a problem. With no structure to his life, no family responsibilities, no school, no farm chores for the first time since he was seven years old, no authoritarian father to keep him in line, Homer—like so many teenage *nisei* boys in camp—ran wild. He spent his days running around in gangs, chasing girls and learning how to smoke cigarettes. He played baseball. He went to dances. For a few hours a day, at his mother's insistence, he worked as an orderly in the camp hospital, as he had in Pinedale. The thirty-four cents a day he made was the first money he had ever been paid for work. He ran out and spent it all on ice cream, candy and cigarettes at the canteen.

Yuka, too, was having a hard time. She started school at Tule Lake as soon as one opened in the fall, but the conditions were far from conducive to the serious learning the Yasuis valued. At first there were no desks or chairs, only an empty barracks room. The students sat on the bare floor, while the teacher perched on a small bench, holding a little blackboard on her lap. There were no books and no supplies of any kind. When she wasn't at school, Yuka spent virtually all of her time with her mother, the two of them fanning themselves on a bench outside the barracks in the oppressive heat or, later, when the weather turned foul, sitting around the potbellied stove in their room. Most evenings they would walk together around the perimeter of the camp, softly singing Shidzuyo's favorite hymn: "This is my father's world/ Oh let me ne'er forget/ That though the wrong seems oft so strong/ God is the ruler yet." Shidzuyo was worried about her youngest daughter. "She is still a sweet child," she wrote to Masuo, "but she feels lonely in a place with no home."

Shidzuyo herself was lonely, with her husband thousands of miles away and her children scattered. But she was also, for the first time in thirty years, free from the grinding work of ministering to a large family and toiling in the fields. She took the opportunity to teach traditional Japanese flower arranging, *ikebana*, to other women. By special permission, four "procurement clerks" were allowed to venture a mile outside camp to collect material for the arrangements. In the summer they gathered cattails, tule grasses, willows and sagebrush. In the winter they had only willow to use. The women met in an empty barracks room, kneeling straight-backed on folded blankets in front of upturned logs that functioned as tables. With one hand they held the stalks, with the other they painstakingly arranged each sprig. Shidzuyo also took English lessons. As she explained to her husband, "A teacher in his teens is teaching us old women with white hair and bad memories." But in between the *ikebana* and the English and her hours with Yuka, she still had plenty of time to worry about her family—and plenty to worry about.

She worried about Masuo, who was being shifted from one Department of Justice detention facility to another. Could he manage to keep up his health, his spirits? With Chop's help, she began to deluge the government with requests for a rehearing of her husband's case, and at first Shidzuyo was convinced Masuo would be "home" for Christmas. But as the months dragged on and the appeals were routinely denied, she began to wonder if they'd ever be reunited.

She worried about Min, her brilliant and strong-willed son, now sitting in solitary confinement at Multnomah County Jail. What would happen to him? How would his principled stand affect his future? Like a good mother, she even found time to worry if her son, already twenty-six, would ever find a woman to marry.

And she worried, along with Chop, about the Yasuis' holdings back in Oregon. As it turned out, they had every reason to be concerned. Due to the wartime economy, Hood River was experiencing a period of unsurpassed prosperity, which, in the words of one local, offered "great incentives" for some Hood River people who leased Japanese land to be "dishonest." Kenneth Abraham, the doctor's son who was then a young lawyer, had the opportunity to scrutinize the wartime books of the Apple Growers Association, and he found glaring anomalies: once highly productive Japanese orchards, now being leased by *hakujin*, were suddenly credited with extraordinarily poor harvests; at the same time, the harvests from the *hakujin*'s own orchards increased dramatically, sometimes a thousandfold. Another Hood Riverite reported that "some people here have no scruples about Japanese property." A man whom the Yasuis had contracted to harvest their considerable asparagus crop —they had been the area's largest producer —wrote instead that the harvest had cost him money. The beetles were bad that year, he said; the crop was thin and scattered. Yields were low from the once productive Willow Flat ranch as well. Shidzuyo and Chop had no way of knowing whether they were being cheated. Some people, on the other hand, were overtly dishonest: a man who leased one of the Yasuis' downtown properties simply stopped paying rent once the family was evacuated.

Hundreds of miles away behind barbed wire, Shidzuyo and Chop could do little to protect the Yasuis' investments. A lawyer in town reported that their 160-acre Mosier property was being severely mismanaged. "The place is in terrible shape," he wrote to them. "The tools are scattered from hell to breakfast." They also learned by letter that the Oak Street store roof was leaking badly, ruining the plaster on the walls of most of the second-floor apartments. Local officials called the building a "serious fire hazard" and insisted that it be cleaned up "without delay." Another report informed them that the Japanese Community Hall, which the Yasuis helped finance and which was built on property they owned, was badly vandalized with "glass broken in every window."

To make matters worse, the family was losing an important local ally. E.C. Smith, the lawyer who befriended Masuo so many years ago, was in failing health and could no longer take an active part in overseeing the Yasuis' property and interests. Instead, he left the family's concerns in the hands of a man the Yasuis had no relationship with, a man who had been assigned by the government to handle all local internees' concerns. Hood River attorney John Mohr did his job, but seemed to have little sympathy for the plight of his assigned clients. When Shidzuyo and Chop were having difficulty figuring out what to do about renting the store building, Mohr replied to their indecision with exasperation. "It is not fair to hold up these deals indefinitely," he wrote. "I cannot continue to keep answering phone calls and having people come into the office to find out about them."

The family's farm and rental income plummeted, but the bills kept coming. There were property taxes to pay, insurance premiums, the interest on notes and mortgages. There were three children in college. There was Min's costly legal battle. And, increasingly, there were offers from Hood Riverites to buy the Yasuis' property at rock-bottom prices. Shidzuyo and Chop, writing regularly to Masuo, tried to balance the family's immediate needs with its hopes for the future. It was not easy.

Closer to home, Shidzuyo was becoming increasingly alarmed by Homer's behavior. Internment had brought him unimagined freedoms, and he was taking full advantage of the situation. He was ready, he told his mother, to "stay in camp forever." She, on the other hand, wanted him out as soon as possible, far from the unwholesome camp environment that was undermining the rectitude and discipline she and Masuo had worked so hard to instill in their children. Shidzuyo was also concerned that Yuka was losing her chance for a normal girlhood and, even more important, her chance to someday go to a decent college. Almost immediately after they arrived at Tule Lake, Shidzuyo and Chop began the tedious, bureaucratic process of applying for educational leaves for the children.

The WRA was willing to release *nisei* from the camps, provided they were accepted as students at schools outside the western military zone. A group of Quakers calling themselves the National Student Relocation Council helped by personally contacting Midwestern and Eastern colleges to ask if they would accept Japanese American students. Many said yes, and by the fall of 1942 the first 250 *nisei* had secured educational leaves, Homer Yasui among them. On September 16, barely two months after arriving at Tule Lake, he and four other young *nisei*, escorted by an armed guard, boarded a bus at Tule Lake's main gate and headed southeast. At Reno he made rail connections and, after an overnight journey, arrived in Denver. Michi and her new boyfriend, Toshio Ando, met him at the train station and took him to the rooming house that would be his new home. Within a week Homer was a freshman at the University of Denver, where Michi was taking graduate courses in education.

It was tougher for Shidzuyo to consider sending Yuka away. Her youngest daughter was her close and constant companion; their relationship strengthened and comforted Shidzuyo. Yuka was only fifteen and far from worldly. Still, Shidzuyo reasoned that her daughter could live in Denver with the three other children. But by early 1943, when Yuka's permit came through, the situation had changed somewhat. Michi had taken a job in Chicago with the War Manpower Commission. Shu had transferred to the University of Wisconsin, hoping that another jump eastward would improve his chances at getting into medical school. Only eighteen-year-old Homer was still in Denver. But Shidzuyo felt she had little choice. For the sake of her own future, Yuka had to go.

On February 25, 1943, with a small suitcase and two hard-boiled eggs in her pocket, Yuka left on a bus to Reno and from there, like her brother before her, boarded a train to Denver. A few days later she was hugging her books to her chest as she walked down the corridors of South Denver High, the school's newest sophomore. At first she shared a basement room with one of Homer's college classmates. But she soon secured a bed-and-board "schoolgirl" position, helping a family with child care, cleaning and cooking—much as her father had done forty years before. Back in Tule Lake, Shidzuyo was lonely and anxious. But she took solace in the fact that Yuka was free.

Meanwhile Chop was spending as little time as possible behind barbed wire by continuing to take a number of temporary agricultural leaves. In the spring of 1943, just a few weeks after Yuka left, he finally secured a yearlong "seasonal pass" for himself, Mikie and baby Joan, and the family headed for Herman Lenz's 250-acre farm near Great Falls, Montana. There Chop harvested sugar beets, threshed grain, dug ditches, repaired fencing and hauled manure for sixty cents an hour and a place to live—a four-room tenant house with no heat, no indoor plumbing, no refrigeration, four chairs and three beds. It was pitch black by the time the family pulled in that first night, and they fell into bed exhausted. The next morning they awoke swollen, red and covered with bites. Neither Chop nor Mikie had ever seen a bedbug before. The Lenzes told them to fill tin cans with kerosene and set the bedposts in them.

Chop worked ten-hour days. Mikie struggled with primitive sanitation as she cared for a baby in diapers. She spent her afternoons preparing big meals for her husband and several other *nikkei* hired hands who lived in neighboring tenant houses. These were hard times, but when they looked out the window, there was no fence. Chop, Mikie and Joan were free, and as it turned out, they never did have to go back to Tule Lake. Before their seasonal permit expired, they were issued "citizen's indefinite leave" cards. Chop had heard of an orchardist in Idaho who needed help. The new job would get him and his family away from Montana's grueling winters and one step closer to Oregon and the Hood River valley.

Shidzuyo was equally eager to leave camp. During the winter of 1942, with Chop on an agricultural leave, Homer already gone and Yuka about to depart, Shidzuyo began the long process of applying for indefinite leave for herself. As an *issei* noncitizen, she had to go through a far more involved procedure than her children. It started with signing a "declaration of declination," stating that she did not want to be repatriated to Japan. Next, she had to fill out in sextuplicate a number of lengthy government forms. Then, as part of a process that would take six months, she had to prove employment or other means of support outside camp, solicit letters attesting to her character and loyalty from Caucasian references and sit for interviews by camp officials.

Shidzuyo met the financial requirement easily by giving camp officials statements from the Hood River branch of the First National Bank that showed the Yasuis still had more than ten thousand dollars in checking and savings accounts. "We have handled your bank account for several years," wrote the manager in a letter of support, "and it has always been very satisfactory. . . . We can assure the Federal Government authorities that you can live independently for quite some time without financial aid from anyone." Shidzuyo also submitted four letters of personal reference to bolster her application. A Methodist pastor called her a "good Christian woman" who was "always sincere, conscientious and dependable." Most important, wrote the minister, "she tried all she could to train her children to be thoroughly loyal American citizens." Another church official called her "a good wife and cultured lady of high character," adding that he was "confident that she had no sympathy whatsoever for the Japanese militarists who are ruining her motherland. . . ." Kindly E.C. Smith wrote that she was "a law abiding, kindly sort of person and hardworking" and concluded that "her standing and reputation in this community is very good." A fourth letter from the bank manager stated that Shidzuyo had "maintained a very excellent reputation in the general community." With that hurdle passed, Shidzuyo was then personally interviewed and evaluated by Tule Lake's leave officer. In a report submitted in January 1943 the camp official noted that Shidzuyo was studying English in camp, had lived in a Caucasian neighborhood in Hood River and "dresses smartly, for an *issei*." With her three boys in college and her daughter working for the government in Chicago, Shidzuyo was deemed "one of the best of the *issei*." Still, it took until the end of March for her to receive clearance to leave camp, and it wasn't the indefinite leave she had hoped for. Officials granted her permission to go to Great Falls, Montana, where Chop and his family were then living, on a temporary pass, but she must return to camp that fall. But in early May, while in Montana, her indefinite-leave papers came through, and she left for Denver to establish a home for her two youngest children.

Min had been against the choice of Denver as a "duration home," as he called it. "Frankly, I don't like the silly place," he wrote to Yuka, hoping she would help persuade their mother to move instead to Kentucky or Virginia. "It's too much of a hick burg, and during war, I'm not so certain about Denver public attitudes." Min had heard that the Denver *Post* was "going to town on the evacuee Japs" who settled there. "There are too many Japs in Denver," he warned Yuka. But Shidzuyo, now fifty-seven years old, was not about to be a pioneer for the second time. She would go where her children were and where the family had contacts. She left for Denver that spring.

By mid-1943, while tens of thousands of other *nikkei* were unhappily settling into their second year of internment, Shidzuyo and all her children were free. Japanese Americans would spend an average of nine hundred days behind barbed wire—Masuo, in fact, was imprisoned for fifteen hundred days—but of the "evacuated" Yasuis, only Chan and Obasan stayed that long in camp. Because of their age, their lack of command of English and their questionable health (Chan had had two eye surgeries), they were not good candidates for early release. And, like most of the *issei*, they had neither the energy nor the heart to start over again at the end of their lives. In the fall of 1943 Chan and Obasan were moved to Minidoka, the southern Idaho internment camp that housed Min after his release from jail. It was there that they quietly sat out the war years.

But regardless of where they were interned or for how long—or even, like Michi and Shu, if they were interned at all—internment was a central, defining experience in the lives of the Yasui family and 110,000 other Japanese Americans. Evacuation wrenched them from their everyday lives, forcibly transporting them hundreds and sometimes thousands of miles from their homes. Internment created a completely segregated, strictly regimented, artificial world of barracks, latrines, barbed wire and armed sentries. For some it was too much. A few days after arriving at Tule Lake a teenage girl had a violent mental breakdown and had to be forcibly restrained. Medical facilities were not yet available. She was tied down to a mess-hall table. Mrs. Hirasawa from Hood River never made it to Tule Lake. When the internment order came, she refused to leave her home and had to be carried by her family to the train. In Pinedale she became "a little hysterical," as one of her friends noted, and was never the same again. Barely in her fifties, she died soon afterward. At least two *issei* committed suicide rather than submit to internment. One was a World War I veteran who, a few months before Pearl Harbor, had been awarded honorary citizenship by his California county.

The psychological effects of internment were both deep and broad: For the *issei*, it was the end of power and control; for the *nisei*, it was the end of innocence. Proud *issei* men, the providers and decision-makers of their families before the war, lost all status behind barbed wire. *Issei* women, the glue that held the family together, lost their place in an environment where the concept of home was meaningless. The older generation was consumed by shame. Rather than blame Roosevelt, the military or their *hakujin* neighbors for their wartime treatment, they turned inward and blamed themselves. "If we had only made ourselves more known to the Caucasians," they told each other. "If we had only been two hundred percent American. It is our fault that they didn't trust us," they said. Instead of being ashamed of the way they were treated, they were ashamed of themselves.

Although for the *nisei*, internment had some benefits—it got them out of their own communities and propelled some of them into leadership positions in camp—it also, and more important, shook their faith in America. Their parents had told them that if they worked hard and studied hard and became good Americans, they would succeed. Internment taught them what their parents didn't or wouldn't: that despite their best efforts, the deck was irrevocably stacked against them. They had played by all the rules—in fact, they had outplayed many of their white contemporaries—yet they had still lost.

Internment taught them also to depend on one another, not on the *hakujin*. America had accused them of a race loyalty that many did not feel. Ironically, the ostracism and segregation of internment helped engender just that loyalty in the *nisei* and led to a protective, postwar "clannishness" that white Americans eyed with suspicion. A half century later, "camp" remained the single, most important reference point for the entire generation.

Internment ended for most Japanese Americans in January of 1945. America was decisively winning the war against Japan, from the taking of New Guinea by the Allies to the Battle of the Philippine Sea, where the imperial forces lost more than four hundred planes, to the dramatic retaking of the island of Guam, which had fallen to the Japanese a week after Pearl Harbor. It never was logical—but now it was no longer reasonable—to publicly sustain and fund a policy based on the immediate threat of Japanese Americans to U.S. security. On December 17, 1944, the War Department announced that the mass exclusion orders against West Coast *nikkei* would be revoked, and the so-called evacuees would be free to go home as of January 2. Had the government not acted, a Supreme Court decision, handed down the very next day, would have ended internment anyway—and publicly embarrassed Roosevelt in the process.

Min Yasui lost his case against the government, as did Gordon Hirabayashi, who also broke curfew, and Fred Korematsu, who failed to report for evacuation. But in the fourth and last *nikkei* case to reach the High Court, that of Mitsuye Endo, the justices ruled that the freedom of loyal citizens could not be abridged. Mitsuye Endo was an interned former Californian who had been carefully selected as a test case by a San Francisco civil rights attorney enraged by the wholesale evacuation. In 1942 he had filed a habeas corpus petition in federal court, challenging the government to prove that it had the right to keep Miss Endo behind barbed wire. At the end of 1944, the case, on appeal, finally made it to the Supreme Court. There, William O. Douglas wrote the Court's unanimous decision, proclaiming that "loyalty is a matter of heart and mind, not of race, creed or color." Justice Frank Murphy concurred: "Racial discrimination of this nature bears no reasonable relation to military necessity and is utterly foreign to the ideals and traditions of the American people."

Internment ended. But it was never forgotten. "My life will never be the same," a *nisei* told a government commission some years later. "I will take this with me until I die."

ABOVE: "Mat" Yasui, as some of the local white businessmen began to call him, was the valley's most successful Japanese entrepreneur. He pioneered the area's asparagus industry and established the Mid-Columbia Vegetable Growers Association to market the vegetable.

BELOW: Renichi ("Chan") took care of the store for more than thirty years, freeing Masuo to develop other business enterprises. This is the interior of the third Yasui Brothers store, a well-stocked, successful downtown concern until Pearl Harbor.

ABOVE: Yukia (left) and Michi, like all *nisei*, lived simultaneously in two worlds. At home they learned to appreciate Japanese customs; at school they were Americanized.

ABOVE: The family gathered in the late 1930s in the living room of the Yasuis' home on Twelfth Street, where Japanese art objects blended with Western furnishings: (seated, from left) Obasan, Michi, Yuka, Shidzuyo, Masuo, Chop, Chan; (standing, from left) Shu, a friend, Min, Homer, a friend, Roku. Masuo and Shidzuyo were looking forward to a quiet, comfortable retirement. Pearl Harbor changed all that.

LEFT: When Chop and Mikie Kageyama, the daughter of longtime valley orchardists, married in August 1939, they had the first Western-style *nisei* wedding in the valley.

ABOVE: After Masuo died, Shidzuyo spent much of her time visiting her children's families and getting to know her many grandchildren. In this 1958 photograph, Grandma Yasui is flanked by Amy Fujikura (Yuka's daughter) and Kip Yasui (Homer's son).

BELOW: The Yasui *nisei* were busy, independent people, but being a Yasui continued to have meaning in their lives. (From left) Michi, Homer, Yuka, Chop, Shu and Min sit behind a banner featuring the family crest at a reunion on the Oregon coast in the late 1970s.

The Yasui *sansei*, the grandchildren
of Shidzuyo and Masuo, don silk-
screened Yasui T-shirts at a family
reunion in 1977. Holly is seated in the
center; Lise is at the far right, standing.

12

Homecoming

Min Asai, Sat Noji and Ray Sato were the first to return to Hood River. The *nisei* sons of established valley orchardists, the three had secured permanent leaves from camp some time before and were working in the Midwest when word came that the exclusion order had been lifted. Considering how the town had reacted in the months after Pearl Harbor as well as the fact that the United States was still at war with Japan, the three figured life would be tough for them if they returned. But the fruit business had been their families' livelihood for close to forty years, and Hood River was the only home they knew. They jumped at the chance to come back.

West Coast residents had feared that the *nikkei* would return by the trainload as soon as they could, but in fact Asai, Noji and Sato were part of what turned out to be a slow trickle of returnees. In January of 1945, when the three came home, only 1,000 of the 85,000 ethnic Japanese still behind barbed wire even applied for release. By March, two months after the order had been lifted, a mere 100 Japanese Americans had returned to Oregon. By midsummer, only 500 of the more than 4,000 *nikkei* who had called Oregon home before the war were back. Some had nothing to come home to; all were being officially discouraged from returning to their prewar homes.

"It would be good for the United States generally and I think it would be good from the standpoint of the Japanese-Americans themselves, to be scattered over a much wider area and not to be bunched up in groups as they were along the coast," War Relocation Authority Director Dillon Meyer told the press. WRA publicists were more blunt. "Go east, young man," they urged the *nikkei*, backing up their advice by establishing regional field offices in major Midwestern and Eastern cities to help with resettlement there. The WRA supervisor for Oregon and Washington assured the residents of the area that the *nikkei* were being "urged to seek other locations than the west coast" even as he officially defended their right to resettle in their old homes.

Economic interests jumped into the fray as well. A group of California produce wholesalers calling themselves the American League of California, "sincerely" suggested that Japanese Americans "demonstrate their patriotism by remaining away from the Pacific Coast." Meanwhile in Hood River the man who was leasing one of the Yasuis' orchards urged Shidzuyo to settle elsewhere. Business would be bad for the family if they returned, he said. The Apple Growers Association would not handle fruit grown by Japanese, he told her.

From the security of the camps or from their temporary "duration homes" away from the West Coast, the *nikkei* cautiously assessed the situation. "The very thought of going back to the West Coast filled us with dread," wrote Jeanne Wakatsuki Houston, then a teenager in camp, in her memoir *Farewell to Manzanar*. Well aware of the antipathy of their erstwhile neighbors, thousands waited for reports from the few who risked early return.

The reports were far from encouraging. Rumors quickly spread through the camps that returning evacuees were being beaten, even murdered. Although the initial accounts were exaggerated, there were in fact more than thirty incidents of terrorism against Japanese Americans in California during the first month of their return, ranging from an attempted bombing to rifle shots fired at a farmhouse to telephoned death threats. Four months after the exclusion order was lifted, Secretary of the Interior Harold Ickes officially reported another twenty-four incidents on the West Coast, including fifteen shootings and one attempted dynamiting. Night riders regularly stalked some farming communities, taking potshots at houses and orchards. Bricks were thrown through windows. Fruit-packing sheds mysteriously caught fire. Many of those who returned reported that their homes had been vandalized in their absence, their carefully stored possessions ransacked and stolen.

Many continued to see the *nikkei* as irredeemably undesirable. In a twenty-four-page self-published pamphlet railing against the Japanese and calling for their complete exclusion from the West Coast, a Seattle-area man asserted that "All men are created equal except those with yellow skins." A national opinion poll in 1946 revealed that almost 90 percent of Americans believed that *nikkei* had spied for the Japanese government during the war.

The Oregon legislature declared its official hostility toward returning *nikkei* by quickly passing an amendment to the old Alien Land Law. The new codicil barred *issei* from engaging in any farming activities by declaring it illegal for the older generation to live or work on land owned by their *nisei* relatives. In Portland local officials let stand until 1947 a statute that barred all *issei* from holding city business licenses. And beginning in early 1945 anti-Japanese groups in Hood River and in the Portland-area agricultural communities of Gresham, Sherwood and Forest Grove began lobbying in earnest for statewide exclusion legislation as well as mass deportation of all ethnic Japanese. In Portland a white man, apparently unprovoked, picked up a *nisei* and threw him through the glass door of a local luncheonette.

More subtle but just as damaging were the economic pressures applied to returning *nisei*. The Teamsters Union in California declared war on returnees by boycotting all Japanese-grown produce until the end of 1945. In Oregon and Washington, the Northwest Produce Dealers Association organized such a systematic and effective boycott that the U.S. secretary of agriculture eventually had to intervene with a cease and desist order. There were countless local boycotts. At Portland's booming East Side Farmers' Market, buyers gave *nikkei*-grown vegetables "a good leaving alone," according to one newspaper account. In fact, the WRA reported that during the spring and summer of 1945 "no person of Japanese ancestry was able to deliver his produce to [Portland-area] wholesalers." Many neighborhood stores refused to carry produce from *nikkei* truck farms or, for that matter, allow *nikkei* customers into the store. Those few establishments that did business with Japanese Americans were often targeted by whites for their own boycott.

Using whatever means they could, anti-Japanese forces in Oregon made certain that returning *nikkei* knew just how unwelcome they were. The goal of these activities, from legislative lobbying to telephoned death threats to economic rebuffs, was bluntly stated in early 1945 by Walter Pierce, an ex-governor and former legislator: "We should never be satisfied until every last Jap has been run out of the United States and our Constitution changed so they can never get back." Anti-Japanese sentiment in Oregon was so virulent during 1945 that the secretary of the interior felt he had to intervene. In a letter to one of the state's several hate groups, Ickes wrote that he was "profoundly disturbed" at the organization's efforts to prevent the peaceful return of Japanese Americans. "[Your] campaign of undisguised economic greed and ruthless racial persecution has shocked and outraged good Americans in every section of the nation," he wrote. The WRA made the letter public, and area newspapers reprinted it, but the group continued its activities unabated. In fact, a month later the same organization legally incorporated itself.

If Ickes was troubled by Oregon's attitude toward its returning *nikkei*, he and other federal officials must have been even more dismayed over what was happening in Hood River. Just as the valley had led the state in race hatred twice before—during the 1910s and the months following Pearl Harbor—it was once again, in the mid-1940s, the epicenter of anti-Japanese activity. In fact, it was nationally famous for it. A *nisei* woman, traveling home to Hood River after years in internment, struck up a conversation with an out-of-state soldier on the train. When she told him she was going to Hood River, he was incredulous. "You're going there? I can't believe you'd go back to *that* place," he said. Apparently men in his military unit who came from Oregon had spread the word.

What happened to the first three *nisei* to return to Hood River was indicative of how the town would treat the several hundred others who followed that year. Asai, Noji and Sato were supposed to arrive in Hood River by train on January 9,1945, just one week after the exclusion order was lifted. Local Legionnaire Penn Crum had already publicly declared in the state's largest newspaper that returnees would not be greeted with open arms. "There is a high feeling against them," he was quoted as saying. "There will be violence." Legionnaires and others somehow got wind of the three *nisei*'s imminent arrival and organized a "reception committee" to meet the men and inform them that they were not welcome in the valley. But when the train pulled in, only the *nisei*'s baggage was aboard. The men themselves were delayed for a few days. When they did arrive on the twelfth, the reception committee was fortunately unable to meet the train. Instead, a sympathetic upper-valley orchardist named Avon Sutton braved the ostracism of his neighbors, met the train and escorted the men to Sato's house, twenty miles south of town. The three *nikkei* decided to temporarily live together, thinking they would be safer that way.

But they didn't feel safe. At night they were afraid to turn on the lights in the house, fearing this would create a visible target for the cars they heard drive by, back and forth, after midnight. They jumped at the creaking of a door or at the sound of mice running in the ceiling. One night they awoke startled and terrified, listening to the crackle of a fire in the kitchen and figuring that someone had set the house ablaze. But it was only a fire gone awry in their own wood cookstove.

When they came into town for supplies, they found that no store would sell to them, and they had to depend on the compassionate Mr. Sutton to buy and deliver their provisions. When they walked down the main street of town, former friends averted their eyes, while the regulars who sat in front of the pool hall stared at them and spat. "What the hell are you doing here?" a man yelled at Min Asai a few days after his return. "I live here," Asai replied. "Well, why don't you go back where you're from?" the man yelled. "But I'm from here," Asai said. "I was born here."

As other *nisei* trickled back into the valley, they were met with increasing hostility. Local vigilantes broke windows, burned a barn and vandalized farming equipment. One Hood River man hired several high school boys to drive through a returning widow's property late at night to try to scare her and her two daughters into leaving town. Min Asai's youngest sister, Mitzi, who returned with her family later in 1945, had a particularly difficult time. One of her rural neighbors lay in wait for her when she passed by the woman's driveway on her way back from school. "Go home, you dirty yellow Jap," the neighbor would yell every afternoon. One day the woman sicced her dog on the terrified eighth-grade girl. The harassment was so severe and persistent that the woman's church thought it prudent to intervene. But even after visits from local clergy and concerned parishioners, the woman still stood across the lane from the Asai house every day, dog at her side, glaring at Mitzi as she walked by.

At school Mitzi and the other young *nisei* were alternately ignored and hectored. No one would play with them during recess or walk home with them in the afternoon. Kids called them names in school, and the youngest and most sensitive of them came home crying every day. In town the principal of Hood River High School asked the returning *nisei* not to participate in any after-school activities. At church no one would sit in the same pew as a Japanese American.

Downtown Hood River was plastered with NO JAPS WANTED signs. Almost every store in town displayed a NO JAP TRADE or NO JAPS ALLOWED poster in the window. Powerful local Legionnaires and their cronies pressured those local merchants who didn't agree with the anti-Japanese stance to display the signs anyway. The penalty for not toeing the line was social ostracism and the risk of a full-scale boycott. The local Standard Oil distributor tried to cut off gasoline supplies to *nikkei* orchardists. The movie theater refused to sell tickets to Japanese Americans. Restaurants would not serve them. Barbers would not cut their hair. One local dentist refused outright to treat *nikkei*, while other dentists and doctors claimed they were "too busy" to see Japanese American patients. People literally crossed the street if they saw a Japanese American walking toward them—a symbolic gesture but also a way for some *hakujin* to avoid interacting with the people they had taken advantage of, in absentia, for the past four years.

During the *nikkei*'s long internment, many homes and orchards did not fare well in the hands of local caretakers and renters. Some homes were vandalized; others were completely stripped of anything of value, from toilet fixtures to windows. Copper wire was ripped from the walls. The farms and orchards had suffered damage it would take years of hard work to repair. Asparagus fields were choked with two-foot-high weeds. Apple trees, unpruned for four seasons, looked like weeping willows, with branches hanging so low that a person could sit on the ground and pick fruit.

As the *nikkei* filtered back, quietly assessing the damage and moving immediately to restore their property, many neighboring farmers were quick to show them that life would continue to be tough. Those *nisei* who managed to bring in a scant first harvest found trouble waiting for them when they delivered their produce to the Apple Growers Association, the cooperative that handled the packing, distributing and marketing of virtually all valley fruit. At first they were routinely pushed out of line while waiting to deliver fruit. Then the association's packers threatened to strike if any Japanese American orchardist even tried to bring in their fruit. The strike was averted when the *nikkei* agreed to deliver their fruit only after all *hakujin* growers had delivered theirs.

Organized opposition to the returnees began early in Hood River. In February of 1945 the Oregon Property Owners Protective Association was formed under the banner of mass deportation of all ethnic Japanese. Short of that, the group worked earnestly toward stripping Japanese Americans of their titles to valley land. In April the Hood River Citizens Committee was formed for the purpose of keeping the *nikkei* from returning to the valley. Later that month a delegation from Hood River traveled to the state capital to lobby for exclusion legislation. But these efforts paled in comparison with the relentless work of local Legionnaire Kent Shoemaker who took it upon himself to be a one-man hate brigade.

JAPS ARE NOT WANTED IN HOOD RIVER, announced the first of Shoemaker's full-page ads in the local paper in early February 1945. Next to a listing of eighty-seven properties owned by *nikkei* (including both Masuo and Chop), Shoemaker wrote: "You Japs listed on this page have been told by some that you would be welcomed back in Hood River. This is not true." To prove his point, Shoemaker listed almost five hundred local citizens who had signed a petition against the *nikkei*'s return. "If you will look over the list," he instructed Japanese American readers, "you will probably find neighbors whom you thought might welcome you back. If you do not find their name this week, keep watching this page . . . and you will eventually find their name."

His next ad, two weeks later, began with this mocking headline: SO SORRY PLEASE. JAPS ARE NOT WANTED IN HOOD RIVER. Again he listed *nikkei*-owned properties, this time accompanied by a long, vitriolic letter that echoed the old racist arguments of the 1910s: The *nikkei* were unalterably foreign and completely unassimilatable. They came to take over the valley, and they still would, if given the chance. "Let us now, while the war is still on, firmly resolve to rid our country of representatives of an alien race who are our enemy and will always be our enemy," he concluded. Below was another long list of Hood Riverites who backed Shoemaker "one hundred percent." A week later, a Shoemaker-sponsored ad, this time signed by 175 people, insinuated that all ethnic Japanese were disloyal to America. "Japs salute the flag and say the pledge of allegiance but this is only lip service. . . ." These ads were followed by others just as pointed. One referred to the *nikkei* as "Japes"—Shoemaker's combination of the words "Japs" and "apes." Another railed against the *nikkei* for coming home to take scarce jobs and suggested that *nisei* who fought in the U.S. armed services did so to lull whites back to their pre-Pearl Harbor slumber. "You bowed and scraped and fooled us once," read the ad, implying that *hakujin* would not be "fooled" again. The ad, which closed "Yours for a Hood River without a Jap," was signed by Shoemaker and one hundred others. Later people would say that they were pressured into signing Shoemaker's petitions, that if they didn't sign they would be labeled "Jap lovers" and their businesses boycotted.

As spring of 1945 took hold in the valley, anti-Japanese rhetoric and action intensified. While Shoemaker was busy spreading his brand of bigotry, Hood River's American Legion Post no. 22 was becoming deeply involved in a controversy that would focus national attention on local racists. The Legion had created a commemorative plaque to honor local men who served in the armed forces during the war. Prominently displayed near the entrance to the county courthouse, the plaque included the names of sixteen *nisei*, fourteen of whom served or were serving overseas, two of whom had been killed in action against the Nazis and ten of whom had been awarded Purple Hearts. The members of Post 22 voted to remove the *nisei*'s names.

The Legion reasoned, if that word could be used, that the *nisei* servicemen (like all *nisei*) were citizens of Japan as well as of the United States. Like a number of other countries in the world, Japan based citizenship on blood—the nationality of one's parents—and not, like America, on place of birth. That meant that *nisei*, born in America of Japanese parents, could theoretically be dual citizens, assuming their birth was recorded in Japan. This hypothetical dual citizenship became, in the minds of the local Legionnaires, tantamount to disloyalty and treachery. Calling American citizens of Japanese descent "American-born Japanese," the local post declared that their return to the West Coast would endanger military operations and increase the danger of "riot, destruction of property and the peace and good order." Removing the names of the *nisei* servicemen was a way to publicly proclaim their "foreignness."

The Legion's long, rambling "Statement on the Japanese" showed, however, that the group's main concern was economic. The local chapter inveighed against the "clever, well organized and well disciplined Japanese minority among us" who carefully orchestrated their prewar success by following the dictates of "Matt Yasui type" leaders, men who "worked for the good of the Emperor" and "were usually agents of the Japanese government." Now these same Japanese were poised for a "victorious return to, and control of, the coveted Pacific slope with all its wealth." The Legion accused the Japanese of implementing a carefully planned strategy to squeeze out white landowners by buying adjoining properties, thus lowering values and "forcing" whites to sell.

The accusations remained a local matter, but the removal of the *nisei* soldiers' names made Hood River nationally infamous. *Collier's* magazine called it "tops in blind hatred." Stories in newspapers across the country and magazines like *The New Republic* and *The Saturday Review of Literature* brought in hundreds of letters, most objecting to the Legion's action. More than three hundred letters came from concerned servicemen, who knew firsthand of the efforts of thousands of *nisei* soldiers. One was from a local boy, marine sergeant David White. "Why did you do it?" he asked the Legionnaires. "We're ashamed to say we're from Oregon now, much less Hood River." Another letter called Post 22's conduct "an outstanding act of narrow-mindedness, hypocrisy and childish intolerance."

The chapter's action was not popular even in American Legion circles. A post in New York showed its disapproval by voting to accept the discredited *nisei* as members of its group. National headquarters issued a directive ordering Hood River to reinstate the *nisei*'s names or face expulsion from the organization. After six weeks, and under great duress, Post 22 knuckled under. Making it clear that the only reason they were restoring the names was that they were directed to do so by headquarters, the Post commander issued a terse statement of compliance that ended by reiterating the group's opposition to the *nikkei*: "[Restoring the names] does not change the sentiment of the Post on the question of the Japanese returning to Hood River."

The actions of the Legion, other organized anti-*nikkei* groups, Kent Shoemaker and assorted vigilantes prompted WRA director Dillon Meyer to make a personal visit to Hood River to chastise its citizens. In a meeting attended by Legionnaires and others, Meyer first spoke generally about the problems returnees were facing and then sternly lectured his audience for using "Hitler and Tojo-like" tactics when dealing with the *nikkei*. The Legionnaires left the room fuming and sputtering, muttering "no government official can do this to us."

Meanwhile, in Fruitland, Idaho, just miles from Oregon's eastern border, Chop and Mikie were watching closely. They had been living and working on a large orchard there for more than a year, marking time until they could return to their own land in the Hood River valley. But as they heard reports of vigilantism, read Shoemaker's invective in the newspaper and followed the American Legion controversy, it seemed to them, in the first few months of 1945, that Hood River was a dangerous and hostile place to be. In fact, although he loved the valley intensely, Chop had just about decided not to return. "You have probably read that Hood River at the present time is not too keen about the returning Japanese," he wrote to a man who owned Idaho orchard land that Chop expressed interest in buying. "I have almost definitely decided to make Idaho my home."

But his childhood home exerted a powerful pull. As the oldest surviving son, Chop felt an obligation to return and reclaim what was left of the family's property and the family name. He felt particularly connected to Willow Flat, where he had worked hard since the early days of high school learning the fruit business from the ground up. It was not a place—or a life—Chop and Mikie could easily turn their backs on. In April of 1945 they loaded up the car and headed west, across the Snake River, across the north-east corner of Oregon and back up to Hood River. Only a half dozen other *nikkei* families had preceded them.

Their plan was to move back to their old house at Willow Flat and begin working the orchards. Before evacuation, Chop had taken care to stipulate in the lease on the property that the house had to be vacated once the *nikkei* were legally permitted to return to the area. But it wasn't that easy. The *hakujin* couple then living in the house refused to leave and, given community sentiment, it was difficult to exert any pressure on them. Instead, Chop, Mikie, almost-three-year-old Joanie and their new baby, five-month-old Tom, stayed in Mikie's parents' house a few miles away. It was five months before they were able to move into their own home. Happy to be there, they were also greatly disheartened at what greeted them.

The orchards hadn't been pruned, fertilized or sprayed in four years. "Decimated" was the word Chop used to describe their condition. It would take several years for the trees to recover, and in the meantime the early harvests were sparse. "All we raised that first year was worms," Chop told a family member. One of the many problems he faced was lack of equipment. When he was forced to abandon Willow Flat, he left a tractor, wagons, mules, harnesses and a variety of tools necessary for the operation of more than a hundred acres of orchard land. In the lease he drafted before evacuation, he specifically noted the fact that the equipment had to be returned in good condition. It wasn't. Much of it was not returned at all. And getting new equipment wasn't easy. Merchants in town, with their NO JAP TRADE signs, wanted no part of Chop's business. He had to drive to the next town or, once, as far as Boise, Idaho, to purchase the supplies he needed.

The house, too, had been stripped bare during the internment years. Chop and Mikie had to replace almost everything, shopping whenever they could afford it in the neighboring town of The Dalles or in Portland. But one item couldn't be replaced: a little knickknack shelf an old *hakujin* neighbor had given Mikie when she got married back in 1939. The shelf represented not only a happy day in her life but also the friendship and acceptance of a white neighbor. She loved it and mourned its disappearance more than anything else in the house. Chop decided to try to track it down. A few days later he found himself in the house of the couple who had leased Willow Flat during the internment. There, hanging on the living room wall, was the little knickknack shelf. He stared at it while the couple told him they had no idea where his property was. That night Mikie urged Chop to do something. But there was nothing to do. He would not go back. He would not beg.

Like the handful of other *nikkei* who had by then returned to the valley, Chop and Mikie at first lived their lives looking over their shoulders, assessing the danger, steeling themselves against the remarks. Once, in the small hours of the morning, they were awakened by the noise of a car driving back and forth in front of the house. Chop went to the window and cautiously peeked out. The car was moving very slowly, its headlights out. Chop went to the closet, got his shotgun, loaded it and waited. If anyone steps out of that car, I'm gonna kill the bastard, he said to himself. After a few more passes in front of the house, the car moved on.

Chop and Mikie dug in their heels. Wrote a friend of those difficult days, "Mikie's good cheer was even more amazing than her supply of physical strength." The two were also spurred on by long-distance pep talks from Masuo, still imprisoned in Santa Fe Detention Center. "I am pleased to know that you are making plans to repair the orchards," Masuo wrote his oldest son. "It will take lots of courage to overcome the present day's turmoil. You have unparalleled opportunities to test your ability. If you pass this successfully, the rest of your life will be much easier." In another letter the father again tried to buoy the son's spirits. "Men and women who can face bravely the present difficult situation can win out the battle of life's struggles." He called this time in Chop's life "the hardest and most difficult examination of the course in the School for Human Life."

The young Yasui family also got a boost that fall when Chan and Obasan were released from Minidoka and eventually came to live with them. Obasan was no stranger to farm work at Willow Flat, but Chan certainly was. He had spent thirty years behind the counter of a store and was, by the standards of the day, a "city slicker." Chop found odd jobs for him to make him feel a part of the operation. On nice days Chan could be seen pushing a red wooden wheelbarrow through the orchards, stopping often to fix the wooden props that prevented heavy, fruit-laden branches from breaking. He also took it upon himself to paint warning signs for the fruit-packing sheds. With *fude*, a traditional Japanese writing brush, and *sumi*, the accompanying ink, he used his fractured English to write: PLEASE DO NOT SMOKING HERE and DANGER FIRE NEVER SMOKING THIS HERE. It didn't matter what Chan did; Chop was delighted to have him around, a constant reminder of a happier time.

In the fall of 1945 Yuka was back in Oregon too, a freshman at the university in Eugene. She had finished high school in Denver and had seriously considered staying in the Midwest for college. But money was a concern. Chop was an Oregon resident, which meant Yuka would have to pay only nominal in-state fees for her education. But the choice was still a difficult one. Yuka knew Oregon was not welcoming home its *nikkei*. University officials had warned her they "couldn't guarantee" student reaction to her presence on campus. In fact, she had a tough time, at least initially. University students from the Hood River area apparently spread rumors that her father was a Japanese spy. "Yuka, please do not worry about what those Hood River kids tell about us in Eugene," Masuo wrote his youngest daughter from his barracks in Santa Fe. "Just ignore them! Our conscience is clear and nothing worries us!" When she continued to express concern about the way she was being treated and hinted that she wanted to leave school, her father urged her to "face the situation calmly and bravely. You are now on trial. Do not act like a coward!" Remember, he instructed her, "we got to take bitter with sweet." On long weekends and holidays Yuka came home to the comfort of her brother's place at Willow Flat. The Yasuis were beginning to be a family again.

The presence of family comforted Chop and Mikie during those difficult days, but so too did the support of several *hakujin* friends who remained loyal. First, of course, was E.C. Smith, Masuo's good friend, who had tried, despite both failing health and public opinion, to protect the Yasuis' personal property during the war. The family's piano sat in his living room; Michi's hope chest was tucked away in his attic. He held the keys to the basement of the Yasui Brothers store, where the rest of the family's possessions were housed. After Chop and Mikie came home, he lent his strong moral support, although increasingly he was coming under fire for being a friend to the returning Japanese. Smith's house was directly across the street from the home of the commander of the local American Legion post, who would sit on his porch and glare threateningly at the Smith place whenever returning *nikkei* came to visit. The situation got so tense for the ailing Smith that he asked Chop to intervene by gently telling other *nikkei* not to visit him. "Choppy, I hardly know how to handle the situation of these Japanese friends coming to our house," he wrote. "I don't like to tell my friends not to come. . . . Yet I do believe their coming stirs up hatred and is doing no good." In another note a week later, he was still troubled by the ethics of the situation. "I would not like to take a chance on hurting the feelings of old friends. Maybe I should ignore these radical neighbors. But the Legion is meeting across the street some nights—and they are talking about me." Chop sympathized, and also got the hint, writing to Smith that he and Mikie would put off their own personal visit "until such time as things have returned to normal, should it be a few months or years hence."

Other people went out of their way to be kind to Chop and Mikie. An old bachelor friend of Mikie's drove out to Willow Flat with a bag of fresh tomatoes and a big box of Ivory soap, two items he apparently considered necessities of life. He knew that many grocers weren't selling to the *nikkei*. One notable exception was R.J. McIsaac, who owned a country store in Parkdale, up the valley from Willow Flat, and remained steadfastly loyal to the Japanese Americans. When disgruntled *hakujin* customers threatened to take their business elsewhere, McIsaac called their bluff, and ended up keeping the business of both contingents.

Throughout the valley the *nikkei* were particularly aware and appreciative of the few people who actively came to their defense: Carl Smith, who kept one family's orchards in fine shape during the owners' internment and welcomed them back in true friendship; Avon Sutton, who showed his support both by escorting the first returnees to their home and, five months later, buying space in the Hood River *News* for a long letter decrying local treatment of the *nikkei*. "Certain forces are at work here, which, if allowed to grow unhampered to full maturity, would be quite up to Nazi standards," he wrote. "The intolerance, prejudice and racial discrimination, which we have tolerated, is causing fair-minded men and women, all over the country to denounce us." Using increasingly passionate rhetoric, he called bigotry un-American and unconstitutional. "Shall we write into the Bill of Rights 'For Caucasians Only' and then piously take our place at the World Peace table and affirm our love for all mankind . . . ?"

A handful of others led by Mrs. Max Moore, wife of the owner of one of the very few downtown stores to refuse to post NO JAPS WANTED signs, and the Reverend Sherman Burgoyne, minister of the Asbury Methodist Church, founded the League for Liberty and Justice to counteract local Legion-inspired activities. The small group vowed to "fight for the democratic way of life in this community." As Mrs. Moore later explained to Chop, "Truly I do not feel that we are being anything more than decent. We honestly believed that our country would be embarrassed if such an un-American program were permitted to prevail so we took a hand to stop the steamroller." In another note, in which she praised Chop for his increasing confidence and good nature, she explained that her group believed "discrimination was fascism under another name." The league had enormous symbolic value for the returning *nikkei*, but its actual accomplishments were few. League members did spearhead a drive to garner signatures for a pro-tolerance petition, and the Reverend Burgoyne used his pulpit to preach against discrimination, but league members mostly showed their support in small ways. Mrs. Moore herself, though obese and slightly disabled, limped from store to store buying provisions for several families. Mrs. Burgoyne publicly greeted one returnee with a big hug and a hearty "I'm so glad to see you" (and was fired from her job at the bank two days later).

Meanwhile, the Reverend was also catching flak for his strong stand. People in Hood River boycotted his small fruit business, which quickly failed. Unhappy parishioners wrote to church officials and asked for his removal. (He was subsequently reassigned to a Willamette Valley community a fraction of the size of Hood River.) But ultimately Burgoyne's principled stance was nationally recognized and publicly rewarded. At a Waldorf Astoria banquet hosted by Eleanor Roosevelt, he was awarded the Jefferson Medal by the Council Against Intolerance. But Burgoyne and the others were a tiny minority. Although a number of other Hood Riverites were distressed with their town's bigotry—their reactions ranged from embarrassment to outrage—most did not follow the Burgoynes' and the Moores' lead. Fearful of losing business, friends and their place in local society, the vast majority of the town's citizens kept silent.

"Time only will resolve these things," Masuo wrote to Yuka when he learned of Hood River's strident opposition to the returnees. "We patiently have to wait." He was right. Ultimately it was not the individual efforts of hardworking *nikkei* nor the actions of a few brave *hakujin* but, rather, time and the course of events that eventually blunted the sharp edge of local racism. Hostility toward returnees subsided somewhat with the defeat and formal surrender of Japan on September 2,1945. But probably of greater local significance, given the decades-old fear of a Japanese "takeover" of the valley, was the fact that many *nikkei* simply did not return to Hood River after internment. In 1940 Hood River County had one of the largest concentrations of Japanese Americans in the state: 462 people, or 4 percent of all residents, according to official census figures. Ten years later, the number had been cut in half. Many *nikkei* had sold their land just before evacuation, during internment or soon after their release. The WRA accurately estimated in early 1945 that after the dust settled, *nikkei* would hold title to only 25 percent of the land they owned prior to the war. Even those who held on to their orchards and returned home came back to much-devalued property and, by virtue of four years of lost income, vastly decreased personal wealth. Hood River's Japanese were not the economic threat they had earlier been perceived to be.

One by one, the NO JAPS WANTED signs began to come down. One local gas-station operator reasoned aloud that there was no difference between a "*nisei* Japanese and a *nisei* German"—and he was a *nisei* German. His sign came down. Another sign disappeared when a former marine captain, who had *nisei* in his outfit, came home and shamed his merchant father into removing it from the window. Kent Shoemaker's own soldier son wrote a letter to the editor of the local paper saying how much he disagreed with his father and how proud he was to have *nisei* friends.

Individual white soldiers had an impact on local opinion, but so too did national news of the all-*nisei* 442nd Regimental Combat Team that distinguished itself in fierce fighting in Italy and France. The regiment's motto was "Go for Broke," and that's what the men did in a bloody effort to prove their—and by extension, their parents'—loyalty to the United States. In seven major campaigns, the legendary 442nd suffered casualties almost three times its original infantry strength and became the most decorated unit of its size, with more than eighteen thousand individual medals, including a Congressional Medal of Honor and fifty-two Distinguished Service Crosses. Although a G.R. Frey of Hood River was unimpressed—"*Nisei* are in the armed services to protect their property rights," he told the local newspaper—the vast majority of people respected the bravery and sacrifices of the 442nd. "The *nisei* bought an awful big chunk of America with their blood," General Joseph Stilwell publicly proclaimed. "I say we soldiers ought to form a pick-ax club to protect Japanese Americans who fought the war with us. . . . We cannot allow a single injustice to be done to the *nisei* without defeating the purposes for which they fought." Hood River listened. Time passed. The grip of the Legionnaires and their ilk loosened.

Still, for the fifty or so *nikkei* families left in the valley, recovery—social, economic and psychological—was slow. Discrimination was still a fact of life. In 1947, a full two years after the *nikkei* returned, one of Chop's friends went into the downtown hardware store to buy a knife only to hear the owner tell him, "We don't want any Jap trade." In 1948 racism was still sufficiently alive in town that the father of a *nisei* soldier killed in the Philippines was worried about hostility toward burying his son in the local cemetery. And it wasn't until mid-1949 that the state legislature finally repealed Oregon's 1923 Alien Land Law along with its more recent amendment. Even then, the repeal had less to do with changed attitudes on the part of the legislators and more to do with the success of a *nisei*-backed legal challenge.

Economic recovery took years as well. Orchardists scraped by, bringing in poor harvests for several seasons. Some orchards never bounced back. And families like the Yasuis had lost too much to ever fully recover from the devastation of forced evacuation. In the late 1940s the U.S. government admitted its responsibility for the *nikkei*'s economic hardships by enacting the Japanese Evacuation Claims Act, which allowed for reimbursement for "damage to or loss of real or personal property" occurring as a "reasonable or natural consequence of evacuation or exclusion." But the bill excluded reimbursement for death, injury, hardship, suffering or lost earned income. From the first payment of $303 for office equipment abandoned by a Los Angeles real estate professional to the last and by far the biggest, a $362,000 settlement for five thousand acres of prime California agricultural land, the government doled out about $37 million to more than twenty-six thousand claimants. But the Federal Reserve Bank estimated that ethnic Japanese had lost more than $400 million worth of property. Government compensation replaced less than one dollar of every ten the *nikkei* lost.

Kenneth Abraham, Min's old law-school friend, handled most of the reimbursement claims for the valley's *nikkei*. In doing so, he had to go through county records and the books at the Apple Growers Association, and neither investigation gained him much popularity in town. People told him he was making a big mistake, that he would not have a successful legal career in Hood River if he persisted. They called him a "Jap lover." Meanwhile Abraham uncovered proof that some *hakujin* had taken unfair advantage of their positions as caretakers of *nikkei* property. Min personally handled the claim for the Yasuis, working hard with Chop to gather what documents they could. But the contents of an entire safe was lost. Before the war the Yasuis' properties and holdings were worth perhaps a half million dollars. After the war, only Willow Flat remained. In the end, Min got what he could for his parents, about thirty-three thousand dollars, one of the better settlements but a fraction of their loss.

Harder to quantify—and recover from—was the psychological toll exacted by evacuation and internment. For years after their return the *nikkei* in the valley didn't socialize much. It was not just that they were too busy working, although that was part of it. It was that the war and its aftermath sensitized them to how their *hakujin* neighbors perceived them. They did not want to be seen as "clannish." They avoided meeting together in large groups. But even as they kept to their homes, they knew that their ultimate acceptance in the valley would be based on their public deeds. They didn't talk about it or intellectualize about it, but they nevertheless understood the dictates of the racism that was so deeply entrenched in the valley: they and their children would have to prove themselves better in order to be merely equal; they would have to mold themselves into a shining, high-achieving "model minority" in order to gain simple respect.

In the late 1940s, as some of the overt signs of prejudice began to disappear, valley *nikkei* made a great effort to become involved in their communities, from school boards to sports teams to charity-fund drives. Leading that effort was Masuo Yasui's oldest surviving son. Chop was not as driven as Masuo. He enjoyed life more, had a good sense of humor and a sociability more like his uncle's than his father's. But Chop picked up the mantle Masuo had dropped, or more accurately, had been snatched from him. This son who had resisted his father's best attempts to steer him into a profession, this happy-go-lucky prankster who had been asked to leave college, now carried the full weight of the family on his shoulders. What the Yasui name would mean in the valley was up to him.

13

Two Hundred Percent American

Masuo and Shidzuyo were happy to be back in the Northwest. They had tried Denver for a few months after Masuo's release from Santa Fe, but the frigid winters and deep snow were just not for them. But neither, anymore, was Hood River. Masuo could not bring himself to go back to the town that had turned its back on him. He had been powerful; he had been, he thought, well liked, even respected, by his fellow businessmen. But now, years after the war, his erstwhile friends were still whispering that he was a Japanese agent, a spy, a top-ranking officer in the Imperial Navy. He could not go home. It was no longer home.

Instead, he and Shidzuyo, now in their sixties, settled in a small frame house in a quiet southeast Portland neighborhood. They retired not so much by choice as by circumstance. Masuo's land was gone, and his business was closed. His long internment had depleted the seemingly endless store of ambition and energy that had fueled his earlier success. At this point in his life he was not interested, and perhaps not capable, of starting a new venture. Luckily, he didn't have to. The Yasuis' savings and investments were enough to support their modest life-style.

The two kept busy with family, church and *nikkei* community activities. Several times a week, Masuo would don his overalls, grab his toolbox and catch a bus to the twelve-unit apartment building he and Shidzuyo had bought as an investment. There he would tinker happily most of the day, doing minor repairs and conversing with the tenants.

Well known in the statewide *nikkei* community from his prewar business successes, Masuo continued to live a somewhat public life. He was one of three area representatives to the first conference of the Association to Attain Naturalization in San Francisco and worked hard for the passage of the McCarran-Walter Act that enabled Asian aliens to apply for naturalized citizenship. When the legislation passed in 1952, Masuo independently organized and taught preparatory classes to fellow *issei*, helping them improve their language skills and instructing them in the basics of American government and the intricacies of the U.S. Constitution. He guided his pupils through the entire process, even accompanying them to the Immigration and Naturalization Service office for their exams.

On July 16, 1953, Masuo escorted one of his best pupils downtown: his wife, Shidzuyo. He and a friend paced the halls of the federal building while Shidzuyo answered in English fourteen questions about the American system of government. She had to, among other things, recite the first ten amendments to the Constitution and name all the principal officers of county government. Twenty-five long minutes later, Shidzuyo emerged from the room smiling. She had had some difficulty understanding the questions and making herself understood in a language she still barely knew, but ultimately she had answered every question correctly. In early September she took the oath of citizenship.

Three months later Masuo stood in front of Alger Fee, the same judge who had sentenced his son Min for violating curfew, and in a clear, firm voice swore allegiance to America, the country that had been his home for half a century. The day before, he had written excitedly to Yuka, "Less than 24 hours from now, I will be an American!" In another letter to his youngest daughter heralding his citizenship, he wrote, "Thanks to God and America for the blessing we receive! Now we of the Yasui family are 100 percent Americans." Taking the oath of citizenship was the "greatest happiness and fortune we have ever received in our lifetime," he told Yuka.

It sounded like hyperbole, but it wasn't, for to Masuo, becoming a citizen was not simply the culmination of an immigrant's dream. Rather it was tangible proof that the American government no longer considered him a "potentially dangerous alien." His record had been thoroughly scrutinized before he was deemed eligible for citizenship. And the record showed, just as Masuo had always insisted, that he was and had always been loyal. "Yes, Yuka, time alone is a good judge, not men," he wrote. "Now I can tell those people who thought I was disloyal to this country to read my record and know better."

Masuo rejoiced, but all was not well with him. Throughout his long years of internment, never knowing when it would end, when he would see his family, or where he would be from month to month, he had written strong, cheerful letters to his wife and children. He never allowed himself to feel scared, lonely, depressed or anxious. Even his personal diary revealed no crack in his armor. But a person—even a Japanese male well schooled in the art of stoicism—can suppress feelings only so long. In the mid-1950s, it seemed that Masuo's psychological past was finally catching up with him. He began to change.

At first it was small things that might be attributed to age. He stopped driving. He became uninterested in travel. Soon he was refusing to venture very far from his Portland home. Yuka, temporarily in town working as a visiting nurse, would sometimes drop by her parents' house in the late afternoon. There she'd find Masuo looking worried and concerned. "Why are you stopping here?" Masuo would ask her. She heard fear and anxiety in his voice. She looked into his eyes and saw a "haunted person." Shidzuyo told her daughter that Masuo was worried that the FBI was coming to get him. "He talks about 'the investigation' and 'the hearing,'" she told Yuka.

When Homer, who had settled in Portland, came to his parents' house for dinner, the place was dark, with the shades down, curtains drawn and lights out. The only illumination in the entire house came from a tiny light above the kitchen stove. "How come you're in the dark?" Homer asked his mother. "Your father insists we turn off the lights," Shidzuyo told him. "He has some idea that someone is after him." Masuo, in fact, was becoming obsessed with the notion that federal authorities would soon knock on his door and take him away. At night, when he felt most vulnerable, he could think of little else. In part, he seemed to be reliving those terrifying days after Pearl Harbor. But he was also creating a special hell for himself out of a real but minor problem in his current life.

Masuo had volunteered to act as treasurer for the Epworth Methodist Church, which served Portland's *nikkei* community. He was a diligent and experienced bookkeeper, but in tallying the books for the year Masuo found minor discrepancies: the books and the church's bank account didn't match to the dollar. Sometimes he would be at a social occasion and a church member would hand him a cash donation. He'd put the money in his pocket and then try to remember later which of the church's funds it was for. Usually—but not always—he remembered correctly. The discrepancy in the books was relatively small, but Masuo, fueled by all the fear and anxiety he had not let himself feel a decade before, imagined the imbalance as a major offense, a serious crime that would bring the FBI to his door. In his mind the slightly askew accounts would provide his enemies with the ammunition they needed to persecute him once again.

Homer and Yuka tried to help with the books. Sometimes late at night Masuo would call his youngest son and plead with him to come over. Homer spent hours in his parents' living room punching the keys on his father's old Burroughs adding machine. "Here's a five-dollar entry, but there's no name and there's no date," Homer told his father. "What's it for?" Masuo couldn't remember. Homer tried to explain that it was impossible to work on the books without such information. "Just try," Masuo begged. So Homer would punch more keys and try different combinations, but the accounts would never come out quite right. "Just explain to them that you've made a mistake," Homer told his father. But to Masuo it was not a mistake; it was a shameful crime.

Increasingly concerned about his father's mental health, Homer insisted that he see a doctor. But after a lengthy examination the doctor said he could find nothing wrong. In fact, Masuo had been so clear and rational and in control of himself during the examination that the doctor suggested it was Homer who had a problem. "You must be imagining your father's condition, or at least greatly exaggerating it," he told Homer. It was true that during the day Masuo seemed to live his life normally, and no one other than his immediate family even suspected he was having problems. Even Chop, who saw his father relatively frequently, did not believe anything was wrong. But Homer and Yuka knew their father was sick. They just didn't realize how sick.

At noon on May 11, 1957, Shidzuyo had just finished fixing lunch and setting it on the table. She called Masuo to come to eat. When he didn't come or reply, she went looking for him, checking the backyard, the basement, the upstairs bedrooms. She called his name, concerned now that she couldn't find him. She began to search the house systematically. Upstairs there was a spare closet. She opened it, and there he was, hanging limp from the clothes rod. Around his neck he had tied a sash she made for him. The other end was knotted around the heavy wooden bar. Because the bar was only five feet from the floor, Masuo had not been able to hang himself properly. Instead, he bent his knees and let his body go limp, waiting for the sash to strangle him. Shidzuyo ran downstairs to the kitchen for a sharp knife. She cut him down, slashing her own fingers in haste. His body fell to the floor. At age seventy, Masuo Yasui was dead.

In Japanese culture, defilement of one's honor is a serious matter. One has the lifelong duty to maintain a spotless reputation, not merely as a matter of personal honor but for the sake of the family name. A soiled reputation—such as the one Masuo imagined he would have because of the unbalanced church books and the one Masuo knew he had from the persistent rumors about his wartime loyalty—could not easily be made clean again. One had to be vindicated, and Japanese culture viewed suicide as the ultimate vindication. The act of taking one's own life erased the shame. One exited the world with a clear conscience and left behind a clean name.

Shidzuyo was crying when Homer and Yuka arrived, but she wasn't the kind of person to fall apart. She was practiced in the art of grief. She wept, but it was she who pulled the family together, she who chose the funeral home, selected Masuo's favorite hymns and handpicked the pallbearers. "It is not how he died," Shidzuyo told Homer and Yuka many times, trying to console them. "It is how he lived. Remember how he lived."

For Shidzuyo, the death of the man she had lived with for forty-five years was a terrible tragedy, but it was also in some ways a release. Masuo's growing obsession had made home life tense; his anxieties had kept the couple housebound. Now Shidzuyo was free to travel, with time to devote to her growing brood of grandchildren. She crisscrossed the country several times, staying at her children's houses and getting to know their young families. In between trips she lived alone in the house she and her husband had shared. It was, for her, an almost happy time. But it was brief.

Just three years after Masuo's death, Shidzuyo was admitted to the hospital for a gall-bladder operation. The operation went well, but in the days that followed, it became clear that she was not going to recover. She couldn't eat. Her liver was failing. She wanted to come home. Homer rented a hospital bed and set it up in a downstairs room of her house. He came by twice a day to check on her and monitor intravenous feeding. Michi, Shu and Roku came to sit by her bedside. A week after coming home, on a spring morning just five days shy of her seventy-fourth birthday, Shidzuyo looked up from her bed and told her children, "*Ashita Papa miru*" (Tomorrow I will see your father). That night she died.

Neither the death of their parents nor the thousands of miles that now separated them kept the Yasui *nisei* from maintaining a strong sense of family. They found time to trade visits several times a year, to stage reunions and to write long letters to one another. They were busy with their own lives and their own families, busy struggling with their own careers, but being a Yasui meant something to all of them and continued to be a focal point of their lives. With Masuo and Shidzuyo dead, the ideal of the hardworking 200 percent American model citizen lived on in the lives of the *nisei* generation. Consistent overachievement had been the family norm for a half century, and the Yasui *nisei* continued the tradition, branching out to establish themselves in professions and in their communities.

Chop, busy tending 140 acres of apple, pear and cherry orchards on the gently rolling hills of Willow Flat, was also busy with his young family. Joan, born at Tule Lake, and Tom, born in Idaho, were joined in 1947 by Philip, quickly nicknamed Flip, the only member of the next generation of Yasuis to claim Hood River as his birthplace. As Chop worked to make Willow Flat profitable again and slowly expand his holdings, he also began to devote time to the community, helping to set up the area's first volunteer fire department and becoming one of the local booster club's most enthusiastic members. His community interests ranged widely, from involvement with the Hood River Music Association to the organization of the valley's version of Little League. A charter member of the Japanese American Citizens League since 1931, he continued his involvement and soon moved into positions of local leadership, eventually serving as chapter president. In 1949 he conducted a one-man house-to-house campaign to sign up more than one hundred new JACL members. He also served as the local chairman for a statewide committee raising funds for a *nisei* war memorial in Portland. He would never have the power, prestige—or wealth—his father had, but his good-hearted gregariousness would win him more friends and wider acceptance. "I'm sorry I wasn't able to be at [the New Year's party]," a *hakujin* acquaintance wrote in a breezy note, "because Chop and fun are like Mary and her little lamb—everywhere that Chop goes, fun is sure to follow."

As the years passed, Chop modestly referred to himself as "just a regular citizen." He was anything but. His early local volunteerism soon spread statewide, then nationwide, as he was elected to serve on thirty-three different boards of directors, from banks to Boy Scouts, insurance companies to government commissions. He started and tirelessly promoted a "sister city" program that established ties between Hood River and a rural Japanese town, in the process helping to heal some of the old wartime wounds in the valley. He worked overtime for agricultural interests, serving as the chairman of the board of directors of Diamond Fruit Company (the erstwhile Apple Growers Association) for fifteen years and almost single-handedly opening Japanese markets to the Northwest cherry industry. His efforts earned him the title of Cherry King and won him a place in Oregon State University's Agricultural Hall of Fame.

A thousand miles away, Min was pursuing an equally active but radically different life from his older brother's. Released from Minidoka in 1944, the Phi Beta Kappa attorney spent a backbreaking summer in Chicago delivering hundred-pound blocks of ice. In the fall he moved to Denver, the city he had tried so hard to dissuade his mother from making the Yasuis' duration home. But now Denver didn't look so bad to him. It was a livable city with a sizable *nikkei* population; Min had both family and friends there. And going back to Oregon was out of the question. After spending nine months in a Portland jail reading newspaper stories that called him a spy, after seeing his father railroaded into four years of imprisonment based primarily on the ill will of his erstwhile friends in Hood River, Min knew that his own future in his home state would be severely constrained by his and his family's past.

In Denver, Min studied hard for the Colorado bar exam and, true to form, earned the highest score of all those who took the test that fall. But the state bar refused to grant him a license to practice, saying that his 1942 curfew case had cast doubts on his status as an American citizen. Min challenged the ruling immediately, bringing the matter to the state supreme court, which soon decided unanimously in his favor. In 1946 he was admitted to the bar, hung out a shingle and married True Shibata, a young woman Michi had introduced him to. During the next few years as True gave birth to three daughters, Min attempted to eke out a living practicing law, building a practice rich in clients—at first *nikkei* whose affairs were in disorder from internment and then a growing number of other racial minorities and working-class people—but poor in accounts receivable. One colleague called him "Denver's first one-man legal aid society."

"*Nisei* lawyers out this way aren't faring too well," Min wrote to Homer in the 1950s, confessing that his practice consisted mostly of "penniless friends who are indebted to us" rather than paying clients. His marginal practice combined with extensive volunteer work—sixty to eighty hours a month for JACL, another twenty to forty hours a month on a civic commission—meant that Min could not measure his success by his income. In fact, his volunteerism put him in serious debt. In the early 1960s he wrote to Homer that he was several months in arrears on his mortgage and had racked up an unpaid heating bill of almost two hundred dollars. "We all try to do the things that seem most important or meaningful to us . . . and I guess the money part is only incidental," he wrote to his brother. "Like you—I'll probably never die rich—as a matter of fact I know darned well that I'll die pretty darned poor."

Min and his family certainly lived poor. When an old Hood River friend flew in for a visit, Min picked her up from the airport in a beat-up sedan. The driver's side door was jammed shut, and Min had to climb in and out through the window. At his house, under the waist-high stacks of newspaper clippings and JACL files, the carpet was worn thin. The windows needed new curtains; the plumbing had seen better days. Min was more concerned with causes than creature comforts; he always had been.

As hard as he worked in the office, with True as his assistant and a baby daughter or two playing on a blanket on the floor, Min worked even harder as a community servant. He founded both the city's Urban League and its first "rainbow" Boy Scout troop, and expended both time and energy fighting for various *nikkei* causes. In 1948 Min took True and their newborn daughter on a barn-storming trip across the country to drum up support for the Japanese Evacuation Claims Act. A few years later he was making the circuit again, this time campaigning for the passage of the McCarran-Walter Act, the legislation that would finally allow his mother and father to become naturalized citizens.

In the late 1950s he gave up his law practice to serve full-time as first a member and then executive director of the Denver Commission on Community Relations. In his twenty-four years on the commission, he initiated and oversaw programs for minorities, youth, the elderly, women and refugees. He volunteered so much of his time to community concerns that the city created a monthly service award in his honor, and the mayor of Denver proclaimed a Min Yasui Recognition Day.

Michi lived a far less public life than her brothers, putting her own career aspirations on hold to raise a large family. She and Toshio Ando, the young law student she had met when she first came to Denver, settled in that city and had six children in nine years. But the Yasui ambition burned in her as well. When the last of her children entered high school, Michi went back to school herself, completing her master's degree in education and beginning a career as a primary-school teacher. During her more than three decades in the Denver public schools, she quietly worked in and out of the classroom to promote cross-cultural understanding, earning the respect of two generations of students as well as a distinguished teaching award from the state.

Roku, the only sibling to escape the family's drive to overachieve, bounced around the country, going from Michigan, where he earned his undergraduate degree to Fort Snelling, Minnesota, where he studied at the army's Japanese Language School, to Japan with the occupation forces and back to Michigan to earn a master's degree. He tried working in Detroit and then Buffalo before he and his wife, an ex-Portlander, settled in Boston to raise their family of three. There Roku at first considered pursuing a doctorate in Far Eastern Studies, but soon turned to what he loved best: working with his hands. He opened a machine-tool shop, repairing equipment and working on his own patented designs.

Shu had also chosen to make his home in the East. The shyest of

the Yasuis, he was in some ways the family's iconoclast. First, he had refused to be evacuated, escaping Oregon just days before the order came
down. Then, during the war, he broke with his past to legally change
his first name. It was 1943, and he was trying unsuccessfully to apply to
medical schools. After writing to twenty schools and receiving responses
from only two, he went to see one of his professors at the University
of Wisconsin. "Your name is a hindrance," the man told him. "You
have to show you're an American. You have to change your name." Shu,
long embarrassed by his Japanese name, listened willingly. "Pick a simple
name," the professor suggested. "What about Robert?" Robert it was.

Robert Yasui was accepted by Temple Medical School in Philadelphia, went on to intern in Allentown and complete his residency in the
small north-central Pennsylvania town of Williamsport, where he was
the only person of Japanese descent. The older doctors liked him because he worked harder and longer than anyone else. He "walked the
extra mile," they said. The insulated community accepted him as one-of-
a-kind, even tolerating to some extent his dating of white student nurses,
including—and soon exclusively—Phyllis Hoffman, a pretty twenty-
one-year-old whose father was a Protestant minister in a nearby town.

Phyllis's friends were openly critical of her relationship with Shu, but
her parents practiced what they preached: Christian love and the broth-
erhood of man. Despite a degree of local censure, the Hoffmans welcomed Shu into their home and their lives. A quiet, industrious, church-
going Christian who clearly had a solid professional career in front of
him, Shu made a good impression on the Hoffmans. But the Yasuis, con-
ditioned by decades of intolerance, were a bit more circumspect about
the match. When Shu and Phyllis announced marriage plans, Homer
wrote to his soon-to-be sister-in-law: "By the very nature of your impending marriage, mixed as it is, you and Bob are going to run into a lot
of problems which sometimes are going to be pretty tough to solve."
But Homer offered both his help and support. "Good luck, Phyllis," he
wrote in closing, "remember, if the going ever gets rough, we're rooting
for you." Masuo may have been skeptical about the marriage, but he too
gave his blessing. "We believe that you will like us and we hope you will
never be disappointed or regret having joined our family," he wrote to
Phyllis. On September 20, 1952, Shu broke the ultimate barrier and became the first Yasui to marry a Caucasian. Phyllis's father married them
in his church. Masuo and Shidzuyo did not come East for the wedding.

Except for two years with the army in Germany, Shu never ventured
far from Williamsport. The town accepted him, and he repaid the debt
by becoming one of its most energetic public servants. For many years

he volunteered his time to serve as the athletic physician for the local college, high school and junior high as well as the annual Little League World Series. He served on the local boards of the American Red Cross, the YMCA, Boy Scouts, Kiwanis and the Firemen's Commission, worked on area political campaigns and was recognized with numerous service awards as well as an honorary doctorate.

Homer followed his brother into medicine and also followed him to Philadelphia, where the brothers lived together for two years while both were students. Homer had applied to ten schools, with grades more than good enough to qualify him for acceptance anywhere, but only Hahnemann Medical College had opened its doors to him. The dean there, known to have a special empathy for minorities, was, Homer suspected, personally responsible for his acceptance. In 1949, degree in hand, he went to Milwaukee for his internship and then Poughkeepsie for a general residency. It was there he decided against specializing in obstetrics—it was too hard on a man who loved to sleep as much as Homer did—and once again followed the lead of his older brother into general surgery. Meanwhile he met and married Miyuki Yabe, a California *nisei* who had been interned in Wyoming and then came East with her mother to relocate.

As the two were considering where Homer would go for his surgical residency—San Francisco was their initial choice—Masuo wrote to his son that it would be nice if he could arrange to come "home," home now being Portland. Still a dutiful son at age thirty, Homer accepted a residency there, dividing his time between surgical duties and his growing responsibilities as a family man. He and Miyuki had two daughters in quick succession and later adopted a baby boy after their own newborn son died in the hospital. After a stint with the navy in Japan, Homer worked hard to establish himself. But it was tough going.

It took him almost five years to create a viable surgical practice in a small town southeast of Portland, a location he carefully chose because there were no other surgeons there. Still, referrals from his *hakujin* colleagues came in very slowly. He made ends meet by conducting physical exams for the Red Cross and the National Guard. He volunteered in the emergency room. "Getting started in any profession is a rough business," Min wrote to his younger brother consolingly. "You have to take a lot of charity cases, and cases of dubious financial rewards. But you have a future before you." In fact Homer's practice did grow, as he ironically began to reap the benefits of reverse prejudice: the Japanese were thought of as superb technicians who were skillful with their hands. According to the stereotype, a surgeon of Japanese descent might be even more desirable than a white doctor. Through the years, Homer found that the vast majority of his patients—like the people in his own neighborhood—were white. But he kept close ties to the *nikkei* community through the JACL. Both he and Miyuki served as local chapter presidents and were involved in some way in virtually every activity and issue that concerned Japanese Americans, from changing the official U.S. abbreviation of Japan ("Jap." with its echoes of past racism, was unacceptable; "Jpn." was the new suggestion) to developing museum exhibits to fighting for national legislation.

Of all the Yasui *nisei*, Yuka alone forged strong ties with her parents' homeland by virtue of her marriage to a Japanese national. After graduating from the University of Oregon in the early 1950s, she went to Yale for a degree in public health nursing, although she would rather have gone to medical school like Shu and Homer. But being both a woman and a Japanese American created one too many obstacles for her in fifties America. At Yale she did well and began a career as a nurse, working in Michigan and then back in Connecticut until a Fulbright took her to Japan to study that country's birth-control policies. There she met a young doctor, Toshio Fujikura, whom she married and accompanied back to America. Until her first child was born, she worked as a visiting nurse while her husband completed a residency in pathology. Later she devoted herself to family-planning causes, spending much of her working life as a full-time volunteer for Planned Parenthood. When her four children were self-sufficient, Yuka and her husband divided their time between their home in the Washington, D.C., area and Japan, where Toshio held a succession of important medical posts. In the land of her ancestors, Yuka learned the language but, with her bold walk, direct gaze and ready laugh, was never mistaken for a native.

Most of the *nisei* generation lived life conservatively, choosing and staying with traditional jobs and establishing themselves firmly in the middle class. They took few chances: Chop stayed in Hood River; Shu never left Williamsport. Michi taught at the same school for thirty years; Homer and Miyuki lived in the same house for thirty-five years. The Yasuis' less than adventuresome lifestyle, like that of their generation, was not a result of the *nisei* having a long and vested interest in the status quo. It was rather, as one writer put it, "a reflection of the price they had to pay to achieve it."

They were the generation who had to prove themselves better in order to be considered merely equal, the "we try harder" generation, as outspoken sociologist Harry Kitano once put it, who came of age behind barbed wire and well understood the fragility of their place in American society. They were the diligent, industrious, law-abiding generation who knew that those who made waves might very well drown in the mainstream. They were, as *nisei* journalist Bill Hosokawa put it, "the quiet Americans." But not Min.

Energetic, combative, always more than willing to stick his neck out for a cause, Min was on the front lines all his life. As a civil rights activist and political gadfly, he fought for the rights of all minorities. But his most important battle was one that helped transform the *nisei* from a silent generation who hid the past from their own children to committed activists who insisted that the federal government publicly apologize for and redress the mistakes of evacuation and internment.

To mount a public fight for redress, the *nisei* had to decide to open old wounds. They knew they risked disapproval, not only of a considerable segment of the white population who continued to believe that the wartime treatment of Japanese Americans was justified, but also of the more conservative *nisei* who didn't want anything to threaten their hard-earned place in American society. If we rock the boat, we will lose what we have, some *nisei* cautioned. In places like Hood River, where the road to acceptance had been long and rocky, there was considerable resistance to the idea of redress and reparations. "I think we've been more accepted by our Caucasian neighbors because we don't really get excited about racial issues," one of Chop's sons told a sociologist. Maintaining a low profile was necessary for continued acceptance, he thought.

But for many, it was not a matter of balancing current levels of acceptance with future risk. It was not a rational matter. Redress was a visceral issue. "All of us had a hard knot of bitterness and anger in our gut," one of the movement's activists once explained. Demanding redress was something they had to do, both for their own self-esteem and as a legacy to their children, the *sansei*. The *sansei* had come of age during the social upheavals of the 1960s, when civil disobedience and mass resistance were seen as viable reactions to government policy. Many couldn't understand—once they finally discovered the "secret" of internment that their parents had kept hidden from them—why their parents hadn't actively resisted evacuation. In fighting for redress the *nisei* were proving to their children that ultimately they did not and would not accept the legitimacy of their wartime treatment. Finally, thirty years later, the *nisei* were saying loudly and publicly: We will no longer be ashamed of what happened to us; you, the government, should be ashamed of what you did to us.

Redress was a fight of the little guy against the government, a fight for principle against great odds. It was Min Yasui's kind of fight. And he was involved almost from the beginning when, in the mid-1970s, JACL started talking seriously about mounting a campaign for national redress legislation. The idea was that the U.S. government should publicly admit wrongdoing and formally apologize for wartime treatment of Japanese Americans. The apology, many thought, should be backed by tangible compensation that proved the seriousness and commitment of the federal government. One wing of the movement called for an immediate congressional vote; another pressed for a class-action suit. Min, who became chairman of the JACL's national committee on redress and traveled thousands of miles to drum up support for the issue, endorsed a more cautious path: lobbying for the establishment of a commission to investigate the effects of evacuation and internment and suggest remedies. A prestigious, congressionally appointed panel, the JACL hoped, would add both visibility and validity to their movement, enhancing its chances of success.

It took Min and others years of exerting pressure on local representatives, years of speech making, lobbying and letter writing before Congress finally, in 1980, voted to establish and fund the nine-member Commission on Wartime Relocation and Internment. Headed by Joan Z. Bernstein, a Washington, D.C., lawyer and former Carter administration official and including an erstwhile Supreme Court justice, three former congressmen, a Philadelphia judge and a Russian Orthodox priest, it was just the sort of blue-ribbon panel the JACL had hoped for. During the two and a half years the members studied America's wartime treatment of Japanese Americans, they examined more than ten thousand documents and conducted twenty-one days of public hearings in ten cities, listening to the often emotional testimony of more than 750 witnesses. The commission's 1983 report, *Personal Justice Denied*, concluded that evacuation and internment was "a grave injustice . . . conceived in haste and executed in an atmosphere of fear and anger." The wartime policy was not justified by military necessity, said the report. Instead, evidence showed that it was prompted by "race prejudice, war hysteria and a failure of political leadership." To compensate in some way for what the *nikkei* had lost during their years of internment, the commission recommended $1.5 billion in reparations, or about $20,000 to each survivor of internment.

The report was a great victory for Japanese Americans, for JACL, as the instigator of the commission idea, and for Min Yasui, who led the charge. But it was only the beginning. Congress had the report, but what would it do with it? Could the *nikkei* drum up enough national support in the Senate and House of Representatives to transform the report's recommendations into legislation that would be enacted? It looked like an uphill battle, but it was one to which Min and others were more than willing to lend their energies. In the mid-1980s, after the report came out, Min devoted himself full-time to redress, stepping down from his position with the Denver Commission on Community Relations and spending as many as 250 days a year on the road speaking, organizing and lobbying. In Portland, Homer and Miyuki joined the fray, leading the local JACL in its efforts to attract congressional support.

But as much time as Min devoted to the cause, for him the redress movement was only part of the total picture. Evacuation and internment represented "a grave moral injustice and an unprecedented abrogation of constitutional protections," Min wrote. But so too did his 1942 conviction, which the Supreme Court had let stand. In the midst of the national fight for redress, Min, with both the financial and moral support of his brothers and sisters, mounted a personal battle to overturn his wartime conviction.

The battle may have been personal, but Min's goal wasn't. Of course he wanted to be vindicated. But his real purpose, like the purpose of his original curfew-breaking, was to use his case to have evacuation be declared unconstitutional. With the help of a team of Asian lawyers headed by an energetic, Vassar-educated young *sansei* named Peggy Nagae, Min filed a petition with the Ninth Circuit Court in Portland asking that his conviction be nullified. "We might not win but we're gonna give 'em hell trying," Min told Peggy.

Min's lawyers, in conjunction with legal teams working in Washington State and California on the other wartime cases of Hirabayashi and Korematsu, decided to mount their challenge based on an obscure legal concept none of them had ever used, or even read about in law school, called a writ of *error coram nobis*. A procedural device, it allowed a case to be reopened if new evidence came to light that would have materially affected the outcome of the case had that evidence been revealed at the time. And in the early 1980s new evidence had come to light: documented proof from the government's own files that high-placed officials, assessing the situation in early 1942, had seen no reason to evacuate Japanese Americans. These memos and letters—from the Office of Naval Intelligence, the FBI and the Justice Department—were suppressed at the time and never became part of the government's official report.

"The entire Japanese problem has been magnified out of its true proportion largely due to the physical characteristics of the people," Lieutenant Commander K. Ringle of the Office of Naval Intelligence reported in a February 1942 memo that never saw the light of day. The same month, both J. Edgar Hoover and the chairman of the Federal Communications Commission wrote memos stating that there was no evidence of "illicit signalling" or unlawful use of the radio waves by any Japanese American. Not only did the government's wartime report on evacuation omit this evidence but it also included direct statements about espionage activities that were categorically denied by the official agencies that investigated them. "There is no doubt these statements were intentional falsehoods," a Justice Department attorney wrote to his boss during the war.

Back in 1943, when the Supreme Court had upheld Min's and the two other men's convictions, it had done so by accepting the government's claim that mass evacuation was a military necessity. But this new evidence showed that a number of ranking officials didn't think it was a necessity. If the Supreme Court had had access to these memos, would it still have upheld the convictions? Min, Peggy Nagae and the other young lawyers thought not. They wanted another day in court.

On January 16, 1984, they got it when the case of *United States of America v. Minoru Yasui* reopened in Portland. Stopping briefly in the midst of a hectic speaking and fund-raising tour for redress, Min addressed the court of Robert C. Belloni, emphasizing the importance of the case. "It is true that I am but an insignificant individual," he told the judge. "But this case does not involve just me as a person, nor does it involve just Japanese Americans. It involves Americans, all Americans, who believe in the dream of equality and freedom and justice."

Peggy Nagae echoed Min's sentiments in her own opening statement. "This is an important case, not simply for Minoru Yasui . . . it is also important for the people, including my parents who are sitting in this courtroom, who were interned during that period of their lives. It is an issue and a case that speaks to every American who believes in democracy, who believes in the rights of individuals. . . ." She told the judge that Min and all Japanese Americans wouldn't be able to put that chapter of their lives behind them unless the court "reaffirms their belief in justice, reaffirms their belief in democracy and the right of each individual . . . to be found guilty on the basis of his actions and not on the basis of his race."

The government admitted that Min "may have been improperly condemned"—in fact, government attorneys did not oppose Min's petition to nullify his conviction—but they did not want the case to turn into a forum for debating America's wartime policies. And they certainly did not want what Min and his lawyers were fighting for: to force the government to admit that evacuation and internment were constitutional violations. "We don't think that it serves any purpose to clear one party by loosely condemning others," government lawyer Victor Stone told the judge.

Belloni agreed. He vacated Min's conviction but refused to consider allegations of government misconduct. He made the decision without opening up the trial to a hearing of the evidence, which was the forum Min and Peggy Nagae were hoping for. An evidentiary hearing was the platform that would have allowed them to introduce the Ringle memo and make the case that war-time restrictions on Japanese Americans, from curfew to internment, were racially and not militarily motivated.

Peggy had trouble getting hold of Min to tell him the verdict. He was on the road for redress again, never in one place for more than a day or two. When she finally did catch up to him with the good news that his forty-year-old conviction for breaking curfew had been nullified, he was sorely disappointed. He told Peggy that the verdict in his favor was "a hollow personal victory" and instructed her to immediately appeal the case to the next judicial level.

It was while the court was reviewing the case, in the summer of 1986, that Min began complaining of a persistent pain in his back. It bothered him in June when he came to Oregon to watch his sister Michi go through the University of Oregon graduation ceremony she had been forbidden to participate in forty-four years before. The university made an event of it, personally inviting all of Michi's siblings and children, honoring her with a special reception and placing her on the stage next to university dignitaries. When she stood to receive her diploma and give a short speech, the crowd, which included all the Yasui *nisei*, responded with a standing ovation.

Min was in pain and feeling tired, but it didn't slow him down. From Eugene, he continued on yet another speaking and fund-raising tour, both for redress and his own case, until late that summer when he stopped in Chicago for the national JACL convention. The pain was getting worse, and he could no longer ignore it. By the time Min made it to the doctor for a diagnosis, his lung cancer had already metastasized below the diaphragm and into his back.

He didn't want to, but he had to give up his grueling schedule as well as his leadership of the redress movement. "I truly deplore quitting the movement at this juncture—but the physical deterioration of my bodily functions needs to be faced realistically," he wrote to a JACL colleague. Soon thereafter he entered a Denver hospital for surgery, where doctors removed as much of the cancer as they could and put him on chemotherapy. He never really regained his strength after the operation. That fall he was shaky and weak, thin, drawn, mostly confined to a wheelchair. But he continued to grant interviews about his case and in September walked unsteadily to a podium to give a speech on redress. He was receiving intravenous chemotherapy at home, but by late October his condition had so deteriorated that he entered the hospital again.

In early November, Homer flew to Denver to sit beside the hospital bed of his seventy-year-old brother. Homer had been a stalwart supporter of Min's *coram nobis* case and had personally headed the fund-raising efforts of a large group of family and friends. He asked his brother what he wanted done with the case. "I want the good battle to the very bitter end," Min told him. A week and a half later Min was dead.

The government moved quickly to dismiss the case, which was stalled at the Ninth Circuit Court of Appeals. The petitioner was dead, the government argued. The case was moot. But Peggy Nagae argued, as she had argued before the district court, that the case was not just about Min. He represented all Japanese Americans who were forced to obey the government's wartime policies. The case was about a larger issue, equality under the law, and should not die with the petitioner. "We will continue to press Min's case," Peggy announced to the media. "That's what he wanted, and that's what we want to do." Two months after Min's death, his widow, flanked by his daughter Holly, Homer, Peggy Nagae and a phalanx of former internees from all ten camps, held a dramatic press conference in San Francisco to plead for the continuation of his case. The event received widespread media coverage but failed to convince the Ninth Circuit Court of Appeals, which dismissed the case that spring.

Still the Yasuis pressed on. In a final attempt, Peggy filed a petition with the Supreme Court, asking it to hear the case. "All of the Yasuis are committed for a goddamn showdown with the Supreme Court," Homer wrote to Peggy in June. Homer could be as stubborn and combative as his older brother. He had a death-bed wish to honor, and he fully intended to honor it. "We will come up with whatever it requires to keep the case alive, no matter how unlikely it is that the Court will grant the writ. Please keep plugging away. . . . If we have to hammer it out toe to toe with anybody, let's do it."

These were fighting words. But while the Yasuis may have been willing to do battle, the Supreme Court was not. In early October the Court denied Min's petition. Homer refused to give up. "We are still committed to carrying this battle as far as the human spirit, heart and mind can take us," he wrote in a letter to members of the Min Yasui Memorial Fund, a group set up to raise money for the case. "Whatever the ultimate outcome . . . may be, everyone should keep in mind that we all gave it the best shot we could."

A few weeks later Peggy filed a second petition with the Supreme Court, asking it to reconsider its original denial. On November 30, 1987, the Court sent back its final word on the subject: it refused to hear the case. All remedial appeals had been exhausted. "We did all we could," Homer told a friend. "We followed it as far as we could, just as he wanted us to." Min had gone down fighting. Homer and the rest of the family had been by his side in life and in death.

The battle over the 1942 conviction was over, but the redress movement, minus Min's leadership, was still going strong. Using the report by the Commission on Wartime Relocation and Internment, congressional allies now carried the torch. During the 1985-86 congressional session, Representative James Wright and Senator Spark Matsunaga had introduced a bill that called for a formal apology and financial reparations to all survivors of internment. In September 1987, not quite a year after Min's death, the House of Representatives voted almost 2 to 1 for the redress bill. In spring of the next year, the Senate approved it by a 70 percent majority.

On August 10, 1988, the long battle for redress officially ended when President Ronald Reagan signed into law the Civil Liberties Act of 1988. It called for the government to issue individual apologies for all violations of civil liberties and constitutional rights, backing up the words with $20,000 tax-free payments to each internment survivor. Even with all that, the government was still hedging its bets. "It's not for us to pass judgment upon those who may have made mistakes while engaged in [World War II]," Reagan told an audience of two hundred of the bill's most ardent supporters gathered to watch the signing. "Yet we must recognize that the internment of Japanese Americans was just that, a mistake." Later in his brief speech the president came on stronger: "What is important in this bill has less to do with property than with honor, for here we admit a wrong. Here, we reaffirm our commitment as a nation to equal justice under the law."

Homer was in the audience listening. He and a JACL contingent had taken the red-eye from Seattle to Washington, D.C., to witness the signing. As Reagan finished his speech the *nikkei* crowd—sedate, undemonstrative middle-aged men and women—began cheering, hugging and kissing each other, pounding one another on the back. Many had tears in their eyes. Homer did too, but it was Min, not the redress bill, he was thinking of at that moment. Min should be here for this, Homer thought. This is Min's moment.

The winning of reparations was in many ways the *nisei*'s swan song. They had proved to themselves and to their children that they could stand up for their rights. Now it was time for the *sansei*, the next generation, to take center stage.

part three

Sansei
The Third Generation

14

Willow Flat

Flip and Tom, Chop's middle-aged sons, sit on the raised brick hearth, their backs warmed by the apple-wood logs burning in the fireplace, their faces lit by the pale morning light of Oregon winter. The light comes in the floor-to-ceiling windows of Flip's Willow Flat home, perched thirteen hundred feet above the floor of the Hood River valley. Out the windows, the view stretches unobstructed for more than forty miles across thousands of acres of fruit orchards, across the town of Odell and the city of Hood River, across the Columbia and well into southwest Washington to the snowy peak of twelve-thousand-foot Mount Adams.

But Flip and Tom hardly ever glance out the windows. And when they do, they don't see the breathtaking panorama, which they take for granted after more than forty years of living in the valley—they see apple trees that need pruning and pear trees that need fertilizing. A thin fog is rolling back up the valley. Outside, the air is ripe with the smell of sheep manure that a crew of Mexican workers is spreading on a nearby orchard. Flip puts a few more logs on the fire. "It'll be sunny by ten-thirty," he announces. Tom nods.

Flip is boyish and trim with a full head of dazzling black hair. He has a wonderful grin, which he mostly keeps to himself. In his usual uniform of grimy mechanic's overalls over jeans and a T-shirt with a baseball cap perched backward on his head, he looks like a kid. He moves with quick self-assurance but is quiet, shy, and uncomfortable around people the way a teenager would be. He's forty-six. Nowhere is he happier than sitting astride his tractor. He loves the land with a passion far beyond that of a man who makes his living from it.

Next to him, Tom, two and a half years his senior, looks like a man from a different class and another generation. The thick glasses and thinning salt-and-pepper hair make him look studious and professional. In his button-down shirt and casual slacks he could be a pharmacist, an insurance agent, a Kiwanis Club regular. In fact, he is at ease dealing with the local business community and its leaders. Unlike Flip, he knows how to chat. Tom works the farm too, but for him it is just a living. He'd rather be drinking coffee at J.R.'s Corral, the local farmers' hangout back down the road in Odell.

The brothers live less than a quarter mile from each other and meet several times a day, but they live very different lives. Flip and his voluble, independent-minded wife, Maija, have three children, two of them in college. They live in what's known as a Northwest contemporary, a casual ranch-style home with a vaulted ceiling in the living room and extensive wooden decks out the sliding glass doors. The house has now gone slightly shabby since Maija designed it fifteen years ago and the two of them built it with the help of local labor, but it's a likable, reassuring shabbiness. It's the kind of place where little kids can jump on the couch, where dishes get done when they get done. It's a house that has comfortably played host to large family gatherings.

Down the road, Tom lives in the same tiny one-bedroom cottage he has lived in since he graduated from college more than twenty-five years ago. The little square house, which has been on the property as long as anyone can remember, is jammed with the accumulation of several lives. Tom and his first wife lived here. Now he and his second wife live here. Several years ago, at age forty-five, Tom became a father for the first time. The baby sleeps in what used to be the laundry room. The laundry is sorted and folded on the living room couch.

Together the brothers farm the 208 acres that is now Willow Flat ranch. Over the years they've added some orchard blocks to the land their father, Chop, worked all his life, the property their grandfather Masuo bought seventy years ago. With its 115 acres of pears, 45 of cherries and 15 of apples, Willow Flat is the valley's third largest family-owned orchard. In a good year, when everything goes right, the business can clear as much as three quarters of a million dollars. But in a bad year, the fruit can be decimated by early frosts or hard rain or no rain or codling moths or pear psylla, or the market can collapse, as it did after the Alar scare. In those years the brothers have to go down to the bank in Hood River and mortgage off pieces of their property just to meet expenses. During the past twenty years, they've had their share of both good and bad years. But in general the nineties have been good. In 1992, the Yasui brothers and their crew of thirty seasonal workers harvested three million pounds of pears and apples and two hundred thousand pounds of cherries.

Regardless of whether the farm makes or loses money, the brothers work hard. In the winter there are almost two hundred acres of pruning to be done. In the spring it's time to clean up the brush, fertilize and spray. Come July the cherries are ready. In August and September it's pears; in October the apples come in. There are seasonal workers to be managed, crews to be overseen, inspectors to be dealt with, books to be kept. From May on, Flip and Tom work many fourteen-hour days, jumping on their tractors as soon as it gets light. Flip, who's in charge of the pear and apple harvests, some of the spraying, managing the crew and keeping the books, works seven days a week and couldn't imagine life being otherwise. Although weekends and traditional vacation times have no meaning for him, he does occasionally steal an hour or two for fishing, an entire morning for hunting or, about every other month, a full day of self-indulgence in Reno. It's an hour by car to the Portland airport, an hour to Reno on a special excursion plane and eight hours of serious gambling before he catches a ten o'clock plane home. The next morning he's up and out on his tractor before dawn.

Tom is also a dedicated gambler who loves Reno, the state lottery games and just about any bet he can get. He works hard during the cherry harvest and does much of the spraying but still takes on a less grueling workload than his younger brother. The inequality is not a source of tension. It's something the brothers have worked out wordlessly over the years. No one has ever heard them argue. In fact, they rarely even discuss decisions. One brother just takes action and then later tells the other brother about it. Somehow it works.

Farming is the only life Flip and Tom know. They grew up on Willow Flat less than a half mile from their present homes and watched their father work the land all through the fifties, sixties and seventies. In those days the farm was fifty acres smaller and, with younger trees and less advanced methods, not as productive as it is today. The farm supported Chop, Mikie and their three children, but they lived modestly in a tidy two-bedroom home that was so small the two boys slept in a trailer permanently parked in the backyard. But Flip and Tom had it much easier than the generation before them. They didn't have to rush home after school to work in the orchards or do hours of chores. There was always enough help at the farm. In the summer they drove tractors and did some picking, but they never had to work as hard or as long as their father and their uncles had to when they were growing up.

By the late 1950s Willow Flat was doing well. Many of the orchards were in their prime, and fruit prices were good and holding steady. Chop and Mikie had squirreled away enough money to build a new house, a modern ranch-style home with a bedroom for each of the children and big picture windows overlooking the valley. They built it just a few hundred feet from their old place and moved in Easter Sunday of 1959.

Both boys went to Wy'east, the rural six-hundred-student high school up the valley, and, like their father, they measured the school year not by courses and exams but by seasons: in the fall, they played football; in the winter, basketball; and in the spring, baseball. Both boys had many friends, most of them Caucasian like the complexion of the school, and both were popular enough to be elected student-body president during their senior years. Unlike Masuo, who pressured his children to do well in school and frequently lectured them on proper behavior, Chop never came down hard on his sons when their grades slipped or they were involved in minor mischief. In fact, he seemed to enjoy their modest teenage rebellions.

The boys' childhood was significantly different from their father's in other ways. Growing up in the decades after the war when so many valley *nikkei* did not return to Hood River, they lived in a much whiter society than their father had, with the Japanese American population less than a quarter of its prewar size. Flip and Tom had few *nikkei* classmates; almost all of their friends, including girlfriends, were white. It was not that Hood River had become color-blind—in fact, Tom was rebuffed in high school by at least one girl solely because of his race—it was that the Japanese population had become so small that there were far too few of them to interact only with one another. There were far too few of them to be threatening.

But it wasn't just numbers. The *nikkei*, now in their third generation in the valley, could no longer be viewed as exotic foreigners. True, they still had Japanese faces, but most of the *sansei* knew as little about Japan and its culture as did their white counterparts. They were about as exotic as the boy next door. Their parents had made sure of that.

Like so many *nisei* who had experienced the trauma of internment, Chop shielded his children from their past. Internment was not a topic of conversation. Wartime hardships were trivialized and laughingly dismissed with comments like "We managed." Chop's children did not learn of their grandfather's suicide until more than thirty years after the fact and then only through the historical investigations of one of their cousins. But it was more than Chop's silence that helped form the world of his children.

The *issei* had wanted their children to be Americans, but they had also wanted to preserve and protect what they considered the best of the Japanese culture. Masuo and his counterparts gave their American-born children Japanese names and sent them to Japanese school to learn the language. They lectured them on the samurai code. They taught and reinforced the psychology and social behavior of the old country. But the *nisei* were far less ambivalent about their own children's Americanism. Chop and most of his generation purposefully distanced themselves and their children from all that was Japanese. Being Japanese was the "crime" that had sent the *nisei* and their parents to the camps. In the decades after the war they did not want their children to grow up being guilty of the same offense. Thus many of the *sansei*, especially those who came of age in virtually all-white communities like Hood River, grew up almost oblivious to their Japanese heritage. Except for preferring rice to potatoes and celebrating New Year's with a special feast, Flip and Tom differed little from their valley classmates. Today, Japanese features notwithstanding, Flip considers himself a person of no particular ethnicity. He shrugs his shoulders when asked about his identity as a Japanese American. He has never thought about it, he says. He's just Flip, a farmer. At the dinner table his Finnish American wife and youngest son sometimes eat with chopsticks. Flip always uses a fork.

For the *sansei*, almost aggressive acculturation at the hands of their parents was a common childhood experience. "The nail that sticks up gets hammered," went the old Japanese proverb. To the *nisei* the saying amounted to a clarion call for assimilation. If they could spare their children the ostracism they had suffered, it would be worth anything, including losing any vestige of their ethnic identity. The *nisei* did such a good job that by the mid-1960s a Japanese American sociologist declared the *sansei* "almost totally acculturated." In the families themselves the push toward assimilation was so powerful that some *sansei* boasted of their cultural ignorance. Wrote *sansei* poet David Mura, born and raised in the Midwest: "I certainly did not want to be thought of as a Japanese American. I was an American, pure and simple. I was proud I didn't know Japanese, that English was my sole tongue."

But the message *sansei* were receiving from their parents was not wholly consistent. "Be proud of your family," the *nisei* told their children. But, at the same time, by hiding their own past, as if internment had somehow been their fault, as if the shame was theirs and not the United States government's, the *nisei* unwittingly taught their children to be ashamed of their own ethnic heritage. "You are an American; you are anyone's equal," they told their children. But the *nisei* also stressed achievement and academic excellence, the silent message being that—as their own parents had taught them—one must outperform one's peers just to be considered their equal.

The confusing double messages they received from home were amplified by their own experiences as they made their way in the world. Few *sansei* were the victims of the kind of direct hostility and overt racism that had plagued their parents and grandparents. In fact, the erstwhile "yellow peril" was now being widely praised as the "model minority." A 1966 *California Living* magazine article invited its readers to "meet the third generation Japanese Americans who face a problem without precedent—they're too good to be true." In the JACL's newspaper, *The Pacific Citizen*, that same year, the *sansei* were heralded as "universally liked and accepted with a better record than any other group in society, including the white majority."

But the very concept of a model minority was racist at its core, and traits the *sansei* were praised for quickly became a straitjacket of stereotypes. They were bookish and obedient, quiet, unemotional and nonthreatening—a stereotype that precluded them from being thought of as having creative or leadership abilities. Told repeatedly by their parents and others that they were fully integrated into mainstream American life, many still had the experience of being complimented by strangers for "speaking English so well." They were third-generation Americans who were not at home in their own country. As one of the *sansei* leaders of the JACL wrote in the late 1980s: "We feel we're a guest in someone else's house, that we can never really relax and put our feet on the table."

Theirs was a schizophrenia just as intense as their *nisei* parents', but because it wasn't acknowledged to even exist, it was potentially more damaging to their identities than the less subtle personality crises of the past generations. Unlike their parents, who knew they lived with a foot in both worlds, the *sansei* grew up believing in their complete Americanism. But it wasn't as complete as they thought, not just because the society around them was racist and looked first at their Japanese faces, but also because, inside themselves, they carried the legacy of their ethnicity.

In the 1960s, sociologists had busied themselves by charting the third generation's remarkable assimilation. But in the decades after the black, brown and red pride movements, when cultural identity became something to herald rather than hide, social scientists began discovering the persistence of "Japanese-ness" in their third-generation research subjects. The *sansei*, it turned out, were more competitive than their white counterparts, but also less aggressive. They had both stronger aspirations for success and a greater fear of failure. They felt a stronger sense of obligation, especially to their parents, than did their white peers, which resulted in closer family ties and greater deference to elders. But none of these traits were as pronounced in the third generation as they had been in the second. In fact, the *sansei* seemed as different from their own parents as they were from their white counterparts. That left them in a limbo every bit as unsettling as the one their parents had experienced in their formative years. Identity crises, some repressed and never acknowledged, others openly explored, were a part of most *sansei*'s experiences.

But despite their common characteristics, the *sansei* are far from being a homogeneous group. In fact, in many ways they are as diverse as the baby-boomer generation of which they are a small part. For some the social upheavals of the late 1960s had lasting effects: among the Yasui *sansei* there is a political activist, an expatriate, a holistic health practitioner and a vegetarian ruralist with children named Sage and Zen. But, among the twenty-seven grandchildren of Masuo and Shidzuyo, there is also a dentist, a doctor, several teachers, a computer analyst, a business administrator, a Hollywood talent coordinator and a drummer in a heavy-metal rock band.

In Hood River, the closed rural enclave that had made life so uncomfortable for two generations of ethnic Japanese, the third generation didn't feel it had the luxury of a full-blown identity crisis. Local *sansei* had only two choices. They could stay in the valley and become invisible, a hammered-down nail—"We have to live here. . . . We can't really say how we feel," a Hood River *sansei* confessed to a sociologist in the late 1980s—or they could leave. Flip and Tom chose the first option; their older sister, Joan, took the second.

Smart, talented and oriented toward achievement, Joan, the first Yasui *sansei*, was just what the sociologists were talking about when they called the third generation a "collective miracle" and an "unprecedented success story." An excellent student who was also developing into a fine pianist, Joan was both the first girl and the first Japanese American to be elected student-body president of Wy'east High School. At the University of Oregon, where she studied sociology, she served in the cabinet of the student government, as secretary of the Associated Women Students and as a dorm leader, all of which won her election to an exclusive women's service honorary. In November of 1962, at the beginning of her junior year, she was crowned homecoming queen. Hoping to pursue a career in social work, she went East to Bryn Mawr, where she earned a master's degree. Joan's younger cousins, especially the girls, were awed and a bit intimidated by what one cousin later called "her talent, her grades, her beauty, her everything." Perhaps her brothers were also somewhat awed.

Beyond following their sister into leadership of the student body at Wy'east, Flip and Tom seemed completely uninterested in accumulating achievements or, as an inordinate percentage of *sansei* were doing, educating themselves for the professions. After high school, both boys went to college more because it was expected of a Yasui than because of some burning intellectual desire or career ambition. They put in their time at Oregon State University, Chop's old school, a quiet outpost almost untouched by the political and cultural ferment of the late 1960s. Other *sansei*, who went to more worldly schools and were exposed to the social-justice movements of the time, emerged from the decade with a raised awareness of their ethnicity that led to a vibrant Asian Studies movement on campuses from Berkeley to Vassar. But Flip and Tom, cloistered rural kids at a cloistered agricultural college in a sleepy Oregon town, were unaffected by the tumultuous sixties. Neither found anything at Oregon State that caused him to question himself or society. Both boys were called to military service and would have served had not health problems—Tom's poor eyesight and Flip's severe allergies—kept them from duty.

During his years at college, Tom changed his major so often that today he barely remembers what he got his degree in. Flip majored in wildlife management, primarily because he loved the outdoors. Both thought briefly about careers other than farming, but soon after graduation, Tom in 1967, Flip in 1969, they came back to Willow Flat to work the land, bringing their new wives with them. Both were Caucasian girls the brothers had dated at college.

Tom's wife, Cheryl, was the daughter of poor farmers who ran some cattle in an arid, remote section of northeastern Oregon. To her, the Yasuis' middle-class life-style seemed sophisticated, almost opulent. Flip's wife, Maija, a local girl he knew slightly from high school, came from a big, close-knit Finnish family that had settled in the valley in the early 1900s. Her father had raised his four children alone on what could euphemistically be called a limited budget. When Flip brought Maija home to meet his parents during spring break of her freshman year, she found herself seated in a formal dining room at a table set with fine china and more silverware than she had ever seen. Four forks lay by her plate. After crab cocktail, Mikie served individual Cornish game hens. Maija was so nervous that she spilled applesauce on the white linen tablecloth. Despite the rocky start, Chop and Mikie loved Maija, who was as warm and sociable as their own son was self-contained. The two were officially engaged that Christmas when Flip arrived at Maija's house with a dozen roses and were married the following summer. Meanwhile, Joan had also married a Caucasian, an eleventh-generation WASP who was a descendant of Ralph Waldo Emerson.

The first Yasui *sansei* had married "out," as the saying goes. And one by one, over the next twenty years, all of their cousins who married followed suit. The Yasui *sansei* chose mostly Caucasians as their spouses, but the new family members also included an Egyptian Jew, an Iranian, an East Indian and a Filipino American. Of the eighteen married cousins, only Tom—much later and the second time around—married a fellow nikkei.

Outmarriage, so much more prevalent among Japanese Americans than any other racial minority in the nation, can be seen as a natural step in the assimilation process, a sign that Japanese Americans are increasingly accepted as equals by white society. Or it can be viewed without any political context: a simple matter of people falling in love with the partners of their choice. But with an outmarriage rate now between 60 and 70 percent (compared with 13 percent for Chinese Americans and 16 percent for Mexican Americans), it seems likely that something else is at work in the lives of the sansei. In fact, it may be that outmarriage, the mingling of the races, is the ironic result of a distinct history of American racism.

The Japanese had always been a tiny minority in the United States, a mere thread in the patchwork quilt. U.S. immigration policy had made sure of that. But prior to World War II, most nikkei lived near one another either in West Coast cities or on nearby agricultural land and had the opportunity to interact with one another in school and ethnic community organizations. They married the men and women whose families they grew up knowing. The *issei* outmarriage rate was barely 1 percent; the more worldly *nisei*, not even 10 percent. But the diaspora following internment meant that many Japanese Americans lived and raised their families in far-flung communities with little or no *nikkei* population, such as Shu's adopted hometown of Williamsport, Pennsylvania. All through high school and into college, the *sansei* dated who was there: Caucasians.

Even those who could pave chosen a *nikkei* mate may have married out in a subconscious effort to raise their own self-esteem (low, according to sociologists) or prove their Americanism (still under question because of their Japanese faces) or improve the chance of their future offspring's acceptance (the more white, the better). As author Jeanne Wakatsuki Houston wrote of her marriage to a Caucasian: "I . . . saw him as my Anglo Samurai, wielding his sword of integrity, slaying the dragons that prevented my acceptance as an equal human being in his world. . . ." For some sansei, marrying out may have been one way to put further distance between themselves and their ethnic roots, just what many of their parents had been telling them to do with their concerted push for assimilation and their shamed silence about the past.

American society, saturated by white images and inundated by white ideals of beauty, helped socialize the third generation. In the world of advertising and mass media, the ideal male mate is a tall, muscular man with hair on his chest—not a short, slender, smooth-skinned Japanese man. The ideal woman is a long-legged, chesty, blue-eyed blonde. As sansei poet David Mura, who himself married a Caucasian, wrote, "[Men] often felt that Japanese women with their *dashi* legs—short and thick like a Japanese radish—square hips and small breasts, lacked the beauty and glamour of white women." But sexist stereotypes work in opposite ways too. Some white men actively seek out *nikkei* women, apparently subscribing to the dual (albeit contradictory) stereotype of the Asian woman as submissive and obedient as well as exotic and sexually available. Whatever the lens through which they viewed one another, sansei men and women outmarry at about the same rate.

Sansei who marry non-Japanese mates not only have looser ties with ethnic organizations and activities but also with their own families. But for the Yasui *sansei*, with their outmarriage rate of 95 percent, the family has remained a focal point. Although all but one of their spouses are non-*nikkei*, although their cultural ties are nearly severed, and although they are scattered across the country—from rural Tennessee to Hollywood, from Seattle to Philadelphia, from Boston to Hood River—being a Yasui continues to have meaning in most of their lives. They have a family crest, several formal versions of the family tree and a self-published family memoir. They stage frequent full-scale reunions, where three generations of Yasuis—the aging *nisei*, the sansei and their partners and now the yonsei, their offspring—all don matching T-shirts silk-screened with the Yasui emblem.

Ironically, family seems less important to Flip and Tom, keepers of the Yasui name and business in the family's American birthplace, than to some of their other distant, citified cousins. Ever since the early years of Flip's marriage, it has been his *hakujin* wife, Maija, who has pursued an interest in Yasui family history, in Japanese culture and tradition.

Flip and Maija married in the summer of 1970 and returned to Hood River, where they lived for a time with Chop and Mikie while fixing up the place on Willow Flat that Chan and Obasan had lived in after the war. It was a small gray house, actually a collection of three tiny cabins, that sat near a wooded hill less than a quarter of a mile from Chop and Mikie's home. Behind the house, in a clearing rescued from a tangle of blackberries and poison oak, was a traditional Japanese rock garden Chan had spent years creating. Back in those days, when Chan, Obasan, Chop and Mikie were working hard to resuscitate the orchards from their wartime neglect, Chan had acquired a new nickname, one that stayed with him for the rest of his life: Uncle Datso. It came from his association with a hired hand on Willow Flat. When he saw the hired man in the fields, Chan would always stop to politely ask him how things were going. Then he would cock his head, listening intently to the reply he only half understood, both because he never became fluent in English and because the hired man stuttered badly. Chan would nod his head encouragingly, every few minutes exclaiming, " 's dat so? 's dat so?" He became Datso to friends and family alike.

When Datso died in 1965 at the age of eighty-two, Mrs. Datso, as Obasan had come to be called, stayed in the house alone until the spring of 1970, when she decided to live out her old age back in Japan. Flip and Maija spent every weekend from March to July working on the old house, which was so crammed with antiques, Japanese artifacts and goods from the old Yasui Brothers Store that at first they had to walk through the house following narrow trails Obasan had forged through the window-high accumulation. Flip and Maija finally moved in the next summer, and soon thereafter began to hear strange noises. They would lie in bed at night in the one downstairs bedroom listening to what sounded like footsteps coming down the creaky stairs from the second floor. The footsteps would jolt them from a sound sleep. Then they'd hear the door at the foot of the stairs swing open. Each night Flip would get out of bed to investigate, and each night he would find nothing. One night, after the footsteps descended and the first-floor door creaked open, the door to their own bedroom swung open. They sat up in bed, silent and scared. Another night they heard the sound of breaking glass upstairs. But when both of them investigated, looking in every room, in every cupboard and on every shelf; they could find nothing broken.

Late that summer they began to be awakened by a new sound, a distinctive noise, half whine, half screech, that seemed to come from outside the house. When they peered out the window, they saw nothing but the rock garden and the blackberry-covered hill rising behind it. For several nights in a row they heard the strange screeching. Then they wouldn't hear it for a week or more; then it would begin again. They joked nervously to each other about ghosts—but didn't believe it for a second. Someone was playing a trick on them, they figured. Then one morning Flip decided to work on the little rock path that skirted the house and went into a nearby shed to look for something to haul gravel in. He found a big old cast-iron wheelbarrow with huge pneumatic wheels. As soon as he pushed it toward the house, he and Maija instantly recognized the noise the unoiled wheels made when they scraped against metal. It was the sound they had been hearing outside their window that summer. Okay, they reasoned, momentarily relieved, someone has been pushing this wheelbarrow through our backyard at night. But the next time they heard the sound and rushed outside to investigate, they saw no one. And the wheelbarrow was still in its place in the shed.

When they told Chop of the wheelbarrow and the "haunting," he laughed. "You know," he told them, "Uncle Datso always used to come up that hill behind your house hauling rocks for his garden in that old wheelbarrow." The rock garden was Datso's passion, he told them. Somehow, the information comforted them, and they began to talk of Uncle Datso's ghost. Fifty years before, Chan had delighted in entertaining his young nephews with hair-raising Japanese ghost tales; now he was the main character in his own story. From then on, when Flip and Maija heard the noises at night, they didn't jump up to investigate. They stayed in bed and called out to the ghost of Uncle Datso. "See, Uncle, it's just us," they would say loudly. "We're fine, Uncle Datso, just go on by." They thought perhaps he was searching the house for his wife. "Obasan's not here, Uncle," they told him.

Finally one night, after they'd been awakened four times by bangs, clicks and creaks, Maija, who was leaving for a trip to Japan that next week, had an idea. "Uncle," she called out from bed. "I'm going to Japan. I'm going to visit Obasan. I will tell her that you're looking for her. But, Uncle, she's back in her old hometown, where she wants to be." Maija felt ridiculous talking to the air at two in the morning. And a few days later sitting with Obasan in a farmhouse outside Okayama, she felt ridiculous telling the old woman about the ghost of Uncle Datso. Obasan clearly thought her grandniece was crazy, but she told Maija that when she died half of her ashes would be buried in her homeland and half shipped back to Hood River to be interred at Idlewild cemetery.

Back home at Willow Flat at Datso's house, the creaking and clanking stopped. Doors stayed shut. The squeaky whine of the wheelbarrow was never heard again. When Obasan died in 1988 at the age of one hundred, Chop went to Japan to carry out her final wishes. Her ashes were laid to rest in the Yasui plot beside her husband.

After Datso's ghost left, life quieted down at Willow Flat. Flip and Tom worked hard in the field, and Chop—who now spent most of his days at Diamond Fruit, where he was president of the board, and virtually every weekend avidly pursuing his hobby of trapshooting—felt it was time to pass along the farm to the next generation. Together the father and two sons worked out a plan to shift ownership, with Flip and Tom using yearly profits to buy out Chop's interest over ten years. That meant that through the 1970s, Flip and Maija and Tom and Cheryl lived close to the bone. One year a silver thaw wiped out an entire orchard. The next year fire blight killed acres of pears. But toward the end of the seventies the farm began to prosper. Still, the sons did not. They had to pay significant sums of income tax on profits and then turn over most of the profits to Chop, leaving them with only a few hundred dollars a month to live on. Flip and Maija survived; Tom and Cheryl didn't. In 1979, the year the boys finished paying off their father, Flip, Maija and their two small children left Uncle Datso's place behind and moved into the house they built on a rise overlooking the valley. Tom and Cheryl divorced.

Back in the early seventies it looked briefly as if Flip and Tom would be following in their father's footsteps when both boys served successively as president of the local JACL. But it quickly became apparent that the two did not have their father's exuberant interest in community service. When they were repeatedly asked to run for a place on the Diamond Fruit Company's board of directors—Chop had served as its president for fifteen years—they steadfastly refused. Neither took up where their father had left off as a regional leader in the cherry industry. Neither expressed much interest in the successful sister-city program their father had developed.

But as the eldest son of the eldest son, Tom could not escape feeling some sense of obligation to the family's name and to its place in the local community. Luckily, like his father, but very much unlike his younger brother, he enjoyed the social aspects of community involvement. Tom became a member of the board for the local volunteer fire department and served for almost a dozen years. He agreed to serve both on the board of directors for a local bank and on the Automobile Association of America's board. But mostly he lives his life as an ordinary farmer, concerned with the spraying and the harvest, with drinking coffee and trading stories with the locals, with bowling on Wednesday night and escaping to Reno as often as he can. More recently he has also been concerned with his young family. In the winter of 1981 Tom became the first and only Yasui sansei to marry another Japanese American. Leslie Sakamoto, the daughter of a local orchardist, labored over her wedding gown for three months, then packed it in a valise and flew to Reno with Tom, where the two got married in a quick ceremony with no friends or relatives attending. In November of 1989 Matthew Thomas Yasui, the family's only full-blooded Japanese *yonsei*, was born.

Just up the road, Flip and Maija were raising their family, which now included three children. Flip continued to pour most of his energy into the orchards, economically if not gustatorially enjoying the fruits of his labor. Oddly, Flip had no taste for most apples and didn't care for pears at all. He ate perhaps one piece of fruit a year, and not happily. Flip coached Little League and was an avid local sports booster, especially during the years his daughter, Kim, played softball and his older son, Corey, played football, but he was steadfastly not a joiner. Service organizations, boards of directors and fraternal groups just meant more meetings to him, more time indoors. "I don't volunteer for anything," he says with an almost stubborn pride. "That's Maija's department."

At their home on Willow Flat the phone rings at least a dozen times a day and visitors come by with a frequency known only in the world of television soap operas. They all want to talk with Maija: Maija, who's been president of the board of directors of the Columbia Gorge Center for the mentally handicapped for nine years; Maija, who heads the fund-raising efforts for a new football stadium for the high school; Maija the three-time PTA president, the Red Cross volunteer, the woman who single-handedly brought a kidney dialysis program to Hood River. Maija, the *hakujin*, who served as president, vice president, historian and social chair of the local JACL, who conducted an *issei* oral history project in the valley, who took over administration of Hood River's sister-city program.

Maija, Flip, Leslie, Tom and their families live in a Hood River that is both startlingly different and essentially unchanged from the place Masuo made his name and fortune more than eighty years ago. The valley is still the "pocket of paradise" its boosters claimed it was a century ago, with its patchwork of meticulously tended orchards, its inspiring mountain views and its tranquil life-style. In spring the air still smells of apple blossoms. Hood River itself is still the two-block-wide town it always was, with streets lined with pretty brick buildings and big old houses on the bluffs overlooking the Columbia.

But today Japanese Americans account for an almost negligible 1.5 percent of the valley's population, down from close to 5 percent in the prewar years. And most of the *sansei* who have remained in the valley or who have come home to nest after testing their wings elsewhere have intermarried. Flip and Maija's younger son, Niko, is one of six half-Caucasian, half-Japanese youngsters in his grade school. There are no full-blooded *yonsei* at the school. "The Japs are not our people," the governor

of Oregon had declared some eighty years before. "We cannot assimilate
them and they cannot assimilate us." "A Jap's a Jap," an Oregon newspaper editor had written around the same time. "The melting pot never
even warms him." What no one could even imagine two generations ago
happened quickly, silently and without fanfare: the *nikkei* in Hood River
wove themselves into the fabric of everyday life.

But the town itself still struggles with its century-old demons of racism, bigotry and discrimination. Only now the bitterness is not directed
toward the Japanese. It is directed toward the Mexicans, who came to
work as seasonal laborers and now stay the year around. It is directed
toward the young, monied Californians who come to wind-surf the Columbia River and walk the downtown streets with their long, scraggly
hair and baggy shorts. It is directed toward the liberals who worked to
have sex education and AIDS prevention taught in the schools and who
are now being fought tooth and nail by a growing contingent of Christian fundamentalists.

A thousand feet above it all, astride his favorite tractor, the fifty-year-
old Ford his father bought just after the war, Flip drinks from a thermos
of hot coffee and drives slowly across the rolling acres his grandfather
planted and his father nurtured. Apolitical, solitary and single-minded,
he is oblivious to it all. None of his children have expressed an interest
in following him into farming, and that's fine with him. He can't imagine ever handing over the reins to anyone. Maija looks out the kitchen
window, catching a glimpse of the tractor as it disappears down the hill.
"Flip will farm this place until he dies or until it kills him," she says.

15

The Past Is Prologue

Fifty people sit on hard wooden seats facing the darkened stage of Seattle's downtown Group Theater. It is a quiet and respectful audience, with a sprinkling of teenagers and a tight knot of octogenarians who sit motionless in the front row. Almost everyone is Japanese American. On stage a single spotlight illuminates a bare iron cot. On the cot sits a young *sansei* actor, small and serious in wire-rimmed glasses and a rumpled suit, reading from a copy of the script he has not yet fully memorized. The cot represents a cell on solitary block in Multnomah County jail. The young actor is playing Minoru Yasui. It is Act III, Scene 2, of *Unvanquished*, and "Min" has just learned from his lawyer that the Supreme Court has ruled against him, upholding the constitutionality of the curfew restriction.

> MIN: I can't believe it.
> BERNARD, the lawyer: Min, this isn't the end. There will be many, many more battles for you and your people. Don't give up.
> YUKA'S VOICE (*offstage*): You have to keep fighting.
> Min turns toward the voice but sees only a dark stage.
> He looks back at Bernard forcing a small smile.
> MIN: No, the war isn't over. I'll keep fighting.
> *Bernard pats Min on the back.*

This is the first reading of the play, and the actor portraying Min is not yet comfortable with his role. He delivers the lines without much conviction. He is still feeling his way into the character of the man he is playing.

In the wings, playwright Holly Yasui, Min's youngest daughter, is pacing and chain-chewing Nicorette gum. She is a striking woman with almost a yard of straight, glossy black hair and her father's high cheekbones and dark piercing eyes. She is slender in the way high-strung, nervous people are slender: tight, sinewy, a coiled spring. Like the man she has written her first play about, Holly is intense, forthright, plainspoken and opinionated. Her father called her "spirited and ornery—like me." She pops another piece of gum in her mouth and listens hard as the actors say their lines. Occasionally she makes notes on her own dog-eared copy of the script.

Holly has been thinking of writing about her father's 1942 arrest since the late 1970s, when she was a film student at the University of Southern California. But she never put words on paper. Min was alive then, and she simply could not write about him. His opinion mattered too much to her. It was too much to risk. But years later, after Min's death and the failure of his resurrected wartime case, Holly began meeting informally with two other women interested in her father. Peggy Nagae Lum, a University of Oregon Law School administrator who was now a lawyer in Seattle, had headed Min's *coram nobis* team and was eager to write a law journal article about her experiences with the case. Barbara Bellus Upp was a Methodist minister who had tended to Hood River's *nikkei* flock in the mid-1980s. She met Min only once, in a Chinese restaurant in downtown Hood River, after Obasan's funeral. Barbara, new to her job, had conducted the services; Min had flown in to attend. At the restaurant the two had struck up a conversation, with Min forcefully describing his case. "I just will not believe that justice will not be done," was the last thing Min had said to Barbara. The next time she heard about him, three months later, he was dead. But his story, and the strength of his convictions, stayed with her. Now she was in graduate school contemplating a doctoral dissertation on Min's legal battles.

The three women began meeting at Carson Hot Spring, a rustic turn-of-the-century hotel on the Washington side of the Columbia River west of Hood River. There they soaked in the mineral baths and talked late into the night about Minoru Yasui. In preparation for one of these meetings, Holly wrote what would later become the prologue and the epilogue for her play. Back in her apartment in Seattle, she suffered through countless false starts, finally pushing herself to write one act and submit it to a local theater group. She was astounded when the group accepted the play for a reading. But there was one problem: there was no play—there was only the one act she had submitted. In a fourteen-day frenzy fueled by coffee and Nicorette gum, Holly completed the final two acts of *Unvanquished* that spring, three and a half years after Min's death. The play's first reading in Seattle—the one that had Holly pacing in the wings—led to a much-revised version that won Seattle's 1991 Multicultural Playwrights

Festival award and was produced by the Northwest Asian American Theater. In 1992, fifty years almost to the day that Min walked the streets of northwest Portland to test the curfew restriction, Holly's play opened a few miles away at the Interstate Firehouse Cultural Center. Later that year, on the strength of the play, Holly was awarded a residency at Hedgebrook Cottages, a Northwest retreat for women writers.

Holly took her father's life and amplified it, making it not only into art—which Min, with his plainspoken ways, may not have appreciated—but also into education, which would have pleased Min greatly. Beyond teaching the audience about Min's case and the larger injustice of wartime internment, the play asked its viewers to follow in Min's footsteps, to keep on fighting the good fight. Yuka gives the final speech, a messianic epilogue in which she updates the audience on Min's battles, from his struggle to be admitted to the Colorado bar to his more than forty years as a civil rights activist to the reopening of his wartime case. Min is now dead, she tells the audience. The *coram nobis* case failed. "But the story continues." The pretty young actress playing Yuka stands alone, center stage, speaking the lines with something deeper than theatrical emotion. "The story continues in the people who remember and redeem the past, in the people who dream and create the future. The story continues. It continues with you."

The play is clearly a tribute to Min that is meant to honor his memory and present his life as a model. In fact, it comes close to canonizing him. Holly knows this, and while the playwright in her wants to create a more complex, flawed main character, the daughter in her won't allow it. Holly is just too proud of her father to do anything other than remember and write him as an unblemished hero. But she wasn't always this proud. She wasn't always this comfortable being Min's daughter or, for that matter, being a Yasui. "I went a long time in my life when I didn't have any heroes," Holly says. "I was embarrassed by my father, embarrassed by my family. They were all so. . . ." She pauses, searching for the right word. "So Japanese."

The last of Min and True's three daughters, Holly was born in 1953 and grew up in an all-white, middle-class neighborhood in south Denver in a modest home the Yasuis could barely afford. They almost lost their house once when an investment Min made went sour. At forty, he had to swallow his pride and ask his father for a loan. In the early years, Min was often several months behind in his mortgage payments because his small law practice, with its list of elderly and indigent clients, just didn't bring in enough money to support a family of five.

So Holly and her sisters grew up middle-class in word and not in deed. Their values were middle-class: education, achievement, family stability, middlebrow culture and proper comportment. But at the same time they were not surrounded by the spoils of middle-class success. Holly wore hand-me-downs from her older sisters and got only one new outfit every year at Easter. The girls had few toys. Their entertainment was family-centered. Their house was plainly furnished, with carpets, sofas and curtains going shabby around the edges. Their father drove a beat-up sedan.

Min and True had a traditional 1950s marriage: he made the money, lived the public life and made the decisions; she followed in his wake, raising the children and supporting his work. True told her daughters that Min never failed to consult her before making a decision. But, she added, through almost forty years of marriage, she never failed to agree with him. The two were an odd couple. Min, gregarious, outgoing and at ease in crowds, enjoyed socializing, hobnobbing, lobbying, delivering fiery extemporaneous speeches—the whole mix of being a public person. True, on the other hand, was a shy, quiet, private woman, who, although she went on the arm of her husband and put on her smiling public face, was never comfortable at social events. She didn't even enjoy entertaining at home. In fact, although Min had an active social life through his work, community involvement and JACL activities, the family itself had little social life. Few people other than Michi and her clan, also living in Denver, were visitors to the Yasui home.

To a great extent, family life revolved around Min's work. Their vacations were really cross-country speaking and fund-raising trips for Min's causes. Their daily routines centered on what Min did. True worked part-time as his secretary, bringing the babies in with her and later, when the girls were in school, arranging her life to accommodate both office work and domestic responsibilities. She was always at home when the girls came back from school. On the many evenings and weekends that Min had to work, the whole family came with him downtown to his Skid Row office. True caught up on the clerical work as Holly and her sisters amused themselves playing on the floor. Later they were old enough to participate in nearby church activities. The city's only *nikkei*-congregation Methodist church was in the neighborhood, as was Denver's one Buddhist temple. And, amid the flophouses and bars, there was a sprinkling of Japanese stores. Walking these streets, Holly looked into the only Japanese faces she ever saw outside her own family.

But if she grew up with few ties to the Japanese American community, she did not grow up completely ignorant of her own *nikkei* past. As

a child, Holly heard a sanitized version of what she later came to think
of as "the Yasui family legend." Min delighted in telling her embroidered
tales of Masuo's pioneer days on the railroad. With the same jocularity
he told her about Masuo's wartime internment. "Oh yes," he would say,
"Grandpa was packed and ready to go. Why, it got to be after a certain
point that if you weren't picked up, you weren't considered important."
He laughed. He made it sound like a lighthearted adventure. He told his
own story the same way, so that while Holly grew up knowing about
"camp" and her father's time in jail, she had little understanding of the
weight and significance of these events.

But there were some stories her father did not tell. She was five years
old when her grandfather hanged himself in the closet of his Portland
home. At her aunt Michi's house, where the Denver Yasuis gathered to
mourn, all the grown-ups were crying. Holly looked around, scared and
confused. Someone told her that Grandpa had died. She remembered
who Grandpa was. His heart stopped; that's what they told her. It wasn't
really a lie. Later she translated that information into an understanding that Masuo had suffered a fatal heart attack. When her own father
had a heart attack in the early 1970s, she was full of anxiety. That's how
Grandpa died, she thought to herself, rushing home from college to
see her father. "I'm really worried about you, Daddy," she told Min.
"Grandpa had a heart attack and died." Min looked up at her from his
hospital bed. "No," he told her quietly, "Grandpa killed himself." Holly
was twenty.

She was older still when she finally learned that her uncle Chop,
whom she had grown up calling "oldest uncle" was not, in fact, the oldest of her father's siblings. In the sanitized version of the Yasui legend,
all traces of Kay had been eliminated. Holly never knew he existed until, during her early college years, she asked her mother whether there
was any history of depression in the family. True told her about Kay,
but True didn't know much. She told her daughter that as a young man
Kay got very depressed and took his own life. Holly could never bring
herself to ask her father directly about his oldest brother. Almost twenty
years later she discovered a few of the details of her long-dead uncle's
life when Maija, Flip's wife, did research on the family.

Until junior high school, Holly maintained a connection to Denver's
small *nikkei* community both through the Japanese Methodist church
she and her family belonged to and through other activities in the mixed-
race neighborhood her father worked in. She would watch Japanese
sword-fighting movies in the basement of the Buddhist church while

her two older sisters took judo lessons. It was there, in the dark, that her
first boyfriend—who would be not just her first but her only Japanese
American boyfriend—gave her her first kiss. But when she stopped going to church at age twelve, and when her father gave up his law practice
to work for the city, her ethnic ties loosened. In her teens she purposefully severed the ties, and for most of the next ten years she steadfastly
denied her own ethnicity. "I was trying very hard to be white," she says
now of those years.

Holly distanced herself from her own heritage any way she could. All
of her friends were white. Her boyfriends were not only white but blond
and blue-eyed as well. While her older sisters took judo lessons, Holly refused, insisting on ballet instead. She actively hated Japanese food while
growing up (Yuka's children shunned it as well, believing that eating
Japanese food would make them look more Japanese) and disliked going
to the one Japanese celebration her family attended, the Obon Festival.
In high school she refused to take a twentieth-century American history
class because, as the only ethnic Japanese in her school, she did not want
to sit in a classroom with all her friends and listen to the teacher lecture
about Pearl Harbor. At sixteen she hated being made to visit Japan. Her
father may have wanted the trip to spur feelings of ethnic identity, but it
had the opposite effect. Holly felt ill at ease, alienated from her Japanese
roots and very much an American.

In high school Holly had so convinced herself that she was white
that it came as a big surprise that she was not permitted to participate
in Denver's desegregation program. Many of her white friends at South
Denver High were being bused out of the district to help achieve a racial
mix at other schools. When Holly asked to be bused too, she was told
that she had to stay put. She was already desegregating a school—her
own home high school.

There was one other Asian in the school, a Chinese American boy
named David. Not only were David and Holly not friends, but they literally ran from each other. If Holly saw David coming toward her down
the hall, she would quickly turn and walk the other way. David did the
same. They were embarrassed to be seen with each other, one person's
Asian face an uncomfortable reminder of the other's ethnic identity.
Holly understands the dynamics now, and shakes her head ruefully. "I
thought if we were seen together everyone would suddenly realize we
were Asian." She laughs. "I just thought I was white, and I didn't want to
be reminded that I wasn't. David reminded me that I wasn't."

In 1971 Holly graduated from high school and headed north thirty-
five miles to Boulder to study fine arts at the University of Colorado.

There, during those black, brown and red power days—heady, empowering times of proclaiming and reclaiming one's racial heritage—Holly inched closer to her own ethnic roots. Her self-exploration, both through personal writing and through academic research, opened the door, at least a crack, to an appreciation of her Japanese American lineage. Still, when she had a chance to go overseas to study, she went not to Japan but to Europe.

It was not until the late 1970s that Holly began to understand who she was and create a strong identity for herself outside white, mainstream society. After Boulder she went west to Los Angeles to study film at USC and there became involved in a two-year documentary project chronicling the city's program of public-school desegregation. Along with a ragtag crew of longhairs, Latinos, Jews and fellow Asians, Holly trekked through Watts and East Los Angeles, listening, looking and filming. She could walk for blocks and never see a white face. What she did see, for the first time in her life, was institutionalized poverty, people sleeping in doorways, gangs, a dead man in the street. During those years she not only observed the effects of racism through the camera lens but felt them personally and forcefully for the first time in her life.

Holly had an African American boyfriend. When the two of them went out filming, they were frequently stopped and questioned by police. But when she went out with one of the white crew members, there was never any interference. She lived in a black-Korean neighborhood that simmered with racial hostility. Undoubtedly mistaken for a Korean, Holly was forced to confront and accept her Asian heritage by others' reactions to her. In her own neighborhood, on the arm of her boyfriend, she was refused service in a restaurant. The African American waitress took one look at her, turned to her boyfriend and spat out, "Why did you bring her in here?" Now when she looked in the mirror, Holly saw what she was: a person of color.

She finished the film but left before completing the degree. The experience of living in Los Angeles had shaken her to the core. "The city was decimating my soul," she says. She escaped inland to Madison, Wisconsin, ostensibly to study at the university there, but really to regain peace of mind. Back in Los Angeles she had read in an encyclopedia that Wisconsin had more cows than people. That's the place for me, she thought to herself. But she found the environment far more intellectually stimulating than she had imagined. While studying for a master's degree in comparative literature and another in communications, Holly dived headlong into the world of Madison's radical politics, from cooperative living to community organizing to Marxist study groups. Through the first half of the 1980s, while she earned two advanced degrees at the university, her real education was taking place elsewhere, in the community and in the study groups. Los Angeles had radicalized her, but Madison taught her the grammar of radicalism, exposed her to its theoretical foundations and in the process gave words to her feelings. But for all its intellectual enrichment, Madison was also, for a Japanese American, a cultural desert. Holly was eager now to find a place with a vibrant Asian community, a place where she could live her politics while strengthening her ethnic ties. She looked West once again, this time to Seattle, where two other Yasui *sansei*, Homer's daughters, had already settled in.

Holly's move to Seattle, just a half hour north of the port of Tacoma, where her grandfather had first set foot on American soil, coincided with what was probably the single most significant event in her life: the death of the father she idolized. Beyond the trauma and the deep sorrow, Min's death propelled Holly into action in behalf of a community she had only recently and tentatively felt a part of and the cause her father had long felt was central to that community—the fight to have wartime internment be once and for all declared unconstitutional. He had fought the battle in two arenas, redress and his own *coram nobis* case. After he died, Holly, along with Homer and other family members, moved in to keep the case alive. "For me personally, the loss of my Dad leaves a terrible empty space in my heart that I can't begin to describe," Holly wrote to her uncle Homer a week after Min's death. "But I also more than ever feel that it is important that Daddy's work be carried on." She carried it on, acting as treasurer for the Min Yasui Memorial Fund, the family-run group that raised significant sums of money to get Min's case to the Supreme Court. She designed mailing materials for the group, helped organize press conferences, gave public speeches and crisscrossed the country accepting posthumous awards for her father.

Her father's death also brought her, for the first time, a deep appreciation of family. "I needed a safety net after my father died," she says. "The center of my world had fallen out. But I came to realize that there was something else out there too, and that was the family." Holly doesn't wax poetic about the Yasuis. For all her pride in her family, she doesn't buy into the Yasui legend. Instead, she sees a large group of people, some interesting, some ordinary, most flawed in some way. "My family is valuable not because we're wonderful people," she says. "It's because we are simply there in a way that so many of my friends' families aren't."

Min's death had yet another profound effect on his daughter: it freed her to write about him. The hard work on the play has been part of her grieving as well as part of her development as a writer. In bringing this episode of her father's life to the stage, not only has Holly honored him and educated others about his case but she has also begun to make a name for herself. She continues to hone the play and plan another, also based on her father's life. In between stage readings, grant writing and time at writers' retreats, Holly supports herself as a desktop publisher, graphic designer, freelance writer and textbook author. It makes for a hectic work life, but not a cushy living. At forty, Holly shares a rented flat with a roommate and cats in a bohemian working-class Seattle neighborhood. She lives simply and drives a rattletrap car not unlike the one her father drove for years.

The Asian community she came West to find has been in some ways a disappointment to her. She considers Japanese Americans in particular too conservative for her tastes. More and more, her own identity comes from her leftist politics. The community she is now a part of is feminist, creative and politically progressive rather than ethnic or racial. Her closest friends are an African American woman and a white woman who share her commitment to social justice. Although she has no close friendships with fellow *nikkei*, she does maintain a number of good working relationships in the Asian community through her volunteer editing of the JACL's Seattle newsletter and by her regular contributions to the city's pan-Asian newspaper, the *International Examiner*.

With her three degrees, four books and award-winning play, Holly is in many ways a model of achievement. But she consciously rejects the "model minority" concept she and her generation were raised with. She sees the whole notion as condescending, racist and damaging to relationships among all people of color. Still, it is very hard to shake. "I almost always feel like I am an example," she says. "With practically everything I do, I am not just another person. I am a Japanese American. I am Holly Yasui."

Three thousand miles away another Yasui *sansei* also has been struggling with her identity, also using art not only for creative expression but as a purposeful exploration of self and family.

Lise Yasui, Shu's oldest daughter, grew up in the quintessential middle-American town of Williamsport, Pennsylvania, with its avenues of well-kept homes, friendly little downtown and numerous and pretty churches. It was a safe, quiet, insular place that once a year went wild when the Little League World Series came to town. As children of a mixed-race marriage, Lise and her four siblings were oddities twice over. They were the only mixed-race children in town and the only children of Japanese ancestry. Although Lise remembers two other Asian families in

Williamsport, her father, Shu, was the only *nikkei*. As the Chinese American poet Alan Lau wrote of his childhood in an all-Caucasian town, "It didn't have to snow for us to know we were surrounded by white."

When Lise was growing up, "family" meant the Hoffmans, her mother's side, a close-knit group of seven blue-eyed siblings and their numerous offspring. She knew little of the Yasui side, which she thought of as "exotic," and even less about her Japanese heritage. Shu did not speak the language or ever talk about his ethnic roots. There were no celebrations of traditional Japanese holidays. And, unlike her Yasui cousins across the country, Lise did not grow up eating Japanese food, for it was her Caucasian mother who did the cooking. Occasionally her aunt Yuka, who had settled some two hundred miles south near Washington, D.C., would send rolls of sushi and what Lise remembers as "stinking Japanese pickles" on a bus to Williamsport. It was a confusing childhood. Surrounded by whites, isolated from half her cultural heritage, Lise looked in the mirror and saw . . . what? A pretty girl with straight dark hair and a hint of Japan around her brown eyes. But she was tallish and creamy-skinned with noticeable Caucasian features. One could see the Yasui in her, but sometimes only barely, as if imagined. What was she? "I never assumed I was a blond WASP," she says. Perhaps she knew what she wasn't. But she did not yet know what she was.

Thousands of miles and a marriage apart from the Yasui clan, Lise was exposed to her father's side of the family through occasional visits with Yuka's family and infrequent stopovers by visiting uncles. She met her uncle Chop for the first time when she was eight. Shu had told Lise that her uncle "lived on a big ranch way out west." She had a hard time reconciling the image this conjured up with the reality of Chop as he walked off the airplane: "a roly-poly Japanese guy with a crew cut," as Lise remembers.

How she really came to know the Yasuis—to the extent she knew them at all as a child—was through the home movies Shu projected on a little screen in their living room. These movies, taken on her parents' cross-country trip to Oregon before she was born, were Lise's main link to her Yasui roots. On the screen she met her tiny grandmother, a wide smile crinkling her round face, and her grandfather, serious and proper in a tan fedora, white dress shirt and tie. She saw her cousins, with their black hair and dark eyes, and began to recognize her own features in their Asian faces. She watched these movies so often as a child that she came to anticipate every frame. Here was Grandma in a summer hat clutching her handbag. Now she'd sit on the swing in the backyard; now she'd look down at the little girl beside her; now she'd laugh.

As Lise watched the home movies, her father offered live narration, telling selected family stories that starred Masuo as the hardworking pioneer railroader, the enterprising young businessman, the pillar of the community, the unblemished hero of the family saga. Shu talked of good times, achievements, successes. Years later Lise came to understand her father's stories and the home movies as "declarations of what he chose to remember." To Lise, as she grew older, the movies represented the boundary between the father she knew and the father whose real feelings might forever remain hidden from her.

After dinner one winter evening in 1965, Shu made a surprising announcement to his family: that evening he—who never watched television—was taking over the TV set to watch a special program. Lise, ten at the time, and her older brother were told to stay out of the room. The show, Shu told Lise and her brother, was about "Japanese Americans who were put in camp during World War Two like Grandpa." Lise had no idea what her father was talking about. She had never heard anything about camps or about her grandfather being taken away. That night, alone, Shu watched the CBS documentary *Nisei: The Pride and the Shame*. It was the first time in two decades that he was confronted with his painful past. Lise filed away the incident, thinking that her father had banned her from watching some show with bad language. He was always protective that way. But her father's comment about internment had piqued her curiosity. "What the son wishes to forget, the grandson"—or, in this case, granddaughter—"wishes to remember." But when she asked her father about the war years, he changed the subject or said nothing at all. The less he said, the more she wanted to know.

At fifteen she found an excuse to get nosy that her father, with his respect for education, would have to respond to: a term paper for a high school history class. She chose internment as her topic. The school library had nothing on the subject, and her own teacher had never heard of it. She went to her father. At first, Shu told Lise only his own story, how he was in college at the outbreak of the war and headed east to avoid internment and complete his education. He told her he was unable to see his family for four years. But Lise, then at the age when getting clear of one's family sounded more like fun than tragedy, didn't think her father's story sounded all that terrible. Surely there must be something more. She urged him to talk. Slowly, tentatively, he filled in some of the gaps, and the more she learned, the more incredible the Yasuis' experiences seemed to her. Here was her heroic grandfather nabbed by the FBI and branded a dangerous enemy alien. Here was her grandmother, alone with two children in a desert prison camp. She learned of her uncle

Min's arrest, of hundreds of acres of orchard lands the family had lost during the war. It confused and angered her. But, most of all, it made her want to know more.

A few years later another history teacher provided her with the opportunity to delve deeper. At the University of Pennsylvania, where she went in the fall of 1973 to study psychology, Lise found herself in a unique and challenging history course. The professor had this idea that the best way to learn American history was by writing family history. Once again, Lise had an excuse to pepper her father with questions. She learned more details, combined historical research with family memories, wrote an A paper, but still felt she had only scratched the surface. There was more to know, and learning it, she thought, might help her find her own place in history.

But she temporarily shelved her curiosity as she finished her bachelor's degree in psychology and worked in the field for close to four years. When she quit an emotionally grueling job at a phobia clinic, she decided to treat herself to a vacation of sorts, a summer studying dance, one of her enduring passions, at Harvard. It was there in an experimental video dance class that she discovered a new passion: filmmaking. Back in Pennsylvania that fall, she enrolled in Temple University's film program and soon began work on a documentary project that would take her deeply, painfully and irrevocably into the lives of the Yasuis.

Originally, she thought she would make the "definitive documentary on internment" for her required master's degree project. But she quickly modified that to focus on internment through the eyes of her father's family. She chased Min around with a camera for a while. She went to Minidoka, the Idaho camp he was sent to after his release from jail. She went with her uncle on a bus tour of Topaz, a Utah internment camp. She took her camera to a conference on internment in Salt Lake City. She trekked to Washington, D.C., to film the signing of the redress bill. Lise shakes her head as she relates her early efforts. "I didn't know what the hell I was doing," she says. "I was just learning how to turn the microphones on. I didn't know how to make a film."

As she was filming anything and everything, her classmates and teachers at Temple began urging her to make a more personal film. She resisted. "I hated personal films. To me they were therapy films, touchy-feely—and I just didn't want to do it." But as she began interviewing her aunts and uncles on tape and found that their versions of the past differed greatly, she realized she had little choice. This would have to be her film, a film not about the past but about her discovery of the past. The pieces would be held together by her perspective and told in her voice.

But this artistic decision didn't make the film any easier to make. Lise felt herself squeezed between her intellect and her emotion. Her schooling had taught her to be aggressive and go after the story. But her experiences with her family, a number of whom were guarded and very protective of their past, warned her to go slowly and be careful. As time went on she herself began to feel protective of these people she was just beginning to know. She felt, as she put it, "frozen behind the camera," unable to ask the questions that needed asking, an observer of lives she might never be able to understand. In a particularly revealing scene she caught on camera during one of her filming trips to Hood River, Chop stops to talk with an *issei* woman who knew Masuo and Shidzuyo. Chop and the old woman converse in Japanese for what seems like a long time. From behind the camera comes Lise's tentative voice. "What is she saying?" she asks her uncle. Chop jams his hands in his pockets and looks toward the camera. "Aw, nothing," he says.

Out in Hood River, Lise filmed cherry orchards in full bloom and sprinklers making rainbows in the sun. "Just incredibly romantic and totally useless stuff," she says. She also tried hard—but not with great success—to get Chop to open up in front of the camera. Whenever her questions turned to internment, his return to Hood River or, most of all, his father's later life, Chop either answered evasively or not at all. What was not being said hung heavy in the air. Lise felt it.

Back home, visiting her parents in Williamsport, Lise stayed up late one night talking to her father as they sat around the kitchen table. She was asking about her grandfather's life after the war. All of a sudden, Shu grew quiet. He was an unemotional man, both by nature and by his physician's training, but Lise could see him fighting for control. He said nothing for a long time, staring at the kitchen table. Then he looked up at her. "Don't you know how your grandfather died?" he asked. His voice was soft. And as soon as he asked the question, Lise somehow knew the answer.

That night Shu told her the whole story of Masuo's suicide, a story he had kept secret from his own wife until the year before. Lise recounts the scene in her film. "I cried because I could see my father's pain," she says in the narration. "And I cried because in that instant my grandfather seemed more real to me than ever before." People, Lise learned, are silent for a reason. They are silent because it holds back the pain. It had taken her father twenty-eight years to tell her the truth about her grandfather, and Lise knew she had to be careful with the information. But as Lise the Yasui *sansei* anguished over her family's pain, Lise the filmmaker thought: Here is the dramatic climax my film needs. Here is the ultimate irony. Even as the thoughts formed she was overcome with guilt for thinking them.

The knowledge of her grandfather's suicide propelled Lise into a series of moral dilemmas. At one point she decided to give up on the film project entirely. She couldn't exclude the suicide from the film because that would be a lie. Yet neither did she feel free to use the information. Her uncle Chop, for one, was dead set against it. He had never told his own children the truth about their grandfather and firmly believed that word of the suicide would besmirch Masuo's and the family's reputation. And Chop was *chonan*, a concept that still meant something in the Yasui family. His word carried weight.

But Lise saw nothing shameful in her grandfather's suicide, and over the course of several months she resolved her own internal conflict, deciding that telling the truth about Masuo's death was essential to understanding her grandfather and the time in which he lived. It took many months of phone calls and letters to convince her uncle and others that she was right. Finally, almost a year after discovering one of the family's closest-held secrets, Lise went back to making her film.

A Family Gathering, as she decided to call her thirty-minute documentary, was the story of her own journey of discovery as she learned about her family's past. It combined the home movies Lise had seen so many times as a child with family photos, historical documents, archival film footage and on-camera interviews with Min, Shu, Homer and Yuka. Lise's matter-of-fact narration told the story with powerful understatement. The film had taken more than five years to make. ("Actually," Lise later told a Philadelphia *Inquirer* reporter, "I've been working on it my whole life, if you look at it psychologically.") But it played with remarkable freshness. The film had been the product of a period of confusion and turmoil, yet it communicated with calm and clarity. Strong and heartfelt, it was also unsentimental.

Lise entered the film in festivals around the country, and not surprisingly, *A Family Gathering* won awards and accolades everywhere it went: a Golden Globe at the San Francisco International Film Festival, a Golden Hugo in Chicago, an invitation to an international festival in Stockholm and another to the first international film festival ever held in Leningrad. In Chicago one of the commissioning editors from WGBH-TV, the Boston public television station that originates the PBS series *The American Experience*, heard of the film and asked Lise to send him a copy. *A Family Gathering* ran thirty minutes, and PBS needed a sixty-minute film for the show, but WGBH loved Lise's tape and offered her funds to expand the film.

She was thrilled, but scared. It was one thing for the film to go out on the relatively obscure festival circuit; it was another for it to be broadcast nationally on public television. "I knew that television critics could write anything they damn well pleased about the film. I had to think hard about what they might say about my family." Lise would not sign a contract with PBS unless all her aunts and uncles gave their permission for their story to be so publicly told. "Things got pretty dicey," she says. It took six months of careful negotiation, then another six months of expanding and reediting the film before it was ready to be aired. Meanwhile Lise had received word of the ultimate accolade: *A Family Gathering*—her first and only film—had been nominated for an Academy Award for best short subject.

The nomination meant her fledgling career as a filmmaker was off to an extraordinary start. But just as important, the nomination quieted the concerns of the family. If other people saw the film, understood it and found it worthy, then the Yasuis' story, and their long-hidden secret, had not been misconstrued. The family name was honored, not muddied. Through *A Family Gathering*, Lise had found her place both in the film community and in her own family.

Late in the film, after the story of internment and Masuo's death has been told, Lise returns to the home movies she grew up watching every Sunday night. "Now when I watch these movies," she says in the film's narration, "I am aware of the history that lies behind these images." On the screen, Masuo is dressed neatly in a gray suit and matching hat. Shidzuyo is wearing a flowered dress. They walk through an arbor and into the dense greenery of their Portland backyard. Their backs are to the camera. A strong sun, filtered through the trees, shines over their shoulders. They are not conscious of the camera. They don't look back. "This is a past my family made for themselves," Lise says in the narration. "It is a past they gave to me."

interview

Homer Yasui
June 20, 2005
Portland, Oregon

Talk about the legacy of your father and mother—that first generation. What did you learn from the life they led? What do you hope readers might learn?

You're talking about my mother and my father and my uncle . . . that whole generation, the *issei*. My father came to this country in 1903 determined that he would stay. He was not going to come to America for just a couple of years, make money and go back to Japan, unlike a number of *issei*. He tried to convince his two brothers to stay also and did manage to convince my uncle Renichi. My father was a very, very determined man. That was one of the things about the *issei* generation, the ones who stayed . . . they were very determined.

The other thing, and this was mainly from the women's side, was that they really stressed education. They thought education was the answer to everything—all the questions and problems that would face them. To that end, both my mother and father wanted us all to go to college. You know, Masuo was not highly educated. He came to America when he was 16, the equivalent to a sophomore in high school. But for the rest of his life he was always studying and trying to better himself. He was mainly self-taught. He didn't take classes. He didn't go to college. But my father and mother wanted all of us to go to college, and so all the Yasui children did go to college, which was not too common in those days. For us, it was not that difficult because my father made enough money to send his children to college. But for most *issei* it was very difficult. But the *issei* generation stressed education so much, and the *nisei* generation listened to their parents and went to college. A lot of them made excellent, wonderful students.

For me the most important legacy was the stress they put on education and character-building. They brought their cultural baggage with them—duty, honor, country. It was a Puritan, Protestant ethic, very similar to the founding fathers of this country. It sometimes boggles my mind the way the white racists in the 1940s used to say that the Japanese were unassimilatable when in fact their character traits were almost identical to the traits of the early Americans.

You are the guardian of the Yasui's history. Why did you take on that role? Why is it important to preserve your family's history?

I am the unofficial family historian. No one appointed me. I am self-elected. When my oldest brother Choppy, Ray, died, there was a whole bunch of stuff left in the barn right next to his house in Hood River. After the funeral, my sister-in-law, Mikie, asked me and my younger sister Yuka, who was in Hood River for the funeral, if we could take a look in the barn and see what we should do with all that material. There was just a vast quantity of material gathering cobwebs and dust. The mice had been chewing on it. Yuka said, "Oh sure, we'll take a look and decide." But Yuka had to get back to Maryland and look after her family, so the responsibility devolved to me. I knew that history. I grew up with it. So it just so happened that I was there, and I was convenient. I lived nearby, in Portland, and I had just retired, so I had the time. One of my sisters-in-law says, "There's always a dumpee in the family. And you're the dumpee on this."

It immediately became apparent to me that there was a great deal of history in that barn. Some of it went back to 1903. So I thought, my gosh, we're talking about 80 years of history here. It would be a sin and a shame to discard that. So I volunteered to take on the responsibility. Yuka helped for about the first ten days until she had to go back home. Then I drafted my good wife. We would go out to Hood River and sit in that cold, drafty, dirty old barn for hours on end sorting through all this stuff just to see what was important. I found it all very rewarding.

Now I'm getting ready to pass on the responsibility to my oldest daughter, Barbara. She's the keeper of the flame now. She says that maybe one in 10 in any given family will take care of this, and she's it in her generation. And that's fine. It's all a work of love.

What's so important about preserving family history?

What's so important? Why I never thought about *why* it was important. You just have to do it. It's the way your children and their children know about their ancestors. Isn't history important to begin with? It's nice for the descendants—however many generations removed—to get a sense of what it was like for the first Yasuis. I mean right now I have the tribal memories, and Yuka too, but we won't be around forever. I think it's important that the descendants know what their roots are, where they came from, what travails and troubles and triumphs their family had. I think it's not only important it's very interesting. Where you came from, what happened in the past, the good things and the bad things — it all reflects on you today.

In addition to family history, there is family identity that is important to the Yasuis. Your father and mother kept all those papers you found in the barn, which is not all that common. The family stays in touch across thousands of miles and multiple generations. You hold big reunions every few years. Someone designs Yasui T-shirts for everyone to wear. What does it mean to be a Yasui? Why is it important to nurture and maintain that identity?

I think it came from my father, the fact that he thought of himself as a person of destiny. He was going to stay here. He was going to succeed. He had this sense of self-importance. He was not always going to be a common railroad laborer. He had this sense of destiny, and I'm sure that spilled over to us.

An interesting thing about that is that so many of the Yasui women have kept their maiden names after marriage. Barbara [Homer's oldest daughter] is still a Yasui. Meredith [his second daughter] is still a Yasui. Kimberly, who is fourth generation [Chop's granddaughter], has kept the name. She's a schoolteacher in Hood River, and she is known as Kimberly Yasui. Most of the daughters have kept the family name.

Part of it may be that Min made the Yasui name famous—or infamous, depending upon your point of view. His defying of the curfew, his case, is very well known. Our name is very well known. Any place you go in the United States to a *nikkei* [people of Japanese ancestry] gathering, people will say, "Oh, Yasui . . . Are you one of the Min Yasuis?" It always comes up. There's really a sense of pride. And you want to do the right thing because you are recognizable, because you are being looked at. The *issei* always said, "Never bring shame to your family." And that's one thing the Yasui family tries not to do.

That sense of identity now goes far beyond any notions of ethnicity or race, doesn't it? So many of the third and now fourth generation Yasuis have not married Japanese Americans. So you can proudly wear the name Yasui and not physically appear to have any Japanese ancestry.

Oh yeah. There are several blond-haired, blue-eyed Yasuis now.

I was thinking about the timing of Pearl Harbor in your life. Just as you were coming into your own as a teenager, just as you were establishing your own identity and beginning to feel your oats, your family was uprooted and interned. What did that feel like to you back then? How do you look at that part of your personal history now?

Well, to answer that honestly . . . I think a lot of *nisei* would get mad at me. I never felt any anger toward the government back then. I mean, I knew it was prejudicial. But for me it was just a very interesting, fascinating period in my life. It was uncomfortable. It was uncertain. We didn't know where we were going or what was going to happen. But for me it was exciting. Here I was herded together with thousands of other people who looked just like me, had the same kind of hair, had the same kind of eyes, same kind of customs, same kind of background. It was fascinating. Intellectually, I knew there were thousands of *nikkei* in the U.S., but I never saw them all together like this. At Tule Lake, I think there were 18,000 of us. My gosh, it was a whole village, people from all over. Like I say, some *nisei* will get mad at me, but I had a good time at camp. I guess I was just too dumb to realize I was deprived.

Would you say that the experiences of the war years affected you long-term?

It did affect me, especially politically. Regardless of how powerful someone is, say in our government, I always listen to what they have to say with a grain of salt. They are our leaders, and we should trust them. But we should always be able to question them, question their motives and their actions. Maybe what I learned in the war years was distrust. All these things that people like President Roosevelt was saying or Earl Warren was saying . . . I mean, these were leaders of our country and they were saying things that, to me, were manifestly untrue. They were saying the Japs were not to be trusted. But hey, I knew I was a trustworthy guy. So I've learned to be cautious, to not be too trustful of our leaders regardless of their level. I sit back and listen carefully, and I think: Is that true? Is that right? I think that's the main thing I learned during the war.

Did you have to go through a process of forgiving your own country for how it treated your family and thousands of other families? How did that happen?

Oh yeah, I did. But for me, even today, it's highly ambivalent. I realize a lot of the people back then said things in the heat of the times, in the heat of emotion. And a lot of people just went along on the bandwagon. Here I am referring specifically to the people who signed the petition that Kent Shoemaker put out in the Hood River *News*. [Shoemaker placed a series of signed ads in the local newspaper in 1945 vilifying those of Japanese descent, calling them "Japes"—his combination of the words Japs and apes—and proclaiming them "an alien race who are our enemy and will always be our enemy."] I find that hard to forgive. But I say, what's the profit in continuing to hold this against people who did these things? There is no profit. To me, it's still sad, and I still think about it sometimes. I still wonder: Why did these people do this? And I don't know the answer. But I think you have to make up your mind that you're going to forgive. Not forget, but forgive. And we should just not let this happen again. And here I am speaking about those people of the Muslim faith right now in our country.

I'm glad you brought that up. Did you feel a déjà vu after 9-11 when we started hearing reports of harassment and discrimination against anyone with an "Arab" face—that same kind of wholesale targeting of a population we experienced after Pearl Harbor?

I think we are better this time. There was no mass round-up of people. There is still a great deal of suspicion and hostility directed against them, but I don't see a move for mass incarceration like the Japanese Americans were subjected to. So to that extent, the United States has learned something. But I'm still a little bit uneasy, especially when there are such things are the Patriot Act and racial profiling.

What do you hope readers will learn from the story of your family?

I hope they learn that with determination and education and the will to keep working despite the odds anybody can succeed, a family can succeed. And I hope they see that families succeed because they work together. They have to help each other. That's a hard lesson. But maybe this book you wrote about our family will show that our family did work together. It was not just giving moral support but physical support. You help sustain your family's drive. The lesson is: You can do it if you try, if you work hard enough. That's the lesson of my father, who was determined to succeed, to make good in the world. And he did—of course, at the cost of his life. But before he died, his family was successful.

My father was not a person to go bragging, especially about his children. That's a Japanese trait: They don't brag about their own family. But I'm sure that my father was inwardly very, very pleased with the success of his children. And it was directly due to his and my mother's efforts to make us kids do the right thing, to go to school, to behave ourselves. In Japanese, it's *maji mena:* Be serious, be straightforward, pay attention.

There's another Japanese expression—*shanto shinasai*—which means: Do things properly! Behave yourself! I heard that a lot from my mother. Those are the values my parents pounded into us. They were part of the cultural baggage they brought over with them. They are good values. And again, it's remarkable how much these values were like those of the founding fathers of this country. I mean, they are identical.

for reading groups and classes

Questions for Discussion

1. Close your eyes, and picture an "American." Describe what you see. What does an "American" look like?

2. Are there distinctly American character traits? What might they be?

3. We are all immigrants. In what ways is your own immigrant past similar or dissimilar from that of the Yasuis?

4. "Give me your tired, your poor, your huddled masses . . . " reads a plaque on the Statue of Liberty, which welcomes immigrants from across the Atlantic to the new land. Why do you think late 19th century European immigrants were welcomed to the U.S. while immigrants from Asia—specifically China and Japan—were not?

5. The Japanese have been called the "model minority." Why? Many Americans of Japanese descent consider this not to be a compliment. Why might they hold this view?

6. What is the American Dream Masui and Shidzuyo dreamed—and so many other millions of immigrants dream—for themselves and their families? Did they achieve it?

7. The Japanese—and many other immigrant groups—put an extraordinary value on education. Why? Is their faith in education justified?

8. Imagine that you had been a neighbor of the Yasuis in 1941, a resident of a small town with a sizable Japanese American population. Imagine you went to high school with several of the Yasui children. Now the newspapers and radio are warning that the Japanese may invade the U.S. and that the people you know as neighbors may in fact be enemy agents. Whom do you believe? How do you act? What would you have done had you been alive during those days?

9. Do you think Masuo Yasui was in any way responsible for his own downfall?

10. Some see the internment of Japanese immigrants and Americans of Japanese descent after Pearl Harbor as a regrettable consequence of wartime hysteria. Others see it as merely the most egregious incident in a long history of racism and intolerance. What are your views?

11. Two metaphors have been used to describe the rich immigrant mix that is the U.S.—a melting pot and a patchwork quilt. How are those metaphors fundamentally different and what do they mean to the way we live as a society?

12. Is it possible to construct a society that both honors the uniqueness of immigrant groups and nurtures a coherent American society? What might that society look like?

13. Each successive generation of an immigrant family deals differently with the process of becoming or being an American as well as the relationship between their immigrant past their American home. What are those distinct generational differences? Can you see them in your own family?

14. What are the advantages and disadvantages of using the story of one family to illustrate the social and political history of a nation?

sources

Chapter 1

Hood River of the early twentieth century has been described in words and presented in photographs and illustrations in a variety of homespun publications including Hood River County Historical Society, *History of Hood River County 1852-1982* (Hood River, Ore.: Hood River Historical Society, 1982); S.F. Blythe and E.R. Bradley, *A Pen Picture of Hood River and Hood River Valley* (August 1900); and Hood River Commercial Club, *Resources and Development of the City of Hood River and the Hood River Valley* (1905).

For the history of the Yasui family in Japan, I have depended heavily on two family trees and accompanying explanations written by Sachiko Yasui Nomura, the daughter of Taiitsuro, Masuo's older brother, as well as a family tree constructed by Homer Yasui. The three versions of Yasui ancestry differ somewhat but not appreciably. Where contradictions could not be resolved, I depended on Homer Yasui's thoughtful interpretations. Both in interviews with me and in correspondence with his family, Homer also provided important details about Yasui ancestry, as did Yuka Yasui Fujikura, Masuo's youngest daughter.

My understanding of pre- and post-Meiji-era Japan came principally from Ronald Takaki's wonderful book, *Strangers from a Different Shore: A History of Asian Americans* (New York: Penguin Books, 1989), and William Peterson's *Japanese Americans: Oppression and Success* (New York: Random House, 1971). Detailed information about "American fever" in Japan came from the *issei* respondents quoted at length in Kazuo Ito's *Issei: A History of Japanese Immigration in North America* (Seattle: Japanese Community Service, 1973) as well as Takaki's book. The respondents in Ito's massive volume also commented in detail on the transpacific voyage.

For the early history of the Japanese in Oregon, I used Barbara Yasui, "The Nikkei in Oregon, 1834-1940," *Oregon Historical Quarterly,* vol. 76, no. 3 (September 1975); Marjorie R. Stearns, *The History of the Japanese People in Oregon* (University of Oregon thesis, July 1937); S. Frank Miyamoto, "The Japanese Minority in the Pacific Northwest," *Pacific Northwest Quarterly,* vol. 54, no. 4 (October 1963); and an unpublished essay, "Issei Pioneers in Oregon: A Short Subjective History," contributed to the Issei Appreciation Committee of the Portland Japanese American Citizens League, September 1973.

Details of life in the Northwest for the *issei* came from the respondents in Ito's book as well as Yuji Ichioka's *The Issei: The World of the First-Generation Japanese Immigrants, 1885-1924* (New York: The Free Press, 1988). I am indebted to Ichioka's "Japanese Immigrant Labor Contractors and the Northern Pacific and Great Northern Railroad Companies," *Labor History,* vol. 21, no. 3 (Summer 1980) for background and details about Japanese railroad crews.

Information about Masuo's first years in Oregon comes from my interviews with his children, principally Chop, Minoru, Homer and Yuka as well as a narrative written by son Robert (Shu) Yasui in a self-published family history, *The Yasui Family of Hood River* (1987). Scattered correspondence between Masuo and his brothers (found in the Yasui Brothers Collection housed at the Oregon Historical Society) was also helpful.

Chapter 2

As a result both of local pride and the national stature of its fruit industry, perhaps more has been written about the small town of Hood River and its valley than other such rural outposts. In addition to the sources consulted for Chapter 1 (Hood River County Historical Society, *History of Hood River County 1852- 1982* [Hood River, Ore.: Hood River Historical Society, 1982]; S.F. Blythe and E.R. Bradley, *A Pen Picture of Hood River and Hood River Valley* [August 1900]; and Hood River Commercial Club, *Resources and Development of the City of Hood River and the Hood River Valley* [1905]), details of both social and business life in Hood River came from several booklets published by the local Commercial Club: *Hood River* (1900), *A Brief Description of the Hood River Valley* (1907), *Views of Hood River, Oregon and its Renowned Fruit Valley* (1908), and *Hood River, Oregon* (1910).

Information (and criticism) about entertainment and recreation came from a master's thesis in education written by a local man, Karl Onthank, "A Survey of the Schools of Hood River County," (University of Oregon thesis, 1915). For local color, I am also indebted to journalist and amateur historian Ruth Guppy, who has been writing about Hood River's history in special supplements to the town's newspaper for the past twenty years, and two other Hood River natives who enriched my understanding of the town's early days: Kenneth Abraham, who enlightened me about "remittance men" and Jane Smithson Irwin, who shared her past with me in numerous, lengthy letters. A number of these same sources were rich in detail about the emerging fruit industry in the valley. Also helpful in this regard was E.H. Shepard, "Success with Apples in Hood River Valley," *Pacific Monthly,* vol. 26, no. 4 (October 1911).

For information about the Japanese in Hood River during the early years, I have depended on local *issei's* stories published in Kazuo Ito's *Issei: A History of Japanese Immigration in North America* (Seattle: Japanese Community Service, 1973) as well as the following unpublished material: "Issei Story," prepared by the Mid-Columbia Japanese American Citizens League, 1961; assorted notes in the "Japanese families" file at the Hood River County Historical Museum; and Prof. Linda Tamura's in-depth interviews with members of the first generation. My own interview with one of the few remaining *issei* women, Mrs. Nakamura (with Mikie Yasui as interpreter), added important detail. Native daughter Mitzi Asai Loftus's autobiography, *Made in Japan and Settled in Oregon* (Coos Bay, Ore.: Pidgeon Point Press, 1990), was also helpful.

For the details of Shidzuyo's life in Japan and the Miyake family, I am entirely indebted to Yuka Yasui Fujikura, who sat through many hours of interviews and shared her memorabilia and pictures. It was she who rediscovered and authenticated her mother's past during trips to Japan, and she who read a translation of Ichiro Miyake's diaries. For background concerning this generation of women, I depended on Mei Nakano's *Japanese American Women: Three Generations 1890-1990* (Berkeley: Mina Press, 1990), Evelyn Nakano Glenn's *Issei, Nisei, War Bride: Three Generations of Japanese American Women in Domestic Service* (Philadelphia: Temple University Press, 1986), and Akemi Kikumura's *Through Harsh Winters* (Nova to, Cal,: Chandler and Sharp, Inc., 1981).

Chapter 3

For background on the transformation from temporary to permanent settlement of the Japanese in America, I have depended on Ronald Takaki's *Strangers from a Different Shore: A History of Asian Americans* (New York: Penguin Books, 1989). Data on the changing demographics of Hood River valley came from the *Thirteenth Census of the U.S., Agriculture,* vol. 3, Table 1—Farms and Farm Properties by Counties; the *Fourteenth Census of the U.S., Agriculture,* vol. 4, Part 3, County Table 1—Farms and Farm

Property; and Wendy Lee Ng's *Collective Memory, Social Networks and Generations: The Japanese American Community of Hood River, Oregon,* (Ph.D. dissertation, University of Oregon, August 1989).

My understanding of Shizuyo, her early days in Hood River and domestic life in the Yasui household came primarily from lengthy interviews with her youngest daughter, Yuka Yasui Fujikura. Occasional glimpses of Shizuyo's place in the *issei* community could be found in Kazuo Ito's *Issei: A History of Japanese in North America* (Seattle: Japanese Community Service, 1973) as well as in letters written by Masuo to friends and business acquaintances. For a general understanding of Japanese women of Shizuyo's generation, of picture brides and of transplanted Japanese family dynamics and structure, I have depended on discussions in Mei Nakano's *Japanese American Women: Three Generations 1890-1990* (Berkeley: Mina Press, 1990); Evelyn Nakano Glenn's *Issei, Nisei, War Bride: Three Generations of Japanese American Women in Domestic Service* (Philadelphia: Temple University Press, 1986); as well as comments made by several of Prof. Linda Tamura's *issei* respondents in her interviews with Hood River Japanese women.

Sources for Masuo's story are more direct. He left behind, and his children preserved, more than one hundred boxes of family papers, the bulk of which relate to Masuo's business dealings. The Yasui Brothers (Y.B.) Collection housed at the Oregon Historical Society contains boxes of invoices, cartons of correspondence, file folders of income tax returns, stacks of account books and a wide variety of other material that shed light on Masuo's life as a storekeeper, fruit rancher and all-purpose entrepreneur. Homer Yasui, Masuo's youngest son, who took on the job of organizing the family papers, offered many important insights about this material in lengthy reports to his family, which he kindly shared with me. Other important business information came from records of Masuo's land purchases and sales at the Hood River County courthouse. Multiple interviews with all of the surviving Yasui *nisei* provided vital insights into Masuo's character. Akemi Kikumura's *Promises Kept: Life of an Issei Man* (Novato, Cal.: Chandler and Sharp, Inc., 1991) provided important context.

Information about the Yasui Brothers Store came from documents in the Y.B. collection at Oregon Historical Society, interviews and extended correspondence with Homer Yasui, and correspondence with several Hood River natives who generously shared their memories: Ruth Crawford, Margaret Smithson Schulz, Jane Smithson Irwin and Kenneth Abraham. Some of the most helpful information about the store, including its layout, came from Masuo's son Chop Yasui, who drew various diagrams of its interior and committed some of his memories to tape before his death. Additional information came from a newspaper article written by Chop Yasui's daughter-in-law, Maija, an energetic amateur historian: "Brothers' store rich cultural center," Hood River *News,* April 17, 1991.

The discussion of Japanese values found in the chapter was based on Ruth Benedict's *The Chrysanthemum and the Sword: Patterns of Japanese Culture* (Boston: Houghton Mifflin Co., 1946), John W. Connor's *Tradition and Change in Three Generations of Japanese Americans* (Chicago: Nelson-Hall, 1977), and Harry Kitano's prodigious work, especially *Japanese Americans: The Evolution of a Subculture* (Englewood Cliffs, N.J.: Prentice-Hall, 1969). I am also greatly indebted to Hisako Yoshinari, a friend of several Yasui *nisei,* who took the time to write me long, thoughtful letters about Japanese culture and values. Her explanations, with their specific connections to the Yasui family, grounded the academic work in reality.

Masuo's relationships, both professional and personal, to the whites of Hood River and elsewhere are well documented in letters found in the Y.B. collection. I owe insights into how some *hakujin* were talking about Masuo to Kenneth Abraham, son of the doctor who ministered to many valley *issei,* and to Shirley Kishiyama, who put me in touch with Mr. Abraham.

Chapter 4

Many books about the American experiences of Asians in general and Japanese in particular deal with the history of the exclusionist movement. I found the following to be the best sources for information about California, where the movement was born and had its greatest successes: William Petersen, *Japanese Americans: Oppression and Success* (New York: Random House, 1971); Harry Kitano, *Japanese Americans: The Evolution of* a *Subculture* (Englewood Cliffs, N.J.: Prentice-Hall, 1969); Roger Daniels, *Politics of Prejudice* (New York: Atheneum, 1968); Ronald Takaki, *Strangers from a Different Shore: A History of Asian Americans* (New York: Penguin Books, 1989). Frank Chuman's *The Bamboo People: The Law and Japanese Americans* (Del Mar, Cal.: Publishers, Inc., 1976) was helpful on immigration laws and Supreme Court decisions. Maisie and Richard Conrat, eds., *Executive Order 9066* (California Historical Society, 1972), a book of photographs dealing with the World War II evacuation and relocation of West Coast Japanese, contains several comments from California nativists, including the quotation from the mayor of San Francisco. Other such comments, including the words of V.S. McClatchy quoted in the chapter, can be found in *U.S. Senate Japanese Immigration Hearings,* 68th Cong., 1st sess., 1924. The report from the Western congressmen who supported California's exclusionist activities is part of House Document no. 89, 67th Cong., 1st sess., 1921. Still the most thoughtful and contextual history of American racism is John Higham's *Strangers in the Land* (New York: Atheneum, 1967), to which I am greatly indebted.

The exclusionist movement in Oregon is much more sparsely documented than that in California, but at least two works offer good summaries: Marjorie Stearns, *The History of the Japanese People in Oregon* (University of Oregon thesis, 1937), and Barbara Yasui, "The Nikkei in Oregon 1834-1940," *Oregon Historical Quarterly,* vol. 76, no. 3 (September 1975). Much of the information about the movement found in this chapter comes from contemporaneous sources, including two state documents, "The Third Biennial Report of the Bureau of Labor Statistics for Oregon" (1909) and Frank Davey, "Report on the Japanese Question" (1920) as well as newspaper articles in the Portland *Oregonian,* Hood River *News,* Prineville *Central Oregonian* and *Oregon Voter.*

Barbara Yasui's research offers helpful information about the Hood River movement in particular. Most of the details about meetings, speeches, citizen reaction and proposals come from stories published in the Hood River *News* and Hood River *Glacier.* Letters and other documents directly related to actions in Hood River (including a copy of the Wilson Ross Winans poem and the Anti-Asian Association's resolution) come from the Y.B. collection at the Oregon Historical Society. Statistics cited are from the *Fourteenth Census of the U.S.: 1920, Population,* vol. 3, Table 7, as well as other government figures reprinted in *Japanese Immigration: An Exposition of Its Real Status* (Seattle, Wash.: The Japanese Association of the Pacific Northwest, 1907). Comments by *issei* concerning their treatment in Hood River during the height of the exclusion movement are quoted in Kazuo Ito's *A History of Japanese Immigration in North America* (Seattle: Japanese Community Service, 1973).

Masuo Yasui's personal involvement in the events of the local exclusionist movement can be traced in occasional stories in the Hood River *News* and the two long interviews in the Idaho *Farmer,* but mostly through correspondence to and from him and other documents (including a Hood River Japanese population survey completed in his hand) found in the Y.B. collection. The poem at the end of the chapter, by Katsuko Hirata, is quoted in Kazuo Ito's book.

Chapter 5

Documents in the Y.B. collection and Homer Yasui's private holdings plus my extensive oral history interviews provided much of the information for this chapter. Masuo's reaction to the triple blows of the early 1920s is evident in his continued business dealings as well as his continued business and personal relationships with whites, both of which are well documented by the letters, invoices and other records in the Y.B. collection. But I am also indebted to Yuji Ichioka's *The Issei: The World of the First-Generation Japanese Immigrants 1885-1924* (New York: The Free Press, 1988) and Ronald Takaki's *Strangers from a Different Shore: A History of Asian Americans* (New York: Penguin Books, 1989) for insights into how the *issei* in general reacted to the restrictions and defeats of the 1920s.

My understanding of the growth of the Yasui family, internal family dynamics and day-to-day family life comes primarily from my numerous interviews with the *nisei* generation. Michi Yasui Ando's recollections, as the oldest girl, were of particular importance, as were Homer Yasui's informal reports written to the *sansei* generation. Ephemera in the Y.B. collection, from miscellaneous magazines to boxes of sporting-goods catalogs to stacks of sheet music, also provided insight into the life of the family. Robert Yasui's self-published *The Yasui Family of Hood River, Oregon* (1987) was an important guide.

All of the *nisei* had especially vivid memories of their uncle Renichi Fujimoto. Of special significance were Homer Yasui's remembrances, told both to me in interviews and to his family through lengthy reports he was kind enough to share with me, and transcripts from tapes made by Chop Yasui in the months before his death in 1989.

A number of secondary sources enriched my understanding of Japanese family culture and made it possible for me to put the Yasuis' experiences in a larger context: Ruth Benedict, *The Chrysanthemum and the Sword: Patterns of Japanese Culture* (Boston: Houghton Mifflin Co., 1946); John W. Connor, *Tradition and Change in Three Generations of Japanese Americans* (Chicago: Nelson-Hall, 1977); Evelyn Nakano Glenn, *Issei, Nisei, War Bride: Three Generations of Japanese American Women in Domestic Service* (Philadelphia: Temple University Press, 1986); Mei Nakano, *Japanese American Women: Three Generations 1890-1990* (Berkeley: Mina Press, 1990).

Masuo's position in the community, the continuing aid and assistance he provided fellow *issei* and his help in establishing the Japanese Community Hall are all documented in letters and occasional press clippings found in the Y.B. collection. Interviews with *nikkei* who grew up in and around the Hood River valley, including Min Asai, Suma Tsuboi Bullock, Hisako Yoshinari and Eiko Tadakuma, confirmed Masuo's special place in his community and the respect he was accorded. Homer Yasui has spent a great deal of time puzzling over the exact nature of his father's awards and the dates they were conferred. I owe my understanding to his deductive reasoning and detective work.

Tracing the ups and downs of Masuo Yasui's business life before and during the Depression was possible because of the extraordinarily detailed records he kept that are now part of the Y.B. collection. Thousands of invoices, together with business ledgers, complete income tax records and copies of letters to and from Masuo help reconstruct how he did business and how the Depression affected him. The numerous and lengthy letters he wrote to W.H. Weber, the man who held the mortgage on the Yasuis' Mosier property, were invaluable. In these letters he not only chronicled his own problems and successes but detailed the state of the Hood River valley fruit business. Also in the collection were newsletters and other communiques from the Apple Growers Association, which helped spotlight local concerns about growing conditions, prices and markets. Much more detailed information about Hood River fruit production and shrinking markets for local produce was found in the Oregon State Planning Board's "Shipment of Apples and Pears from Oregon, 1927-1934" (report submitted to the Oregon state legislature, June 31, 1936). Masakozu Iwata's *Planted in Good Soil: Issei Agriculture in the Pacific Coast States* (unpublished paper prepared for the JACL Committee on Redress, undated) provided good general back-ground.

Chapter 6

Much has been written about the ten War Relocation Authority (WRA) internment camps that housed virtually all the West Coast ethnic Japanese during the war years. (These works are discussed in the notes for Chapter 10, which deals with this wholesale internment.) But very little has been written about the facilities operated by the Department of Justice that housed those *issei* like Masuo Yasui who were considered "dangerous enemy aliens." The exceptions, Paul Clark's *Those Other Camps: An Oral History of Japanese Alien Enemy Internment* (M.A. thesis, California State University/Fullerton, 1980) and John Christgau's *Enemies: World War II Alien Internment* (Ames: Iowa State University Press, 1985) were therefore extraordinarily helpful. Several other books, while not focusing on enemy alien internment, also offered important insights: Roger Daniels, *Concentration Camps, USA: Japanese Americans and World War II* (New York: Holt; Rinehart and Winston, 1972); Richard Drinnon, *Keeper of Concentration Camps: Dillon S. Meyer and American Racism* (Berkeley: University of California Press, 1987); Peter Irons, *Justice at War* (New York: Oxford University Press, 1983).

But most of the information about Masuo's internment came from primary sources. A ten-page handwritten "Record of Japanese Detention at Fort Missoula, Montana" was an exciting find at the University of Washington's Suzzalo Library special collections. These remembrances of an *issei* incarcerated in Montana for much longer than Masuo offered specific details on the organization of Fort Missoula and the routines of camp life. Most helpful was material obtained from both the FBI and the Department of Justice through the Freedom of Information Act: the sworn statement taken from Masuo in Multnomah County Jail on December 13, 1941; the March 6, 1942, order of internment; an INS report on "internee behavior"; the Enemy Alien Special Hearing Board report and other reports, reviews and documents. Of enormous assistance in tracking Masuo's internment was a detailed index to a now nonexistent Department of Justice file, with names, dates and subject matter, of all correspondence concerning Masuo from his arrival at Fort Missoula to his release from the Santa Fe Detention Station. Although I was unable to obtain a transcript of Masuo's original enemy-alien hearing, I was fortunate enough to have Minoru Yasui's personal memoir on the subject. Present throughout the hearing, Min wrote a detailed first-person version of the proceedings, complete with verbatim dialogue between one of the government officials and Masuo.

Masuo wrote numerous letters to family members—and vice versa—during the four years of his internment, some of which are in the personal collection of Yuka Yasui Fujikura, others of which can be found in the Y.B. collection. Some of these letters are quoted from directly; others provided insights into the routines of camp life, family concerns, etc. Masuo's telegrams to Min and Shidzuyo as well as Taiitsuro Yasui's telegrams to his brother are also part of the collection.

Details of the Yasuis' life in the days immediately after Pearl Harbor came from oral history interviews with Homer Yasui and Yuka Yasui Fujikura, the two children still at home during the time. Information on Hood River's attitudes toward the Japanese and especially the rumors circulating about Masuo and others came from oral history interviews with local citizens. Paul Keir was particularly helpful.

Chapter 7

Details of the Yasuis' childhood, and particularly the lives of the three oldest boys, came from both family members and their Hood River contemporaries. In-depth interviews with Chop, Min, Michi, Shu, Homer and Yuka provided many of the specific anecdotes. A number of *nisei* who knew the Yasui children in the 1920s and 1930s also sat for interviews or corresponded with me: Hisako Yoshinari, Kumeo Yoshinari, Eiko Yamaki Tadakuma, Frances Maeda, Suma Tsuboi Bullock, Suma Kobayashi and Min Asai. The Yasuis' *hakujin* classmates and friends shared their memories and impressions: George Jacobson, Don Nance, Frieda Paasche Barnes, Kenneth Abraham, Ruth Guppy, Bonnie Parker Edstrom, Malcolm Kresse, Robert Hackett, Elburna Volstorff, Jane Smithson Irwin, Margaret Schulz, Margaret Cooper Annala, Ruth Finney Crawford.

Dr. Robert Shu Yasui's self-published book about his family, *The Yasui Family of Hood River, Oregon* (1987), provided important detail, and a variety of material in the Y.B. collection was helpful. Kay's papers helped me to understand something of his wide-ranging interests; Chop's personality test gave me an insight into his character I never would have had. Masuo Yasui's letters to Kay, Min, Michi and Yuka were extremely helpful. Stories in the Hood River High School *Guide* marked the various activities and achievements of the three brothers. The *Mascot,* the high school yearbook, was also helpful in developing a picture of school life.

I did depend on a number of secondary sources to put the Yasuis' experiences in context and to enrich my understanding of *nisei* life. In that regard, portions of Wendy Lee Ng's doctoral dissertation on the Hood River *nikkei* community, *Collective Memory, Social Networks and Generations* (August 1989), were particularly helpful, as was Mitzi Asai Loftus's story of her Hood River family, *Made in Japan and Settled in Oregon* (Coos Bay, Ore.: Pidgeon Point Press, 1990). Monica Sone's autobiographical *Nisei Daughter* (Boston: Little, Brown and Co., 1953) provided important emotional insights. Ronald Takaki's *Strangers from a Different Shore: A History of Asian Americans* (New York: Penguin Books, 1989); Harry Kitano's *Japanese Americans: The Evolution of a Subculture* (Englewood Cliffs, N.J.: Prentice-Hall, 1969); and Bill Hosokawa's *Nisei: The Quiet Americans* (New York: William Morrow and Co., Inc., 1969) all added to my general understanding of this pivotal generation.

I was once again indebted to Ruth Benedict's *The Chrysanthemum and the Sword: Patterns of Japanese Culture* (Boston: Houghton Mifflin Co., 1946) and John W. Connor's *Tradition and Change in Three Generations of Japanese Americans* (Chicago: Nelson-Hall, 1977) for their discussions of Japanese values. Mamoru Iga's "Cultural Factors in Suicide of Japanese Youth with Focus on Personality," *Sociology and Social Research,* vol. 46, no. 1 (October 1961), provided interesting speculations not only on the place of suicide in Japanese culture but also on the personal attributes of youth most likely to take their own lives. Jennifer Ulum and Dr. Richard S. Urbanski, both of Sacred Heart Hospital, Eugene, Ore., helped educate me about strychnine poisoning.

Chapter 8

Most of the information about the lives of the Yasui *nisei* came from the children themselves in extensive oral history interviews. Chop, Min, Michi, Shu, Homer and Yuka were all consistently generous with their time. It was Homer's detailed drawing of the house on Twelfth Street that helped established a sense of place. Marcia Stone, Ruth Finney Crawford and Hisako Yoshinari, friends of the Yasui children during their years in Hood River, offered important insights and anecdotes.

Once again, the Y.B. collection was of enormous importance. Chop, Min, Michi and Roku wrote home from college regularly, and Masuo saved every piece of correspondence. They sent him monthly expense accounts, which were also carefully filed. Many copies of Masuo's letters to his children are also part of the collection. In addition to correspondence, the collection also includes occasional report cards and notebooks from Hood River schools, clips from the student newspaper and boxes of Michi's piano music. Yearbooks from Hood River High and the University of Oregon helped corroborate the Yasuis' school activities as well as add to my general understanding of campus life.

Finally, Shu's self-published book on the family was once again an important source. His chapter on himself was particularly revelatory and helped me develop more insightful questions about his experiences.

Chapter 9

Min Yasui related the story of his decision to break curfew and his subsequent arrest, imprisonment and trial to a variety of people during his lifetime. The most detailed narratives, all of which coincide with one another on the major points, were used to piece together the story here: my interview with Min, October 1986; transcript of Holly Yasui (daughter) interview with Min (un-dated); Min Yasui biography, videotape project, Japanese American Citizens League, January 20, 1983; Min Yasui, "Thoughts of Evacuation," a memoir prepared for the National Committee on Redress, August 25, 1982.

Min's memory for detail was extraordinary, but the narrative was further enhanced by a number of letters, documents and poems in the Y.B. collection that chronicled Min's moods and thoughts during his nine months in jail. My interviews with Tomo Saito and Kats Nakayama, two of Min's closest friends during those days, added detail; so too did conversations with Frances Maeda, one of Min's principal correspondents during his time in jail, and William Bernard, son of Min's attorney Earl Bernard.

Virtually every book on the Japanese American experience makes some mention of Min Yasui's trial, but Peter Irons's *Justice at War* (New York: Oxford University Press, 1983) offers not only the most detailed account but also a thoughtful analysis of the trial and the behind-the-scenes maneuverings. I am indebted to Professor Irons's careful work, especially his major contribution to the scholarship of the era: the documents and memos related to the decision to intern the Japanese that Irons secured through Freedom of Information Act requests. Samuel Walker's *In Defense of Liberty: A History of the ACLU* (New York: Oxford University Press, 1990) was helpful in sketching in that group's changing position toward contributing to wartime internment cases.

Information about Min's trial is readily available. The lower court decision can be found in *US v Min Yasui* 48 F. Suppl. 40 No. 16056; the complete verbatim transcript of the lower court trial can be found in the Supreme Court transcripts of *Yasui v US* 20 US 115 (1943). An account of the oral arguments before the Supreme Court, with verbatim questions and answers, can be found in *US Law Week* 3344-47 (1943). I am indebted to Seattle attorney Peggy Nagae Lum, who headed Min's later *coram nobis* case, for explaining the intricacies of the law involved in both the lower and Supreme Court cases.

Chapter 10

Most of what has been written about the Japanese in America has focused on their evacuation and internment during the World War II era. I found the following works most helpful in gaining an understanding of what happened during the months between Pearl Harbor and the forced evacuation: *Personal Justice Denied: Report of the*

Commission on Wartime Relocation and Internment of Civilians (Washington, D.C.: The Commission, 1983); U.S. War Department, *Japanese Evacuation from the West Coast, 1942: Final Report* (New York: Arno Press, 1978); Dorothy S. Thomas and Richard S. Nishimoto, *The Spoilage* (Berkeley: University of California Press, 1946); Arthur Hansen, ed., *Japanese American World War II Evacuation Oral History Project* (Westport, 1991); Roger Daniels, *Concentration Camps USA: Japanese Americans and World War II* (New York: Holt, Rinehart and Winston, Inc., 1971); Maisie and Richard Conrat, *Executive Order 9066* (California Historical Society, 1972). These books also contained the quotations from government and military officials used in this chapter. The quotations from Oregon citizens and state officials come from the published proceedings of the Tolan Committee (U.S. Congress, Select Committee Investigating National Defense Migration, *Hearings,* 77th Cong., 2nd sess., Parts 29, 30 and 31 [Washington, D.C., 1942]).

For insights into life in Hood River after Pearl Harbor, I have depended on my interviews with Mikie, Homer and Yuka as well as Paul Keir and Eleanor Middleton. For other details, including local reaction, federal government and military involvement in Hood River, and Hood River's evacuation chronology, I have depended on published reports in the Hood River *News*. Mitzi Asai Loftus's *Made in Japan and Settled in Oregon* (Coos Bay, Ore.: Pidgeon Point Press, 1990) also provided insights about life in post-Pearl Harbor Hood River. Interviews with Shu and Michi provided the information on their last few months at the University of Oregon. Additionally, files at the University of Oregon's archives were helpful in tracking Dean Onthank's efforts to help Michi attend her own graduation. Shu's book, *The Yasui Family of Hood River, Oregon* (1987), offered excellent detail on his flight from Eugene to Denver.

Chapter 11

A number of excellent books concerning evacuation and internment helped me understand this all-important period in the lives of Japanese Americans. In addition to some of the works cited in the notes for Chapter 10 *(Personal Justice Denied: Report of the Commission on Wartime Relocation and Internment of Civilians* [Washington, D.C.: The Commission, 1983]; Dorothy S. Thomas and Richard S. Nishimoto, *The Spoilage* [Berkeley: University of California Press, 1946]; Roger Daniels, *Concentration Camps USA: Japanese Americans and World War II* [New York: Holt, Rinehart and Winston, Inc., 1971]; Maisie and Richard Conrat, *Executive Order 9066* [California Historical Society, 1972]), I found the following works of particular value: Richard Drinnon, *Keeper of Concentration Camps* (Berkeley: University of California Press, 1987); Michi Weglyn, *Years of Infamy* (New York: William Morrow, 1976); John Tateishi, *And Justice for All: An Oral History of the Japanese American Detention Camps* (New York: Random House, 1984); Allen H. Eaton, *Beauty Behind Barbed Wire* (New York: Harper and Brothers, 1952); Raymond Okamura, "A Pilgrimage Guide to the American Concentration Camps," *Pacific Citizen,* December 21-28, 1979; Raymond Okamura, "The American Concentration Camps: A Cover-up Through Euphemistic Terminology," *Journal of Ethnic Studies* vol. 10, no. 3 (1982); "Pride and Shame," an evacuation and internment project completed by the Seattle chapter of the Japanese American Citizens League, 1971.

Published personal remembrances from those interned were also of tremendous value, especially Jeanne Wakatsuki Houston and James D. Houston's memorable *Farewell to Manzanar* (San Francisco: San Francisco Book Co./Houghton Mifflin, 1973). Mine Okubo's *Citizen 13660* (Seattle and London: University of Washington Press, 1983); Laura Maeda's "Life at Minidoka," *The Pacific Historian,* vol. 20, no. 4 (Winter 1976) and Mitzi Asai Loftus's *Made in Japan and Settled in Oregon* (Coos Bay, Ore.: Pidgeon Point Press, 1990) all added important insights. Also of great interest was a small oral history update conducted by a social scientist who was part of the original University of California team that interviewed internees during the war: Rosalie H. Wax, "In and Out of Tule Lake Segregation Center: Japanese Internment in the West, 1942-1945," *Montana, The Magazine of Western History,* vol. 37, no. 2.

For specifics on camp life, I consulted the Pinedale *Logger,* the center's mimeographed weekly newspaper, the *Tulean Dispatch* and *Newell Star,* the camp newspapers, as well as Harry Inukai's *Tule Lake Directory and Camp News* (Hood River, Ore.: Inukai Publishing Co., 1988).

As always, the Y.B. collection was extraordinarily helpful, including letters back and forth between family members, correspondence between Hood River authorities and the Yasuis and numerous documents pertaining to the family's internment and leave applications. Interviews with Chop, Homer and Yuka were of obvious value.

Chapter 12

The period after internment when the *issei* and *nisei* returned—or chose not to return—to their prewar homes has been written about relatively sparsely compared with earlier periods. On the national level I found helpful material in William Petersen, *Japanese Americans: Oppression and Success* (Washington, D.C.: University Press of America, 1971); Bill Hosokawa, *Nisei: The Quiet Americans* (New York: William Morrow and Co., Inc., 1969); Mei Nakano, *Japanese American Women: Three Generations* (Berkeley: Mina Press, 1990) and Eileen Sunada Sarasohn, *The Issei: Portrait of a Pioneer* (Palo Alto: Pacific Books, 1983).

For information and insights on life in Hood River after internment, I am greatly indebted to Stefan Tanaka's *The Return of a People: The Japanese Americans in Oregon after World War* II (undergraduate thesis, Linfield College, 1974); Barbara Yasui's "From Seed to Blossom: The Japanese in Hood River, Oregon" (history paper, Stanford University, 1971); Wendy Lee Ng, *Collective Memory, Social Networks and Generations: The Japanese American Community in Hood River, Oregon* (Ph.D. dissertation, University of Oregon, 1989); and Mitzi Asai Loftus's *Made in Japan and Settled in Oregon* (Coos Bay, Ore.: Pidgeon Point Press, 1990).

Press coverage in both the Hood River *News* and the Portland *Oregonian* supplied information about the activities of anti-Japanese groups in Hood River and elsewhere in the state. Among the national media coverage devoted to Hood River's infamous behavior, I found the following to be the most insightful: Ralph G. Martin, "Hood River Odyssey," *The New Republic,* December 16, 1946; Richard Neuberger, "Their Brothers' Keepers," *The Saturday Review of Literature,* August 10, 1946.

Much of the information about life in Hood River after January 1945 and, in particular, life for the Yasuis came from oral history interviews, including two completed by others: Maija Yasui's interview with Asai, Noji and Sato, the first three *nikkei* to return to the valley in 1945; and Chop Yasui's extensive taped statement (1971) for his niece Barbara Yasui. The interviews I conducted with Mikie and Chop Yasui, Min Asai, Kenneth Abraham, Paul Keir, George Jacobsen and Frieda Barnes were of enormous assistance in recapturing the mood of those days. I also relied on letters to and from Masuo, Chop and Yuka found in the Y.B. collection.

Chapter 13

Much of the material concerning the lives of Masuo, Shidzuyo and their children comes from my lengthy interviews with the Yasui *nisei,* including Mikie and Miyuki who married into the family. I am particularly indebted to Homer and Yuka, who spoke so candidly about their father's illness and suicide. Ruth Benedict's *The Chrysanthemum and the Sword: Patterns of Japanese Culture* (Boston: Houghton Mifflin Co., 1946) and John W. Connor's *Tradition and Change in Three Generations of Japanese Americans* (Chicago: Nelson-Hall, 1977) helped me understand the meaning of suicide in Japanese culture. Letters, documents and photos found in the Y.B. collection were of considerable help in piecing together the individual and collective lives of the Yasuis in the decades after the war. Robert (Shu) Yasui's self-published book about his family, *The Yasui Family of Hood River, Oregon,* helped fill in some blanks.

For background on the redress and reparations issue, I have depended on Peter Irons, *Justice at War* (New York: Oxford University Press, 1983); *Personal Justice Denied: Report of the Commission on Wartime Relocation and Internment of Civilians* (Washington, D.C.: The Commission, 1983); William Hohri, *Repairing America: An Account of the Movement for Japanese American Redress* (Pullman: Washington State University Press, 1988); as well as documents and letters in the Y.B. collection dealing with Min's and Homer's involvement in the movement. Stories in newspapers from the New York *Times* to a variety of West Coast dailies, chronicled some of the movement's highlights. Wendy Ng's dissertation, *Collective Memory, Social Networks and Generations: The Japanese American Community in Hood River, Oregon* (Ph.D. dissertation, University of Oregon, 1989), offered important insights into how some of the people in Hood River viewed the redress movement.

For my understanding of Min's *coram nobis* case, I owe a major debt to Peggy Nagae Lum, who headed Min's legal team. Not only did she patiently and repeatedly explain the case, but she opened her personal files to me as well. Court proceedings, memoranda, letters, press releases, newspaper clippings and other material that helped chronicle the long legal battle came both from Peggy's files and from the Y.B. collection.

Chapters 14 and 15

These two chapters about the Yasui *sansei* owe a great debt to the *sansei* themselves: Chop's sons, Flip and Tom; Min's daughter Holly; Shu's daughter Lise; and Homer's daughter Barbara—all of whom sat for lengthy, and in some cases numerous, interviews. Holly allowed me to read the very first version of her play, *Unvanquished,* and personally invited me to all its showings. Lise sent me videotapes of both the thirty-minute and sixty-minute versions of her film, *A Family Gathering.* Lengthy interviews with Maija Yasui, Flip's wife, and Barbara Bellus Upp, former Hood River pastor, were extremely helpful. Both Shu, who sent me piles of clippings about the accomplishments of his children, and Miyuki Yasui, Homer's wife, who gave me thumbnail sketches of all the *sansei,* were of great assistance.

I depended on the work of a number of social scientists for insights into third-generation Japanese Americans. Among the most helpful works were: Stephen S. Fujita and David J. O'Brien, *Japanese American Ethnicity: The Persistence of Community* (Seattle: University of Washington Press, 1991); Fumiko Hosokawa, *The Sansei: Social Interaction and Ethnic Identification Among Third Generation Japanese* (San Francisco: R & E Research Associates, 1978); Harry Kitano, *The Evolution of a Subculture* (Englewood Cliffs, N.J.: Prentice-Hall, Inc., 1969); Daniel Montero, *Japanese Americans: Changing Patterns of Ethnic Affiliation Over Three Generations* (Boulder, Colo.: Westview Press, 1980); Wendy Lee Ng, *Collective Memory, Social Networks and Generations: The Japanese American Community of Hood River, Oregon* (Ph.D. dissertation, University of Oregon, August 1989); David O'Brien and Stephen Fujita, *The Japanese American Experience* (Bloomington and Indianapolis: Indiana University Press, 1991).

I found myself depending on more subjective material as well, including parts of Joann Faung Jean Lee's *Asian American: Oral Histories of First to Fourth Generation*

Americans from China, the Philippines, Japan, India, the Pacific Islands, Vietnam and Cambodia (New York: The New Press, 1991) and Jeanne Wakatsuki Houston's thoughtful *Beyond Manzanar: Views of Asian American Womanhood* (Santa Barbara, Cal.: Capra Press, 1985). Especially helpful were Lydia Yuri Minatoya's *Talking to High Monks in the Snow* (New York: HarperCollins, 1992) and David Mura's *Turning Japanese: Memoirs of a Sansei* (New York: Atlantic Monthly Press, 1991). I also turned to the poetry and fiction of *sansei* writers for insight into that generation's search for identity. Garrett Hongo's *The River of Heaven* (New York: Knopf, 1990), Ruth Sasaki's *The Loom and Other Stories* (St. Paul, Minn.: Graywolf Press, 1991) and various selections from Frank Chin et al., eds., *Aiiieeeee! An Anthology of Asian American Writers* (New York: Mentor Books, 1991), taught me much.

index